The Trajectory of Trumpism

The Trajectory of Trumpism

Talking about Racism, Fascism, Civil War, and Beyond

Sanford F. Schram

OXFORD
UNIVERSITY PRESS

OXFORD
UNIVERSITY PRESS

Oxford University Press is a department of the University of Oxford. It furthers the University's objective of excellence in research, scholarship, and education by publishing worldwide. Oxford is a registered trade mark of Oxford University Press in the UK and in certain other countries.

Published in the United States of America by Oxford University Press
198 Madison Avenue, New York, NY 10016, United States of America.

CIP data is on file at the Library of Congress

ISBN 9780197827406

ISBN 9780197827390 (hbk.)

DOI: 10.1093/9780197827437.001.0001

Paperback printed by Marquis Book Printing, Canada

The manufacturer's authorized representative in the EU for product safety is Oxford University Press España S.A. of Parque Empresarial San Fernando de Henares, Avenida de Castilla, 2 – 28830 Madrid (www.oup.es/en or product.safety@oup.com). OUP España S.A. also acts as importer into Spain of products made by the manufacturer.

For Kay Brown

Contents

Acknowledgments viii

1. **Trumpism: The Discourse of a Movement** **1**
2. **The Trajectory of Trumpism** **41**
3. **Racism** **76**
4. **Fascism** **111**
5. **Civil War** **148**
6. **Prosecutions as Persecutions: Trumpism as a Cult** **179**
7. **Alternative Futures of Trumpism** **202**

Index 233

Acknowledgments

Some time in my freshman year in college, my first-year English professor Kay Brown assigned our class Orwell's essay on politics and the English language. It made a lasting impression (even if I do not necessarily agree with parts of it). (Years later, as a professor myself, I spent a year on sabbatical studying with Murray Edelman to further my studies on politics and language.) From my first year in college going forward, I continued to be fascinated with the role of language in politics, especially the language of demonization.

After years of writing about the politics of demonization in American politics, in the spring of 2023, I thought I was done. But something happened that changed all that. I was driven to write this book in spite of myself. At the time, I was winding down getting ready to retire when I attended a colloquium where my good colleague Robyn Marasco was presenting a draft book chapter. Afterwards, she asked what I was working on. I said: "nothing." I explained I was transitioning into a relaxing retirement. Robyn protested that I should keep writing. I went home, thought about it, and remembered this book that was rattling around in my mind about being continually frustrated with the success of Donald Trump and his followers in spreading lies in order to cling to power. The floodgates opened and out-poured this book. After about nine months, a rough draft of the manuscript came into shape. Then came another year of editing and then updating. And then it was done. Robyn made me do it! I thank her for encouraging me.

A number of friends and colleagues read parts or all of this manuscript at various stages and I want to thank them especially for their recommendations for changes. I want to express my heartfelt thanks to Mary Bellhouse, Mette Christiansen, Phoebe Cohen, Micaele Di Leonardo, Alan Draper, Tom Duffin, Lenny Feldman, Stanley Feldman, Rich Fording, Max Fuerderer, Florence Goff, Alex Herz, Leonie Huddy, Bettina Leibetseder, Joe Lowndes, Andrea Masters, David Osten, Bruce Piasecki, Frances Fox Piven, Robyn Rowe, Cathy Schneider, Joe Soss, Roni Strier, Ida Susser, Carl Swidorski, Barbara Tsairis, and Charles Tien, all who read parts or all of the manuscript or discussed the book with me at length. I especially want to note the help of Jeffrey Isaac and John Massaro in providing detailed comments on the entire manuscript. Their suggestions improved the book substantially, as did the suggestions of two anonymous reviewers. Ryan Schram consistently offered important insights for improvement that are most appreciated, especially regarding the main thesis of the book. I also want to acknowledge Padmapriya Arumugam who ably managed the production of this book. Once again, Angela Chnapko proved to be the best editor. She supported the book from beginning to end, shepherding it through the entire process, including critical editing. She is wise and gets right to the point in her advice. As usual, I had extensive discussions with Joan Schram that were critical in forming the broad outlines of the book. She is a real trooper, and I love her for it.

1

Trumpism

The Discourse of a Movement

I have studied the politics of demonization for several decades now.[1] For years, I focused primarily on the targeting of those living in poverty, especially the disproportionately non-White single mothers with children receiving welfare assistance from the US government. I originally thought that this politics of welfare demonization was somewhat of a side issue, even if important in its own right, but still not consistently, let alone centrally, involved in shaping mainstream politics. Nonetheless, over time, I became convinced that welfare demonization was very much fundamental to mainstream politics. In order to gain public support, even the most prominent candidates for public office used racial and gender stereotypes to vilify the poor as the cause of their own poverty.[2] Today this is called gaslighting, as it deflects attention away from the embedded structures of power that oppress people living in poverty while creating economic advantages for many others.[3] This gaslighting significantly deemphasizes the actions of nonpoor people, in power and out, who also are very much complicit in the perpetuation of policies and practices, inside and outside of government, that reproduce inequity and oppression.[4]

[1] See Sanford F. Schram, *Words of Welfare: The Poverty of Social Science and the Social Science of Poverty* (University of Minnesota Press, 1995). Also see Sanford F. Schram, *Becoming a Footnote: An Activist-Scholar Finds His Voice, Learns to Write and Survives Academia* (SUNY Press, 2013).

[2] See Sanford F. Schram and Joe Soss, "Demonizing the Poor," *Jacobin* (September 3, 2015), (originally titled "Lobster Is the New Red Herring: How It Pays to Demonize the Poor in the Neoliberal Age"), https://jacobin.com/2015/09/welfare-republicans-sam-brownback-race-corporations. Also see David Firestone, "How to Use the Debt Ceiling to Inflict Cruelty on the Poor," *New York Times*, May 17, 2023, www.nytimes.com/2023/05/17/opinion/debt-ceiling-republicans-poor.html?action=click&module=Well&pgtype=Homepage§ion=Editorials.

[3] The term gaslighting refers to getting people to question their own thinking by manufacturing a false alternative. It has only in the last decade come into popular use but is derived from George Cukor's 1944 film *Gaslight*. See Ben Yagoda, "How Old Is 'Gaslighting'?" *The Chronicle of Higher Education*, January 12, 2017, www.chronicle.com/blogs/linguafranca/2017/01/12/how-old-is-gaslight/. The newer uses of "gaslighting" simply imply it to be about deflection, while older versions, including feminist ones, emphasize that gaslighting involves long-term abuse by way of systematic deception. See Stephanie Sarkis, *Gaslighting: Recognize Manipulative and Emotionally Abusive People* (Da Capo Press, 2018).

[4] On using a "relational approach" to understanding poverty not as a condition but as a relationship between the poor and the nonpoor, see Matthew Desmond, *Evicted: Poverty and Profit in an American City* (Crown Publishers, 2016); and *Poverty, By America* (Crown Books, 2023).

The Trajectory of Trumpism. Sanford F. Schram, Oxford University Press. © Oxford University Press (2026).
DOI: 10.1093/9780197827437.003.0001

Stigmatization of the welfare population saves society the money it would have to spend to create economic opportunities for those who need assistance. But it does so much more. It also provides solace that it is not society or the nonpoor who need to change but "the poor" themselves who need to learn to behave differently. This framing actually is very nostalgic as it suggests that if everyone were to adhere to "traditional" (i.e., White, middle-class) work and family values, there would be no or little poverty for us to worry about. This type of thinking especially overlooks how issues of race, class, and gender create barriers for families living in poverty.[5] In the end, mainstream society is absolved of any need to invest in changing the way things are. Instead, all we need to do is demand that people living in poverty conform to social standards that we claim were supposedly always adhered to by mainstream society in the past. An "us vs. them" dynamic, based on a tendentious reading of history, is at the core of this narrating of issues of welfare and poverty, where the "us" of mainstream society can rest on its unearned laurels and the "them" of those who need to rely on public assistance must change their ways.[6]

Trumpism: The Discourse of a Movement

In one sense, welfare demonization is paradigmatic of what is central to the resurgent White Nationalist movement that Donald Trump had led while going on to win the presidency in 2016 and then again in 2024.[7] Over time, Trumpism has become a movement representing a constellation of grievances, and Trump's incendiary way of demonizing his enemies proved to help him win votes from many people including those disaffected and unhappy people who might not have been specifically motivated to vote based on racial considerations. Yet, Trump's governing coalition for his second term was filled with billionaires, led by the authoritarian-leaning Elon Musk, who seemed most keen on exploiting the movement for fulfilling

[5] For a book that inadvertently ties the politics of welfare demonization to the broader demonization of non-Whites and other outgroups, see Lawrence M. Mead, *Burdens of Freedom: Cultural Difference and American Power* (Encounter Books, 2019). Much of Mead's previous writings was about how the non-White welfare population needed to learn to behave more like White, middle-class Americans.

[6] See Sanford F. Schram, "The Deep Semiotic Structure of Deservingness: Discourse and Identity in Welfare Policy," in *The Argumentative Turn Revisited: Public Policy as Communicative Practice*, ed. Frank Fischer and Herbert Gottweis (Duke University Press, 2012), 236–58. Also see Ron Eyerman, "Jeffrey Alexander and the Cultural Turn in Social Theory," *Theses Eleven* 79, no. 1 (2004), 25–30: https://doi.org/10.1177/0725513604046953.

[7] See Richard C. Fording and Sanford F. Schram, *Hard White: The Mainstreaming of Racism in American Politics* (Oxford University Press, 2020), Chapter 1; and Lisa Lerer, "America Hires a Strongman," *New York Times*, September 6, 2024, https://www.nytimes.com/2024/11/06/us/politics/trump-election-analysis.html?smid=nytcore-ios-share&referringSource=articleShare.

their own anti-democratic goals and not unrelated financial gain for themselves and their oligarchic allies.[8] Nonetheless, Trump's initial ascendancy in mainstream presidential politics occurred when he assumed leadership of the racist birther movement. This movement claimed that President Barack Obama was an illegitimate president because he was not born in the United States and was probably not really a Christian but instead a Muslim born in Kenya.[9] White racists and many others who opposed Obama as the first non-White president were thrilled to follow Trump, given these audacious claims. Trump then initiated his 2016 presidential campaign with his most frequently repeated slur, demonizing immigrants crossing the southern border as a threat:

> The U.S. has become a dumping ground for everybody else's problems. … When Mexico sends its people, they're not sending their best. … They're bringing drugs. They're bringing crime. They're rapists. … It only makes common sense. They're sending us not the right people. … It's coming from more than Mexico. It's coming from all over South and Latin America, and it's coming probably—probably—from the Middle East.[10]

The MAGA Movement to "Make America Great Again" that Trump formed in his successful 2016 presidential bid had the "us vs. them" divide at its core. It encouraged a vengeful form of nostalgia where it is the White "us" that is called to take back the Nation from those "other" people, who are seen as needy and threatening, and are increasingly populating a diversifying America. It was a classic discursive move to forge unity and identity in opposition to supposedly threatening others.[11]

A popular Trump slogan promised to put "America First"; it was an explicit invocation of the original America First Committee of the 1930s that opposed war with Germany, espoused White Nationalist ideas, and was populated by many Nazi and fascist sympathizers.[12] That racist, nativistic, isolationist, and essentially anti-democratic movement was deeply embedded in long-standing currents of hostility toward non-Whites and non-Christians. The America First movement ultimately fizzled as the United States entered World

[8] Jamelle Bouie, "The Dubious History of America's Most Famous Monarchist," *New York Times*, January 22, 2025, https://www.nytimes.com/2025/01/22/opinion/trump-vance-yarvin-monarchy.html.

[9] See Christopher S. Parker and Matt A. Barreto, *Change They Can't Believe In: The Tea Party and Reactionary Politics in America* (Princeton University Press, 2013).

[10] "Here's Donald Trump's Presidential Announcement Speech," *Time*, June 16, 2015, https://time.com/3923128/donald-trump-announcement-speech/.

[11] Rodney Barker, *Making Enemies* (Palgrave MacMillan, 2007).

[12] Krishnadev Calamur, "A Short History of 'America First,'" *The Atlantic*, January 21, 2017, https://www.theatlantic.com/politics/archive/2017/01/trump-america-first/514037/.

War II.[13] Yet it contributed to what became the Nazi-aligned post–World War II movement ultimately led by the anti-communist fearmonger Sen. Joe McCarthy (R-WI). McCarthyism was widely known for having demonized Jews, gays, and others in the government as communist spies. Yet, his movement was about much more. A popular slogan among those on the Far Right in those years came from the then-prominent New York State Sen. Merwin Hart (R): "Taking America Back."[14] It is similar to Trumpism's call to "Take America Back." McCarthy mobilized millions of Americans on the political Right, including fascist and Nazi sympathizers, but the minority and explicitly anti-majoritarian and anti-democratic movement ultimately failed in seeking to rig the Electoral College to make McCarthy president. This ploy to insist on taking back the Country from interlopers became a strategy prominently deployed by Trumpists.

Trumpism has proven to be much more successful than its predecessor, though it uses similar tactics, such as telling one Big Lie after another, and exploits similar prejudices, such as stoking fear of the "other," to promote what became its own backward-looking, anti-democratic agenda. The Movement's agenda is centered on opposing liberal efforts to move the United States to be a more inclusive social democracy. For sure, anti-liberal resistance to an inclusive liberal democracy has been present since the founding of the constitutional order, ebbing and flowing in its influence over time. Significantly, Trumpism has sustained itself as an extension and accentuation of that resistance movement as it has evolved, capturing one of the two major political parties, and with Trump winning back control of the White House and eventually much more.[15]

Various factors led to Trumpism's success in mainstreaming its extremism. In this book, I focus on not just what was said, but also how. I demonstrate the importance of the way Trumpism has operated as a discourse that normalizes its extremist rhetoric. Led by Trump but eventually followed by others,

[13] See Rick Perlstein, "American Fascism," *The American Prospect*, January 24, 2024, https://prospect.org/politics/2024-01-24-american-fascism-john-ganz/; Rachel Maddow, *Prequel: An American Fight Against Fascism* (Crown, 2023); and John Ehrenberg, *White Nationalism and the Republican Party: Toward Minority Rule in America* (Routledge Press, 2022).

[14] See David Austin Walsh, *Taking America Back: The Conservative Movement and the Far Right* (Yale University Press, 2024). For the Electoral College strategy, see Rachel Maddow, *Ultra*, Season 2, Episode 7, July 29, 2024, https://www.msnbc.com/msnbc-podcast/rachel-maddow-presents-ultra/transcript-rachel-maddow-presents-ultra-season-2-episode-7-mobilized-rcna164071.

[15] For the argument that Trumpism grows out of an enduring strain of anti-liberalism that from the founding on has always opposed the liberalism that undergirds the US constitutional order, see Robert Kagan, *Rebellion: How Anti-Liberalism is Tearing America Apart-Again* (Penguin Random House, 2024); and Damon Linker, "Get to Know the Influential Conservative Intellectuals Who Help Explain G.O.P. Extremism," *New York Times*, November 4, 2023, www.nytimes.com/2023/11/04/opinion/sunday/conservative-intellectuals-republicans.html.

Trumpism has normalized extremism in unprecedented ways in national political discourse. Trumpism most critically provides supporters with a permission structure to deny reality while dehumanizing opponents.[16] Trump himself was said to be a savant in "grooming" the public and the press to learn to consider his outrageousness normal.[17]

For instance, it became okay to lie that immigrants were literally eating people's pets, or to figuratively suggest that they were poisoning the blood of the Country, or other outrageous claims.[18] It became acceptable to smear Republican-appointed judges who tried to block Trump's unconstitutional attempts to assert unilateral power in his presidency.[19] Trumpism arguably has made anti-democratic and autocratic talk acceptable in US politics to an extent never previously experienced.[20] It not only made autocratic talk acceptable, but it also proved it can be a winning electoral strategy in a Country that prides itself on being a model democracy. Now, political adversaries could be referred to as an "enemy within" who needed to be taken down by the US military.[21] Trumpism crossed a line in political discourse but did so in ways that proved politically successful. It opened up the question of how it could be that so many of the American public were not for but against basic democratic aspirations that create an inclusive democracy genuinely committed to principles of equal opportunity. But, before I turn to Trumpism as a politically effective discourse, I provide here background on the factors that led to the ascendancy of Trumpism as a movement.

The Rise of Trumpism

In less than a decade, Trumpism has proven surprisingly influential as an extremist movement in reshaping mainstream politics. It took Trump to the

[16] Hanna Rosin, "Autocracy is in the Details," *The Atlantic*, October 17, 2024, https://www.theatlantic.com/podcasts/archive/2024/10/autocracy-is-in-the-details/680273/.

[17] Sherrilyn Ifill, October 5, 2023, https://www.instagram.com/thetnholler/p/CyBKjrvuCsW/.

[18] Edward Helmore, "JD Vance Admits He Is Willing to 'Create Stories' to Get Media Attention," *The Guardian*, September 15, 2024, https://www.theguardian.com/us-news/2024/sep/15/jd-vance-lies-haitian-immigrants.

[19] Amanda Taub, "'This Is Worse': Trump's Judicial Defiance Veers Beyond the Autocrat Playbook," *New York Times*, March 20, 2025, https://www.nytimes.com/2025/03/20/world/europe/trump-courts-defiance-autocrats-playbook.html.

[20] Anne Applebaum, "Trump is Speaking Like Hitler, Stalin, and Mussolini," *The Atlantic*, October 18, 2024, https://www.theatlantic.com/politics/archive/2024/10/trump-authoritarian-rhetoric-hitler-mussolini/680296/.

[21] Alice Herman, "Trump Warns of Enemies "within our Country" to Christian Media Gathering," *The Guardian*, February 23, 2024, https://www.theguardian.com/us-news/2024/feb/23/trump-national-religious-broadcasters-enemies-within-country.

White House in 2016 and back there again in 2024. Even after losing reelection in 2020 and eventually getting indicted for trying to stay in office and block the peaceful transfer of power, Trump remained atop the Republican Party with his outrageous claims that the 2020 election was stolen. He continued to dominate the Party with most Republican officeholders reluctant to criticize him and became the 2024 nominee, eventually going all the way to winning reelection. Grover Cleveland is the only other president to lose a reelection bid and then win reelection four years later. It is important to stress that Trump's successful navigation of this unusual situation was in no small part the result of the undying loyalty of the Movement Trump came to lead. As a result, Trumpism's persistent influence on mainstream politics came in spite of the extremist views it pushes. There are a variety of reasons for this shocking development. The shock comes from a constellation of forces cohering as needed to make that happen.

First, it is true that Trump was building off well-established but growing hostility among disenchanted Whites toward the liberalism that flows from founding political principles of the US constitutional system. The history on this point runs deep. Robert Kagan has written:

> The American Revolution did not just produce a new system of government dedicated to the protection of the rights of all individuals against government and community, the first of its kind in history. It also produced a reaction against those very liberal principles, by slaveholders and their white supporters, by religious movements, by those many Americans who have sought to preserve ancient, traditional hierarchies of peoples and beliefs against the leveling force of liberalism. This struggle between liberalism and antiliberalism has shaped international politics for the last two centuries and dominates the international scene today. But the same struggle has also been fought within the American system since the time of the Revolution. The idea that all Americans share a commitment to the nation's founding principles has always been a pleasing myth, or perhaps a noble lie. We prefer to believe we all share the same fundamental goals and only disagree on the means of achieving them. But, in fact, large numbers of Americans have always rejected the founders' claim that all men are created equal, with "unalienable" rights to life, liberty, and the pursuit of happiness, and they have persistently struggled against the imposition of those liberal values on their lives. Great numbers of Americans, from the time of the Revolution onward, have wished to see America in ethnoreligious terms, as fundamentally a white, Protestant nation whose character is an outgrowth of white, Christian, European civilization. Their goal has been to preserve a white, Christian supremacy, contrary to the founders' vision, and they have

tolerated the founders' liberalism, and the workings of the democratic system, only when it has not undermined that cause.[22]

In recent years, this hostility has intensified among segments of the White population, particularly in reaction to the successes of the Civil Rights Movement, increased efforts at promoting racial inclusion in US politics, and movement toward a multicultural society more generally.[23] American politics moves forward with one movement countering another.[24] Since the 1960s, there has been what many people have called the "culture war" that involved pushback by conservatives opposing the liberal changes in various issues including especially the issue of race, but also gender and religion.[25] The conservative pushback eventually was associated in particular with growing antipathy toward the federal government as a force for progressive change in the wake of the Civil Rights Movement and aligned progressive change efforts coming out of the 1960s. This antipathy began intensifying with the presidency of Ronald Reagan in the 1980s. Reagan's rhetoric, and that of others who followed him, like Pat Buchanan, led to white extremists becoming more active in expressing their opposition to a federal government working to make society more equitable and inclusive, rather than perpetuating a class-based society with hierarchies of privilege that favored White, male, heterosexuals.[26]

This anti-federal government movement was there for the taking by someone ready to step forward to shape that hostility into a coherent political movement. Trump, as the force that he has become in mainstream politics, would not have been possible without a ready-made base prepared to follow his lead. By the time Trump rose to prominence in national politics, the two major political parties were already increasingly sorted along opposing cultural lines. One was a largely White, Christian, male-dominated, conservative,

[22] See Kagan, *Rebellion*, 7–8.

[23] See Katherine J. Cramer, *The Politics of Resentment: Rural Consciousness in Wisconsin and the Rise of Scott Walker* (University of Chicago Press, 2016); and Jeff Sharlet, *The Undertow: Scenes from a Slow Civil War* (W.W. Norton, 2023).

[24] David S. Meyer and Suzanne Staggenborg, "Movements, Countermovements, and the Structure of Political Opportunity," *American Journal of Sociology* 101, no. 6 (1996): 1628–60. Also specifically regarding American politics, see Sidney M. Milkis, "Review Essay: Donald Trump, Charismatic Leadership and the "Deep State," *Political Science Quarterly*, March 2024, https://doi.org/10.1093/psquar/qqae018; and Suzanne Mettler and Robert C. Lieberman, *Four Threats: The Recurring Crises of American Democracy* (St. Martin's Press, 2020).

[25] See James Davidson Hunter, *Culture Wars: The Struggle to Define America* (Basic Books, 1991).

[26] Sean Wilentz, "American Carnage," *New York Review of Books*, August 17, 2023, https://www.nybooks.com/articles/2023/08/17/american-carnage-homegrown-jeffrey-toobin/. On Reagan, Buchanan, and others, Wilentz writes: "their stark themes of isolationism, lost national greatness, immigrant invasion, and racial fear provided a template for Donald Trump's MAGA campaign a quarter-century later. 'American carnage' [the title of Trump's inauguration speech] was the favored Far-Right image at least two decades before Trump."

non-central city party favoring corporate elite interests and stoking resentments about being left behind or left out in a changing society. The other was a racially, ethnically, religiously diverse, and gender-affirming, liberal big city, pro-free trade party that attracted support from the more educated in the populace while often making gestures to uplifting the poor and enabling working families to thrive. The reinforcing lines of division hardened partisan identities and ultimately made for an "affective polarization" where emotional party allegiance and deeply branded partisan identities overshadowed policy attitudes.[27] As a result, supporting your side to win power has become an end in itself.

Second, even though Trumpism's roots in American history are deep, it is also associated with a relatively recent global trend. The extremism of Trumpism is associated with the rise of reactionary movements in political parties around the developed world more generally, as the issue of global immigration has induced resistance to allowing foreigners, often non-Whites from poorer nations, seeking entry.[28] The United States itself has an uneven history in encouraging immigration. With the 1965 immigration reform, the United States greatly loosened quotas, allowing more immigration from non-Western European countries.[29] But in the United States, pushback against the resulting diversification of the US population has now led to the United States increasingly getting caught up in the global reaction sweeping over the developed world. The immigration issue has operated as an accelerant to reactionary movements, allowing them to gain seats in national legislatures and parliaments. It has now come to affect elections in the United States. This global trend emboldens Trumpism and has added to its growing support among various groups, but especially White people of European descent.

Third, we should recognize the importance and uniqueness of Trump himself.[30] There had to be someone who was willing to step up, cross the line, break the code, and go where others dared not to lead such a movement that has created space for a variety of extremists.[31] As an outsider with a long-time interest in breaking into mainstream politics, Trump was ready to step forward when the right opportunity presented itself. Trump further

[27] See Lilliana Mason, *Uncivil Agreement: How Politics Became Our Identity* (University of Chicago Press, 2018), 17–18.

[28] Pippa Norris and Ronald Inglehart, *Cultural Backlash: Trump, Brexit, and Authoritarian Populism* (Cambridge University Press, 2019).

[29] Jia Lynn Yang, *One Mighty and Irresistible Tide: The Epic Struggle Over American Immigration, 1924-1965* (W. W. Norton, 2020).

[30] Corey Robin, *The Reactionary Mind: Conservatism from Edmund Burke to Donald Trump*, 2nd ed. (Oxford University Press, 2017), 269.

[31] See Philip Rucker and Carol Leonnig, *A Very Stable Genius: Donald J. Trump's Testing of America* (Penguin Press, 2020).

had the background, upbringing, and personality that enabled an extremist anti-liberal movement to move to the front, despite his prior liberal political positions. He was very transactional about it, but also saw everything in zero-sum terms, where all relationships always have a winner who wins at the expense of a loser, whether it was in real estate, sexual relationships, race relations, or international trade.[32] Even compared to most professional politicians, Trump has exhibited a shamelessness that has insulated him from criticism of his uninhibited quest for power, especially to dominate his perceived enemies.[33] He lies like no other president or presidential candidate that came before him.[34] He mangled language and luxuriated in viciousness and vulgarity in unprecedented ways. He has not shied away from celebrating his supporters' devotion to him in what has essentially become an authoritarian personality cult.[35] Trump exploited every opportunity, including even a dramatic assassination attempt that he shamelessly used to raise more money for himself as well as his campaign.[36] Trump could never, it seems, resist exploiting his movement's resentments to seek retribution for his own personal sleights.[37] As a second-term president, he faced no opposition from his supporters as he used his power like an autocrat to initiate criminal prosecutions of his political enemies. Along the way, Trump continued to push the agenda of the White resistance movement to the liberal order.

Fourth, success in mainstreaming the Movement was due to being better than past efforts at exploiting deficiencies in the liberal democratic political institutions of the United States, whether it is an Electoral College that allows someone with less than majority support to ascend to the presidency, or the extreme gerrymandering of congressional seats enabling anti-majoritarian features of the fragmented federal system at all levels of government.[38] The deficiencies have helped allow the Republicans in particular to get control of various parts of the government, with the result being more often than

[32] See Jamelle Bouie, "The Tariff Saga is About One Thing," *New York Times*, April 9, 2025, https://www.nytimes.com/2025/04/09/opinion/trump-tariffs-rationale-power.html.

[33] See David Keen, *Shame: The Politics and Power of an Emotion* (Princeton University Press, 2023).

[34] Paul Krugman, "Why Trump Is Lying about Disaster Relief," *New York Times*, October 3, 2024, https://www.nytimes.com/2024/10/03/opinion/trump-biden-hurricane-helene.html.

[35] Perlstein, "American Fascism."

[36] Jessica Piper and Ursula Perano, "Trump Sends Fundraising Appeal: 'I Will Never Surrender',"*Politico*, July 14, 2024, https://www.politico.com/live-updates/2024/07/14/trump-rally-shooting-updates/trump-fundraising-appeals-00168147.

[37] Jamelle Bouie, "Trump Promised Retribution. Turns Out He Had a Very Big Target in Mind," *New York Times*, March 5, 2025, https://www.nytimes.com/2025/03/05/opinion/trump-revenge-american-people.html.

[38] See Jamelle Bouie, "Something's Got to Give," *New York Times*, May 5, 2023, https://www.nytimes.com/2023/05/05/opinion/constitutional-amendments-supreme-court.html?smid=nytcore-ios-share&referringSource=articleShare.

not reactionary policies at the state level but also a paralyzing polarization that has stymied efforts to make federal policy supported by a majority of the American people.

Trumpism exploited anti-majoritarian features of the governmental system to resounding success. Trumpism as a movement has proven way more influential than the limited size its base of supporters would suggest. Trump himself has never been that popular with the majority of Americans.[39] Nonetheless, he inflamed simmering resentments to get elected president in 2016 while losing the popular vote, then went on to remake the Republican Party, and forced party elites to *kowtow* to his wishes in part by maneuvering through loopholes checking presidential power.[40] When he claimed he was robbed of victory in his 2020 reelection bid, Trump stoked opposition to the existing constitutional system. Eventually, he won reelection in 2024, winning this time not just the Electoral College but also the popular vote. He then relied on the worst demonizations and lies against his enemies and outgroups to justify taking illegal and unconstitutional action once back in office to concentrate power in his presidency.[41]

Fifth, while disinformation and demonization have always been prevalent in US politics, as well as elsewhere,[42] there is the changing media landscape that, in a variety of ways, has distinctively given Trump and his acolytes unfiltered access to spread lies and contrived grievances to faithful followers.[43] The Balkanization of the media makes for a more intense tribalism in politics today. Trumpists seem unsurpassed in their willingness to exploit what amounts to a post-Truth information landscape.[44] Whether it is social media like Twitter and Trump's own ironically named Truth Social or mass media outlets like Fox News, Newsmax, and One America News Network, the siloing and creation of isolated information bubbles allow Trumpism's disinformation to often go unchallenged.[45] The growing influence of social media

[39] Ewan Palmer, "Donald Trump Is Not as Popular as Everyone Thinks," *Newsweek*, March 6, 2024, https://www.newsweek.com/donald-trump-super-tuesday-results-nikki-haley-1876330.

[40] Peter Wehner, "The Party of Malice," *The Atlantic*, January 21, 2024, https://www.theatlantic.com/ideas/archive/2024/01/haley-trump-gop/677212/.

[41] Nick Jachim, "When Was the Last Time the Republican Party Won the Popular Vote?" *The Hill*, September 6, 2024, https://thehill.com/homenews/nexstar_media_wire/4976301-when-was-the-last-time-the-republican-party-won-the-popular-vote/; and "Trump's Test of the Constitution," *New York Times*, February 1, 2025, https://www.nytimes.com/2025/02/01/opinion/trump-fired-accountability.html.

[42] See Sanford F. Schram and Philip T. Neisser, eds., *Tales of the State: Narrative in Contemporary U.S. Politics and Public Policy* (Rowman and Littlefield, 1997), 1–16.

[43] James Slotta, "The Annotated Donald Trump: Signs of Circulation in a Time of Bubbles," *Journal of Linguistic Anthropology* 29, no. 3 (2019): 397–416.

[44] See Steve Benen, *Ministry of Truth: Democracy, Reality, and the Republicans' War on the Recent Past* (Mariner Books, 2024).

[45] Joel Achenbach, "Science is Revealing Why American Politics Are So Intensely Polarized," *Washington Post*, January 20, 2024, https://www.washingtonpost.com/science/2024/01/20/polarization-science-evolution-psychology/; and Michael Tomasky, "Why Does No One Understand the Real Reason Trump

platforms like Twitter has changed how people, especially on the Right, think and talk. As David French noted regarding the growing influence of Twitter, "There are several consequences of this reality. It's altering the way the right speaks. ... Social media doesn't create a marketplace of ideas so much as a gallery of takes, where you can spend hours doomscrolling through short videos and snappy retorts. ... This transformation has the effect of further radicalizing the right. There's a "Can you top this?" dynamic to posting that pushes people to extremes."[46]

Last, there is the main focus of this book: how Trumpism as a distinctive discourse operates to make even the most outrageous positions seem mainstream, normal, and legitimate. Heather Cox Richardson has noted that the key to the rise of authoritarians is their use of language.[47] Authoritarian demagogues consistently use a language of resentment to appeal to people in a once dominant group, who see changes in society as a sign they are being left behind. They encourage the populace to demonize the chosen scapegoats as illegal newcomers or interlopers or discredit and threaten minority groups who are the cause of their supposed declining status. People then buy into the lies, misinformation, and conspiracy theories to justify their resentments. Yet, I would add that the key here is how the most extreme accusations get normalized so that those more in the mainstream end up going along. For me, this normalization is what is most critical about the role of discourse (more on this later).

All these factors helped make Trumpism a uniquely successful extremist movement in the United States. From a broader historical perspective, there have been a number of significant political movements in the United States organized around resentments toward various outgroups, including especially nativistic and racist movements against people of color, immigrants, Jews, and others.[48] Yet, Trumpism is arguably different in its contradiction, and that helps explain its success in mainstream politics. Today, in the post–Civil Rights era, such a movement is more likely than previously to be rejected by mainstream society when it is explicit about its racism or xenophobia and therefore must maintain deniability while communicating its hostility. Admittedly, political movements that focused on mobilizing people primarily based on appealing to deep-seated resentments have, to varying degrees, especially in recent decades, had to contort their language to

Won?" *The New Republic*, November 8, 2024, https://newrepublic.com/article/188238/trump-won-voter-perception-2024.

[46] David French, "Why Elon Musk Is the Second Most Important Person in MAGA," *New York Times*, March 3, 2024, https://www.nytimes.com/2024/03/03/opinion/musk-x-maga-trump.html.

[47] Heather Cox Richardson, *Democracy Awakening: Notes on the State of America* (Penguin Books, 2024), xvi.

[48] Nell Irwin Painter, *The History of White People* (W.W. Norton, 2010).

disingenuously imply they were not doing so.[49] Trumpism shares this quality in its discourse.

Given the increased brazenness with which it lies to appeal to deep-seated resentments of a frustrated base, Trumpism's disingenuous contortions to deny what it is saying invariably intensify. In appealing to the broader public and not just its committed base, Trumpism arguably intensifies this process in a vicious cycle.

On the other hand, in spite of its disingenuousness, or more likely because of it, Trumpism proved to be more successful than other historical precedents in mainstreaming White extremism. The southern resistance against integration extended from post-Reconstruction until the successes of the Civil Rights Movement. The Democratic Party in the latter part of the nineteenth century and early twentieth century included the significant influence of the Ku Klux Klan. The Second Klan, as it was called, was reinvigorated in the early twentieth century by growing opposition to immigration, in particular, to spread well beyond the South. But it was building off established White racism more than mainstreaming it. Trumpism's uniqueness lies in its ability to mainstream its extremism more generally even when most people oppose it.

Trumpism might have initially built a base off opposition to the Obama presidency, but has morphed into what prominent observers came to see as a broader anti-democratic, insurrectionist, and increasingly authoritarian movement.[50] This historically significant development became but a noteworthy moment in the country's long tug of war over the move toward an inclusive liberal democracy.[51] In other words, the back and forth over the direction of the country's politics in recent decades brought on a resurgent backlash increasingly desperate to counter the successes of the Civil Rights Movement.[52] It is this back and forth that today makes for an important context in shaping the uniqueness of Trumpism, especially the discourse.[53]

[49] For instance, see Jefferson Cowie, *Freedom's Dominion: A Saga of White Resistance to Federal Power* (Basic Books, 2022). Cowie says about George Wallace the leader of Massive Resistance in the 1960s against the enforcement of Civil Rights laws: "The buzzwords of the 1968 campaign may have been 'law and order,' but the symptoms were 'fear and frustration and anger.' Wallace was the strong man who could return America to the heartland it once was. And, to take his own language seriously, he was willing to use physical violence to restore it. His version of freedom revealed itself as a form of latent violence and suppression of not just Creek Indians and African Americans but those with whom one has fundamental political disagreements" (468).

[50] Perlstein, "American Fascism."

[51] See Fording and Schram, *Hard White*, Chapters 8–9.

[52] Rogers M. Smith and Desmond King, *America's New Racial Battle Lines: Protect versus Repair* (University of Chicago Press, 2024), 8.

[53] Steve Bannon, the former Chief Executive Officer of the 2016 Trump presidential campaign, and subsequent White House Chief Strategist, and eventually top MAGA cheerleader, is a big believer in the

Today, when we say "Trumpism," it could mean the political movement that Trump leads, or it can imply a political ideology, but, contrary to most other studies, I think it is important to also focus on how Trumpism is a discourse, specifically as a rhetorical discourse—that is, a way of speaking that incites action.[54] It is both a way of narrating what is happening and a course of action implied by those words (making for a *dis-course*).[55] This book focuses on key examples that illustrate how distinctive features of the rhetorical discourse of Trumpism operate as a part of the effort to mainstream the resentful politics of the Movement.

The Undertow

There is no question that the old cliché asking what is more important, the movement or the message, haunts our ability to understand what has made Trumpism the political force it has become.[56] Trumpism as a movement of people organized for political action was built among various disaffected groups with their particular resentments.[57] Today it is giving expression to an increasingly wide range of animosities that have been bubbling up in the post–Civil Rights decades, with intensifying focus against the federal government, democratic institutions overall, and the broader society that moves furtively toward a more inclusive, multiracial democracy.[58]

Part of the shock of the rise of Trumpism as a movement is this underappreciated "Undertow" of seething resentment—both overlooked and despised.[59] The Undertow today is a prime force in pulling the country apart politically, and it represents a constellation of emotions tied together by the claims of various, if somewhat overlapping, underappreciated groups: Whites, especially Christians and males, but others of various backgrounds who see themselves

idea that there are cycles to political history and Trumpism represents a historically significant countermovement. See Isaac Arnsdorf, "How Steve Bannon Guided the MAGA Movement's Rebound from Jan. 6," *Washington Post*, April 4, 2024, https://www.washingtonpost.com/politics/2024/04/04/steve-bannon-maga-january-6/.

[54] See Jennifer Mercieca, *Demagogue for President: The Rhetorical Genius of Donald Trump* (Texas A&M University Press, 2020).

[55] On discourse as creating new "headings" that allow us to go in new directions, see Jacques Derrida, *The Other Heading: Reflections on Today's Europe* (Indiana University Press, 1992). On the use of language as a form of action that actively imparts meaning to the words, see Ludwig Wittgenstein, *Philosophical Investigations; The English Text of the Third Edition* (Prentice Hall, 1968), 23.

[56] Marshall Ganz, "The Power of Story in Social Movements," in *The Proceedings of the Annual Meeting of the American Sociological Association*, Anaheim, California, August 18–21, 2001.

[57] See Cramer, *The Politics of Resentment*; and Wilentz, "American Carnage."

[58] For historical context, see Ganz, *When the Clock Broke.*

[59] Sharlet, *The Undertow.*

as increasingly disadvantaged by shifts in American society, culture, economy, and our increasingly polarized politics.[60]

Among the various groups in the Trump coalition, there are the many conservative Evangelical Christians who see Trump leading a Christian Nationalism to enshrine their religious fundamentalism as the primary basis for the nation's public policies. It is noteworthy that Trump has strong Evangelical support despite his long history of philandering and his transparent lack of commitment to Christian values more generally.[61] Religious extremists among Catholics have likewise flocked to Trump in support of his agenda on abortion and a conservative cultural agenda more generally. Trumpism includes many males who feel threatened by the rise of feminism. The religious zealots have been leaders in propagating wild conspiracy theories on any number of issues like transgender rights, the killing of infants, and other incendiary nonsense.[62] Going further, Trump's incessant norm violating has added to his coalition another distinctive constituency of those who want affirmation for their own norm violations.[63] Beyond those with an explicit commitment to racism, there are those Whites in particular who are attracted to Trump based on their more amorphous status anxiety in a diversifying society.[64] Then there are the many economically disenchanted members of the White working class, including many veterans who feel they have been neglected in spite of their service. This is true of various others who support Trump and his movement in spite of how little Trump has done for them as president to uplift them economically.[65] The Trump coalition includes non-Whites who are attracted not just to his economic nationalism but also his

[60] For an in-depth examination across a range of resentments that by 2020 had come to be enfolded into Trumpism, see Lawrence Rosenthal, *Empire of Resentment: Populism's Toxic Embrace of Nationalism* (New Press, 2020).

[61] Tim Alberta, *The Kingdom, the Power, and the Glory: American Evangelicals in an Age of Extremism* (Harper, 2023).

[62] Eric Sammons, "Trump Wins: Let the Work Begin," *Crisis Magazine*, November 6, 2024, https://crisismagazine.com/editors-desk/trump-wins-let-the-work-begin.

[63] Michael Crowley, "As Election Nears, Trump's White House Grows Bolder in Flouting Ethical Norms," *New York Times*, July 16, 2020, https://www.nytimes.com/2020/07/16/us/politics/trump-goya-ivanka.html.

[64] See Daniel Martinez HoSang and Joseph E. Lowndes, *Producers, Parasites, and Patriots: Race and the New Right-Wing Politics of Precarity* (University of Minnesota Press, 2019); Biko Koenig, "Politicizing Status Loss Among Trump Supporters in 2020," *RSF: The Russell Sage Foundation Journal of the Social Sciences* 8, no. 6 (2022): 69–86; and Diana C. Mutz, "Status Threat, Not Economic Hardship, Explains the 2016 Presidential Vote," *Proceedings of the National Academy of Sciences* 115 (2018): E4330–39.

[65] For an in-depth statistical analysis on economic disenchantment and racial resentment combining among some Trump supporters, see John Sides, Chris Tausanovitch, and Lynn Vavreck, *The Bitter End: The 2020 Presidential Campaign and the Challenge to American Democracy* (Princeton University Press, 2023). For an analysis of how economic disenchantment has prompted many in the White working class to move away from the Democratic Party, see Justin Gest, *The New Minority: White Working Class Politics in an Age of Immigration and Inequality* (Oxford University Press, 2016). Also see Arlie Russell Hochschild, *Strangers in Their Own Land: Anger and Mourning on the American Right* (The New Press, 2018).

authoritarianism, xenophobia, anti-feminism, and opposition to according sexual minorities full rights in a liberal society.[66] At the other end of the economic spectrum are the many wealthy in the corporate and investor class who are prepared to tolerate Trump's extremism in exchange for policies that undercut liberal reforms and thereby allow them to continue to accrue excessive profits in an increasingly unequal society.[67] The coalition includes many White women disenchanted with the liberal drift of society. All told, Trumpism today brings together a wide variety of largely White people with a diversity of resentments, old and new, to build a solid but limited base of support for the grievance politics championed by Trump and allies.

As it has evolved, the Movement at times has gone beyond Trump himself to feature new hatemongers; opinion leaders have stepped forward to further the expressions and variety of grievances. While still a movement led by people who are given to expressing or tolerating the racism of the White Nationalist movement, or other less explicit forms of racial resentment, Trumpism has evolved to broaden its membership and widen its focus. This constellation of resentments ultimately has come to be reflected in an increasingly aggressive authoritarian turn in rhetoric. Trump himself came to promote this authoritarian turn, most especially once back in office, if for no other reason than his personal interest in acquiring power by emulating authoritarian leaders around the world.

The Authoritarian Turn

Over time, Trumpism has widened its purview in politically disturbing ways. As a discourse, it has proven particularly disturbing for some observers, especially in its mainstreaming of radical rhetoric that threatens the existing constitutional order. The growing interest in pursuing authoritarianism is still critically related to the issue of racial resentment and anxiety about multicultural diversification associated with immigration. As it was rising, Trumpism increasingly opposed majority rule and even the idea that the United States should be a democracy. Much of this was arguably related to the fear that White Americans would become a minority. Further, Trumpism has, since 2021, been about seeking revenge against those who have sought to hold Trump accountable for his misdeeds (which grew in number while

[66] See Daniel Hosang Martinez and Joe Lowndes, eds., *The Politics of the Multiracial Right* (NYU Press, 2024).

[67] Jamelle Bouie, "There's a Reason Trump Has Friends in High Places," *New York Times*, June 11, 2024, https://www.nytimes.com/2024/06/11/opinion/trump-business-capitalism-democracy.html.

he was in office during his first term). These currents in Trumpism continue to undermine the existing democratic features of the political system and move in a more authoritarian, or even fascist, direction (as witnessed at the start of his second term).[68] The 2024 presidential campaign, in fact, became preoccupied with whether a Trump victory would mean the end to liberal democracy in the United States. Conversation parried back and forth about whether Trumpism was instigating an existential threat to the constitutional system or was, as Trump claimed, a radical antidote to saving democracy from a litany—in Trumpspeak—of liberals, progressives, socialists, Marxists, communists, or some concatenation of all those who were said to be the real fascists.[69] Trump himself went so far as to refuse to say whether he opposed violence should he lose the 2024 election.[70] This type of incendiary talk continued even after both parties suggested a cooling of rhetoric after the failed assassination attempt against Trump in July 2024. The overheated rhetoric of Trumpism piloted him to win the popular vote in the 2024 election; the Country then waited to see what he would do once back in power. An authoritarian power grab quickly ensued.

Trumpism succeeded in reframing the liberal push for a more inclusive democracy as itself a threat to White power. Trumpism had already successfully tapped into anti-democratic attitudes among Whites with high levels of racial and other resentments.[71] But now those racial anxieties were being inflamed in support of authoritarian rule. Trump, however, was interested in being more than just a strong leader in a liberal democracy. By the time of the 2024 presidential campaign, he began talking about wanting to be an authoritarian much like those authoritarian leaders in other countries. This authoritarian turn had been developing for some time. Back in his Veterans Day statement of November 2023, Trump stated: "We pledge to you that we will root out the Communists, Marxists, Fascists, and Radical Left Thugs that live like vermin within the confines of our country, lie, steal, and cheat on Elections, and will do anything possible, whether legally or illegally, to destroy America, and the American dream."[72] Soon after this inflammatory

[68] Charles Homans, "Donald Trump Has Never Sounded Like This," *New York Times*, April 27, 2024, https://www.nytimes.com/2024/04/27/magazine/trump-rallies-rhetoric.html?smid=nytcore-ios-share&referringSource=articleShare&sgrp=c-cb.

[69] Swan and Haberman, "One of Trump's Oldest Tactics in Business and Politics: I'm Rubber. You're Glue."

[70] Eric Cortellessa, "How Far Trump Will Go" *Time*, April 30, 2024, https://time.com/6972021/donald-trump-2024-election-interview/.

[71] See Steven Miller and Nicholas Davis, "The Effect of White Social Prejudice on Support for American Democracy," *Journal of Race, Ethnicity and Politics* 6, no. 2 (2020): 334–51.

[72] Trump as quoted in Jamelle Bouie, "Trump Wants Us to Know He Will Stop at Nothing in 2025," *New York Times*, November 14, 2023, https://www.nytimes.com/2023/11/14/opinion/trump-stephen-miller-immigration.html. Trump has said to others that he is willing to invoke presidential power under the

declaration to use the powers of the presidency to extract retribution from his opponents, Trump thrilled his supporters by saying that he was set on being a dictator (if only temporarily), once he got back into office.[73] As time went on, he increasingly heaped praise on authoritarian leaders like Viktor Orban in Hungary as well as Jinping Xi in China and Vladimir Putin in Russia.[74] And once back in office, he initiated a series of authoritarian moves against his political opponents, the federal bureaucracy, the media, the universities, and others, shifting the political system away from liberal democracy in a dramatic fashion.[75] The connection between authoritarian rule and White racial hostility was hidden in plain sight. With this focus, the intensity of resentments grew and diversified with Trump's continued prominence in national politics. These resentments led to increased demonizing of immigrants and others that transcended what now seems like the almost quaint race-baiting and sexual demonization that have been at the core of welfare discourse—or in fact just about anything progressive proposed in the post–Civil Rights era. Those living in what Jeff Sharlet calls the "Trumpocene," where the Undertow tugs hard, in fact at times had gone well beyond Trump's original catcalls in ratcheting up the rhetoric, demonizing their opponents, and blaming them for their grievances.[76]

At times, it seems the Movement's growing intensity came to be on autopilot, evolving to find new targets of resentment. Part of the reason for the ongoing intensification of vengeful rhetoric is the growing frustration over being unable to fully overturn modern, liberal, multicultural society. As a result, there is a persistent ratcheting up of the rhetoric demanding ever more extreme actions to turn back the clock. Rick Perlstein calls this the "authoritarian ratchet."[77] Trump's most prominent supporters often sound as vengeful as Trump himself.[78] And as Trump continues to seek to have his Movement

Insurrection Act of 1792, as amended, to call up the military to put down protests against his presidency should he get back into office. David French, "It's Time to Fix America's Most Dangerous Law," *New York Times*, December 3, 2023, https://www.nytimes.com/2023/12/03/opinion/insurrection-act-trump-president.html.

[73] Marina Pitofsky, "Donald Trump Repeats Comment He Would Be a Dictator 'for One Day' if Reelected in 2024," *USA Today*, December 11, 2023, https://www.usatoday.com/story/news/politics/elections/2023/12/11/donald-trump-dictator-one-day-reelected/71880010007/.

[74] Maegan Vazquez, "Trump Meets with Orban, Hungary's Autocratic Leader," *Washington Post*, March 9, 2024, https://www.washingtonpost.com/politics/2024/03/09/trump-viktor-orban-autocrat/.

[75] Ryan D. Enos and Steven Levisky, "Harvard Must Take a Stand for Democracy," *The Harvard Crimson*, March 6, 2025, https://www.thecrimson.com/article/2025/3/6/enos-levitsky-harvard-trump-democracy-fight/.

[76] Sharlet, *The Undertow*, Chapter 6. Sharlet gets the term "Trumpocene" from Jeffrey Ruoff.

[77] Rick Perlstein, "My Political Depression Problem—and Ours," *The American Prospect*, May 29, 2024, https://prospect.org/politics/2024-05-29-my-political-depression-problem/.

[78] Prominent among the most vengeful Trumpists is Marjorie Taylor Greene. See Trudy Ring, "11 Times Marjorie Taylor Greene Was the Worst," *Advocate*, August 8, 2022, https://www.advocate.comdo/politics/2022/8/12/11-times-marjorie-taylor-green-was-worst. Key advisor to Trump Steve Bannon sees

behind him, he continues to be a leader in intensifying the authoritarian rhetoric.

With Trump's reelection victory, the resentments of Trumpism crystallized into a populist rage against liberal elites dictating, via the federal government, inclusivity. The groundwork for this turn was established well before Trump's victory. Running alongside the Trump 2024 presidential campaign was Project 2025, housed in the Washington think tank, the Heritage Foundation. It laid out a blueprint for an authoritarian, anti-democratic, and xenophobic agenda for Trump, should he be reelected.[79] The project was led by various Republican administrators, including Russell Vought, the former Director of the Office of Management and Budget during Trump's time as president, and Mike Davis, a former staff attorney working with Sen. Chuck Grassley (R-IA) as the Senate Judiciary Committee Chairman. Others leading the project included Paul Dans, Spencer Chretien, John McEntee, and many others formerly from the Trump administration. These project leaders are examples among many working for Trump who, more on the basis of loyalty than ability, went from being obscure staffers to prominent political activists championing Trumpism in its most radical form. Their pronouncements emphasized that Project 2025 would enact a Right-Wing version of what is called the "unitary executive theory" to consolidate power in the presidency and enable Trump to remake the government by unilaterally enacting a wide variety of extremist policies. Vought has gone so far as to characterize Project 2025 as creating a "post-constitutional" government, founded on principles of Christian Nationalism.[80]

As Project 2025 gained more visibility and criticism, Trump disavowed it, though people aligned with him were behind the project from the beginning.[81] In July 2024, while Trump was preparing to move to the center politically as the Republican presidential nomination convention neared, Kevin Roberts, President of the Heritage Foundation, stated that "we are in

Trumpism lasting well beyond Trump's time in politics, and he says that Trump is really a moderate in the MAGA Movement. See Alex Griffing, "Bannon Warns 'Trump is a Moderate' in the MAGA Movement and in the Future the Left Will 'Pine' to Have Him Back," *Mediaite*, November 13, 2023, https://www.mediaite.com/news/bannon-warns-trump-is-a-moderate-in-the-maga-movement-and-in-the-future-the-left-will-wish-to-have-him-back/?fbclid=IwAR3hy6rUmmx5_Oyph2oe-M4YOuTcwtJtZQyNUet_FYyFsgY-fuT3B-C-i4g.

[79] Robert Kagan, "A Trump Dictatorship Is Increasingly Inevitable. We Should Stop Pretending," *Washington Post*, November 30, 2023, www.washingtonpost.com/opinions/2023/11/30/trump-dictator-2024-election-robert-kagan/.

[80] Will Bunch, "The Scariest Word in America is 'Post-Constitutional,'" *Philadelphia Inquirer*, June 11, 2024: https://www.inquirer.com/columnists/attytood/trump-post-constitutional-american-russell-vought-20240611.html.

[81] See Will Bunch, "Mike Davis Wants to Cage Kids, Put Trump's Enemies in a 'Gulag': He Could Be Our Next AG," *Philadelphia Inquirer*, November 19, 2023, https://www.inquirer.com/opinion/commentary/mike-davis-trump-attorney-general-20231119.html.

the process of the second American Revolution, which will remain bloodless, if the left allows it to be."[82] Trump later posted on his social media platform Truth Social: "I know nothing about Project 2025. I have no idea who is behind it. I disagree with some of the things they're saying and some of the things they're saying are absolutely ridiculous and abysmal. Anything they do, I wish them luck, but I have nothing to do with them."[83]

Nonetheless, Project 2025 was in fact part of a long-term plan by those on the Right to stay in power over the long term, and growing numbers of Trump enablers and supporters voiced support for the plan.[84] In fact, Trump seemed all fine with it at first. In late April 2024, once talk about Project 2025 showed there was growing support among his base, Trump explicitly endorsed some of the most extreme proposals for an authoritarian takeover of the federal government, including politicizing the judiciary, weaponizing the Justice Department to prosecute his enemies, pardoning January 6th insurrectionists, using military troops, some from abroad, to place millions of undocumented immigrants in deportation camps, replace civil service bureaucrats with politically loyal henchmen, take control of the Federal Reserve and other independent regulatory agencies, and get around the 22nd Amendment so that Trump could serve additional terms as president.[85] Trump eventually followed through on many of these moves with a slew of executive orders and over 1,500 pardons for the insurrectionists, all executed on his first evening back in office on January 20, 2025.

It had already become clear that Trumpism's authoritarian turn included defending its strongman leader in cult-like fashion.[86] While defending himself in court from charges of obstructing the peaceful transfer of power on January 6, 2021, Trump insisted that presidents have "absolute immunity." This squares with his interest in claiming dictatorial powers and his insistence on projecting an unchallenged right to dominate.[87] In fact, the US Supreme Court ruled in July 2024, just before Project 2025 started to get criticized

[82] Adriana Gomez Licon, "Trump Disavows Project 2025 Transition Plan after a Key Official Calls for a New American Revolution," *AP News*, July 5, 2024, https://apnews.com/article/trump-project-2025-biden-9d372469033d23e1e3aef5cf0470a2e6.

[83] Ibid.

[84] Barrington Salmon, "Project 2025, If Allowed, Will Cement America as a Rightwing Authoritarian State," *Michigan Advance*, January 16, 2024, https://michiganadvance.com/2024/01/16/project-2025-if-allowed-will-cement-america-as-a-rightwing-authoritarian-state/; and Ruth Ben-Ghiat, "The Permanent Counterrevolution," *The New Republic*, May 16, 2024, https://newrepublic.com/article/181265/permanent-counterrevolution.

[85] Cortellessa, "How Far Trump Will Go."

[86] Isaac Arnsdorf, *Finish What We Started: The MAGA Movement's Ground War to End Democracy* (Little, Brown and Company, 2024).

[87] M. Steven Fish with Laila M. Aghaie, *Comeback: Routing Trumpism, Reclaiming the Nation, and Restoring Democracy's Edge* (Rivertown Books, 2024).

widely, that the president did possess near absolute immunity for "official acts" taken as president.[88] The Court had created a legal foundation for an authoritarian president to enact this agenda.[89] Trump's claim that the president always has absolute immunity was never credible, but by having the Supreme Court seriously consider it and then substantially, if not entirely, go along with the claim, Trump has succeeded in normalizing his authoritarian strategy.[90] Gaining credibility by way of the Supreme Court only further rallied support for installing Trump as a president with extraordinary power.

This became a fait accompli and seemed in retrospect to have emboldened Trump that he could be that authoritarian strongman president he seemed always inspired to be. This decision showed how deep the commitment among the Right had grown to align with Trump's vision of an authoritarian strongman government as a bulwark against sharing power in a democracy. As a result, Trump's quest to have his Trumpists concentrate their energies on protecting their leader against the supposedly all-powerful oppressive liberal "regime" (as it is often now called) succeeded; and it encouraged mainstream conservatives to continue to back him.[91] With Trump returning to power, he was ready to move quickly to take steps to replicate the "authoritarian breakthrough" that other elected autocrats around the world have achieved where they use their constitutional powers to destroy the elected democracy that put them in office.[92]

Trumpism as an anti-democratic movement poised to undermine the constitutional system ended up with Trump winning the popular vote in the 2024 election. The "authoritarian ratchet" ended up not as an act of desperation but as a road to consolidating power. It was aided by the process of normalizing the authoritarian tendencies in Trumpism to the point that a near-majority of voters accepted Trump's candidacy. Right-Wing extremist politics to undermine the rule of law moved to the top of the agenda. It was all part of a pushback against the effort to move to a more inclusive multiracial democracy. In the process, Trumpism evolved from a movement stoking White resentment to one slavishly dedicated to protecting its leader.[93] The intensity of these efforts has taken Trumpism to yet another level. With a popular vote victory in the 2024 election, the Country was poised to, in

[88] *Trump v. U.S.* (2024), https://www.nytimes.com/interactive/2024/07/01/us/scotus-immunity.html.

[89] Charlie Savage, "Immunity Ruling Escalates Long Rise of Presidential Power," *New York Times*, July 2, 2024, https://www.nytimes.com/2024/07/01/us/politics/immunity-president-supreme-court.html.

[90] See Ruth Ben-Ghiat, https://twitter.com/ruthbenghiat/status/1783516548184826319.

[91] See Patrick J. Deneen, *Regime Change: Toward a Postliberal Future* (Sentinel, 2023).

[92] M. Gessen, "This Is the Dark, Unspoken Promise of Trump's Return," *New York Times*, November 15, 2024, https://www.nytimes.com/2024/11/15/opinion/donald-trump-orban-putin.html.

[93] Jennifer Rubin, "The Media's Worst Lapse: Refusing to Identify Trump as a Cult Leader," *Washington Post*, January 12, 2024, https://www.washingtonpost.com/opinions/2024/01/12/media-trump-cult/.

fact, install a democratically elected autocrat.[94] In other words, the Undertow that sustains Trumpism had become a Riptide, and mainstream politics ended up drowning in it.[95] Trump's first weeks of his second term saw his administration moving quickly to implement the Movement's authoritarian, anti-democratic agenda with illegal and unconstitutional actions on a wide variety of issues including attacks on the federal bureaucrats and liberal public policies, the media, the universities, the exercise of free speech, and the rights of immigrants.

Exemplifying the Discourse of Trumpism

Over time, Trumpism, either as a movement, ideology, or discourse, has not had one singular focus, emerging as it has from a variety of sources with diverse targets for its resentments. The trajectory of Trumpism, as it arced across different inflection points, nonetheless manifested a coherent discourse and consistent style of expression reflective of prior efforts to mainstream extremist claims in a post–Civil Rights society. In fact, the coherent and consistent style of expression highlights what it takes for the mainstreaming of extremism to gain traction with the public.

In what follows, I focus on particular points of controversy in the trajectory of Trumpism as it has evolved from the rhetoric of racism, to talk that is more reflective of an American-styled fascism, to calls for civil war and then implacable opposition to the constitutional order, if that is what is needed to protect their leader from legal accountability for various crimes, including his attempt to block the peaceful transfer of power upon losing the 2020 election. I will focus on key examples in each case to illustrate how Trumpism as a coherent discourse consistently operates in service of attempts to normalize, mainstream, and legitimize its extremist claims.

My interest is not primarily in who supports Trump or why, though White males remain a key constituency. Nor is it who exactly are the leading practitioners of the Trumpist discourse, though that would be Trump himself. Neither is it about whether Trumpism as a discourse gets adopted by most followers in the Movement, though Trump has many emulators, if none are as prominent. Last, it is not about whether the discourse of Trumpism has proven to be always successful in mainstreaming its demonizations, lies, and mischaracterized grievances, though Trump won reelection in 2024 after

[94] Lerer, "America Hires a Strongman."

[95] Jamelle Bouie, "Trump Is Playing with Fire," *New York Times*, January 12, 2024, https://www.nytimes.com/2024/01/12/opinion/trump-political-violence.html.

being defeated in 2020. Instead, my analysis focuses on key examples of how the discourse has operated by consistently employing certain discursive techniques that are designed, if not always successfully, to defuse opposition and normalize and legitimate the outrageous things being said. I focus on these features of Trumpism as a discourse to illustrate how it does not just energize the base but also gets deployed in efforts to win over enough support in the mass public to become as politically successful as it has in the post–Civil Rights society.

The examples I provide are paradigmatic in the sense that they are representative of the general pattern of the discourse of Trumpism.[96] These examples not only highlight a consistent style of expression as Trumpism has arced across different inflection points. They also serve to illustrate how that consistent style of expression aims to legitimate its demonizations, lies, and mischaracterized grievances. I do give attention to the possible effectiveness of these discursive practices. But my primary focus is to illustrate how Trumpism as a discourse operates in practice for purposes of normalizing, mainstreaming, and legitimating its claims.

The analysis that follows lays the groundwork for concluding that Trumpism as a discourse has likely contributed significantly to Trump and his acolytes remaining such a force in mainstream politics, including their successful remaking of the Republican Party and the eventual return of Trump to the White House.[97]

The Discourse Matters

In the chapters that follow, I will examine distinct inflection points in the increasingly overheated rhetoric of Trumpism as it has cycled through its racism, fascism, civil war talk, and then how it gave voice to an authoritarian cult bent on insulating its leader from legal accountability. Consistently across these different inflection points, Trumpism has exhibited a style of expression that significantly operates to normalize the overheated rhetoric.[98] My examples will illustrate this consistency in discursive practices. They are designed to legitimate and normalize resentments that have been there previously but

[96] Bent Flyvbjerg, "Five Misunderstandings about Case-Study Research," *Qualitative Inquiry*, 12 (2006): 219–45.

[97] See Jonathan Karl, *Tired of Winning: Donald Trump and the End of the Grand Old Party* (Dutton, 2023); and Julia Azari, "Trump's Dominance in the GOP Isn't What It Seems," *Politico*, May 18, 2023, https://www.politico.com/news/magazine/2023/05/18/donald-trump-paradox-gop-00097458.

[98] Michael C. Bender, Lisa Lerer, and Michael Gold, "Trump Signals an Election Year Full of Falsehoods on Jan. 6 and Democracy," *New York Times*, January 6, 2024, https://www.nytimes.com/2024/01/06/us/politics/jan-6-trump-biden.html.

now with Trumpism have found a way to become more prominent in mainstream politics. This consistent style of Trump speak, what I am calling the discourse of Trumpism, is, I would argue, a significant contributing factor to understanding the success of Trumpism as a movement.[99]

There have always been those who dismiss the idea that we should take seriously the overheated rhetoric of Trump and his supporters.[100] As late as December 2023, after Trump was criticized for calling immigrants "vermin" and saying they were "poisoning the blood of our country," US Senator and diehard Trump supporter Lindsey Graham (R-SC) said "I could care less what language people use."[101] Graham had his own reasons for wanting to deflect away from focusing on the language of Trumpism. Yet, he was not alone. In fact, for years now a number of Trump critics have suggested that we should just stop encouraging "them" by shining a light on their outrageousness. They suggest that if we ignore Trumpism as a discourse, it would lose its potency for its failure to "own the libs." But just look where that has gotten "the libs."

Trumpism has become its own self-sustaining fear-mongering machine, thriving on the constant ratcheting up of its lies, conspiracy theories, and demonizations. Trumpism, however, accomplishes more than mobilizing Trump voters to cast their ballots based on resentments they may have been previously reluctant to express. Trumpism as a discourse has also proven to act as a form of "dangerous speech" or "stochastic terrorism" as in speech that encourages people to go on and commit illegal acts, including violence, in the name of acting out those inflamed resentments.[102] It pushes bullets as well as ballots as a way of exercising political power. The fact that Trump got reelected in 2024 does not mean there will be less violent behavior by his supporters (as the initial months of Trump's second term already indicated).

[99] On the role of language in politics overall, see Murray Edelman, *The Symbolic Uses of Politics* (University of Illinois Press, 1967); William E. Connolly, *The Terms of Political Discourse* (Princeton University Press, 1974); and Michael J. Shapiro, *Language and Political Understanding: The Politics of Discursive Practices* (Yale University Press, 1981).

[100] Dan Balz, "Voters Must Take Trump Seriously and Literally. The Stakes Are That High," *Washington Post*, November 18, 2023, https://www.washingtonpost.com/politics/2023/11/18/trump-second-term-plans/. Also see Jamelle Bouie, "Want to Know What Trump Will Do? Listen to What He Says," *New York Times*, March 19, 2024, https://www.nytimes.com/2024/03/19/opinion/trump-immigration-poisoning-rhetoric.html.

[101] Lauren Sforza, "Graham Blows off Trump Migrant 'Poisoning' Remark: 'I Could Care Less What Language People Use,'" *The Hill*, December 17, 2023, https://thehill.com/homenews/senate/4364611-graham-blows-off-trump-migrant-poisoning-remark-i-could-care-less-what-language-people-use/.

[102] Jonathan Leader Maynard and Susan Benesch, "Dangerous Speech and Dangerous Ideology: An Integrated Model for Monitoring and Prevention," *Genocide Studies and Prevention: An International Journal* 9, no. 3 (2016): 70–95; and David Corn, "Donald Trump, Stochastic Terrorist," *Mother Jones*, September 29, 2023, https://www.motherjones.com/politics/2023/09/donald-trump-stochastic-terrori-milley-violence-muskst/. There is also "harmful speech"; see David Beaver and Jason Stanley, *The Politics of Language* (Princeton University Press, 2023).

When he won in 2016, there was a sharp uptick in acts of domestic terrorism committed by White Nationalists and others who could be said to be aligned with Trumpism.[103] We saw it again now that Trump had been reelected.

Trumpism as a Metapragmatic Discourse: The Road to Normalization

The focus of this book is on Trumpism as a "metapragmatic discourse" that reframes points of political contention to make its political aims more acceptable.[104] I want to highlight that the distinctive discursive practices of Trumpism form its own disturbing path to normalizing extremism.[105] Trumpism is in fact a profoundly dangerous discourse that I will show has evolved in just a few short years right before our eyes. It continues to evolve as the efforts of Trump and his supporters to seize power grow ever more threatening to not just rational political dialogue but also to the constitutional order that makes that possible and even politics overall as an alternative to violence.[106]

The irony is not to be missed. Trumpism increasingly became a threat regardless of whether all the loose talk should be taken seriously or literally.[107] And it is a real threat not just because Trumpists gained more power. The threat also intensified because Trump and his followers became increasingly desperate about losing what power they have had. Trumpism is an extremist movement of resentful Whites, males, Christians, and other followers, led by a narcissistic leader who is himself anxious about his status, legal as well as political, and therefore too willing to give voice to their grievances in exchange for their support. Trumpism as a discourse seeks to mainstream, normalize, and legitimate extremism on issues such as race, democracy, and even the constitutional authority of states in the federal system. Depending on which Trumpist opinion leader articulates these extremist views, they were often doubling down in the face of increased criticism.

[103] Vanessa Williamson and Isabella Gelfand, "Trump and Racism: What Do the Data Say?" *Brookings*, August 14, 2019, https://www.brookings.edu/articles/trump-and-racism-what-do-the-data-say/.

[104] On metapragmatic discourse, see Ryan Schram, "Independent Declarations: Attributions of Peoplehood in News Narratives," *Signs and Society* 10, no. 3 (2022): 287–313; and Michael Silverstein, "Metapragmatic Discourse and Metapragmatic Function," in *Reflexive Language: Reported Speech and Metapragmatics*, ed. John A. Lucy (Cambridge University Press, 2000), 32–58.

[105] See Mercieca, *Demagogue for President: The Rhetorical Genius of Donald Trump.*

[106] Michael Feola, *The Rage of Replacement: Far Right Politics and Demographic Fear* (University of Minnesota Press, 2024), 56.

[107] Salena Zito, "Taking Trump Seriously, Not Literally," *The Atlantic*, September 23, 2016, https://www.theatlantic.com/politics/archive/2016/09/trump-makes-his-case-in-pittsburgh/501335/.

Trumpism as a metapolitical discourse operates at two levels: the pragmatic and the metapragmatic.[108] First, there is the pragmatic level where the questionable claims of Trumpism are used *in particular contexts*. It is this contextual issue that makes the first level pragmatic. Trumpism gives voice to the smears, lies, and mischaracterizations that resonate with the particular concerns that a minority coalition of resentful Americans seeks to express. Trump himself has for some time now been a leader in popularizing these pragmatic speech acts that push people's emotional buttons. And his supporters have proven most appreciative of what they say is his forthrightness, indicating that they like that he is not reluctant to "tell it like it is."[109] Other prominent Republicans and opinion leaders on the Right have joined with Trump in pursuing this discourse of demonization and lying, distinctive relative to what has been the norm in mainstream politics in recent years.[110]

Yet, Trumpism also operates at a second metapragmatic level where the original claims are *recharacterized in misleading ways*.[111] I label this second level metapragmatic because the metapragmatic function of language is manifested in instances where a speech act references another speech act.[112] Metapragmatic language is not just contextual, it is also "intertextual" in invoking what has been previously enunciated but now recharacterized.[113] Since Trumpism is giving voice to views rejected by most Americans, it must engage in various metapragmatic recharacterizations to mainstream, normalize, and legitimate its claims. Both levels are important. While the Trumpist discourse of demonization, lying, and mischaracterizing grievances might enable one to win a primary with the support of those siloed in the Trumpian information bubble, they need to engage in a metapragmatic discourse to win the general election. They need to recharacterize their earlier statements to

[108] Silverstein, "Metapragmatic Discourse and Metapragmatic Function," 32–58.

[109] "Election 2016: Trump Voters on Why They Backed Him," *BBC*, November 9, 2016, https://www.bbc.com/news/election-us-2016-36253275.

[110] For instance, people like Tucker Carlson, formerly of Fox News, and Marjorie Taylor Greene, a Republican member of Congress from Georgia, are among the many acolytes who have seemingly self-consciously practiced what I am calling Trumpism as a discourse. There are many others even at the highest levels of the Republican Party like Elise Stefanik (R-NY) in House who, in pursuit of advancing politically, have not only aligned themselves with Trump but have distinctively used demonizations and lies in the metapragmatic ways that Trump has.

[111] For instance, see Aurora Donzelli, "On Metapragmatic Gaslighting: Truth and Trump's Epistemic Tactics in a Plague Year," *Signs and Society*, 11, no. 2 (Spring 2023): 173–99.

[112] See Michael Silverstein, "Shifters, Linguistic Categories, and Cultural Description," in *Meaning in Anthropology*, ed. Keith. H. Basso and Henry A. Selby (University of New Mexico Press, 1976), 11–56.

[113] Intertextuality was a term coined by Julia Kristeva in 1966. See Julia Kristeva, "Word, Dialogue, and Novel," in *Desire in Language: A Semiotic Approach to Literature and Art*, ed. Leon S. Roudiez, trans. Thomas Goraet (Columbia University Press, 1980), 64–91.

inoculate themselves from criticism with the mass media and the broader public.[114]

Trump himself often offers his own overheated version of the two-step. There is the metapragmatic reinterpretation of a prevailing understanding, but Trump also then turns to demonize those who oppose his doing so (often the people who offered the original understanding). A paradigmatic example is when Trump rejected a reporter's factual assessment of Trump with the retort: "you are fake news."[115] Trump is recharacterizing the news as fake, but he is also personalizing it. In so doing, Trump trolls the reporter with a popular meme and simultaneously puts a face on the critique. Once the "enemy of the people" (as Trump often labeled the mainstream press, invoking a Nazi term) is identified and demonized, a political target is isolated, and mobilization of supporters is made that much easier. Trump's own distinctively personalizing and simplifying metapragmatic discursive moves such as these lie at the heart of this strategy for normalizing outrageous claims and are critical in making his combative approach to politics so effective with his supporters.[116]

More often however the two-step of Trumpism as a discourse seeks not to boomerang a critique as much as to gaslight understanding to soften the extremist statements with forms of deniability, as in "that is not what was meant." Trump's surrogates often enact this move on his behalf as his vice presidential (VP) candidate J. D. Vance did in serial fashion throughout the 2024 campaign. Vance inverted the classic role of VP candidate as attack dog and often sought to minimize or explain away Trump's extremist statements.

Therefore, language and how it is expressed are something that really do matter and do so in a very particular way for Trumpism as a discourse. I want to show why we should not minimize its political significance. My focus goes beyond highlighting Trumpism's rhetoric of resentment. I intend to show not only that it is important to examine what is being said, but also how. I will demonstrate that a consistent style of expression has been present even as Trumpism has evolved to feature different resentments. Most importantly, I will show that more often than not, the two-step of Trumpism has been

[114] On how the media have often been complicit in normalizing Trumpism, see Chris Lehmann, "The 'Is Donald Trump a Fascist?' Debate Has Been Ended—by Donald Trump," *The Nation*, November 14, 2023, https://www.thenation.com/article/politics/donald-trump-fascist-vermin/.

[115] Amber Jamieson, "'You are Fake News': Trump Attacks CNN and BuzzFeed at Press Conference," *The Guardian*, January 11, 2017, https://www.theguardian.com/us-news/2017/jan/11/trump-attacks-cnn-buzzfeed-at-press-conference.

[116] See Angelo Fichera, "The Method Behind Trump's Mistruths." *New York Times*, April 8, 2024, https://www.nytimes.com/interactive/2024/04/08/us/politics/trump-speech-mistruths.html.

expressed in ways that seek to mainstream its extremist claims by maintaining deniability.

Trumpism as a discourse has roots in the changing forms of communication associated with an age where social media has become dominant. For instance, it has important features consistent with the style of expression known as trolling that has been popularized in social media in recent years, where people often express themselves disingenuously in order to disrupt and disturb others who are trying to make factual claims that they find to be threatening.[117] Rather than accept the facts or try to counter them with other facts, trolls, as they are called, deflect them with various discursive moves. This type of disingenuous expression allows the troll to continue to insist on their point of view without having to actually engage in a serious exchange of ideas. Trumpism's style of expression is very much consistent with the growing popularity of disingenuous trolling on the internet. The internet creates a congenial platform for the disingenuousness of Trumpism and is consistent with the growing tendency in recent years, especially among Trump and his supporters, to authorize transgressing standards of truth in the quest for political ascendancy.[118]

Trumpism's style of expression builds off the popularity of trolling to maintain its outrageous lies, conspiracy theories, and misguided beliefs.[119] A leader in this regard was the internet-savvy Steve Bannon, who was a major force in the Alt-Right Movement, came to head Trump's 2016 campaign, and then got appointed for a short time as White House advisor, before becoming a popular podcaster where he continued to troll in order to mainstream and legitimate Trumpism.[120] Though led by Bannon, Trump is its most prominent performer. He is the ultimate "edgelord of strategic irony" when it comes to constantly blowing smoke on the internet and elsewhere.[121]

Whether it is about how immigrants are "poisoning the blood of our country" or how he promises to be a dictator (if only on the first day of returning

[117] Commentators on Right-Wing mass media outlets like Fox News prominently also practice trolling. See Brian Stelter, *Network of Lies: The Epic Saga of Fox News, Donald Trump, and the Battle for American Democracy* (Simon and Schuster, 2023), 217–18.

[118] See Frank Fischer, *Truth and Post-Truth in Public Policy: Interpreting the Arguments* (Cambridge University Press, 2021); and Benen, *Ministry of Truth*, 187.

[119] Henna Paakki, Heidi Vepsäläinen, and Antti Salovaara, "Disruptive Online Communication: How Asymmetric Trolling-like Response Strategies Steer Conversation Off the Track," *Computer Supported Cooperative Work* 30 (2021): 425–61.

[120] See Naomi Klein, *Doppelganger: A Trip into the Mirror World* (Farrar, Straus and Giroux, 2023), Chapter 7.

[121] Kathryn Joyce and Jeff Sharlet, "Losing the Plot: The 'Leftists' Who Turn Right," *In These Times*, December 12, 2023, https://inthesetimes.com/article/former-left-right-fascism-capitalism-horseshoe-theory?fbclid=IwAR13IT3HD1Ax8JVbwCXeZHvvIMc0tZiL7J2hJ-NZ82qNEp8rUtpK4yYImfs.

to the presidency), Trump's discursive strategy includes repeating the outrageousness, if simultaneously recharacterizing it so as to normalize it. The repetition makes the outrageous seem less shocking over time. The repetition can also prove effective in reinforcing misinformation, not so much to be believed as to be deferred to by followers.[122] As an authoritarian practice, Trump's repetition of lies and smears not only makes them commonplace but also forces people to choose whether to defer or risk retribution. Further, the repetitions also work to "flood the zone" and overwhelm opponents who get preoccupied with having to constantly call out repeated falsehoods when they should be doing and saying things related to advancing their own agenda. Last, Trump's repetitions increase the possibility of people actually acting out in response to these reprehensible statements.[123]

Bannon repeatedly emphasized that Trump deflects criticism by saying his critics are the real culprits, thereby inoculating himself from criticism.[124] For instance, if you are accused of undermining democratic deliberation by spreading misinformation, smears, lies, and conspiracy theories, deflect the criticism, adopt the democratic rhetoric of your opponents, and turn the tables to accuse your accusers of being the ones who are undermining democracy in trying to limit free speech. There is even a network of Trump-related organizations and Republicans in Congress that have gone as far as suing in court on First Amendment grounds to stop academic research in order to normalize the right to spread disinformation.[125] Normalizing, mainstreaming, and legitimating smears, lies, and contrived grievances on First Amendment grounds is one thing, but using the First Amendment to get the judicial system to bar academic research so that you can keep smearing and lying and contriving really shows the audaciousness of these upside-down Bannon-inspired efforts to mainstream Trumpism. Using the First Amendment against itself is just the kind of dangerous irony promoted by the two-step of Trumpism as a discourse.

[122] Sarah E. Parkinson, "Acting 'as if' during Pandemic: Information and Authoritarian Practice in White House," *Items*, June 25, 2020, https://items.ssrc.org/covid-19-and-the-social-sciences/democracy-and-pandemics/acting-as-if-during-pandemic-information-and-authoritarian-practice-in-white-house/. Regarding "as if" speech as an authoritarian practice, see Lisa Weeden, *Ambiguities of Domination: Politics, Rhetoric, and Symbols in Contemporary Syria* (University of Chicago Press, 1999).

[123] David A. Graham, "Trump Isn't Bluffing: We've Become Inured to His Rhetoric, but His Message Has Grown Darker, *The Atlantic*, December 7, 2023, https://www.theatlantic.com/magazine/archive/2024/01/trump-veterans-day-speech-vermin-reelection/676137/.

[124] Swan and Haberman, "One of Trump's Oldest Tactics in Business and Politics: I'm Rubber. You're Glue."

[125] Philip M. Napoli, "Agnotology, Free Speech and the Precarious Politics of Media Research" (a paper presented at the annual meeting of the Southern Political Science Association, New Orleans, LA, January 13, 2024); and Cat Zakrzewski and Naomi Nix, "Trump Allies Crush Misinformation Research Despite Supreme Court Loss," *Washington Post*, July 24, 2024, https://www.washingtonpost.com/technology/2024/07/14/trump-allies-disarm-misinformation-researchers-ahead-election/.

The Three Horsemen of Trumpism: Gaslighting, Boomeranging, and Co-opting

In what follows, I focus on select examples preceding the 2024 election from Trump and other key proponents of Trumpism. This group includes sympathetic mass media commentators from outlets like Fox News, who employ select metapragmatic moves that are prominent features of the two-step of Trumpism as a discourse. I highlight how these discursive maneuvers operate to mainstream, normalize, and legitimate their extremist claims in the face of criticism. These examples are designed to be illustrative rather than definitive as to the leading practitioners of Trumpist discourse and how frequently and successfully they have employed these discursive techniques. My analysis will focus most specifically on several powerful discursive practices of Trumpism as it has arced over time that have helped not just normalize but also legitimate its extremism. Working at times separately but also in combination, these discursive practices help create what Naomi Klein calls an alternate reality "Mirror World" that simultaneously invalidates criticisms and provides cover for Trump and his supporters to evade accountability.[126] The key discursive practices featured in my examples are reflective of Bannon's primary recommendation to deflect, accuse your accusers of what they accuse you of doing, and adopt their rhetoric to make you appear to be the good guy. In other words, I focus on what in contemporary parlance is called gaslighting, boomeranging, and co-opting.

To be explicit, gaslighting is deflecting criticism by suggesting something or someone else is the problem.[127] Trump has repeatedly said he did not get to remain as president at the end of his first term because Joe Biden and the Democratic Party "stole" the 2020 election. Boomeranging is to invert criticism that has been already made about you and to apply it to the opponent, thereby invalidating their criticism as hypocritical. During the 2016 presidential campaign, Bannon arranged for women who had accused Bill Clinton of sexual harassment or worse to appear at the front of the audience for the debate between Hillary Clinton and Trump. This happened just two days after Trump was first excoriated for the Access Hollywood tape in which he said that women allowed him to grope them because he was a "star."[128]

[126] Ibid.

[127] Emma Brockes, "I am Grateful to Trump for One Thing: Mainstreaming 'Gaslighting,'" *The Guardian*, December 2022, https://www.theguardian.com/commentisfree/2022/dec/01/trump-mainstreaming-gaslighting-word-of-the-year.

[128] Matt Flegenheimer, "What Donald Trump's 'Access Hollywood' Weekend Says About 2020," *New York Times*, July 12, 2020, https://www.nytimes.com/2020/07/12/us/politics/donald-trump-access-hollywood.html.

Many other boomerangs would follow over the next eight years.[129] When done subconsciously, boomeranging is a form of projection, where projection is unconsciously anticipating the criticism to suggest it is a valid concern about the opponent.[130] Last, co-opting is to take up various terms that the opponents use to describe what they are trying to do and steal them for oneself (if often to use them pejoratively or even defiantly).[131] Probably one of the most dramatic instances of co-optation in the twentieth-century political history was actually by the Civil Rights Movement. "Racism" was a relatively recent term, if not a new practice, in the 1930s when White Supremacists imported it from the Nazis' assertions of the superiority of the "Aryan race." Civil Rights activists subsequently inverted it to cast opprobrium on White Supremacists for believing that Blacks were inferior.[132]

Gaslighting, boomeranging, and co-opting are metapragmatic discursive moves in that they all are speech acts that refer to other speech acts.[133] They are representative of what arguably makes language distinctive as the only form of communication that has the capacity to refer to itself.[134]

[129] On how Trump boomerangs "fascist" back at his critics so as to neutralize that criticism about him, see Rachel Maddow as interviewed by Chris Hayes, *Why is This Happening?* https://www.msnbc.com/msnbc-podcast/why-is-this-happening-chris-hayes#:~:text=Every%20week%20on%20the%20podcast,unprecedented%20moment%20in%20world%20history%3F. Boomeranging, for some political scientists, is the failed attempt to disabuse people of their extremist views only to have the extremists double-down on those views. See Andreu Casas, Ericka Menchen-Trevino, and Magdalena Wojcieszak, "Exposure to Extremely Partisan News from the Other Political Side Shows Scarce Boomerang Effects," *Political Behavior* (February 2022), https://link.springer.com/article/10.1007/s11109-021-09769-9. Yet boomeranging can more commonly be seen as a *tu quoque* response to criticism when the people being criticized fling the criticism back at the critic as in "I am not the perpetrator of racist lies but instead you are." A noteworthy example of boomeranging was when Trump's 2024 reelection campaign staff resisted his instruction to hire Laura Loomer, who was not just a devout Trump supporter but also a self-identified Islamophobe. She had long perfected the art of boomeranging: "In 2018, she was barred from Twitter for violating its hateful conduct policy. To protest the ban, Ms. Loomer, who is Jewish, affixed a yellow Star of David to her clothes—just as 'Nazis made the Jews wear during the Holocaust,' she said—and handcuffed herself to the entrance to Twitter's New York headquarters." See Maggie Haberman and Jonathan Swan, "Trump Wanted to Hire Laura Loomer, Anti-Muslim Activist," *New York Times*, September 7, 2023, https://www.nytimes.com/2023/04/07/us/politics/trump-laura-loomer.html?smid=nytcore-ios-share&referringSource=articleShare. Also see Jeremy Diamond, "Donald Trump and the Art of the Boomerang Insult," *CNN*, September 16, 2016, https://www.cnn.com/2016/09/14/politics/donald-trump-boomerang-insult/index.html.

[130] See John Avlon, "Trump's Absurd Projection Reveals His Anxiety, *CNN*, September 24, 2019, https://www.cnn.com/2019/09/24/opinions/trumps-absurd-projection-reveals-his-anxiety-avlon/index.html.

[131] See Caroline Mala Corbin, "A Critical Race Theory Analysis of Critical Race Theory Bans," *UC Irvine Law Review* 14, no. 1 (March 2024): 95, https://scholarship.law.uci.edu/cgi/viewcontent.cgi?article=1630&context=ucilr.

[132] Linda Gordon, *Seven Social Movements that Changed America* (Liveright, 2025), 5.

[133] Silverstein, "Shifters, Linguistic Categories, and Cultural Description," 11–56.

[134] Roman Jakobson, the prominent twentieth-century linguist, emphasized language as a distinct and superior form of communication. He was also a mentor to Michael Silverstein, who coined the term "metapragmatics" in referring to speech acts that are indexical to other speech acts, i.e., where the speaker's language references other language in use. For Silverstein, metapragmatics highlight the distinctiveness of language as the only system of communication that has the capacity to reference itself. See Silverstein, "Shifters, Linguistic Categories, and Cultural Description," 16–17; and Miyako Inoue, "'Shake Well Before Using': The Dialectics of Michael Silverstein (1945–2020)," *Journal of Sociolinguistics*, 26 (2022): 177–91.

Generally, but especially for Trumpism as a discourse, they are a second level of discourse that is often designed to mainstream, normalize, or legitimate the controversial statements that are being referenced.

These particular metapragmatic discursive moves become especially important for Trumpism once we consider the contemporary political context. The context is important in shaping both the trajectory and the character of Trumpist discourse—not just what is said but how. As I have suggested, it is important to highlight that Trumpism is evolving in the post–Civil Rights era, making it at its base or core a minority movement that must work to mainstream, normalize, and legitimate its questionable pronouncements, especially its demonizations, lies, and contrived expressions of grievance. It is in many ways a movement driven to counter the Civil Rights Movement and the changes it has helped bring to society. Now people cannot make explicit White Supremacist statements on the floor of the US Senate as senators did for many decades.[135] The Undertow, as a loose collection of the disaffected and resentful, had already been expressing many of the resentments prominently articulated in Trumpist discourse and doing so in ways that sought to mainstream them. Some of these ways of expressing resentments in fact are long-standing. Trumpism as a discourse has assimilated these practices and intensified them. For instance, Trump has also brought back prior efforts from segregationists to deflect criticisms of racism. He does this by suggesting that resistance was not about racism as much as it was about the federal government dictating what people could or could not do. Now Trumpism is often about denying its opposition to multiculturalism per se and instead saying it is resisting the "Deep State" and singling it out for undermining people's rights.[136] In the post–Civil Rights society, subterfuge is more than ever necessary in order to mainstream and legitimate the Far-Right hate that lies behind them.

Gaslighting, boomeranging, and co-opting are not mutually exclusive but at times are distinguishable.[137] They often work together simultaneously, as some of my examples will seek to demonstrate. For instance, Democrats have long claimed to stand for the "common man" against the "elites," but Trump succeeded in co-opting that dichotomy while boomeranging charges that he is a rich man who favors the wealthy by emphasizing that he is an outsider working against the Establishment and the Elites (which he used

[135] See Ira Katznelson, *Fear Itself: The New Deal and the Origins of Our Time* (Liveright, 2014), Chapter 5.

[136] For a devastating critique of how White resistance to the power of the federal government has long been a deflection of charges of racism, see Cowie, *Freedom's Dominion*.

[137] See Ronald Brownstein, "The Limits of Trump's Identity Politics," *The Atlantic*, August 15, 2019, www.theatlantic.com/politics/archive/2019/08/trump-2020-democrats-racism/596155/.

interchangeably).[138] To be sure, Trumpists are not alone in using some of these metapragmatic moves. A boomerang that involved both co-opting criticism and inverting it came when Biden became "Dark Brandon" in response to "Let's Go Brandon" that Trumpists used as code for "F∗ck You Biden." When Biden was a guest on the TV show "Late Night with Seth Meyers," Meyers noted that Biden had "coopted Dark Brandon" into a meme of his supernatural powers.[139] Yet the more outrageously deployed metapragmatic moves are much more common among Trump and his allies. For instance, when talk of Trump "smelling" down below circulated among his critics, Trump supporters began attending his rallies wearing diapers that said "Diapers over Dems."[140] Weird but metapragmatic co-optation, nonetheless. The hallmarks of trolling were visible in this discursive move, suggesting that whatever you call our man, we will not be moved to be less supportive.

One of the most politically volatile metapragmatic moves came after the attempted assassination of Trump in July 2024. After years of well-documented and numerous cases of Trump encouraging political violence against his opponents,[141] Trump and others immediately boomeranged that it was Biden and the Democrats who were encouraging violence against Trump.[142] The assassination attempt created a pretext for Trump to boomerang charges that Biden and the Democrats were practicing what had by then come to be called "stochastic terrorism," that is, essentially encouraging violence by virtue of using inflammatory rhetoric. Boomeranging this charge not only sought to put Biden on the defensive, but it also held out the prospect of normalizing that kind of incendiary rhetoric that Trump and his acolytes commonly used to make it seem it was something everyone does. Trumpism operated as a metapragmatic discourse to recategorize and thereby legitimize extremism by dismissing it as normal. Immediately after the assassination attempt, there were calls for moderation or coming together

[138] See Michael Kruse, "Trump Reclaims the Word 'Elite' With Vengeful Pride," *Politico*, November/December 2018, www.politico.com/magazine/story/2018/11/01/donald-trump-elite-trumpology-221953/.

[139] See Tommy Christopher, "Biden Has Prop Ready When Late Night Host Asks Him About 'Dark Brandon' and Taylor Swift," *Mediaite*, February 27, 2024, https://www.mediaite.com/entertainment/biden-has-prop-ready-when-late-night-host-asks-him-about-dark-brandon-and-taylor-swift/.

[140] Anna Rascouët-Paz, "Fact Check: Photos Purportedly Show Trump Supporters Wearing Diapers at Rallies. Here's What We Found," *Snopes*, May 9, 2024, https://www.yahoo.com/news/fact-check-photos-purportedly-show-174100807.html.

[141] Mike Levine, "'No Blame?' ABC News Finds 54 Cases Invoking 'Trump' in Connection with Violence, Threats, Alleged Assaults," *ABC News*, May 30, 2020, https://abcnews.go.com/Politics/blame-abc-news-finds-17-cases-invoking-trump/story?id=58912889.

[142] Jeffrey Isaac, "Republican Feigned Outrage About Violence Must Not Be Allowed to Buoy Trump," *Democracy in Dark Times*, July 14, 2024, https://jeffreycisaacdesign.wordpress.com/2024/07/14/republican-feigned-outrage-about-violence-must-not-allowed-to-buoy-trump/?fbclid=IwZXh0bgNhZW0CMTEAAR1U8uYunHUEqJ5nNuMQTb9bt6yVx0YHEmw6GG2ujlTxUZg3KrDIEZrqDg4_aem_9qwXwBoA5w0fWVutxMdAaw.

in unity, but Trump and his acolytes continued to practice Trumpism as a two-step metapragmatic discourse that featured incendiary rhetoric.[143] This is just another, if very dramatic, instance of Trumpism's constant inflammatory refrain, always remaking extremism as normal and legitimate by boomeranging the criticism back at your enemies.

These metapragmatic moves are not exclusive to Trumpism, but they are prominently featured in Trumpist discourse as the chapters that follow will illustrate in detail. They are also not just satirical but more seriously share in Trumpism's insistent effort to win the broader emotional battle in the increasingly fraught struggle of US domestic politics in a post–Civil Rights era. In fact, a popular discursive move among Trumpists is to co-opt the rhetoric of the Civil Rights Movement and even go so far as to say they are reenacting the righteous resistance to the abusive power of the government that is denying them their civil rights. Civil Rights activists did this in demonstrations, sit-ins, and other forms of direct action against southern White government oppressors.[144] Trump outrageously called the African-American Republican gubernatorial candidate Mark Robinson in North Carolina "Martin Luther King on steroids," even though Robinson's extremist statements included calling for murdering opponents.[145] By deflecting attention (gaslighting), parrying back what is said about you by your critics (boomeranging), or reusing your opponents' terms for your side or against them (co-opting), the metapragmatics of Trumpism help legitimate its demonizations, lies, and contriving of grievances. The practical consequences go well beyond making harsh rhetoric acceptable. Instead, it can also exonerate Trumpism by denying its political indiscretions, proving that Trumpists are not the deplorables but the downtrodden. It thereby inverts victimhood and exculpates Trumpism against claims that it is racist, fascist, promoting a new civil war, or seeking to override the rule of law and overthrow democracy. Instead, it suggests that those characterizations better apply to the other side. As a result, the trajectory of Trumpism is then better able to sustain itself as its extremism evolves beyond these inflection points.

[143] Matt Dixon, Allan Smith, and Katherine Doyle, "Republican Convention Aims for Unity—But Keeps Some of the Old Red Meat," *NBC News*, July 15, 2024, https://www.nbcnews.com/politics/donald-trump/republican-convention-aims-unity-keeps-old-red-meat-rcna162020?fbclid=IwZXh0bgNhZW0CMTEAAR14RlwK_vwqBT-aqpQcyyepe1OmAR8mDmndcDLok75s03RTNhlJMrJzli4_aem_lnX2OD-FGAOHfhIGPQKTVw.

[144] Klein, *Doppelganger*, 254.

[145] Alec Hernández and Jake Traylor, "Trump Calls GOP Candidate with a History of Offensive Remarks 'Martin Luther King on Steroids,'" *NBC News*, March 2, 2024, https://www.nbcnews.com/politics/2024-election/trump-compares-north-carolina-lt-gov-mark-robinson-martin-luther-king-rcna141523; and Bill Church, "When You're Running for Governor, What You Say Matters," *Raleigh New & Observer*, July 13, 2024, https://www.newsobserver.com/news/local/article290008164.html.

There is the argument that these metapragmatic moves of Trumpism equate to the distinction between lying and bullshitting.[146] Lying is knowingly telling untruths, but bullshitting is about spouting them without regard to their veracity. Yet, my argument is that Trumpism does more than pollute public discourse. It does so in order to normalize its extremism. Trumpism therefore arguably has a strategic value that is its most important feature.

The metapragmatics of Trumpism go beyond what is said to also involve who is saying what. For instance, one increasingly popular metapragmatic move for Trumpism is to have women project strength and a desire to dominate, as exemplified by congressional representatives Marjorie Taylor Greene (R-GA) and Lauren Boebert (R-CO). In this way, the penchant for cruelty, popular among Trumpists, is softened by having it delivered by a female. A controversial case is that of former Gov. Kristi Noem (R-SD), who before becoming Trump's Secretary for Homeland Security, was seeking to be chosen as Trump's 2024 VP running mate and published a memoir that described her shooting and killing her puppy for being allegedly untrainable.[147] The public reaction was swift. Noem was widely criticized for what was seen as her extreme cruelty. Yet the metapragmatics of this move were also visible. As a woman and a mother, Noem claimed she was acting aggressively but on behalf of her children and for ensuring safety on her farm. Her aggression, preference for using guns, and acting violently were to be softened via her gender. Or so it seemed. But the level of her cruelty was so high that her gendered responsibilities as a mother and a woman could not balance the cruelty and make it seem acceptable. It appeared that it was the goal. The two-step metapragmatic discourse of Trumpism was hidden in plain sight. The cruelty that was popular among Trumpists got repudiated in this instance, but it was a metapragmatic move in service of normalizing extremism, nonetheless.

Trump himself has proven to be the most profligate user of a wide variety of these combative metapragmatic discursive moves, often in service of evading accountability for his extreme behavior as well as extreme statements.[148] A good case can be made that Trump's constant deployment of these metapragmatic moves has helped popularize them; others who have been pushing Trumpism forward as a political movement have, with increasing frequency, employed these rhetorical devices. Then again, given that they all are

[146] Paul Rosenberg, "Six Big Lies That Won the Election: How Donald Trump Gaslit America," *Salon*, November 9, 2024, https://www.salon.com/2024/11/09/six-big-lies-that-won-the-election-how-donald-gaslit-america/.

[147] The story about killing her puppy Cricket was excised from the book just after its first printing. See Sarah Fortinsky, "Noem Suggests Biden's Dog Also Should Have Been Shot," *The Hill*, May 6, 2024, https://thehill.com/homenews/4646010-noem-suggests-bidens-dog-also-should-have-been-shot/.

[148] See Mercieca, *Demagogue for President*.

listening to each other and often seeing each other on Fox News, the media outlet that was for a long time the main source for promoting Trumpism, it is hard to know who is learning from whom. It can be yet again another vicious cycle, much like the "authoritarian ratchet," central to the dynamics of Trumpism.

Trump was always comfortable practicing this sort of double-talk, given that it is consistent with his preexisting personal penchant for maintaining deniability for his culpability for the many questionable things he says and does.[149] For instance, for a long time, he often used *enthymeme*, the practice of not finishing sentences, and leaving your audience to fill in the missing idea or words for you.[150] In this way, the speaker maintains deniability if needed by saying they were misinterpreted or that he was only saying what others were saying. Trump liked to also distance himself from what he was suggesting by saying "people are saying" or "lots of people have said," etc. In other words, he was in still another way only reporting on what others were saying, but in this case reserving the right to say he was not saying it himself. It was like his preference to re-tweet White Nationalist memes and then say they were "only" re-tweets when criticized. In his view, he could leave it open for others to decide whether the racist meme should be embraced or not.[151]

Yet, Trumpism evolved beyond enthymeme and innuendo. The metapragmatic discursive moves of gaslighting, boomeranging, and co-opting became the critical forms of expression that enable Trump and his supporters to engage in verbal combat with the other side. Maintaining innocence and denying culpability remain important, but they are now to be achieved through these more combative moves. In this way, Trumpism is profoundly Orwellian, where up is down, and Whites are the real victims of racism. Trump, as an ex-president indicted for trying to illegally stay in power, was the real victim for being denied the office he claimed he still legitimately held. He claimed not to be trying to undermine democracy but seeking to save it by preventing an election from being stolen. It had gotten to the point where the gaslighting, boomeranging, and co-opting frequently combined to create an alternate reality his supporters had bought into. Now most Trump supporters believe the 2020 election was indeed stolen, in spite of the lack of evidence to

[149] Aaron Blake, "Plausible Deniability: The Thing President Trump Can't Stop Abusing," *Washington Post*, July 4, 2017, https://www.washingtonpost.com/news/the-fix/wp/2017/07/04/plausible-deniability-the-drug-that-president-trump-cant-stop-abusing/.

[150] Emily Flitter, "Trump is a——: White House Hopeful Plays Fill-in-the-Blanks with Voters," *Reuters*, February 16, 2016, https://www.reuters.com/article/us-usa-election-trump-language/trump-is-a-white-house-hopeful-plays-fill-in-the-blanks-with-voters-idUSKCN0VQ035. Also see Sanford F. Schram, "You Tell Me: Trump and the Politics of Denial," *Public Seminar*, August 16, 2016, https://publicseminar.org/2016/08/you-tell-me-trump-and-the-politics-of-denial/.

[151] "Trump Calls Dubious Post 'Just a Retweet,'" *WKBW Buffalo*, February 23, 2016, https://www.wkbw.com/news/us-news-world/democracy-2016/trump-repeats-dubious-posts-says-it-was-just-a-retweet.

suggest it was. In the end, Trump was reelected in part by convincing enough people to buy in or in some cases at least tolerate his insistence on an alternate reality.

There is merit in the claim that Trump himself has always just blustered wildly to defend himself: "Trump has treated his own words as disposable commodities, intended for single use, and not necessarily indicative of any deeply held beliefs. And his tendency to pile phrases on top of one another has often worked to his benefit, amusing or engaging his supporters—sometimes spurring threats and even violence—while distracting, enraging or just plain disorienting his critics and adversaries."[152] Nonetheless, over time, a consistent pattern to employ the metapragmatics of gaslighting, boomeranging, and co-opting, even if done unconsciously as a reflective self-defense mechanism, can be detected. And these discursive moves, as will be shown in the chapters that follow, have become prominent across the board for Trumpist supporters, among the political leadership, mass media commentators, and other aligned actors. Therefore, while it is always true, it is especially important to study not just what is said but how in the case of Trumpism.

I will focus on these metapragmatic discursive moves, operating often in concert, over the course of the trajectory of Trumpism as it has moved through initial phases and beyond, where themes of the preceding phase are carried forward while new ones are added. My goal is not to determine if all those associated with Trumpism are actually racist in one way or another, or fascists committed to using violence to overthrow the government, or are really ready for a real white-hot civil war, or even in the end ultimately invested in supporting Trump in a quest to become a dictator. Nor do I seek to show that all speech acts committed by Trumpists merit vituperation. Instead, I seek to point to particularly noteworthy instances where prominent Trumpers, like Trump himself or others aligned with the Movement, in the Party, on TV, or social media, invoked the two-step of Trumpism as a discourse in order to legitimate some of the more outrageous claims of Trumpism. I track the consistency of the two-step discourse as it evolved from featuring primarily racist concerns, to fascistic calls to promote violence, seize power, and undermine democracy. This includes, eventually, talk about the need for a new civil war, given the extreme polarization in US politics in recent years, and then about rallying around Trump to protect him from being brought to justice for his crimes and ultimately about overriding the rule of law.

[152] Maggie Haberman and Jonah E. Bromwich, "Trump's Trial Could Bring a Rarity: Consequences for His Words," *New York Times*, April 28, 2024, https://www.nytimes.com/2024/04/28/us/politics/trump-trial-words.html.

I examine the metapragmatics of Trumpism as it continued to evolve during the 2024 presidential campaign toward a blustery "copycat fascism," as in following today's autocrats like Viktor Orban.[153] As Jason Stanley has noted, fascists have consistently practiced a discourse of saying incendiary things to their base supporters and then denying those statements to assuage others, so as to normalize and legitimate the initial incendiary rhetoric. "You do it and then you deny it and it's just systematic, over and over and over again. The people who want to hear it hear it, and it signals the direction you want to go in. [The subsequent denial is] a way of lying to themselves and telling themselves [and others] this is not what's really going on."[154] The two-step metapragmatics of Trumpism are entirely consistent and make for a copycat fascist discourse, which includes even toying with encouraging violence against government officials and subversion of the current constitutional system.

Throughout the entire analysis that follows, I focus on the discursive practices associated with attempts at mainstreaming by way of subterfuge. Further, I will go on to show where evidence is available how this mainstreaming has real material effects on public opinion and the political behavior of Trump's supporters. For instance, it has gotten to the point where growing numbers of people not only believe that the 2020 election was stolen but also that immigrants at the border are a serious threat to the safety and economic well-being of the country and that the Democratic Party is responsible for most of the Nation's problems. I also highlight a number of vicious cycles in Trumpism as a movement. In particular, I emphasize how Trump and the movement more generally enact a desperation to stay popular. As a result, the discourse becomes more outrageous, and the discursive moves to maintain deniability become more prominent. I ultimately focus on the evolution of Trumpism into an authoritarian cult dedicated to protecting its leader at all costs. I end with assessments on the dangers posed by the trajectory of Trumpism, now with a victorious Trump back in the White House.

What Follows

Chapter 2 focuses on what has driven the trajectory of Trumpism as a discourse as it has arced from inflection points of racism, fascism, civil war,

[153] Dana Milbank, "Trump's Fascist Talk is What's 'Poisoning the Blood of Our Country,'" *Washington Post*, May 24, 2024, https://www.washingtonpost.com/opinions/2024/05/24/trump-fascist-rhetoric-reich-policy/.

[154] Ibid.

and eventually undermining the constitutional system to help its beloved leader evade legal accountability. Then I offer three chapters that highlight the specific legitimating discursive moves of gaslighting, boomeranging, and co-opting as related to key inflection points regarding racism, fascism, and civil war in Trump discourse. In each chapter, I provide evidence of how these discursive moves facilitate Trumpism's anti-democratic politics, policies, and practices, both nonviolent and violent. Each chapter provides a discourse analysis and research on corresponding responses to grasp more fully the trajectory of Trumpism as discourse that prompts political behavior. I conclude with a chapter considering the future of Trumpism now that Trump has won reelection and quickly moved to implement an authoritarian agenda.

Why It Matters

Trump's successful 2024 reelection campaign featured rhetorical moves that persistently repeated his denials by way of metapragmatics that suggested that not he but his opponents were the threat who needed to be taken down. Trump and his followers boomeranged the charge of weaponizing the justice system, and therefore served as justification for him to do the same should he get back to the White House.[155] The result of metapragmatic moves like this was that his supporters quickly became ever more agitated and less supportive of existing political institutions.[156] Whether Trump's winning the popular vote in 2024 changed their support for American democracy is an open question. Yet, given their past complaints, their support was most likely contingent upon how they could exploit its limitations and in fact see Trump inflict revenge on his opponents.

This, however, is not just an American story. This state of affairs is ever more fraught, as it is increasingly clear that regardless of its origins, the rise of Trumpism in the United States is now undoubtedly part of a global phenomenon where authoritarian leaders who rose through electoral processes, sometimes by winning back office after getting booted out, are emboldened

[155] Jonathan Swan, Maggie Haberman, and Charlie Savage, "The G.O.P. Push for Post-Verdict Payback: 'Fight Fire With Fire,'" *New York Times*, June 5, 2024, https://www.nytimes.com/2024/06/05/us/politics/trump-conviction-gop-revenge.html.

[156] Sarah Ellison and Josh Dawsey, "Despite Trump's Guilty Verdict, His Attacks Take Toll on Judicial System," *Washington Post*, May 31, 2024, https://www.washingtonpost.com/politics/2024/05/30/even-judicial-system-finds-trump-guilty-his-attacks-take-toll/.

to break with the rule of law.[157] Trumpism is finding allies around the world in his quest to undermine constitutional democracy in the United States.[158] As Kim Scheppele has noted:

> By now, we know the pattern: A constitutional democracy, flawed but in reasonably good standing, is hit by a transformative election. A charismatic new leader comes to power, propelled by the growing impatience that the electorate feels with things as they are. The leader promises to sweep away the dysfunctions of partisanship, gridlock, bureaucracy. … [R]ound the world, liberal constitutionalism is taking a hit from charismatic leaders like these whose signature promise is to not play by the old rules. But such hits have been long foretold. In one constitutional democracy after another, publics have grown increasingly discontent with their political institutions. This decline in public trust is particularly pronounced in countries that were hit hard by the global financial crisis of 2008 and after. But while the Great Recession made matters worse, democratic decline was already underway because the number of countries that could call themselves democracies in good standing began to drop before the economic crisis hit. Democratic malaise has economic correlates, but the causes go beyond economics. Something even bigger must be going wrong with democracy across many countries at once.[159]

Trump and his allies have indicated a willingness to be part of this global trend through their repeated expressions of appreciation for Orban's "illiberal democracy" in Hungary, where a popularly elected leader uses his power to impose authoritarian rule.[160] It is an open question whether the United States and other liberal democracies will continue to see more of what is euphemistically called "democratic erosion."[161] Trump's initial moves for a second term as an anti-democratic president are ominous.[162] An important question related to the specific instance of Trumpism concerns whether its discourse of deniability is helping bring about more democratic erosion in the United States

[157] Fintan O'Toole, "Letting It All Hang Out," *The New York Review*, November 7, 2024, https://www.nybooks.com/online/2024/11/07/letting-it-all-hang-out-november-5-election-fintan-otoole/.

[158] Anne Applebaum, "The New Propaganda War," *The Atlantic*, May 6, 2024, https://www.theatlantic.com/magazine/archive/2024/06/china-russia-republican-party-relations/678271/?gift=hVZeG3M9DnxL4CekrWGK3zpgN-PM-Vcu-tWJWxdvrdU&utm_source=copy-link&utm_medium=social&utm_campaign=share.

[159] Kim Lane Scheppele, "Autocratic Legalism," *The University of Chicago Law Review* 85, no. 2 (March 2018): 545–46.

[160] Vazquez, "Trump Meets with Orban, Hungary's Autocratic Leader."

[161] Steven Levitsky and Daniel Ziblatt, *How Democracies Die: What History Reveals About Our Future* (Penguin Books, 2019).

[162] Franklin Foer, "Corruption Unbound," *The Atlantic*, December 5, 2023, https://www.theatlantic.com/magazine/archive/2024/01/trump-second-term-mafia-state/676128/.

by erroneously claiming to be trying to save democracy. What happens when so much of political discourse becomes metapragmatic, where the debate is not about the substance of the original claims but instead about the gaslighting, boomeranging, and co-opting? Does this itself constitute the form of democratic erosion where political discourse increasingly denies the populace engaging with the substantive issues of democratic governance? In other words, to say once again for emphasis, it is important to study not just what is being said, but how. For then we might be able to better grasp the insidious way in which Trumpism is legitimating whatever authoritarian actions it promotes and its leader gets to enact.

2

The Trajectory of Trumpism

In this chapter, I provide background on what I see as the increasingly fraught trajectory of Trumpism. I trace the trajectory right up through the Movement becoming focused on rallying behind Trump as an indicted ex-president, who while running for reelection claims that he was the real victim for being selectively prosecuted for his alleged crimes to steal documents, overturn the 2020 election, and other wrongdoings. I focus on Trumpism and not Trump himself, though he is at the center of it all, because, given its success, Trumpism has such momentum as a reactionary movement that it is likely to remain prominent on the Right for some time even after Trump is gone.

For now, I begin with an overview of what drives the trajectory of Trumpism focusing first on the key role played by Trump himself and his relationship to the Movement he has come to lead. I go on to provide context for understanding how Trumpism as a discourse has come to be practiced. Then I provide an overview of key initial inflection points in the trajectory of Trumpism that help exemplify those practices. In subsequent chapters, I will examine these examples in detail to demonstrate how the specific discursive practices of gaslighting, boomeranging, and co-opting have operated consistently to help mainstream Trumpist claims associated with the different inflection points in the discourse of Trumpism.

The Vicious Cycle: The Trump in Trumpism and the Trumpism in Trump

The trajectory of Trumpism has been increasingly disconcerting as Trump and his followers have become more than strident and successful in mainstreaming their rhetoric and the ideas behind them. What we can call the critical vicious cycle of Trumpism however involves not just the interplay of words and actions. It also involves what amounts to the spiral between Trump and his followers, where it is not always clear who is leading whom, as Trump feeds off the reactions he receives from his supporters. Trump's personal insecurities loom large in this relationship. His narcissistic need to be loved seems unquenchable. In addition, Trump's own self-absorbed behavior increasingly

The Trajectory of Trumpism. Sanford F. Schram, Oxford University Press. © Oxford University Press (2026).
DOI: 10.1093/9780197827437.003.0002

led him to a plethora of personal legal and political woes,[1] and, as a result, his personal jeopardy made for an increasingly desperate discourse of demonization directed at his enemies that continued with even more recent episodes like the crisis over releasing files about Trump's long friend and pedophile Jeffrey Epstein The rhetoric has become ever more extreme as Trump faced continued assaults on his character, outrageous claims and deleterious policies.[2] Clinically speaking, it is a mistake not to include this psychological dimension in the examination of the trajectory of Trumpism as it arcs over US politics. In fact, many specialists have emphasized the importance of Trump's personality as a factor explaining the extremism of the Movement overall and its rhetoric. It is wise not to ignore these assessments.[3] We just cannot ignore the Trump in Trumpism. His personality ultimately looms large in affecting the political agenda for the country.[4]

Political scientists have long studied pandering politicians, but Trump has shown his willingness to go beyond what most pandering politicians are willing to do to appeal to voters.[5] Trump's personality leads him to seek the adulation of his followers, regardless of how many of them come from the fringes of our society. We therefore need to resist normalizing Trump's style of politics even as he tries to normalize his rhetoric and outrageous claims about stolen elections, his adversaries, and just about everything that has stood in his way to regaining power. With this personal approach, Trump's political posture is consistent with that of the classic demagogue who stokes fears and resentments among his base in order to secure his own hold on power.[6] Yet, Trump's demagoguery is distinctive in his indiscriminate willingness to give voice to even the most extreme groups in society just in order to secure his base of support. Political Science has yet to catch up in this regard to what Trump has done to mainstream political discourse. In fact, early assessments minimized the significance of Trumpism in this regard.[7]

[1] Sarah K. Burris, "George Conway Explains Why 'Narcissistic Sociopathic' Trump is Flailing and Lashing Out," *Raw Story*, March 23, 2023, www.rawstory.com/trump-online-freakout-indictment/?xrs=RebelMouse_fb&ts=1679665075&fbclid=IwAR313Q3MEdby6hUF13OgQknGeivpDUsDgVsOsQFW1SjJYWUKGDibQ5A8oHU.

[2] Karen Tumulty, "Donald Trump Is Promising the Apocalypse, *Washington Post*, March 28, 2023, https://www.washingtonpost.com/opinions/2023/03/28/trump-2024-battle-apocalypse-rhetoric/.

[3] Jennifer Senior, "We Are All at the Mercy of the Narcissist in Chief," *New York Times*, October 11, 2019, https://www.nytimes.com/2019/10/11/opinion/trump-narcissism.html.

[4] Michael C. Bender and Shane Goldmacher, "Trump Puts His Legal Peril at Center of First Big Rally for 2024," *New York Times*, March 26, 2023, www.nytimes.com/2023/03/25/us/politics/trump-waco-texas-speech.html.

[5] See Lawrence R. Jacobs and Robert Y. Shapiro, *Politicians Don't Pander: Political Manipulation and the Loss of Democratic Responsiveness* (University of Chicago Press, 2000).

[6] See Jennifer Mercieca, *Demagogue for President: The Rhetorical Genius of Donald Trump* (Texas A&M University Press, 2020).

[7] For a thoughtful but dismissive early assessment of Trump's ability to effectively enact an agenda on behalf of extremism, see Corey Robin, *The Reactionary Mind: Conservatism from Edmund Burke to Donald Trump*, 2nd ed. (Oxford University Press, 2017), 265–72.

Trump's willingness to align with extremists arguably was initially born of weakness and his inability to create a dominant majority coalition that could gain power without appealing to the fringe.[8] Yet, it is a mistake to see this weakness as meaning the anti-democratic threat posed by Trumpism is less than it is. Instead, it is this weakness that leads to Trumpism becoming entrapped in a downward spiral of intensifying hate and resentment in order to more aggressively mobilize more supporters to rally around the cause. Eventually, that ratcheting up of authoritarian rhetoric succeeded.

Originally, with his extreme rhetoric in his 2016 bid for the presidency, Trump pushed out many mainstream conservatives from the Republican Party. He lost the popular vote by a large margin but surprisingly won a narrow victory in the Electoral College. Yet, as president, he declined in the polls, and he appealed to even more extreme elements among the disenchanted in order to replenish his dwindling base of support and try to win reelection.[9] Losing his reelection bid in 2020 only intensified the quest to use more extreme rhetoric to continue to keep his frustrated base of support. Rather than walk away, he doubled down and stayed atop his Movement and the Party. It is the need to never admit losing, and to stay popular with whoever he needs to be seen as victorious. This is what drives Trump and the trajectory of Trumpism overall as a Movement that has tied its fate to its leader. All the while, Trump always tried to deny what he said in order to maintain support with the broader public. Therefore, it seems undeniable that it is Trump's extremely narcissistic personality that is a big part of what has helped make the trajectory of Trumpism so dangerous, pushing to the extremes in order to continue to collect supporters. It is the key vicious cycle of Trumpism.[10]

As a result, we have witnessed the increased role of his most extreme followers in setting the trajectory of Trumpism. Trump's seeming need to be loved by his followers, I would argue, is what led him to cycle through embracing racists, fascists, and proponents of civil war, in his personal quest to achieve glory and power. He always needed the adulation of his supporters as the political leader who helps mainstream their resentments and enable them to gain traction in US politics. Resultingly, their outrage at the existing society becomes something Trump must unavoidably add to his own (even at risk of further undermining his standing in mainstream society). Throughout this process, Trump consistently relied on his preferred response

[8] Corey Robin, "Trump and the Trapped Country," *New Yorker*, March 21, 2024, https://www.newyorker.com/news/our-columnists/trump-and-the-trapped-country.

[9] James Bickerton, "Fox Displays Poll Showing 61% of People Don't Want Donald Trump Back," *Newsweek*, March, 29, 2023, https://www.newsweek.com/fox-displays-poll-showing-61-people-dont-want-donald-trump-back-1791107.

[10] On the dynamic relationship between Trump and his base, see Jamelle Bouie, "Imagine if Trump Loses," *New York Times*, January 9, 2024, www.nytimes.com/2024/01/09/opinion/trump-republicans-democracy-hope.html.

each time he was called out for his inflammatory rhetoric—he engaged in projection and boomeranging in particular, spitting back that his critics were the racists, fascists, or proponents of a civil war tearing the Country apart.[11] Consciously or not, he was deflecting what was true about his own words and behavior in order to avoid being called into account. This denialism only further authorized his supporters to continue to up the ante in their politics of demonization.

Given the contradictions, Trump is at best half-hearted in these endeavors, often denying he is racist or fascistic or a proponent of civil war or has dictatorial ambitions. He sometimes is caught reluctantly backing down, as in taking down re-tweets on Twitter or re-postings on his social media platform, Truth Social, to avoid being held accountable for the resulting actions he promises or has actually taken by his supporters.[12] He cycles between seeking approval of extreme positions for rightist adulation, then denying them. Trump's personality is therefore part of a fraught dynamic. Trump aspires to be a popular leader in pushing MAGA resentments to the forefront of mainstream politics, but he is afraid of being outed as a true believer. He pushes to the extreme to energize his base but backs down as a politician who seeks elected office when it starts to hurt him in the polls.

As a result, Trump must work both levels of Trumpism as a discourse: He needs to give voice to extremist views in order to keep the base happy, but he must distance himself at times from those views via key metapragmatic moves in order to maintain deniability with the broader American public.[13] It is like he needs the first to win the primary in his political party and then the second to win the general election. This two-step explains why Trump often ended up sounding so contradictory. It is an open question whether it will stay that way, given he has won reelection and has pursued an authoritarian agenda as president.

For much of his short time at the forefront of national politics, it has been a fraught dynamic since Trump was first and foremost afraid of losing his base of support while still trying to win elections. This dynamic is actually reflective of the fundamental tensions between movements and political parties historically in the United States. Movements can be effective politically without having to create large coalitions that parties need for winning elections

[11] Peter Beinart, "The Projection President," *The Atlantic*, July 14, 2017, https://www.theatlantic.com/politics/archive/2017/07/the-success-of-smoke-and-mirrors/533706/.

[12] David Neiwert, "Trump's Dance Around the Racism, Violence Drawn to His Campaign Appears to Encourage It," *SPLC*, August 9, 2016, https://www.splcenater.org/hatewatch/2016/08/09/trumps-dance-around-racism-violence-drawn-his-campaign-appears-encourage-it.

[13] Michael Gold, "'I'm Not Going to Have Time for Retribution,' Trump Says at Town Hall," *New York Times*, January 11, 2024, https://www.nytimes.com/2024/01/10/us/politics/trump-town-hall-fox.html.

in the US two-party, winner-takes-all type of election system. As a result, Trump's hold on the Movement he commandeered was not guaranteed.[14] Trump needed to remain loyal to his followers as much as he expected them to remain loyal to him. When he initially announced his bid to run again for the presidency again in late 2022, Trump gave a tepid speech as if to signal that he would not continue to seek to inflame his base with overheated rhetoric. Yet, it was not well received by disappointed supporters. After he had Christmas dinner with Ye (formerly, Kanye West) and the avowed neo-Nazis Nick Fuentes (and others), Trump seemed to respond to their prodding that the base wanted him to continue to be the flamethrower who had thrilled them previously. After that, Trump returned to form and also began an ascent in the polls. Trump eggs on his base with strong rhetoric, but he also feels obligated to give the base what it wants for fear of losing popularity.[15]

This particular vicious cycle between the leader and his followers leads to an evolution in the rhetoric from first emphasizing racism, then fascism, and then later still civil war as distinct inflection points or phases in the trajectory of Trumpism, as Trump found new extremists to appeal to in trying to consolidate power while rallying more potential supporters, extremists, and others to his cause. Trump found ever more allies as he fell under increasing legal jeopardy for his many crimes.[16] His personal resentments began to loom even larger than previously. After losing his reelection bid in 2020 to Joe Biden, Trump's postings on social media went viral with his Big Lie urging his supporters to "Stop the Steal." He subsequently egged on supporters to storm the Capitol on January 6, 2021, to stop Biden's victory from being certified by Congress. Trump at that point ultimately elevated his personal resentment campaign to be the central cause of the Movement, when, in his speech in March 2023 before the Conservative Political Action Committees, he characterized his candidacy to run for President yet again in 2024: "In 2016, I declared: I am your voice. Today, I add: I am your warrior. I am your justice. And for those who have been wronged and betrayed: I am your retribution."[17] As Trump transitioned to being back in the White House in late 2024, his

[14] David French, "MAGA, Not Trump, Controls the Movement Now," *New York Times*, March 26, 2023, https://www.nytimes.com/2023/03/26/opinion/donald-trump-waco-rally-speech.html?smid=nytcore-ios-share&referringSource=articleShare.

[15] John Bowden, "Neo-Nazi Trump Dinner Guest Nick Fuentes Laments Kanye's Antisemitism Apology," *Independent*, December 27, 2023, https://www.independent.co.uk/news/world/americas/us-politics/nick-fuentes-kanye-trump-apology-b2470199.html.

[16] See William E. Connolly, *Aspirational Fascism: The Struggle for Multifaceted Democracy under Trumpism* (University of Minnesota Press, 2017), 7–8.

[17] David Smith, "'I am Your Retribution': Trump Rules Supreme at CPAC as He Relaunches Bid for White House," *The Guardian*, March 4, 2023, https://www.theguardian.com/us-news/2023/mar/05/i-am-your-retribution-trump-rules-supreme-at-cpac-as-he-relaunches-bid-for-white-house.

rhetoric may have cooled momentarily a bit at first, but his promises to seek retribution against his enemies remained.

All along, Trump was explicitly making his resentments synonymous with the Movement's and vice versa.[18] One cannot exist without the other. On the one hand, Trump had gained the undying loyalty of many of his followers. On the other hand, Trump also personally embodied their victimhood by making his own threatened status the primary complaint of his movement. But this constant enlargement of outrage and victimhood could become its own debilitating cycle. The base emboldens Trump, and he responds by authorizing them to be their worst selves.[19] He then cannot afford to go against the resentments he himself inflamed.[20] As president yet again, Trump now risked losing control of the Movement he came to command. Increasingly, the lies, conspiracy theories, and demonizations bubbled up from his base, whether the absolutely bonkers Q-Anon theories about baby-eating Democrats, or the Trump campaign's outrageous lies about Dominion voting machines flipping votes from Trump to Biden, or even what reactionary propagandists called by co-opting the Black Lives Matter terms so as to criticize "woke" teachers indoctrinating elementary school students in "Critical Race Theory."[21] Trump had amplified much of it, perhaps not at first but with time, increasingly embracing very extreme ideas from the fringes of his Movement, often seemingly just in order to stay on top. As things progressed, the varying resentments revealed the breadth and depth of those resentments that went into making the Trump coalition. Yet it also suggested a preoccupation by the Movement's coalition partners in clinging to power in the face of possibly losing it. Yet, given Trump's remarkable staying power, as the Republican electoral losses mounted first in the 2018 midterm elections, then in the 2020 presidential election, there has never been any sort of course correction, except maybe with that failed reelection campaign announcement speech. Instead, as it evolved, the lies, conspiracy theories, and demonizations only continued to get employed—whether about who won the 2020 election, whether Trump has committed various crimes, or sundry other

[18] Hannah Knowles and Meryl Kornfield, "Loyalty, Long Lines, 'Civil War' Talk: A Raging Movement Propels Trump," *Washington Post*, January 21, 2024, https://www.washingtonpost.com/politics/2024/01/21/trump-supporters-republicans-presidential/.

[19] Both the prominent civil rights attorney Sherrilyn Ifill and Donald Trump's niece, Mary Trump, were among those who emphasized this dynamic early on in Trump's rise to power.

[20] David A. Graham, "Trump Is Caught in a Double Bind: The Former President's Winning Strategy Is Also a Losing One," The Atlantic, September 7, 2022, https://www.theatlantic.com/ideas/archive/2022/09/trump-qanon-post-2022-republican-midterms/671354/.

[21] Ken Bensinger and Maggie Haberman, "Trump's Evolution in Social-Media Exile: More QAnon, More Extremes," *New York Times*, January 28, 2023, https://www.nytimes.com/2023/01/28/us/politics/trump-social-media-extremism.html. Also see Rosenthal, *Empire of Resentment*.

political and personal matters, often all mixed together in a jumble that perhaps only makes sense as part of an effort just to stay on top. In the end, the increasingly outrageous rhetoric proved to be part of a successful presidential reelection campaign, but whether Trump, now victorious, would continue to follow through remained unclear until suddenly it was not.

Trump's personal history was relevant to understanding the nature of Trumpism as a discourse, starting with Trump's tawdry history as a sex abuser. Like other sex abusers, Trump practices what psychologist Jennifer Freyd called DARVO (deny, attack, reverse, victim, and offender).[22] DARVO employs gaslighting, boomeranging, and co-opting in its patented process. For Trump, however, it is no longer limited to targeting women who accused him of sexual abuse. He has gone on to widen his targets when applying this metapragmatic process of denying misdeeds and accusing his accusers of having been the ones to actually commit those misdeeds. Further, the Movement has joined him, and DARVO has become the generic metapragmatic move for Trumpists in general. Sidney Blumenthal writes, "Though Trump ranks among the greatest living specimens of misogyny, his Darvo blame-casting extends to foes of any gender in every one of his conflicts. Trump's syndrome has become the core of his politics. Just as he is the Maga icon, even exalted as a god, his derangement is the golden calf for his followers. They worship by imitation. His gaslighting about his sexual violence has morphed into the essence of his pseudo-ideology of a debauched party."[23]

In These Times: The Context Matters

The foregoing suggests that it is important to recognize there is a lot of Trump in Trumpism and vice versa. This dynamic relationship has evolved, and so has the discourse. Yet, this means that the fraught arc of Trumpism as a discourse is not just due to Trump's personality and his need to frequently lie and deceive in support of the increasingly diversified extremist elements of his coalition in order to achieve his own personal and political success. It arguably is also a sign of the times. We live in an era of extreme "negative partisanship," where politics is largely conducted via demonizing opponents as an irredeemable enemy while not countenancing any division on your side.[24]

[22] Sidney Blumenthal, "Deny, Attack, Reverse—Trump has Perfected the Art of Inverted Victimhood," *The Guardian*, February 1, 2024, https://amp.theguardian.com/commentisfree/2024/feb/01/trump-victim-political-strategy-manipulation.

[23] Ibid.

[24] Rachel Bitecofer, *Hit 'Em Where It Hurts: How to Save Democracy by Beating Republicans at Their Own Game* (Crown, 2024).

Partisan success in winning elections goes to the more united party that is more intensely focused on demonizing the other side as an existential threat to the Country.

There is however a more pronounced tendency on the Right—definitely more so than on the Left—for politically active people, among leaders and followers, to seek to outdo each other by offering ever more cynically inspired outrageous claims about the other side.[25] The Right is given to practicing Rick Perlstein's "authoritarian ratchet," where their failure to deliver the change promised by their extremist rhetoric leads to an intensification of that rhetoric to assure their base of supporters that they are willing to go further to achieve the promised extremist changes.[26] According to the best research available, these claims are reflective of how the asymmetrical polarization of party elites today (more among Republicans than Democrats) can feedback and affect the emotions of the party rank-in-file (i.e., "affective polarization" where emotional identification supersedes ideological and policy commitments).[27] Yet, these claims are also associated with the well-established "paranoid style in American politics" (as Richard Hofstadter called it) that thrives when selected groups feel they are losing their privilege and being displaced by newcomers and upstarts.[28]

The ascendency of the politics of demonization today is most pronounced on the Right (it is in that sense asymmetrical). Nonetheless, the Left is undoubtedly not perfect. There is a tendency on the Left at times for those on the Far-Left to vilify liberals as sellouts capitulating to working within the capitalist system, but this is far more benign compared to what we are seeing on the Right in the Age of Trump.[29] On the Right, just about anyone these days who is tagged as disloyal to the cause of expressing extreme resentment to mainstream politics is subject to being demonized as beyond the pale and open to being dehumanized or at the least being called a RINO (i.e., Republican in name only), as has happened to some of the most prominent Republicans like Senate Minority Leader Mitch McConnell or former

[25] John Knefel, "The New York Times Continues Its Ahistorical 'Tough-on-Crime' Coverage as Trump and DeSantis Attempt to Outdo Each Other with Racist Dog Whistles," *Media Matters for America*, March 31, 2023, https://www.mediamatters.org/ron-desantis/new-york-times-continues-its-ahistorical-tough-crime-coverage-trump-and-desantis.

[26] Rick Perlstein, "My Political Depression Problem—and Ours," *The American Prospect*, May 29, 2024, https://prospect.org/politics/2024-05-29-my-political-depression-problem/.

[27] Naomi Ehrich Leonard, Keena Lipsitz, Anastasia Bizyaeva, Alessio Franci, and Yphtach Lelkes, "The Nonlinear Feedback Dynamics of Asymmetric Political Polarization," *Proceedings of the National Academy of Science*, December 14, 2021, doi:10.1073/pnas.2102149118.

[28] On the paranoid style of politics, see Richard Hofstadter, "The Paranoid Style in American Politics," *Harper's Magazine* (November 1964): 77–86.

[29] See Samuel Moyn, *Liberalism Against Itself: Cold War Intellectuals and the Making of Our Times* (Yale University Press, 2023).

Vice President Mike Pence. McConnell condemned the January 6th insurrection and Pence was targeted for hanging that day for failing to go along with Trump's plot to overturn the 2020 election. McConnell ultimately decided to step back from leadership in the Senate while still endorsing Trump's 2024 bid to return to the presidency. Pence ran against Trump in the 2024 primary but was reluctant to criticize him, though ultimately he would not endorse his reelection. In both cases, they had, as early as 2020, lost favor with the MAGA base of the Party.

On the Left, things are civil in comparison. The anti-capitalist Left is not about to take up arms against more moderate liberals and in fact those on the Far-Left tend to still see them as allies, even if it is recognized that partnering with liberals inevitably means there will be a profound sense of disappointment about the possibilities for radical change.

Nonetheless, history has shown the Left has its own trajectory of distancing itself from our less than fully democratic constitutional order. The Labor Movement of the late nineteenth and early twentieth centuries came to include communists, socialists, anarchists, and others who were demonized as terrorists, leading some to be deported while others were killed.[30] By the 1960s, the Anti-War Movement included the Far-Left radicals, such as the Weathermen and the Weather Underground whose extreme alienation led to violence including isolated killings.[31] A broader swath of the Movement then expressed growing distrust of a federal government that lied about US involvement in the Vietnam War. The revelation of the FBI's illegal Cointelpro program of spying on American anti-war protesters intensified that alienation.[32] The FBI's assassination of Fred Hampton, a young civil rights activist and a prominent member of the Black Panthers, did much to further the Left's disenchantment with the rule of law in the United States.[33] Many other crimes, whether inflicted on individuals, groups, or society, got attributed, not always correctly, to the government, including the killing of Martin Luther King Jr., the rise of mass incarceration, the failure to eliminate poverty, and so on, all furthering the Left's alienation. The Left's alienation in fact has continued right through to today to contribute to the declines in the

[30] Ahmed White, "100 Years Ago, the First Red Scare Tried to Destroy the Left," *Jacobin*, December 23, 2019, https://jacobin.com/2019/12/red-scare-industrial-workers-of-the-world-iww.

[31] Maurice Isserman, "Weather Reports: The Radical Individualism of the New Left Was Hardly Un-American," *The Nation*, January 24, 2008, https://web.archive.org/web/20150223212010/http://www.thenation.com/article/weather-reports.

[32] David Garrow, *The FBI and Martin Luther King, Jr.* (Yale University Press, 2006).

[33] Bryan Burrough, *Days of Rage: America's Radical Underground, the FBI, and the Forgotten Age of Revolutionary Violence* (Penguin, 2016), 84–85.

already low levels of trust in the federal government among the US population more generally.[34]

Today, the similarities and differences in Left–Right alienation from the federal government are complicated by the movement of a minority of fringe Leftists over to supporting Trump as their new champion for disaffection toward the federal government.[35] The award-winning Left-Wing critic Naomi Klein wrote about how she was often confused for another prominent writer, Naomi Wolf, even though it was only Wolf who became a mirror image of herself in switching from being a Left-Wing critic of the abuses of power to a Hard-Right Trump-like critic of the federal government.[36] Robert Kennedy Jr. became a reverse image of his family's political persona, as champions of the common people, when he ran first for the 2024 Democratic presidential nomination and then as an independent candidate, posing in ways that led him to gain support from COVID deniers and anti-vaxxers and ended up being praised by the Trump Guru Steve Bannon and other MAGA leaders while gaining traction with their followers.[37] Kennedy ended up in Trump's second term cabinet spreading lies about vaccines, fluoridation, and the federal government's failed Deep State of compromised scientists. The old "horse-shoe theory" that the extreme Left and Right have a lot in common regained some currency in the Trump era.

Yet, even in these destabilizing times, the doppelgangers who become the Right-Wing mirror images of their former Left-Wing selves are a distinct minority. A more common problem is that, at times, it does seem to be the case that a non-trivial number on the Left have fallen prey to feeling obligated to respond to growing extremism on the Right with their own set of over-the-top responses. We are at risk of becoming "reverse marionettes, where the other side's alleged outrage orchestrates our own exaggerated response."[38] I do believe it is driven mostly by one side, which is to say this is yet another contrapuntal vicious cycle that seems particularly specific to living in an era where Trumpism has perverted politics. It is yet another example of a vicious cycle that afflicts our politics today in an age of growing polarization.

One troubling development is that both sides increasingly feel obligated to police their coalitions to marginalize those in their ranks who do not toe that line for fear that internal divisions will weaken their ability to win out

[34] Pew Research Center, "Public Trust in Government: 1958-2022," June 6, 2022, https://www.pewresearch.org/politics/2022/06/06/public-trust-in-government-1958-2022/.

[35] Kathryn Joyce and Jeff Sharlet, "Losing the Plot: The 'Leftists' Who Turn Right."

[36] Klein, *Doppelganger*, Chapter 7.

[37] Ibid.

[38] Ibid., 117.

against their main opponents in tight elections. More generally, "cancel culture," as the Right likes to label it, unfortunately does manifest itself on the Left at times.[39] At times, there has been overheated rhetoric from the Left about Trumpism, and there have been instances where Left-Wing extremist agitation has led to violence, but this rarely happens, especially compared to the escalation of Right-Wing extremism.[40]

"Both-sideism," as a thoughtless response to today's political discourse in the context of increasing affective polarization, is however the much larger problem. If the Left has at times been overheated in reacting to Trumpism, it pales to what Trumpism is doing all on its own. Instead, today, the trajectory of Trumpism is largely a self-sustaining echo-chamber of hate, barreling down its own hyper-resentful version of the "highway of despair."[41] The Movement increasingly sees itself as being unfairly criticized as dangerous and defamatory, and the leader himself is increasingly seen that way as well. Yet the result is a stubborn doubling down, with an intensification of the discourse of demonization, the related conspiracy theories, the outrageous lies, and resulting increased demands for ever more radical changes to mainstream society, the culture, and our politics. The intensification of demonization exacerbates ongoing political polarization, widening the gap between political adversaries, turning them into enemies. As enemies, those on the other side become combatants in war. This situation opens the door to legitimizing violence against the other side. It is as if the base has an insatiable well of resentment, and when attempts to amplify their resentment fail to work politically, the only solution is to draw more deeply into that well. At times, it seems that Trumpism is increasingly not about policy victories as much as it is about inflicting pain on the other side. It is more about getting and keeping power, about winning, so as to ensure that liberals lose and do not get the power to enact their policies. Trumpism remains primarily about enacting the demonizations associated with "affective polarization." Even calls for tempering the rhetoric after the first failed assassination attempt on Trump largely fell on deaf ears, and the 2024 campaign continued to be highly combustible.

[39] See Eric Levitz, "David Shor's Unified Theory of American Politics," *Intelligencer*, July 17, 2020, https://nymag.com/intelligencer/2020/07/david-shor-cancel-culture-2020-election-theory-polls.html.

[40] Jeffrey Isaac, "Reflections on the New Anarchy and the Real Danger of MAGA Republicans," *Common Dreams*, April 4, 2023, https://www.commondreams.org/opinion/anarchy-and-the-real-danger-of-maga-republicans.

[41] On how Hegel's "highway of despair" can serve as a frame for a generic critical tendency especially in Left-Wing political theorizing, see Robyn Morasco, *The Highway of Despair: Critical Theory After Hegel* (Columbia University Press, 2015).

The Arc of Trumpism

This intensifying trajectory of Trumpism could have been just another example of the inevitable tendency of all political movements to burn out and decline beyond a certain point. This actually happens whether they succeed in having an impact on mainstream politics or not.[42] Social movement theory tells us that social movements are transitory mobilizations in attempts to influence mainstream politics, whether they form in neighborhoods, nationally, in person, online, or otherwise.[43] Their networked character suggests they emerge out of overlapping alliances. They go through stages, rising and inevitably declining.[44] The role of leadership is important in affecting these changes.[45] Yet Trumpism is its own unique phenomenon, and its trajectory is arguably specific to this Movement and the current era. The sustained trajectory of Trumpism could be in part caused by Trump's long-standing quest to achieve greatness for himself, or it could be something inherent in the Movement he ended up coming to helm. It is also probably a bit of both. Yet, when a movement's leader is preoccupied with their own survivability, it can go into decline or go off the rails.[46]

As Frances Fox Piven and Richard Cloward famously argued decades ago, political movements in general, especially protest movements, do not endure if those in power can co-opt them with concessions (which is often followed by repression).[47] Decline often follows. Further, Charles Tilly and others have argued that social movements more generally, including those not involved in staging mass protests, often deteriorate over time for a variety of reasons, including when they achieve a modicum of success and the intensity to get some kind of change dissipates.[48] This decline may be in the future for Trumpism, whether Trump leads the Movement or not. That decline may be looming

[42] See Lilliana Mason, *Uncivil Agreement: How Politics Became Our Identity* (University of Chicago Press, 2018), Chapter 7.

[43] John Scott and Gordon Marshall, *A Dictionary of Sociology* (Oxford University Press, 2009).

[44] On the theory that all social movements transition through stages, see Herbert Blumer, "Social Problems as Collective Behavior," *Social Problems* 18 (1971): 298–306; and Armand L. Mauss, *Social Problems as Social Movements* (Lippincott, 1975). Also see Charles Tilly, *Social Movements: 1768-2004* (Paradigm Publishing, 2004); and Doug McAdam, Sidney Tarrow, and Charles Tilly, *Dynamics of Contention* (Cambridge University Press, 2001).

[45] Aldon D. Morris and Suzanne Staggenborg, "Leadership in Social Movements," in *The Blackwell Companion to Social Movements*, ed. David A. Snow, Sarah A. Soule, and Hanspeter Kriesi (Blackwell Publishing, 2004), 171–96.

[46] On the role of leadership in producing the decline of a social movement, see Mayer N. Zald and Roberta Ash, "Social Movement Organizations: Growth, Decay and Change," *Social Forces* 44, no. 3 (March 1966): 327–41, https://doi.org/10.1093/sf/44.3.327. Also see Jerrold M. Post, "Narcissism and the Charismatic Leader-Follower Relationship," *Political Psychology* 7, no. 4 (December 1986): 675–88.

[47] Frances Fox Piven and Richard A. Cloward, *Poor People's Movements: Why They Succeed, How They Fail* (Vintage Books, 1977), 65–68.

[48] See Tilly, *Social Movements: 1768-2004*, 148–51.

and affect how people act in anticipation. But Trumpism has proven quite enduring up to now.

Then again, movements are almost always overtaken by counter-movements.[49] The constant push and pull of movement politics is central to what makes for the cyclical character of politics more generally.[50] It is like the defining characteristic of politics as the struggle between opposing groups for power. Critical to understanding the trajectory of Trumpism is how it represents a counter-movement to the Civil Rights Movement. Trumpism has emerged to be the vanguard of a Second White Redemption (the first came after the end of Reconstruction after the Civil War and successfully rolled back many advances to accord African Americans full rights as citizens).[51] Political movements and their counter-movements may always have a trajectory that ultimately leads to decline. Yet, today, we confront the extremely unusual case that a Right-Wing movement led by a demagogue who got elected president persists in clinging to power and in fact has become resurgent. It is difficult to find precedence to normalize that as something that recurs in American political history.

The distinctiveness of Trumpism, however, lies well beyond the fact that it has become more than an episodic protest movement. In fact, it is unusual for a political movement to have transitioned from being an outside force to taking over one of the two major political parties and coming to exercise state power.[52] The Trumpist Movement has captured the Republican Party, taken hold of a number of state legislatures, and continues to influence the decision-making of members of Congress.

The success of Trumpism as a movement that has taken over the Republican Party is however likely to become increasingly fraught. As political scientists like Julia Azari have noted, political movements and parties have often worked at cross purposes as much as they work together.[53] In the past, parties had to be cautious in their relationships with movements that

[49] David S. Meyer and Suzanne Staggenborg, "Movements, Countermovements, and the Structure of Political Opportunity," *American Journal of Sociology* 101, no. 6 (1996): 1628–60. Also specifically regarding American politics, see Sidney M. Milkis, "Review Essay: Donald Trump, Charismatic Leadership and the "Deep State," *Political Science Quarterly*, March, 2024, https://doi.org/10.1093/psquar/qqae018; and Suzanne Mettler and Robert C. Lieberman, *Four Threats: The Recurring Crises of American Democracy* (St. Martin's Press, 2020).

[50] Sanford F. Schram, *The Return of Ordinary Capitalism: Neoliberalism, Precarity, Occupy* (Oxford University Press, 2015), Chapter 1. On the cyclical nature of racial politics specifically, see Michelle Alexander, "The Injustice of This Moment Is Not an 'Aberration,'" *New York Times*, January 17, 2020.

[51] Serwer, *Cruelty Is the Point*, 6–14.

[52] Cathy Schneider provided this important insight.
https://journals.sagepub.com/doi/epub/10.1177/00027642241267933.

[53] Julia Azari, "Trump's Dominance in the GOP Isn't What It Seems," *Politico*, May 18, 2023, https://www.politico.com/news/magazine/2023/05/18/donald-trump-paradox-gop-00097458.

could help build their electoral coalitions but also push the party to take more explicit positions that could alienate Independents and moderate voters whose support was needed to win elections.[54] This was true for Democratic Party and groups like the Women's Movement or the Civil Rights Movement and for the Republican Party with the Pro-Life Movement and the Gun Rights Movement.[55] Going forward, the emerging fissures between the Movement and the Party need to be watched closely.

As partisanship has become stronger with an increasingly polarized electorate and as parties have become weaker as institutional gatekeepers determining who gets nominated, political movements have become even more influential in party politics.[56] Under these conditions, it becomes more possible for the unprecedented to happen, as when extremist movements like Trumpism take over the Republican Party. When a highly energized movement like Trumpism enters the nomination process, party elites are vulnerable to being displaced. While ironically called RINOs (Republicans in name only) by Trumpists, the Republican Party establishment increasingly got marginalized with Trump's ascendency. Trumpists become the "real" Republicans in the transformed party.

For much of the post–World War II history, each of the two major political parties aligned with movements for the purposes of primarily strengthening the party in order to enact an agenda that the movements supported to varying degrees depending on their cause.[57] Yet Trumpism's success in taking over the Republican Party signals an inversion where the party is being used to strengthen the movement. Presidential candidates often neglected party building while concentrating on their own electoral prospects. Trump has gone further in that direction than his predecessors, at times seeming more interested in using the party to enrich himself, his campaign, and his movement. Trump has always been more of a movement leader than a party builder, and for that reason he most often favors welcoming extremists into the Party conditional on them supporting him. He actually seems not to care about the status of the Republican Party beyond what it enables him to do as

[54] On the relationship of movements to political parties, see Sanford F. Schram and Richard C. Fording, "Racial Liberalism Resurgent: Connecting Multi-Racial Protests and Electoral Politics Today," *Journal of Race, Ethnicity and Politics* 6, no. 1 (2021): 97–119; and Nella Van Dyke, Kyle Dodson, Paul Almeida, and Jaqueline Novoa, "Social Movement Partyism and Congressional Opposition to Certifying the 2020 Presidential Election Results in the United States," *American Behavioral Scientist* 68 (November 2024): 1761–81, https://journals.sagepub.com/doi/epub/10.1177/00027642241267933.

[55] Sidney M. Milkis and Daniel J. Tichenor, *Rivalry and Reform: Presidents, Social Movements, and the Transformation of American Politics* (University of Chicago Press, 2019).

[56] Nicholas F. Jacobs and Sidney M. Milkis, *What Happened to the Vital Center? Presidentialism, Populist Revolt, and the Fracturing of America* (Oxford University Press, 2022).

[57] Azari, "Trump's Dominance in the GOP Isn't What It Seems."

the leader of a movement that sometimes seems to want to remake the entire Country. Trump's nomination of Sen. J. D. Vance (R-OH) as his vice presidential candidate underscored how Trump was more interested in sustaining a legacy of the Movement beyond his time in office.[58] It was a nomination for the Movement more than the Party. Trumpism has had a fraught relationship with the Republican Party, sometimes backing extreme candidates and policies that lead the GOP to defeat. The Trumpists often seem not to care because they are interested in the more fundamental change of tearing down the established institutions, including the Republican Party. As long as Trump and others aligned with him emphasize the Movement over the Party, Trumpism will not likely pass away any time soon. And throughout it all, there has been a consistency: Trumpism as a discourse employed metapragmatic discursive moves to help normalize some of its most outrageous claims across various inflection points.

Examining the trajectory of Trumpism, as a movement or as a discourse, I would argue, reveals that Trump's desire to be an all-powerful leader of a loyal movement of supporters led him to align himself with more than just racially resentful Whites. Trump's emphasis on the movement's emotional calls for standing up for the "real America" over the party's emphasis on policy priorities is consistent with the rise of authoritarians in the Western world in the twentieth century and beyond.[59] In the process, Trump ultimately came to embrace those with anti-democratic and seditious tendencies and eventually those whose resentment led them to seek the end of the US governmental system altogether by calling for civil war. But he also pandered to those who were just mad at the liberals. Trump himself of course ended up supporting all this because it aligned with his interests in staying in power and his fantasy of going down in history in the pantheon of all-powerful strongmen. In the process, the Republican Party has been replaced by an authoritarian personality cult that encourages the extremists on the Right to set the agenda.

Therefore, the trajectory of Trumpism, fueled as it is by Trump's quest to seize/maintain/not lose and ultimately win back power in whatever ways he could, can be seen as having its own phases, with pivotal moments or inflection points, demarcating significant shifts as the Movement came to accommodate diversifying elements to the coalition. The diversifying coalition avoided tension for the most part, as all, to varying degrees, shared a commitment to having Trump in power to enact his authoritarian agenda

[58] Meryl Kornfield and Marianne LeVine, "Trump Chooses Sen. J.D. Vance, a Former Critic, as His Vice-Presidential Pick," *Washington Post*, July 15, 2024, https://www.washingtonpost.com/politics/2024/07/15/jd-vance-trump-vice-president-announcement/.

[59] See Hannah Arendt, *The Origins of Totalitarianism* (Harcourt Brace, 1949), Chapter 8.

on their behalf. Reflective of political developments and events that enabled Trump and his followers to broaden their coalition, there were corresponding discursive shifts.

The End of Entryism: Trumpism Amplifies Racism

Trump's entry into mainstream politics was initially propelled by a racist discourse about how non-Whites, in the inner cities, but especially as immigrants, were a real threat to America as a White Nation. Trump's initial 2015 campaign announcement featured this kind of racially resentful rhetoric. This marks the first inflection point in the trajectory of Trumpism as an inflammatory discourse that ironically had mainstreaming effects. The White Nationalist Movement in America has demonstrated its violent potential for a long time, but in recent years it practiced "entryism," focusing on gaining entrance to mainstream politics by reducing its hateful rhetoric.[60] Yet, this seems to have reversed once Trump became their ostensible leader and was able to capture the Republican Party on his way to winning the White House. Rather than toning things down in order to achieve success in mainstream politics, Trump constantly encouraged his supporters to express their resentments. It was an unexpected development when it proved to be a winning strategy.[61] The result has been a diffusion of hate throughout the Trumpist movement with more moderate Republicans willing to be complicit in tolerating the mainstreaming of an intensified politics of resentment as the core of the Party's ideology in exchange for building a winning coalition.

Before Trump, in the post–Civil Rights Era, it had become verboten for candidates to make explicitly racist statements for fear of being discredited by the political mainstream. In order to appeal to White people's racial resentments, candidates had to "dog-whistle" (i.e., make only implicit racial references).[62] Trump broke new ground for leading Republican presidential candidates and as a result surprisingly gained followers, even as he turned off others, for initially saying the quiet part out loud regarding various outgroups, non-Whites, noncitizens, and non-Christians in particular.[63] In this phase, Trump was aligning himself with a White Nationalist Movement, whose leaders included Steve Bannon, who became a top official in both

[60] See Fording and Schram, *Hard White*, 75.

[61] Lilliana Mason, *Uncivil Agreement: How Politics Became Our Identity* (University of Chicago Press, 2018), 2.

[62] See Tali Mendelberg, *The Race Card: Campaign Strategy, Implicit Messages, and the Norm of The Race Card: Campaign Strategy, Implicit Messages, and the Norm of Equality* (Princeton University Press, 2001).

[63] See Fording and Schram, *Hard White*, 174–78.

the Trump campaign and the White House, only to get fired because of his own incendiary racist statements.[64] Trump continued in the White House to align himself with the White Nationalist Movement, as he did in his irresponsible statements about there being good people on "many sides" after the counter-protesters were violently attacked by the White Nationalists who led the "Unite the Right" march in Charlottesville, Virginia, in 2017.[65]

Back in this initial racist phase of the emergence of Trumpism as a movement, implicit and explicit racist and xenophobic statements were prominently used, if also subsequently denied, to rally resentful Whites to the Trump cause, while seeking to avoid the broader public's condemnation in a post–Civil Rights era where explicit calls to racism had come to be seen as beyond the pale.[66] Even here at this initial point in its trajectory, Trumpism practiced what I would define as a broadly construed, but largely implicit, racism. Rather than emphasizing White Supremacist views of racial inferiority of non-Whites, it most often only intimated such views. The racism of the Trump Movement is also more about racial resentment where non-Whites are seen as a threat rather than insisting that non-Whites are inferior (though there is at times the suggestion that inferiority is itself a threat to sustaining the White culture that allegedly makes America great).[67]

The racism of the Trump Movement cast its net broadly to include a wide variety of allegedly threatening outgroups. This more generalized resentment is perhaps better characterized as White outgroup hostility.[68] African Americans, especially those holding office or voting in central cities, in critical swing states, were targeted to be sure. Yet a full panoply of additional outgroups got targeted as well in the quest to attract as many voters as possible among those whose targets for their resentments varied. This racism of a more generalized outgroup hostility remains prominent and has not faded but instead carries over to the additional phases as the trajectory of Trumpism evolved and expressed broader animosities against democracy itself and against the political opposition.[69]

[64] Joshua Green, *Devil's Bargain: Steve Bannon, Donald Trump, and the Storming of the Presidency* (Penguin Press, 2017).

[65] Fording and Schram, *Hard White*, 12.

[66] Fording and Schram, *Hard White*, Chapter 1.

[67] See Mead, *Burdens of Freedom*. Amy Wax is another prominent defender of the idea that White Anglo-American culture is under assault. See Joe Patrice, "Amy Wax Defends Herself by Admitting Most of the Allegations Against Her," *Above the Law*, April 17, 2023, abovethelaw.com/2023/04/amy-wax-admits-most-allegations/.

[68] Fording and Schram, *Hard White*, Chapter 2.

[69] Joseph Lowndes, "Far-Right Extremism Dominates the GOP: It Didn't Start—and Won't End—with Trump," *Washington Post*, November 8, 2021, www.washingtonpost.com/outlook/2021/11/08/far-right-extremism-dominates-gop-it-didnt-start-wont-end-with-trump/. Also see Fording and Schram, *Hard White*, 222–24.

A "color-blind" or "laissez-faire" racism that features an emphasis on standing up for White identity rather than seeking to subordinate non-Whites is also part of the generalized White ethnocentrism prevalent in Trumpism today.[70] Anti-woke campaigns, such as Gov. Ron DeSantis' (R-FL) efforts to erase the study of racism from the Florida schools, also are added to mix. These forms of racial discourse help allow people who wish to not be associated with blatant racism to align themselves with the Movement. Supporting controversy-free public education can seem to be unrelated to racism. Protecting students from learning about the racist past of a state, region, or even the Country can seem to be also not about reinforcing White privilege. Trumpism has featured discursive moves associated with each of these variants of racialized gesturing that have been aided by the metapragmatic moves of gaslighting, boomeranging, and co-opting such that the racism embedded in Trumpism maintains deniability, and gets normalized and legitimated.

To maintain deniability, Trumpism was already commonly employing metapragmatics. A major example was casting Whites as the new victims of racism, thereby co-opting the victim status often associated with people of color who continued to face racial discrimination. Lying that Black Haitian immigrants are eating people's pets, as Trump and his vice presidential candidate J. D. Vance did in the 2024 campaign, and then saying it was just to get people to take the issue of immigration seriously, was gaslighting in a highly metapragmatic way where extremist lies get normalized in a two-step process.[71] This kind of gaslighting traded on beliefs of the superiority of White Christian culture in America, and often was associated with tacit claims of standing up for the "real America" or espousing support to put "America First" as in attempts to limit immigration by non-Whites and non-Christians. These examples and others will be provided in the next chapter where we examine the metapragmatics of Trumpism in inflaming but also mainstreaming racism.

The Patriot/Militia Movement and the Fascism in Trumpism

The second inflection in the trajectory of Trumpism points to a fundamental shift in Trumpism, both as a movement and as a discourse, to include appeals

[70] Fording and Schram, *Hard White*, Chapter 1.

[71] Edward Helmore, "JD Vance Admits He Is Willing to 'Create Stories' to Get Media Attention," *The Guardian*, September 15, 2024, https://www.theguardian.com/us-news/2024/sep/15/jd-vance-lies-haitian-immigrants.

to other extremists who were, for some time, organizing apart from the White Nationalist Movement. Prominent among these other extremists was what is often called the Patriot Movement.[72] Some members of various Patriot groups were and are racists and align with the White Nationalist Movement, but others do not. What is critical about members of the Patriot Movement is that they universally consider themselves the real patriots committed to defending the real Americans and the federal government officials are not. These groups can be highly focused on committing acts of violence. A small cell that went by the name "the Wolverine Watchmen" was arrested for plotting to kidnap and kill Michigan Governor Gretchen Whitmer in October 2020.[73] Groups like the Wolverine Watchmen identify themselves as part of the Patriot Movement, the Patriot Militia, or just the Militia Movement. The Whitmer kidnap plot is but one instance of the fascistic (if not outright fascist) orientation of the Militia Movement for its willingness to use violence to overthrow the existing government.

The Patriot/Militia Movement came to be intimately involved in promoting Trump. Trump's willingness to align with the Movement began when he went as far as actually expressing sympathy for the Wolverine Watchmen when they were arrested. Trump did this as president and prefaced his remarks by intimating that Whitmer and he were political adversaries.[74] The next development was when the elements of the Patriot Movement came to be involved with the anti-federal government lockdown protests that Trump expressed support for during the early stages of the COVID-19 pandemic. By the spring of 2020, protests in Michigan and elsewhere were often led by various Patriot/Militia groups, including most prominently the Oath Keepers, whose leaders including the head, Stewart Rhodes, were later convicted for plotting a seditious conspiracy as part of the January 6, 2021 insurrection.[75] During the height of the lockdown protests, Trump was still President, and supposedly leading the battle against the pandemic, when he began to tweet in support of the anti-lockdown protestors.

[72] Malachi Barrett, "Who Are Michigan's Militias? Armed 'Patriot' Groups Resurface during Anti-Government Climate," *m.live*, January 21, 2021, https://www.mlive.com/politics/2021/01/who-are-michigans-militias-armed-patriot-groups-resurface-during-anti-government-climate.html?outputType=amp.

[73] Ibid.

[74] Maegan Vazquez and Nikki Carvajal, "Trump Appears to Give a Pass to the Domestic Kidnapping Plot Against Whitmer," *CNN*, October 27, 2020, https://www.cnn.com/2020/10/27/politics/trump-gretchen-whitmer-kidnapping-michigan/index.html.

[75] Dakota Adams, "How I Left the Far Right," *Raw Story*, July 12, 2022, https://www.rawstory.com/dakota-rhodes/.

Trump had been overwhelmed by the pandemic. It was simply beyond his abilities as to how to respond.[76] At first, he claimed be all-powerful as president and would be the ultimate decider on the government's response. But then just as quickly, he reversed himself saying it was up to the states regarding lockdowns, masking and other policies.[77] In early 2020, for several critical months, Trump delayed invoking the Defense Production Act that could have accelerated the manufacture of masks, gloves, ventilators, and other emergency equipment. When Trump was asked why, he said that governors, not the president, were responsible for emergency supplies and that telling "companies what to do" might upset the "business community."[78]

Trump persisted in hoping that it would all just go away, and the economy and everyday life would go on as it had before the pandemic. He also evidently worried he would be held accountable for the rising death toll and the government's inability to contain the spread of the disease. He was preoccupied with controlling appearances and suppressing bad news. Ultimately, he preferred being the outsider who wailed against state government regulations. He appeared to be focused primarily on making himself look good and on the side of his base supporters who were suspicious of government regulation and limitations on personal freedom. Almost by sheer happenstance, Trump's anxiety about how he would personally suffer standing in the eyes of his supporters who opposed the government's lockdowns led him to become a natural ally of the Patriot/Militia Movement. Trump had already refused to denounce the conspiracy theory network QAnon by saying he did not know anything about them "other than I understand they like me very much" and "it is gaining in popularity."[79] It was Trump's priority with keeping himself as popular as possible with his supporters that made the rise of these extremist groups, as an important part of the Trump coalition, a non-problem for him.

Trump's alignment with the Patriot/Militia Movement is the beginning of the second phase of the trajectory of Trumpism. Those anti-lockdown protestors were not primarily White Nationalists. All kinds of protesters were involved. Many were very much into conspiracy theories about vaccines, the federal government, and much else. Many also did not resist demonizing

[76] William Saletan, "The Trump Pandemic: A Blow-by-Blow Account of How the President Killed Thousands of Americans," *Slate*, August 9, 2020, https://slate.com/news-and-politics/2020/08/trump-coronavirus-deaths-timeline.html.

[77] Ibid.

[78] Ibid.

[79] Zeke Miller, Jill Colvin, and Amanda Seitz, "Trump Praises QAnon Conspiracists, Appreciates Support," *AP*, August 19, 2020, https://apnews.com/article/election-2020-ap-top-news-religion-racial-injustice-535e145ee67dd757660157be39d05d3f.

all kinds of outgroups, but their primary target was what they saw as a federal government that now sought to take away the rights the Right likes to emphasize about individual freedom from government control, including the right not to have to get vaccinated, wear a mask, or shutdown schools and businesses.

Previously, Trump's position on the pandemic was rather nonpartisan and supportive of government measures to stop the spread. He also was supportive of Dr. Anthony Fauci's effort to direct the government's campaign against the pandemic. Yet, after he tweeted in support of the anti-lockdown protests, Trump turned against his own administration and aligned himself with the protesters, who, it turns out, were often led by Patriot/Militia Movement members. It was the beginning of a concerted effort by Trump to appeal to groups like the Oath Keepers, the Proud Boys, etc. These groups already supported Trump, but he had not appealed to them explicitly, though, as is his style. After being challenged on his alignment with them, he refused to renounce them in his presidential debate with Biden in September 2020. Rather than agree to tell them to stand down, he told them to "stand back and stand by," as if saying they should be ready to use violence to come to his defense (which they eventually did).[80]

In this phase of Trumpism, while the targeting of outgroups continued, efforts to rally support frequently took on an anti-democratic and especially anti-federal government focus, most especially during the pandemic. There were increasingly less than veiled references that democracy in the United States was an anti-White practice being enforced by a "Deep State" that required White people to have to give up their rights and share power with other people.[81] In this case then, the appropriate response was to oppose democracy, even the rule of law, including the Constitution of the United States, in order to resist having to share power. This type of thinking eventually came to buttress Donald Trump's insistence that people needed to take action in response to what he said was the voter fraud in largely non-White central cities in key swing states that denied him reelection in 2020. The lies, conspiracy theories, and demonizations put out in response to Trump's "Stop the Steal" campaign energized his supporters to storm the Capitol on January 6, 2021, to try to stop Congress' certification of Joe Biden as president. Prominent among the insurrectionists on that day and in other instances were

[80] Dean Obeidallah, "Trump's Proud Boys 'Stand Back and Stand By' Debate Moment Was More than a Dog Whistle," *NBC News*, September 20, 2020, www.nbcnews.com/think/opinion/trump-s-proud-boys-stand-back-stand-debate-moment-was-ncna1241570.

[81] For example, see Miller and Davis, "White Outgroup Intolerance and Declining Support for American Democracy."

members of the Patriot/Militia Movement who were already committed to violently resisting the federal government.[82]

Trump's Big Lie was similar to that which Hitler used to ascend to power in Germany by blaming the Jews for the country's loss in World War I.[83] Trump's gaslight was that he had actually won the election, but the Democrats, especially in Black-led central cities in swing states, had flipped votes from Trump to Biden. It was yet again a metapragmatic move that denied the initial reports that he had lost and instead recategorized the final result as a stolen election produced by deviant others that mainstream society should not trust.[84] And like the Nazis, Trump did more than lie; he exhorted his followers to use force to keep him in power. After weeks of harping on the Big Lie and failing to win any significant court battles, he incited the mob he had implored to come to Washington, DC, on January 6, 2021, to sack the Capitol and stop the peaceful transition of power to Joe Biden, his democratically elected successor. The Proud Boys and the Oath Keepers led the most violent parts of the mob to try to stop Congress' certification of Biden as president. Trump's own version of stormtroopers sought to use violence to keep him in power.

Trump's willingness to align himself with the most violent and anti-democratic elements of the anti-government Patriot/Militia Movement was demonstrated when he held his first rally for his 2024 campaign to be president yet again in Waco, Texas, where the FBI's fifty-one-day siege of the Branch Davidian compound in 1993 eventually led to a fire that killed seventy-six people (including twenty-six children), making them martyrs of the Patriot Movement.[85] That site had become a shrine to martyrs of the Militia Movement, and Trump was transparently tipping his hat to them and calling for their continued support by holding his campaign-kickoff rally there.

[82] Jaclyn Diaz and Rachel Treisman, "Members of Right-Wing Militias, Extremist Groups Are Latest Charged in Capitol Siege," *NPR*, January 19, 2021, www.npr.org/sections/insurrection-at-the-capitol/2021/01/19/958240531/members-of-Right-Wing-militias-extremist-groups-are-latest-charged-in-capitol-si.

[83] Matthew Rozsa, "Trump's Big Lie and Hitler's: Is This How America's Slide into Totalitarianism Begins? Hitler Undermined Democracy by Lying about World War I; Trumpists Want to do it by Lying about the 2020 Election," *Salon*, April 11, 2021, https://www.salon.com/2021/04/11/trumps-big-lie-and-hitlers-is-this-how-americas-slide-into-totalitarianism-begins/.

[84] For an analysis of how metapragmatic moves like gaslighting suggest a deviant "other" that serves to legitimate your claim to be part of the mainstream, see Bart Cammaerts, "The Abnormalisation of Social Justice: The 'Anti-Woke Culture War' Discourse in the UK," *Discourse and Society*, 33, no. 6 (November 2022): 730–43. On semiotics of othering as fundamental to the cultural pragmatics of politics generally, see Jeffrey Alexander, *The Performance of Politics: Obama's Victory and the Democratic Struggle for Power* (Oxford University Press, 2010).

[85] Charles Homans, "A Trump Rally, a Right-Wing Cause and the Enduring Legacy of Waco," *New York Times*, March 24, 2023, https://www.nytimes.com/2023/03/24/us/politics/donald-trump-waco-branch-davidians.html.

Throughout Biden's presidency, Trump continued to practice projection and boomeranging, railing against the "fascists" in power, even as his supporters engaged in further instances of violence against non-Whites, Jews, immigrants, member of the LGBTQ+ community, and even attacks on the FBI. President Biden ultimately felt the need to call out the fascists' turn in the trajectory of Trumpism. In a televised address to the Nation, Biden homed in on the danger of Trump promoting what Biden gingerly, if somewhat infelicitously, called a "semi-Fascism."[86] Trump boomeranged that charge right back at Biden, dropping the "semi-" and accusing Biden of being a full-fledged fascist.[87] The trajectory of Trumpism had turned a fraught corner with hateful rhetoric encouraging anti-democratic maneuvering and even acts of violence to resist the rule of law. According to the Anti-Defamation League, "right-wing extremist terror" incidents in the United States had been increasing since the mid-2000s, at a growing rate. "There were just seven right-wing terror incidents in the period 2005–2007, but by 2017–2019 there were 27, which increased to 40 in 2020–2022."[88] Trumpism was amping up a trend of increasing Right-Wing political violence.

Nonetheless, throughout the 2024 presidential campaign, Trump continued to want to have it both ways. He continued to deny that he was really a fascist or an authoritarian but instead mocked the idea by claiming he would only be a dictator for one day if he got back into the presidency.[89] Instead, he boomeranged repeatedly that President Biden was the real threat to democracy, not him. Regarding the possibility of being barred from being on the presidential ballot in some states due to his instigating the January 6th insurrection, he threatened that if he were prosecuted, then there would be "bedlam."[90] When asked, he refused to say he would denounce any violence that might occur. Yet, he also would subsequently say that if he got back in, he would be too busy governing to spend time trying to inflict the retribution he promised for his enemies. All the while, he claimed he had

[86] Federico Finchelstein, "Biden Called Trumpism 'Semi-Fascism': The Term Makes Sense, Historically," *Washington Post*, September 1, 2022, https://www.washingtonpost.com/made-by-history/2022/09/01/biden-called-trumpism-semi-fascism-term-makes-sense-historically/.

[87] Johanna Chisholm, "Video Resurfaces of Trump Calling Democrats 'Fascists' as Conservatives Rage over Biden Speech," *Independent*, September 3, 2022, https://www.independent.co.uk/news/world/americas/us-politics/trump-clip-democrats-fascists-b2159062.html.

[88] "Right-Wing Extremist Terrorism in the United States," *ADL*, November 15, 2023, https://www.adl.org/resources/report/right-wing-extremist-terrorism-united-states.

[89] Marina Pitofsky, "Donald Trump Repeats Comment He Would Be a Dictator 'for One Day' if Reelected in 2024," *USA Today*, December 11, 2023, https://www.usatoday.com/story/news/politics/elections/2023/12/11/donald-trump-dictator-one-day-reelected/71880010007/.

[90] Devan Cole, "Trump Lawyers Warn Supreme Court of 'Chaos and Bedlam' If States Are Allowed to Bar Him from 2024 Ballot," *CNN Politics*, January 18, 2024, https://www.cnn.com/2024/01/18/politics/14th-amendment-supreme-court-trump-colorado/index.html.

"absolute immunity" as president (something the US Supreme Court eventually, if shockingly, in large part affirmed). Trump's claims that he could not be prosecuted for using his office to seek retribution gained credibility, and their resulting normalization heightened the growing concern about what he would do if he got back in power. Trump was always trying to have it both ways, using metapragmatic statements to disavow his threats while making those threats more credible. He was agitating his base while trying to defuse opposition on the grounds that he would only do what the law allowed. His metapragmatics were designed to enable him to use the law against itself, a tried-and-true fascist tactic. His efforts ultimately paid off with his prosecutions being dropped upon his winning reelection and then his ultimately pardoning the January 6th insurrectionists, with them likely becoming his loyal militia standing by as needed.

The New Civil War

If this was not enough, a third inflection point in the trajectory of Trumpism began to gain visibility, enhancing the racism and fascism rhetoric but including an emphasis on reanimated rightist culture wars.[91] For Trump, this shift may have begun when he joined others to complain about what he called political correctness when it came to such trivial things as whether you were supposedly being denied the right to say "Merry Christmas" (as exclusionary) and should only say "Happy Holidays" (as multicultural inclusionary terminology suggested). Yet, the Culture War was always about much more than the niceties of political correctness.[92] Over time, the trajectory of Trumpism has led to the suggestion among his supporters that culture wars on various fronts must necessarily lead to an all-out civil war where our differences call for creating separate countries, divided by opposing stands on a whole raft of issues such as abortion, sexual identity, religious freedom, public education, and even the role of the federal government in our lives regarding such matters as social welfare and economic regulation. Yet this talk only intensified as Trump came to be indicted by the government for various crimes (again underscoring how he had successfully tied his fate to the movement's).

[91] For analyses that see the Right leading the way, but some on the Left also anticipating the need to use violence in the new civil war, see Sharlet, *The Undertow*. See Adrienne LaFrance, "The New Anarchy: America Faces a Type of Extremist Violence It Does Not Know How to Stop," *The Atlantic*, April 2023, https://www.theatlantic.com/magazine/archive/2023/04/us-extremism-portland-george-floyd-protests-january-6/673088/; Stephane Marche, *The Next Civil War: Dispatches from the American Future* (Avid Reader Press/Simon and Shuster, 2022); and Barbara F. Walter, *How Civil Wars Start: And How to Stop Them* (Viking, 2022).

[92] See James Davidson Hunter, *Culture Wars: The Struggle to Define America* (Basic Books, 1991).

Frustration over Trump's 2020 election loss intensified this third inflection point that prominently featured gaslighting about the alleged new civil war that falsely implied that "both sides" were going to extremes in seeking to undermine the existing governmental system.[93] It was this kind of "both-siderism" that made "civil war" a convenient gaslighting because it was the Right, especially its political leadership, that was increasingly extremist—something that was happening to a far lesser degree on the Left.[94] Invoking "civil war" suggested that as a country, the United States is so polarized into two opposing increasingly extremist political camps who were ready to attack each other. The idea of a coming civil war implied both sides could no longer work together and some kind of divorce or separation was necessary, but exactly how is usually not specified.[95] When prominent Trumpists like Rep. Marjorie Taylor Greene (R-GA) talked of a coming civil war, it seemed as if it were an excuse to demonize adversaries as irredeemable enemies. The talk of civil war continued into the rallying behind Trump as a former president who was running to be reelected in spite of his being indicted by the government for his efforts to overturn the prior election.

This talk of a new civil war inevitably echoed in the politically convenient mentions of the original Civil War, as in Trump outrageously suggesting he had a "fascination" about whether the Civil War could have been "negotiated," or in how his 2024 primary opponents like Nikki Haley in her campaign rhetoric fumbled over whether the cause of the Civil War was slavery or Ron DeSantis in his education policies as Florida's governor had downplayed the horrors of being a slave.[96] It was all posturing to appease people who want to rationalize why the South had every right to rebel. It was taking the opportunity to dog-whistle support for racists and their beliefs. Opposing the liberals, the "Deep State," or even the mainstream culture more broadly, had become the "New Lost Cause."[97] Yet, Haley's failure to mention slavery as the cause of the Civil War and instead suggest it was more about states' rights in a federal system has a particular poignancy today. Today's new civil war is very much about states getting to undercut the federal government and enact their own reactionary policies.

[93] See Peter Wehner, "Marjorie Taylor Greene's Civil War," *The Atlantic*, February 23, 2023, https://www.theatlantic.com/ideas/archive/2023/02/marjorie-taylor-greene-secession-civil-war/673142/.

[94] Nancy LeTourneau, "The Gaslighting Effect of Both-Siderism," *Washington Monthly*, October 8, 2018, https://washingtonmonthly.com/2018/10/08/the-gaslighting-effect-of-both-siderism/.

[95] Wehner, "Marjorie Taylor Greene's Civil War."

[96] Toluse Olorunnipa, "Civil War Talk in Presidential Contest Reveals Fresh Divisions on Race," *Washington Post*, January 13, 2024, https://www.washingtonpost.com/politics/2024/01/13/haley-trump-civil-war-history/.

[97] Eleanor Clift, "The Big Lie Is the South's New Lost Cause," *Daily Beast*, January 13, 2024, https://www.thedailybeast.com/the-big-lie-is-the-souths-new-lost-cause.

In the meantime, a growing number of Trump supporters were ready to pull the civil war trigger (literally as well as figuratively). Trumpism had reached the point where the inflections of racism, fascism, and civil war fold into each other. Trumpist had joined Trump in mourning martyrs to the overall struggle. Ashli Babbitt, who was killed trying to storm the Capitol on January 6, had become the key martyr among Trump supporters who call for civil war. Trump himself repeatedly invoked her death as an important marker as if to align himself with the struggle. He has gone on to call January 6 a "beautiful day" and the African American police officer who shot Babbitt a "thug."[98] Trump has also promised to (and eventually did) pardon all who have been convicted of participating in the insurrection in open defiance to the rule of law. Trump was joined by Rep. Elise Stefanik (R-NY), Chair of the House Republican Conference, in referring to the imprisoned January 6th insurrectionists as "hostages."[99] In fact, others have joined in the call for pardons, some even suggesting that the pardons should include one for Trump should he need one.[100] The call for pardons is yet another gaslight, trying to absolve people for their seditious acts and to simultaneously mainstream Trumpism as a patriotic stand against the opposition that threatens to prevent America from becoming great again. The gaslight that the insurrectionists are the real patriots standing up for the Constitution boomerangs the opposition's argument in a way that makes violence a legitimate political tactic for Trumpism. Trump's own statements about pardons do the same. Yet, Trump's cowardice meant he cagily had not gone as far as his followers in making explicit calls for civil war (though in expressing outrage over his indictments regarding the insurrection and the Stop the Steal campaign he came close).

Instead, as I show in Chapter 5, the civil war inflection point eventually drew in Trump to get involved when some of his most outspoken followers supported Texas Governor Greg Abbott (R-TX) when he sought to assert states' rights to use military force to patrol the State's southern border to the point of confronting federal officials in violation of the U.S. Constitution.[101]

[98] Graig Graziosi, "Trump Calls Police Officer Who Shot Ashli Babbitt a 'Thug' During CNN Town Hall," *Independent*, May 11, 2023, https://www.independent.co.uk/news/world/americas/us-politics/trump-ashli-babbitt-thug-cnn-town-hall-b2337214.html.

[99] Greg Sargent, "Elise Stefanik's Ugly 'Hostages' Barb Points to Serious GOP Mayhem Ahead," *New Republic*, January 12, 2024, https://newrepublic.com/article/178044/elise-stefanik-jan-6-hostages-gop-mayhem.

[100] L. Z. Granderson, "DeSantis Is Reckless to Dangle Pardons for Trump and the Jan. 6 Rioters," *Los Angeles Times*, May 26, 2023, https://www.latimes.com/opinion/story/2023-05-26/desantis-is-reckless-to-dangle-pardons-for-trump-and-the-jan-6-rioters.

[101] John Moritz, "Abbott Keeps up Border Security Fight after Supreme Court Rules Feds Can Cut Razor Wire," *USA Today*, January 24, 2024, https://www.usatoday.com/story/news/nation/2024/01/24/supreme-court-razor-wire-texas-biden-border/72330906007/; Lauren Irwin, "Trump Calls for States to

Yet the more consistent calls for civil war independent of Trump came from those in MAGA Republicans in Congress, such as Taylor Greene.[102] While Greene and other members of Congress, like Rep. Thomas Massie (R-Ky), gaslight the public with talks about how they fear a coming civil war brought on by both sides, some commentators also buy into the "both sides" argument.[103] Still others on the Far Right co-opt the terminology of the Far Left to suggest that their followers should "accelerate" the movement toward tearing down the existing constitutional system.[104] Far-Right groups among those in the Militia Movement like the Boogaloo Bois talk of "accelerationism," previously an obscure idea among some neo-Marxists to accelerate capitalism's collapse by intensifying its contradictions.[105] Accelerationism has been co-opted to become a term of art among Right-Wing proponents of civil war who seek to intensify division through acts of violence, making society ungovernable and necessitating dissolution of the constitutional system. Beyond that popular strategy to retrofit Left terminology for Right-Wing purposes is the art of projection and boomeranging that had for some time been perfected by Trump himself, as demonstrated by the Fox News commentator Mark Levin, who in response to Trump being indicted for one of his many crimes said: "I just want the audience to know that we are staring in the face of tyranny, that the Democrat Party is a totalitarian party." Levin added that the Democrats were turning the United States into two irreconcilably separate countries (a less than veiled reference to civil war).[106]

As witnessed by these calls for civil war, there is a *sotto voce* dimension to Trumpism where its leaders, Trump, and the others, who incite the followers, reserve room for their deniability because they do not explicitly say "burn the house down" or "storm the Capitol." Instead, there is the increasingly prevalent stochastic terrorism, where their hatemongering inspires others, acting as individuals or in groups, to respond with violence. And when it happens, the leaders then can disavow that they were calling for violence against the targeted groups, be it non-Whites, immigrants, other outgroups, or the Democrats in Congress. There are even attempts to say that the incidents of

Deploy National Guard to Texas Amid Border Feud," *The Hill*, January 25, 2024, https://thehill.com/homenews/state-watch/4430262-trump-calls-states-deploy-national-guard-to-texas-amid-border-feud/.

[102] Wehner, "Marjorie Taylor Greene's Civil War."

[103] For a critique of the "both sides" perspective on the growing divisiveness that some are calling a new civil war, see Isaac, "Reflections on the New Anarchy and the Real Danger of MAGA Republicans."

[104] Sharlett, *The Undertow*, Chapter 9 ("The Great Acceleration").

[105] Also see Jared Thompson, "Examining Extremism: The Boogaloo Movement," *Center for Strategic & International Studies*, June 30, 2021, https://www.csis.org/blogs/examining-extremism/examining-extremism-boogaloo-movement.

[106] Media Matters Staff, "Fox Host Mark Levin Calls Trump Indictment 'a grotesque, Stalinist, Maoist-type action,'" *Media Matters for America*, March 30, 2023, www.mediamatters.org/mark-levin/fox-host-mark-levin-calls-trump-indictment-grotesque-stalinist-maoist-type-action.

domestic terrorism were "false flag" events or that the January 6th insurrection was not violent. Or that it was its own false flag staged by the FBI.[107] The two-step in Trumpism as a discourse was once again on full display, where the insurrection was both justified but also actually staged by the government to make Trump and his supporters look guilty. It is all classic Trumpism of maintaining deniability via gaslighting, boomeranging, and co-opting. In the meantime, the Country becomes ever more polarized and moves closer to where violence gets mainstreamed as a way for Trumpism to continue its quest to seize and cling to power. The growing clash between Red and Blue states on issues like abortion, gun control, immigration, and other hot-button issues suggested a country that was pulling apart in ways that suggested a cold civil war.[108]

Trumpism as a Cult Defending Its Outlaw Leader at All Costs

A noteworthy, if acute, inflection point came as the 2024 presidential election campaign intensified, as Trump was also preoccupied with fending off his multiple prosecutions, including his being charged with seeking to obstruct the peaceful transfer of power on January 6, 2020. Trump had by then hit upon the idea that he could use his prosecutions to make himself out to be the martyr. He boomeranged the status of who is the real victim, claiming the prosecutions were undermining his ability to campaign. He claimed his legal prosecutions were actually political persecutions.

In the first criminal trial of a former president, Trump continually violated a gag order to intimidate witnesses, like Michael Cohen, his former lawyer, and Stormy Daniels, the porn-star paramour Trump paid off to "catch and kill" her story about their brief liaison. It was suggested by many that Trump was actually hoping to get jailed for the gag-order violations so as to improve his standing as a martyr who was being persecuted for standing up to the despised "Deep State."[109] Yet, it also seemed that he was hoping to mobilize supporters to help undermine his prosecutions. He was blurring the boundary between law and politics and seeking to use the court cases for political

[107] "Jan 6 Tapes Revive False Claims of FBI Involvement," *NDTV World*, November 22, 2023, https://www.ndtv.com/world-news/us-capitol-attack-jan-6-tapes-revive-false-claims-of-fbi-involvement-4598285.

[108] David Dayen, "The Cold Civil War," *The American Prospect*, October 7, 2024, https://prospect.org/politics/2024-10-07-cold-civil-war/.

[109] William K. Rashbaum, "Could Trump Go to Prison? If He Does, the Secret Service Goes, Too," *New York Times*, April 23, 2024, https://www.nytimes.com/2024/04/23/nyregion/trump-trial-hush-money-prison.html.

effect while leveraging political support for his attempts to extricate himself from his legal entanglements.

In fact, his polling seemed to improve each time legal developments went against him. His base was rallying around their leader.[110] His legal jeopardy was being interpreted as their shared political peril. Trump had said his enemies were actually out to attack his supporters, but he was standing in their way. Trump had come to suggest he embodied the Movement and his supporters at times verged on deifying their leader as the spiritual embodiment of the Movement. Trumpism was at that point operating more like an authoritarian personality cult that was first and foremost dedicated to defending its leader at all costs.[111] Chapter 6 details this dynamic that became the central focus of Trumpism as an authoritarian personality cult. In these battles, Trump has amplified his chosen persona as an outlaw who is opposing the established order not to undermine democracy but to realize it.[112] This itself is its own metapragmatic move, suggesting his defiance of law and order is actually in the name of overcoming the oppressive legal system of the establishment in order to give the people real justice. His constant fighting in court is not, as it seems, to save himself from punishment for his alleged crimes, but instead to stand up against how the established order oppresses his supporters and people in general. It is at this point where Trumpism's rogue defiance of the established order gets positioned not as an authoritarian cult leader but as the leader of a genuine democratic movement on behalf of "real" Americans.

Trump was in this sense the MAGA Robin Hood or Jesse James, the people's outlaw fighting for them. This is gaslighting in the name of justifying a power grab. Trump positions himself as the people's outlaw, with his mug shot on coffee cups. "If Mr. Trump can manage to convince voters that he is an outlaw hero, then the usual criticisms of him won't stick. His vices, however grave, will be seen as expressions of the democratic character, bound up with the political system his critics purport to defend."[113] Using the logic analogous of the Nazi theoretician Carl Schmitt, Trump's attempt to impose

110 Jason Lange, "Trump Indictment: Reuters/Ipsos Poll Shows Most Republicans Think Charges Are Politically Motivated," *Reuters*, June 14, 2023, https://www.reuters.com/world/us/poll-trump-holds-double-digit-lead-after-federal-indictment-reutersipsos-2023-06-12/.

111 Thomas B. Edsall, "The Deification of Donald Trump Poses Some Interesting Questions," *New York Times*, January 24, 2024, https://www.nytimes.com/2024/01/17/opinion/trump-god-evangelicals-anointed.html; David Ramsey, "How Donald Trump Became God," *Baptist News Global*, January 27, 2022; and Martin Pengelly, "Sarah Palin Denies Then Seems to Confirm That Trumpism Is a Cult," *The Guardian*, June 15, 2023, https://amp.theguardian.com/us-news/2023/jun/15/sarah-palin-trumpism-cult-confirmation.

112 Matthew Schmitz, "Trump Embraces Lawlessness, But in the Name of a Higher Law," *New York Times*, May 2, 2024, https://www.nytimes.com/2024/05/02/opinion/trump-trial-2024-election.html.

113 Ibid.

dictatorship could be justified as the way to fully realize democracy, where the dictator rises above the liberal democratic order to give the real Americans what they really want.[114] Whether this metapragmatic two-step will help overturn the constitutional system remains to be seen, with Trump now having won reelection.

Normalizing Trumpism on Display

Trumpism continued to evolve right through the 2024 presidential campaign beyond these inflection points; however, throughout the full arc of Trumpism as it morphed from one inflection point to another, there had been a consistent style of expression conducted in service of normalizing the most extreme claims. The two-step discourse of Trumpism constitutes an important form of signaling not just to its base but also the broader public.[115] The signaling is at times tongue-in-cheek with a dash of irony as if to imply it is all normal and pushback is unjustified. This signaling can occur via images as well as words and where words and images can reinforce each other.[116] Whether it is misleading photographs of staged events or memes on social media, Trumpism operates as a self-rationalizing discourse that is readily available to public inspection. To be sure, the later inflections in the trajectory of Trumpism are not always so quiet or playful whether they are about trying to undermine the rule of law or rallying around Trump as the leader who must be shielded from being held accountable for his crimes. At various points, the quiet part gets said out loud. The stridency of Trumpism sometimes overtakes the discourse in seeking to mainstream outrageousness. That stridency seems increasingly available for visual inspection in images displayed in the changing memes posted by Trump's acolytes. Back in the day, early on, there was not so subtle dog-whistling of the White Nationalist "OK" hand signal (see Figure 2.1). Its ambiguity led some to see this as not a racist dog-whistle, but others saw its ambiguity as a way to "own the libs" by getting them to accuse the signalers

[114] Jennifer Szalai, "The Nazi Jurist Who Haunts Our Broken Politics," *New York Times*, July 13, 2024, https://www.nytimes.com/2024/07/13/books/review/carl-schmitt-jd-vance.html.

[115] Yang Liu and Amir Zeldes, "Discourse Relations and Signaling Information: Anchoring Discourse Signals in RST-DT," *Proceedings of the Society for Computation in Linguistics* 2, no. 35 (2019), DOI: https://doi.org/10.7275/vh3w-4240.

[116] See Sanford F. Schram, *The Return of Ordinary Capitalism: Neoliberalism, Precarity, Occupy* (Oxford University Press, 2015), 63–65. Also see John Muse, "Preoccupations: Looking at Pictures with Judith Butler" (paper presented at Bryn Mawr College, November 9, 2011). Michel Foucault emphasized texts imply images and vice versa, calling the text/image imbrication a "calligram." See Michel Foucault, *This Is Not a Pipe*, trans. James Harkness (University of California Press, 1983 [1969]). Also see W. J. T. Mitchell, *Picture Theory: Essays on Verbal and Visual Representation* (University of Chicago Press, 1993).

Figure 2.1 Patriot Prayer and Proud Boys flash the OK sign in Portland, Oregon

of being racists for showing a mere friendly "OK."[117] Either way, the ambiguity is what is important for it highlights that at this stage in the trajectory of Trumpism, there was a reticence to some degree in saying the quiet part out loud. This changes as Trumpism evolves. Trumpism was always about willing to say politically incorrect things, but the gestures toward anti-democratic politics and calls for violence became more explicit over time.

Figure 2.2 speaks more loudly even as it underscores the mainstreaming. If you can believe it, it is from a holiday greeting posted by Rep. Tom Massie with his family all holding AR-15s, which had become the symbol of the movement's defense of gun rights.[118] While Trumpists had started calling liberals "groomers" for allegedly supporting teaching children about gender issues, the picture suggests Massie and his wife were proud to be seen as if they were grooming their children for a life where it is totally acceptable to be an owner of the increasingly popular assault rifle that is also preferred by people who were committing the rising number of mass killings (often in schools).[119] In a Christmas card, no less. This, despite the fact that White Nationalist

[117] David Neiwart, "Is that an OK Sign? A White Power Symbol? Or Just a Right-Wing Troll?" *SPLC*, September 19, 2018, https://www.splcenter.org/hatewatch/2018/09/18/ok-sign-white-power-symbol-or-just-Right-Wing-troll.

[118] Christina Wyman, "A Christmas Card with Guns? Lauren Boebert and Thomas Massie Start a New Culture War," *NBC News/Think*, December 19, 2021, https://www.nbcnews.com/think/opinion/christmas-card-guns-lauren-boebert-thomas-massie-start-new-culture-ncna1285709.

[119] Editorial Board, "No One Needs an AR-15—Or Any Gun Tailor-made for Mass Shootings, *Washington Post*, March 28, 2023, https://www.washingtonpost.com/opinions/2023/03/28/ar-15-assault-rifles-magazines-ban/.

Figure 2.2 Rep. Thomas Massie, R-Ky, posted a "Holiday" photo of his family on Twitter

Trump supporters were increasingly reported to be using this weapon in mass killings at synagogues, churches, supermarkets, bars and nightclubs, and elsewhere, especially targeting non-Whites, Jews, Muslims, Latinos, LGBTQ+ people etc. The trajectory of Trumpism had moved to glorify violence with its key symbol now an automatic weapon (the AR-15), which is not just the most popular gun purchased in recent years but is associated with the most horrific killings. An AR-15 type weapon was used in the failed assassination attempt of Donald Trump in July 2024 at a Pennsylvania campaign rally.

At first blush, the Massie Christmas Card appears to be designed to shock and offend those who are not part of the Gun Culture. It looks like a brazen attempt to threaten. Yet, upon reflection, it just might be more about normalization (the goal that lies at the heart of Trumpism as a metapragmatic discourse). The AR-15 might be the gun commonly used by those committing the growing number of mass killings in America. But that is not so much an aberration practiced by mass murders as it is due to the fact that the AR-15 has become the most frequently purchased gun in the Country overall.[120] The Massie Christmas Card is not about shocking people as much as celebrating how mainstream owning weapons of war have become and how normal their ownership should be seen.

[120] James Bandler and Doris Burke "How a Maine Businessman Made the AR-15 Into America's Best-Selling Rifle," *ProPublica*, November 21, 2023, https://www.propublica.org/article/how-bushmaster-made-ar-15-into-best-selling-rifle-us.

This normalizing includes legitimating the idea of being gun-toting revolutionaries. The idea of being part of a rouge movement to upend the constitutional order seems to follow logically among the supporters of Trumpism. The normalizing of efforts to overturn the constitutional order does not, however, have to necessarily include violence. In fact, Trumpism today includes increased moves to undermine forms of democratic accountability to resist sharing power with these outgroups and, in the ultimate act of opposition to democratic processes, calls for abolishing the government via some form of nonviolent civil war, via litigation and lawmaking, often referred to as lawfare.

Talk of dissolving the Union has also come to be associated with increased attention to legal maneuvering like supporting the preexisting calls on the Right for a constitutional convention. Such a convention could end up making separation more likely or give states more freedom to ignore the federal government.[121] The only precedent for such a convention in US political history is the rouge convention called under the Articles of Confederation, which ultimately led to the drafting of an entirely new Constitution (which remains in effect to this day, but now seems in jeopardy). As allowed by Article V of the US Constitution, a requisite number of states (currently thirty-four) can call for a constitutional convention. Today, while some on the Left have supported the call for an Article V Constitutional Convention, support comes primarily from the Right.[122] The origins of the Right's efforts pre-date the rise of Trumpism but receive support from the Right-Wing extremists with whom Trump has aligned himself for his own political advantage. These calls are often grounded in racism and anti-democratic maneuvering featured in the earlier phases of Trumpism. Yet they have become louder with the trajectory of Trumpism now prominently claiming the need to dissolve the US constitutional system as we know it; and if not that, then at least commandeering the government to implement an authoritarian agenda.[123]

Nonetheless, the metapragmatics of Trumpism enable claiming to be upholding the law while actively undermining it. Not testifying under oath to prove your false claims about stolen elections or delaying your trial about

[121] See Travis Waldron, "A Radical Right-Wing Dream to Rewrite the Constitution Is Close to Coming True," *HuffPost*, April 27, 2021, https://www.huffpost.com/entry/mark-meckler-article-five-constitutional-convention_n_6086c380e4b09cce6c143b10.

[122] Michelle Goldberg, "A Leading Law Scholar Fears We're Lurching Toward Secession," *New York Times*, September 23, 2024, https://www.nytimes.com/2024/09/23/opinion/electoral-college-presidential-election.html.

[123] Over the course of US history, many groups across the political spectrum have called for an Article V Convention, but one has never been held. See Jamelle Bouie, "There Is a Way to Break Out of Our Constitutional Stagnation," *New York Times*, November 18, 2022, https://www.nytimes.com/2022/11/18/opinion/midterms-states-constitutions.html.

obstructing the peaceful transfer of power is justified because prosecutors are weaponizing a constitutional system that is rigged against you. The late stages of Trumpism have come to be centered on seeking to overthrow the liberal elite that allegedly dominate just about everything from the culture, the economy, the major political institutions and society writ large. As Timothy Snyder has said, Trumpism as a movement includes both "breakers" who seek to overthrow the constitutional order and "gamers" who seek to manipulate it for anti-democratic ends.[124] These developments in fact did not go away but intensified with Trumpism evolving into a cult dedicated to defending at all costs its leader evading legal accountability to go on to become authoritarian strongman atop an anti-democratic regime.

Other prominent images powerfully reinforced the view that Trump is a heroic outlaw who cannot be stopped. There is mugshot upon being charged in Georgia for election interference and then there is the picture of him raising a fist shouting "fight, fight, fight" after being shot at his Pennsylvania rally in July 2024. Trumpism more generally is all about posturing in defiance of the established order. We see pictures of this posturing by Trumpists again and again.

Nonetheless, the popularity of elected officials posing with weapons of war guns reminds us that a penchant for violence is a deeply troubling part of Trumpism.[125] It is a violence that is being legitimated by the discourse's normalizing two-step style of expression. The trajectory of Trumpism is not just the changes in its grievances but how they are consistently expressed in words and images designed to normalize and legitimate the extremism at the heart of these grievances. Yet, the collateral damage of those words goes well beyond the pollution of political discourse. Even as Trumpism fails to achieve all of its political objectives, its demonizing discourse may prove to be fatal for the targets of Trumpism. Trumpism includes stochastic terrorism.[126]

The metapragmatic moves to rationalize whatever violence that might come will then prove perhaps the most difficult to sustain. This is happening while Right-Wing domestic terrorist killings continue to rise.[127] The number of death threats against Democrats in elected office, prosecutors, judges, election workers, and others has also increased at an alarming rate.[128] At some

[124] Timothy Snyder, "The American Abyss," *New York Times*, January 9, 2021, https://www.nytimes.com/2021/01/09/magazine/trump-coup.html.

[125] See Adam Serwer, *Cruelty Is the Point: Why Trump's America Endures* (One World, 2020).

[126] Corn, "Donald Trump, Stochastic Terrorist."

[127] Mike Levine, "'No Blame?' ABC News Finds 54 Cases Invoking 'Trump' in Connection with Violence, Threats, Alleged Assaults," *ABC News*, May 30, 2020, https://abcnews.go.com/Politics/blame-abc-news-finds-17-cases-invoking-trump/story?id=58912889.

[128] Jack Forrest, "Capitol Police Chief Says Threats Against Members of Congress 'Still too High' Despite Drop in Case Numbers," *CNN*, January 17, 2023, https://www.cnn.com/2023/01/17/politics/congress-threats-decline-capitol-police/index.html.

point, the two-level discourse might not work to normalize all this and we will have to address what is to be done at that point. Also, whether the threats toward the "enemy within" continue with Trump reelected remains to be seen.

Before we turn to that topic, in the next four chapters, I examine case studies on how Trumpism as a discourse has consistently used metapragmatic moves at key junctures in the trajectory of Trumpism as it has arced from across different inflection points involving racism, fascism, and civil war talk and then rallying around Trump as a persecuted cult leader. All before he triumphantly returned to the White House.

3
Racism

For years, Donald Trump has said: "I am the least racist person." He sometimes adds: "who you have ever interviewed," as when responding to reporters' questions about his calling African nations "shithole countries," or "in this room," as when debating Joe Biden during his 2020 reelection campaign, or "in the world," as he did in 2019 when taking to Twitter to defend himself while calling CNN commentator Don Lemon (who is African American) for being the "dumbest person on television."[1] Not everyone believed Trump when he denied his racism.

Whether Trump is really a racist or just pandering to get support from racially resentful Whites is a frequent question. Trump's personal history of discriminating against African American tenants or vilifying the Central Park 5 for a beating they were eventually exonerated for are but two of many examples of his racist behavior that occurred in his pre-presidential past. The many statements he made as a candidate that invoked racist stereotypes add additional evidence. His racist statements and actions as president provided further proof.[2]

Yet, regardless of whether Trump actually believes in White racial superiority whenever he talks about people having "good genes," or when he demonizes non-Whites for lacking in intelligence or good values, Trump played the Race Card to win the White House and continued to do so after losing it.[3] At the height of the 2024 campaign, Trump continued to emphasize the threat of immigration as a question of allowing people to pollute the gene pool in the United States.[4] Trump first gained political success by becoming the hero of today's White Nationalist Movement by championing

[1] John Wagner and Colby Itkowitz, "Trump Renews Attacks on Intelligence of CNN's Don Lemon, One of the Moderators of the Democratic Debate, *Washington Post*, July 31, 2019, https://www.washingtonpost.com/politics/trump-renews-attacks-on-intelligence-of-cnns-don-lemon-one-of-the-democratic-debate-moderators/2019/07/31/0192a6cc-b382-11e9-8949-5f36ff92706e_story.html.

[2] See Richard C. Fording and Sanford F. Schram, *Hard White: The Mainstreaming of Racism in American Politics* (Oxford University Press, 2020), Chapter 1.

[3] German Lopez, "Donald Trump's Long History of Racism, from the 1970s to 2020," *Vox*, August 13, 2020, https://www.vox.com/2016/7/25/12270880/donald-trump-racist-racism-history.

[4] Philip Bump, "Saying Immigrants Bring 'Bad Genes' Echoes Trump's History—and the World's," *Washington Post*, October 7, 2024, https://www.washingtonpost.com/politics/2024/10/07/trump-finally-just-says-that-some-immigrants-are-genetically-inferior/.

The Trajectory of Trumpism. Sanford F. Schram, Oxford University Press. © Oxford University Press (2026).
DOI: 10.1093/9780197827437.003.0003

the birther controversy that Barack Obama was not born in the United States and therefore was an illegitimate president. Based on that effort and his consistent campaigning by inflaming racial resentment, Trump helped return White racism to mainstream presidential politics in ways that were shocking for people who thought that it was no longer possible in the post–Civil Rights era.

This was the first phase of Trumpism; its trajectory has taken it beyond just racism, but still carries that racism forward while allowing other simmering resentments to rise to the top. Yet, the first inflection point is significant for being just that. The racism was always there in mainstream politics before Trump though expressed most often covertly in the post–Civil Rights era. It was peeking out periodically in more explicit terms as with the Tea Party Movement that emerged in reaction to Barack Obama becoming the first non-White president in US history.[5] Yet, Trump gave a full-throated endorsement to White Nationalist resentment, thereby significantly changing mainstream politics when he started to rise to power. Perhaps then, it does not matter what Trump really believes, especially since he is disseminating racist tropes, even if only to make him popular, successful, and powerful.[6] Trumpism as a discourse has arguably proven successful in mainstreaming racism in no small part due to the metapragmatic subterfuges of gaslighting, boomeranging, and co-opting.

Therefore, the goal in this chapter is not to determine what kind of racist Trump is. Nor is it to determine the extent to which Trumpism today is a movement led by people who are committed to enshrining White superiority as the law of the land. Instead, my goal is to show how in a post–Civil Rights era the Trumpist discursive practices of gaslighting, boomeranging, and co-opting race talk have contributed to legitimizing the White Nationalist sentiment that helps drive Trumpism to new heights politically.

Racism has long been a prominent dimension of Right-Wing politics in the United States, including Right-Wing, reactionary populist politics practiced by demagogues like Trump. For a long time, White Supremacy was hailed in speeches in Congress.[7] That changed with the successes of the Civil Rights Movement, as witnessed by how racists like George Wallace denied their racism and deflected criticism by saying their ire was directed at the federal government that was requiring integration.[8] Today, US Senator Tommy

[5] See Christopher S. Parker and Matt A. Barreto, *Change They Can't Believe In: The Tea Party and Reactionary Politics in America* (Princeton University Press, 2013).

[6] See Fording and Schram, *Hard White*, Chapter 6.

[7] Ira Katznelson, *Fear Itself: The New Deal and the Origins of Our Time* (Liveright, 2014), Chapter 5.

[8] See Jefferson Cowie, *Freedom's Dominion: A Saga of White Resistance to Federal Power* (Basic Books, 2022), Chapter 21.

Tuberville (R-AL) is fairly unique when his bluntness about White Nationalists has him saying the quiet part out loud. He comes close to old-fashioned racism but still denies it when he says: "Democrats are attacking our military, saying we need to get out the White extremists, the White nationalists ... Well, they call them that. I call them Americans."[9] Today, the racism of the Trump Movement appeals to hardcore racists to be sure, but it gains more legitimacy and potency by denying its very existence. Now, perhaps more than ever, successful mainstreaming of racism is achieved by actually denying it, gaslighting it, projecting it onto the opposition to boomerang critiques back at them, and co-opting the rhetoric of those opponents. Such is what the post–Civil Rights context requires, and that is exactly what Trumpism provides.

This is what most significantly makes the racism of today's Trumpist movement different. There are specific discursive practices of Trumpism that help mainstream its racism by denying it. Some of these were already in use, others are newer. "Color-blind" racism, for instance, is a long-standing practice that gets enacted to claim no racial bias is being propagated but ends up reinforcing racial hierarchy by insisting that you are only enforcing meritocratic principles in favoring those who score or are ranked the highest. What is unstated is that this practice most often fails to account for preexisting advantages and disadvantages. Trumpism includes its own *sotto voce* racial privileging that is welcoming to people who want to align with Trumpism but not be associated with explicit racism. It is not quite "written under erasure" (which implies the label of racism is inaccurate), but more like it is "hidden in plain sight" (which suggests it can still be seen by both opponents and supporters).[10]

Today's post–Civil Rights era political context leads to a racism that wants to have it both ways, where it can be denied to opponents even as it is affirmed for supporters. There is a Trumpian uncertainty principle where camouflaged racism is both present and absent simultaneously. If we want to understand why Trumpism is such a prominent dimension of US politics in recent years, we need to account for the ways the discursive practices of Trumpism have helped make that happen in a post–Civil Rights era.

[9] Azi Paybarah, "GOP Senator Says of White Nationalists in the Military, 'I Call Them Americans,'" *Washington Post*, May 11, 2023, www.washingtonpost.com/politics/2023/05/10/tuberville-military-extremists/.

[10] "Written under erasure" was originally a phrase invoked by Martin Heidegger. See Jacques Derrida, *Of Grammatology* (Johns Hopkins University Press, 1967). "Hidden in plain sight" is usefully deployed in Kathleen O. Kane, "Hidden in Plain Sight: Gender and Death," (PhD diss., University of Hawai'i, Honolulu, 1994); and Kathy E. Ferguson and Phyllis Turnbull, *Oh, Say, Can You See? The Semiotics of the Military in Hawai'i* (University of Minnesota Press, 1998), xiii; and Micaela di Leonardo, *Exotics at Home: Anthropologies, Others, American Modernity* (University of Chicago Press, 1998), Prologue.

Moving From Race to Culture: An Insidious Metapragmatic Move

The (unattainable) desire to "have your cake and eat it too" is a long-standing proverb (i.e., locution) in idiomatic English (supposedly originally from a letter written by the Duke of Norfolk to Thomas Cromwell).[11] Its relevance here is that it speaks to the Right-Wing insistence on being able to express racist ideas but still hold on to the claim that you are not a racist. There may be a variety of ways that Trumpists have tried to do this, but one prominent way is to say they are expressing so-called uncomfortable truths about non-Whites that are not based on hate or prejudice. That is how someone can claim they are the "least racist person in the world" while still casting aspertions about non-Whites and other outgroups. In this way, the hatemonger can express hate while still asserting that they really have no animosity that is based on racial prejudice. It is by no means an easy thing to do, but it receives appreciative support from like-minded people (who may or may not consciously harbor racial prejudice), when it is done well (as I will show later in this chapter).

Publicly proclaiming you are not a racist while expressing racist resentment is an important performative act in the post–Civil Rights era, where being outed as a racist can be devastating to your standing in a society that has come to want to deny legitimacy to racist thinking.[12] Many people who still have some form of racial resentment on what they insist are nonracist grounds (as in opposition to affirmative action) will likely appreciate the double-talk as affirming their policy preferences as legitimate and not deserving of public condemnation.[13] Still others insist they are not racist, but instead harbor resentment about a Country that seems to be leaving them behind.[14] Then again, there are others who wish not to make public their racist views but who can also, and probably more greatly, appreciate the racism-denying performance. And nonracists who simply are conservative on policy but get mistaken as racists will undoubtedly be among the most appreciative. As an outspoken politician who engages in this sort of discursive performance, you

[11] *Letters and Papers, Foreign and Domestic, Henry VIII, Volume 13 Part 1: January-July 1538* (p. 189 ref. 504), *British History Online*, Vol. 13. *Institute of Historical Research*, 176–92, https://www.british-history.ac.uk/letters-papers-hen8/vol13/no1/pp176-192.

[12] See Ian Haney Lopez, *Dog Whistle Politics: Strategic Racism, Fake Populism, and the Dividing of America* (Oxford University Press, 2013).

[13] On the issue of whether racial resentment as measured by survey researchers is related to racism, see Stanley Feldman and Leonie Huddy, "Racial Resentment and White Opposition to Race-Conscious Programs: Principle or Prejudice?" *American Journal of Political Science* 49 (2005): 168–83.

[14] Thomas B. Edsall, "Trump Has Turned It Up to 11," *New York Times*, October 16, 2024, https://www.nytimes.com/2024/10/16/opinion/trump-racism-immigrants.html.

can increase your following by creating a public space for a variety of people in this way. For the hardcore racists, this is most important, for public shame, if not the private guilt, of their racism is absolved in the two-step dance of opinion leaders publicly denying racism while expressing it.[15]

Trump tried largely unsuccessfully to deny the racism of his Alt-Right supporters when they marched with torches in the "Unite the Right" rally in Charlottesville, Virginia, early in his presidency on August 11, 2017.[16] The marchers included known leaders of various factions of today's White Nationalist Movement. They wore preppy clothing, khaki pants, and polo shirts especially, in response to neo-Nazi leader Andrew Anglin's call for them to look "appealing," in an effort to try to mainstream their cause.[17] Anglin was quoted as saying to those planning to attend, "I cannot stress the point hard enough—I'm hitting italics again—we need to be extremely conscious of what we look like, and how we present ourselves. That matters more than our ideas. If that is sad to you, I'm sorry, but that is just human nature. If people see a bunch of mismatched overweight slobs, they are not going to care what they are saying."[18]

The Charlottesville marchers were accused of co-opting the look of suburban Americans in their quest for acceptance. This actually was a longstanding practice among white racial extremist hate groups, often referred to as "suit-and-tie racism."[19] But they chanted "Jews will not replace us," which came across as much more threatening than any reassurances their appearance provided. Words and images collided disastrously. And the next day, a counter-protester, Heather Heyer, was killed by a neo-Nazi driving a car into a crowd of counter-protesters.

Trump tried to have his cake and eat it too, yet again, despite the neo-Nazi murder of a peaceful counter-protester. Instead of a direct condemnation of his supporters for instigating this situation, Trump ambivalently stated that there were in fact "many good people" at the rally and "both sides" should be condemned for fomenting the violence.[20] He was gaslighting, deflecting attention away from what his supporters said, and trying to whitewash their

[15] See David Keen, *Shame: The Politics and Power of an Emotion* (Princeton University Press, 2023).

[16] Fording and Schram, *Hard White*, 12.

[17] Alice Newell-Hanson, "Why White Supremacists Are Co-opting Khaki Pants," *Vice*, August 24, 2017, https://i-d.vice.com/en/article/paaqwn/why-white-supremacists-are-co-opting-khaki-pants.

[18] Ibid.

[19] Ibid. Alice Newell-Hanson quotes Kelly Baker as referring to "suit-and-tie racism." See Kelly Baker, *Gospel According to the Klan: The KKK's Appeal to Protestant America, 1915–1930* (University Press of Kansas, 2011).

[20] Adrienne Dunn, "Fact Check: Meme on Trump 'Very Fine People' Quote Contains Inaccuracies," *USA Today*, October 17, 2020, www.usatoday.com/story/news/factcheck/2020/10/17/fact-check-trump-quote-very-fine-people-charlottesville/5943239002/.

hate, just as their appearance in khakis and polo shirts was designed to do. He boomeranged the charges of instigating violence back at the counter-protesters. Trump went on to say many of his supporters were there to simply oppose the taking down of a statue of Confederate General Robert E. Lee because they had a legitimate complaint that this was an attack on their cherished cultural heritage. Trump himself defended Lee on the grounds that he was a genius and a great general.[21] This odd statement deflects attention from Lee's commitment to slavery and the South's insistence on the right to own Black people as property.

Trump tried to shift the ground away from the racism of supporters and paint them as defenders of cultural heritage. Of course, that heritage was one of White Supremacy. Trump was making the discursive moves that today's racism required in a post–Civil Rights era where blatant embrace of White Supremacy is verboten. Trump gave it his best effort, but it was not universally accepted and his repeated attempts to clarify his position seemed to suggest he knew it was not working.

Even as late as spring 2024, standing outside the courtroom where he was on trial for the election interference-hush money case involving Stormy Daniels, Trump digressed to minimize the Charlottesville riot as a "little peanut" compared to the student protests against the Israeli war on Gaza that were occurring at the time.[22] Trump was boomeranging back against Biden who had previously said he ran for the presidency against Trump because of Charlottesville. Now Trump was pushing back, saying Biden was failing to control the student protests against Israel. In the process, Trump was employing a metapragmatic move in order to normalize his support for racists, who in turn were committed to putting him back in the White House.

Yet, as Trumpism has evolved, it has proven an unattainable desire that these discursive moves on their own will indemnify racists as upstanding members of mainstream society and in the process make their rhetoric uncontroversial. Many people who are appropriately keen to repudiate hate speech will see through the performance as unimpressive whitewashing of the soiled expressions of hate. The self-contradictory performative act of denying the hateful speech you just expressed will not do the trick. On its own, it does

[21] Trump continued to try to shift the issue of Charlottesville away from race to culture throughout his presidency and beyond. See Myah Ward, "Trump Praises Robert E. Lee While Denouncing Statue's Removal in Virginia," *Politico*, September 8, 2021, https://www.politico.com/news/2021/09/08/trump-lee-statue-removal-510732.

[22] Ivana Saric, "Trump: Charlottesville Rally Was a 'Little Peanut' Compared to Pro-Palestinian Protests," *Axios*, April 24, 2024, https://www.axios.com/2024/04/25/trump-charlottesville-rally-peanut-palestine-protests.

not make sense. More is needed to justify it. There must be some kind of underlying discourse that makes these discursive moves plausible.

As already suggested, these moves are perhaps most welcomed by supporters who are not racist. Many people who align with Trump and Trumpism are not comfortable with trying to promote White Nationalism or other explicit racist movements even if they are concerned about the declining status of the assumed dominant groups in a diversifying society.[23] Still others plausibly argue that they are not racist but are concerned about how different people with different values and culture are coming to the United States and threatening the established White culture.[24] Many Whites are primarily concerned about how they are being left behind in a diversifying America that seems to lead to fewer opportunities for Whites.[25] This sort of posturing has become more prominent with increased diversity in the immigrant population coming to the United States in today's globalizing world.[26] Racial anxiety has itself evolved. For much of US history, racism was primarily a matter of animosity toward African Americans, even as Native Americans, Asians, and others were also subject to racist attacks. But today racial resentment often takes the form of a more generalized hostility toward a diversity of outgroups, including not just African Americans but also Latino immigrants, Muslims, Asians, and others. In the process, these additional outgroups often get racialized, lumped in with others as non-Whites. Further, this outgroup hostility is often also associated with animosity toward the LGBTQ+ community, non-Christians generally, not just Muslims, and even women. What holds together these different kinds of group-based anxiety is fear of diversity and the threat to the status of people who were assumed to be the dominant or privileged group.

Denials of racism or the more generalized outgroup hostility are not always convincing depending on who is making them and why, though efforts have been made to insist otherwise. Amy Wax, a law professor at the University of Pennsylvania, called herself a "racial realist" when charged with making racist statements to non-White students.[27] She said she was just stating facts about how it is important to recognize that Anglo-American culture, based on Judeo-Christian values, was essential to American greatness and needed

[23] Biko Koenig, "Politicizing Status Loss Among Trump Supporters in 2020," *RSF: The Russell Sage Foundation Journal of the Social Sciences* 8, no. 6 (November 2022): 69–86; and Diana C. Mutz, "Status Threat, Not Economic Hardship, Explains the 2016 Presidential Vote," *Proceedings of the National Academy of Sciences* 115 (2018): E4330–39.

[24] See Ashley Jardina, *White Identity Politics* (Cambridge University Press, 2019).

[25] Arlie Russell Hochschild, *Stolen Pride: Loss, Shame, and the Rise of the Right* (New Press, 2024).

[26] See Fording and Schram, *Hard White*, Chapter 1.

[27] Vimal Patel, "UPenn Accuses a Law Professor of Racist Statements. Should She Be Fired?" *New York Times*, March 13, 2023, https://www.nytimes.com/2023/03/13/us/upenn-law-professor-racism-freedom-speech.html.

to be defended by limiting non-Whites and non-Christians who were undermining that culture. "Racial realism" can be a way of expressing prejudicial ideas while denying your prejudice.[28]

Ultimately, some sort of context about who is making the denial and why is needed to make these denials plausible.[29] The relationship of narrative to discourse is relevant here. I would suggest that discourse is something that is broader and deeper than specific narratives. All narratives have structure, to be sure, but the most common form of narrative is a story. Stories have structure too, but it is most often in the form of a plot with characters whom we follow from beginning to end. Stories never tell the whole story; they trade on implied understandings that are drawn from the wider and deeper discourse in which readers partake (and therefore share) with the authors of those stories. From this perspective, we could say that a discourse is needed to provide an underlying template of intelligibility that makes specific narratives plausible to the point they can provide needed context for the people making the denials.[30]

The underlying discourse today that most commonly gets invoked to facilitate denialism is one like racial realism that shifts the focus from race to culture. The argument is that non-Whites, including African Americans, but also Latino immigrants and other foreigners, and Muslims too, are adherents to cultures that are not consonant with the Anglo-American, Christian culture most White Americans are steeped in, and which has been the mainstream culture of the United States from its inception. In other words, focusing on the alleged threats to the dominant White culture takes the focus off race, deflects attention away from the issue of opposing racial diversification, and absolves people like Amy Wax of the charge of racism. And further, if you are to then still insist that she and others like her are racist, that charge boomerangs back on you as the real racist who is projecting your racial focus on people who have a legitimate concern about what they see as a cultural threat independent of racial considerations. Yet, once culture is the focus, then the issues

[28] Joe Patrice, "Amy Wax Defends Herself by Admitting Most of the Allegations Against Her," *Above the Law*, April 17, 2023, https://abovethelaw.com/2023/04/amy-wax-admits-most-allegations/. For an alternative view, see Aaron Sibarium, "Inside the University of Pennsylvania's Precedent-Setting Effort to Revoke Tenure From Its Most Controversial Professor," *The Washington Free Beacon*, February 13, 2023, https://freebeacon.com/campus/inside-the-university-of-pennsylvanias-precedent-setting-effort-to-revoke-tenure-from-its-most-controversial-professor.

[29] For the argument that all successful social movements, progressive as well as reactionary, must articulate narratives that resonate with the dominant culture, see Deva R. Woodly, *The Politics of Common Sense: How Social Movements Use Public Discourse to Change Politics and Win Acceptance* (Oxford University Press, 2015).

[30] See Sanford F. Schram, "The Deep Semiotic Structure of Deservingness: Discourse and Identity in Welfare Policy," in *The Argumentative Turn Revisited: Public Policy as Communicative Practice*, ed. Frank Fischer and Herbert Gottweis (Duke University Press, 2012), 236–58.

go beyond conflict between Whites and Blacks. It opens the door to seeing Latino immigrants, Muslims, and others as part of the threat. This is in fact the trajectory of Trumpism over time, the diversification of targets to demonize as not real Americans (i.e., people who are not White, Christian, heterosexual, etc.). Yet, shifting the focus from race to culture also opens the door to enlisting, as part of Trumpism, non-Whites who agree with the need to preserve the dominant American culture.[31] By turning to culture, the very idea of racism is complexified, and Trumpists and their resentments ironically then resist clear categorization.

The shift from race to culture took on a profoundly disturbing turn in the 2024 campaign when Trump and his vice presidential candidate J. D. Vance lied that Black Haitian immigrants were eating people's pets. Vance ultimately made the metapragmatic move of saying the lying was just to get people to take the issue of immigration seriously. It was gaslighting in a highly metapragmatic way where the extremist lie gets normalized in a two-step process.[32] In some ways, the turn from race to culture is itself metapragmatic where culture is just a stand-in for race, allowing racial smears to get normalized as allegedly just an honest debate about culture.

The Great Replacement Theory: Racial Realism Underwrites Racist Denialism

Of most relevance here is the story that has resonated so well with Trumpists: The Great Replacement Theory. The discourse of racial realism undergirds the story of The Great Replacement Theory. Leaders of the Alt-Right popularized this "theory" in the years leading up to the rise of the Trumpist Movement. Prominent among them was once again Steve Bannon, who, as already noted, became a top official in the Trump 2016 presidential campaign and in the Trump White House. Bannon, but also top Trump White House speechwriter Stephen Miller, both repeatedly implored people to read *The Camp of the Saints*, a 1973 French dystopian novel by Jean Raspail.[33] That book tells a parable about how elite inaction led Indian immigrants to overtake the indigenous French people to eventually overrun the entire continent.

[31] See Daniel Hosang Martinez and Joe Lowndes, eds., *The Politics of the Multiracial Right* (NYU Press, 2024).

[32] Edward Helmore, "JD Vance Admits He Is Willing to 'Create Stories' to Get Media Attention," *The Guardian*, September 15, 2024, https://www.theguardian.com/us-news/2024/sep/15/jd-vance-lies-haitian-immigrants.

[33] Elian Peltier and Nicholas Kulish, "A Racist Book's Malign and Lingering Influence," *New York Times*, November 22, 2019, https://www.nytimes.com/2019/11/22/books/stephen-miller-camp-saints.html.

Bannon in particular suggested that it was a model of how we should look at what was happening in the United States, where allegedly increasing numbers of non-White immigrants were joining with African Americans to lead the United States to soon become a country where White people were a powerless minority. This apocryphal story continued to be pushed by Trumpists in the 2024 election campaign when Gov. Kristi Noem (R-SD) posted on Twitter: "Countries like Venezuela are emptying their prisons, their mental institutions, and sending them to America. The White House is facilitating this invasion. They're doing it on purpose. Joe Biden could stop it—but he hasn't."[34]

Yet this lie that there is a plan for immigrants to replace Whites in America only makes for concern among those White people who insist we should be leery of immigrants because the United States must be a strictly White, and most often also Christian, country. Only then do non-Whites and non-Christians pose a threat. Only then does the idea of replacement make sense. Other people do not buy into the idea of replacement because they emphasize that the United States historically has had increasingly diverse waves of immigration and its commitment to a pluralistic society celebrates diversity. A xenophobic discourse of White Nationalism or belief in the superiority of White Christian Anglo-American culture that is implicit in racial realism discourse is needed to make the narrative of The Great Replacement Theory plausible.

Today, the underlying discourse that is often conveniently used to whitewash xenophobia and racism is that very same "racial realism" that Amy Wax invoked. It is the idea that people are not really racist; they are just concerned about how people from different backgrounds pose a threat to the dominant culture, which deserves to be protected from those threats. When we hear "racial realism," we must appreciate that, given the trajectory of Trumpism, the definition of racism has changed with the shift to emphasizing the cultural threat. Today, the focus is on people who do not embrace Anglo-American Christian culture and who are the threat.

"Racial realism" is arguably best seen as tagging an underlying discourse that assumes the superiority of Anglo-American (Christian) culture.[35] It informs narrative stories about the immigrant threats to the mainstream culture when they are simply practicing their religion. It is also reflective of a discourse that sees non-Whites, immigrant or not, as not sharing values of Whites regarding traditional work and family values, leading them to be less

[34] https://twitter.com/KristiNoem/status/1765513039795601862.

[35] On the superiority of Anglo-American culture, see Mead, *Burdens of Freedom*.

hard-working and less committed to forming stable families, and thereby posing an increased burden on society by relying on public assistance. For all these reasons, White culture is threatened and the viability of the United States to sustain its greatness is thrown into doubt.

Therefore, the discourse of racial realism helps make the narrative stories of immigrants or non-Whites as a threat more credible. The underlying discourse does this because of its assumptions about White Supremacy and/or Anglo-American cultural superiority. Within this context, the two-step of racial denialism can gain traction. Without the underlying discourse, the story of the immigrant or non-White threat falls flat. But with those stories discursively fortified, racists can have their cake and eat it too. Trump can only be seen as the least racist person in the world when we buy into the underlying discourse associated with racial realism. Accordingly, fighting the threat to White Christian America becomes not deplorable but heroic.[36]

With a generalized White, American ethnocentrism becoming a resurgent kind of contemporary racism that is especially popular on the Right, Trump was able to start to attract support to mobilize a base of supporters to win the presidency in good part by railing against the perceived threats. Further, there was a positive feedback loop at work in energizing the initial phase of Trumpism. It is true that public opinion was already trending in this direction, but it accelerated with the rise of Trump and his willingness to push that button. He arguably was critical in helping it become more legitimate among his base to not trust people who come from suspect places or have suspect backgrounds.

Yet, for Trumpists, race and ethnicity are supposedly irrelevant or, if not that, then merely coincidental. The cultural threat is what counts. Putting aside the denialism, the failure to fully account for the context is what makes the threat narratives and their relationship to the underlying discourse so questionable. The idea that we must stop these other people from overtaking the White culture, whatever that may be, fails to recognize that in our globalizing world, US diversification is all but inevitable. A major reason for this is that a declining birth rate has for a long time increased the need to import a growing number of people who can fill openings in the workforce. Other shifts including changing cultural norms regarding inter-racial and inter-ethnic marriage, increased advancement of women in the workforce, and liberalization of attitudes toward sexual minorities, all help shift the cultural landscape to increase diversification. It is inevitably a losing battle for

[36] See Darragh Roche, "Trump Responds to Meme Saying He's the 'Savior of Western Civilization,'" *Newsweek*, February 10, 2023, https://www.newsweek.com/trump-meme-savior-western-civilization-1780370.

those Whites who try to make America a cultural citadel impervious to the changes that diversification is bringing.

The Camp of the Saints: A Story of The Great Replacement Theory

As noted, *The Camp of the Saints* is a story about how people come to an island off the coast of France but end up overrunning the whole continent. This is somewhat of a tell, suggesting an "island mentality," where a people seek to insulate themselves from the rest of the world.[37] Japan may be the paradigmatic example, but regardless of how long Japan can insist on its ethnic homogeneity, the United States historically has wrestled with this issue, with pluralism winning more often than not. It is this history that the White Nationalist Movement has for a long time been so agonized about, and the increase in diversity in recent years only has heightened the anxiety. The island mentality might not be un-American, but it is a losing proposition, nonetheless.

The aporias of the White Nationalist narrative make racial realism discourse less than convincing. Denialism among Trumpists regarding issues of diversity inevitably becomes vulnerable to charges of duplicity. Yet, as is the way with Trump and Trumpism, once it becomes clear that the majority of Americans do not embrace this kind of prejudicial thinking, there is no explicit admission but instead a doubling down. Rather than openly back away from the less than plausible denials of racism, instead we get more gaslighting, boomeranging, and co-optation.

Sorry, Not Sorry Racism

Probably the most prominent proponent of the US version of The Great Replacement Theory was Fox News' Tucker Carlson. During its six-year run, Carlson's prime-time cable news show, "Tucker Carlson Tonight," regularly promoted White Nationalist themes, including that the 2020 election was stolen in part because African American–led cities allowed for manipulation of the votes. He consistently suggested that the Democrats were allowing for massive illegal immigration of Latinos to vote for them and keep Trump out

[37] Bertram Gregory Liyanage, "Island Mentality, Where Darkness Matters," *Medium*, April 21, 2020, https://medium.com/@liyanagebg/island-mentality-where-darkness-matters-6d67402492b7.

of power. He suggested that many other lies about non-Whites and immigrants were true. He accused members of the press who disagreed of being fascists. Throughout it all, he consistently sought to smear Trump's opponents as anti-American. Black Lives Matter protesters against police violence were continually vilified as terrorists, but the insurrectionists of January 6 were nonviolent protesters. Fear of the other was the main theme for Carlson's nightly show on Fox News.

Carlson boomeranged the charge that the Militia Movement operated like Trump's Stormtroopers on January 6. For Carlson, the Militia Movement groups at the Capitol on January 6 were countering the anti-fascist groups who identified with ANTIFA (anti-fascism) because they were essentially, to Carlson, the Democratic Party's "armed militia."[38] In other words, our armed militia were the good guys defending democracy, but your armed militia were the bad ones threatening it. The insurrection was, however, for Carlson more likely an inside job and the government's spies were the ones undermining the rule of law. Many of the people he demonized, whether they were elected officials, police officers, poll workers, or ordinary citizens, got constant death threats, at times needing to sell their homes or get paid security. Carlson framed all this around the idea that White people were under assault and at risk of being replaced by non-Whites and foreigners, and it was all being abetted by the Democratic Party and a federal government that could no longer be trusted to stand up for real Americans (i.e., White people).[39] Also, we were constantly being reminded by Carlson that the Democratic Party was now the party of the elite establishment that was oppressing ordinary people by gaining power via the immigrant vote.

In spite of leaked emails indicating at times a tiring of Trump and his Movement, Carlson was overall deeply committed to Trumpism as a Movement and was periodically rumored to be a possible choice by Trump to be his running mate even as late as 2024.[40] Therefore, it is no surprise that with Carlson's show, the discursive techniques of Trumpism were on nightly display. Carlson gaslighted, boomeranged, and co-opted his way to legitimating Trumpism's hate for the benefit of his audience and Trump's base, who were already primed to embrace it. Carlson was the master of these discursive practices

[38] Tucker Carlson, "Antifa Is the Armed Militia of the Democratic Party and Is Back in Force," *Fox News*, January 23, 2023, https://www.foxnews.com/opinion/tucker-carlson-antifa-armed-militia-democratic-party-back-in-force.

[39] Nicholas Confessore, "How Tucker Carlson Stoked White Fear to Conquer Cable," *New York Times*, May 4, 2022, https://www.nytimes.com/2022/04/30/us/tucker-carlson-gop-republican-party.html?smid=nytcore-ios-share&referringSource=articleShare.

[40] Dominick Mastrangelo, "Trump Jr. Says Tucker Carlson 'Certainly' a VP Contender," *The Hill*, January 18, 2024, https://thehill.com/homenews/campaign/4416145-trump-jr-tucker-carlson-vp-contender/.

that made White Nationalism seem an unimpeachable All-American belief system that should not have been seen as threatening. As Nick Confessore explains how Carlson perfected these discursive moves over time:

> Mr. Carlson has constructed what may be the most racist show in the history of cable news—and also, by some measures, the most successful. Though he frequently declares himself an enemy of prejudice—"We don't judge them by group, and we don't judge them on their race," Mr. Carlson explained to an interviewer a few weeks before accusing impoverished immigrants of making America dirty—his show teaches loathing and fear. Night after night, hour by hour, Mr. Carlson warns his viewers that they inhabit a civilization under siege—by violent Black Lives Matter protesters in American cities, by diseased migrants from south of the border, by refugees importing alien cultures, and by tech companies and cultural elites who will silence them, or label them racist, if they complain.[41]

Carlson was an expert practitioner of the discursive moves needed to maintain deniability in the post–Civil Rights era. He became famous for monologues that were "only asking questions" but actually were ushering in racist speculation as publicly accepted facts.[42] Trumpism had found its megaphone for legitimating extremist racist talking points for a Republican Party that had long been keen to get the votes of disenchanted Whites. Many of Carlson's stories came from the darkest corners of the internet where hate metastasized unchallenged. He was Trumpism's most prominent White Nationalist spokesperson on TV. And he provided cover for the White Nationalist Movement specifically by gaslighting denials, boomeranging criticisms, and co-opting the anti-elite rhetoric of the Left. Throughout it all, he maintained deniability, calling White Supremacy a "hoax."[43]

Then, suddenly, Carlson and Fox announced on April 24, 2023, that "Tucker Carlson Tonight" would no longer air. It was shocking news since Carlson's show was at the time the highest rated news show on cable TV and earned Carlson reportedly something like $35 million a year in salary.[44]

[41] Ibid.

[42] Matt Wilstein, "Seth Meyers Nails Tucker Carlson's 'Just Asking Questions' Nonsense," *Daily Beast*, October 14, 2021, https://www.thedailybeast.com/seth-meyers-nails-tucker-carlsons-just-asking-questions-nonsense.

[43] Tim Elfrink, "'It's not Actually a Real Problem in America': Tucker Carlson Calls White Supremacy a 'Hoax,'" *Washington Post*, August 7, 2019, https://www.washingtonpost.com/nation/2019/08/07/tucker-carlson-white-supremacy-hoax-lie-not-real-problem/.

[44] Alison Durkee, "Here's What Tucker Carlson Said in Lawsuits that Reportedly Led to His Firing," *Forbes*, April 26, 2023, https://www.forbes.com/sites/alisondurkee/2023/04/25/heres-what-tucker-carlson-said-in-lawsuits-that-reportedly-led-to-his-firing/. Also see Federick Brown, "Tucker Carlson Net Worth 2023," *CA Knowledge*, March 28, 2023, https://caknowledge.com/tucker-carlson-net-worth-salary-cars-house/.

Carlson had become a powerhouse propagandist that people followed to hear the most extreme White Nationalist memes getting mainstreamed into public discourse. But then it all abruptly ended.

Carlson and Fox, it was said, had agreed to part ways amicably.[45] Yet there was suspicion that this too was a lie. There had been wide discussion in the press just prior to the show's end that Carlson had become a huge embarrassment in a variety of ways. In particular, recent court documents in a Dominion Voting Systems defamation case against Fox showed that Carlson was a serial liar who in private conversations with other Fox News talking heads confessed that he did not like Donald Trump at all and was looking for the day when he did not have to defend him on air (something he had been doing for years).

Carlson's firing was though likely due to a variety of additional contributing factors, including abuse of power associated with misogyny in his treatment of female employees, his bullying of Republican elected officials, members of the press, and ordinary citizens, as well as, not insignificantly, his disloyalty to the Fox leadership.[46] Yet, his firing also looked like punishment for his revealing the duplicity behind Fox's news reporting. Carlson ultimately had failed to practice effectively the metapragmatics of Trumpism. The Carlson revelations seemed to make too public that he, along with his Fox colleagues, wanted to have their cake and eat it too. They wanted to make boatloads of money providing their viewing audience of diehard Trump supporters just what they wanted to hear, but they did not want to have to ever admit publicly whether they believed the lies they spread. That was too much honesty for a disingenuous discourse.

After Fox News agreed to a record-breaking settlement of $787.5 million to end the defamation lawsuit regarding lies about the 2020 election, those court documents seemed to have been critical to Carlson's dismissal, though a long line of irresponsible statements and actions by Carlson likely contributed as well.[47] For its part, Fox News admitted as part of the settlement that it had publicized lies about Dominion machines flipping votes from Trump to Biden. But it never apologized. Instead, Fox's statement read, "We are pleased

[45] Melissa Quinn, "Tucker Carlson Is Leaving Fox News, Network Announces," *CBS News*, April 24, 2023, https://www.cbsnews.com/news/tucker-carlson-leaving-fox-news/.

[46] Durkee, "Here's What Tucker Carlson Said in Lawsuits that Reportedly Led to His Firing"; and Oliver Darcy, "Fox News' Sudden Firing of Tucker Carlson May Have Come Down to One Simple Calculation," *CNN*, April 25, 2023, https://www.cnn.com/2023/04/25/media/fox-news-tucker-carlson-reliable-sources/index.html.

[47] Jeremy Peters, Katie Robertson, and Michael M. Grynbaum, "Tucker Carlson, a Source of Repeated Controversies, Is Out at Fox News," *New York Times*, April 24, 2023, www.nytimes.com/live/2023/04/24/business/tucker-carlson-fox-news/tucker-carlson-fox-news?smid=nytcore-ios-share&referringSource=articleShare.

to have reached a settlement of our dispute with Dominion Voting Systems. We acknowledge the Court's rulings finding certain claims about Dominion to be false. This settlement reflects FOX's continued commitment to the highest journalistic standards. We are hopeful that our decision to resolve this dispute with Dominion amicably, instead of the acrimony of a divisive trial, allows the country to move forward from these issues."[48]

It was "sorry, not sorry" (as they say on Twitter).

Fox News Gaslights Racism

The "sorry, not sorry" duplicity reached its zenith when a Tucker Carlson text message was leaked by someone who suggested it was the main reason Carlson was fired right after the settlement. Carlson's text has him saying he saw a video of Trump supporters ganging up on an "Antifa kid." Carlson is self-reflective about how he felt guilty that he was hoping the Trump supporters might even kill the Antifa kid. He however also complained that: "It's not how White men fight."[49] The racism was explicit, and the guilt was as well. Once again, the discursive move is to maintain innocence even while expressing racism. If Fox News actually fired Carlson because of this text message, then it too was practicing the discourse of Trumpism in a post–Civil Rights era. Fox News had long allowed Carlson to spew racism on his highest-rated cable news show. But it could not afford to be seen as having his back when he was expressing the desire that the "Antifa kid" be killed. It is less likely that Fox was concerned that Carlson felt guilty because the White Trump supporters had the Antifa kid outnumbered. That expression of guilt would be consistent with the metapragmatics of Trumpism, and it would be a way for Fox to still practice "sorry, not sorry" racism.

The metapragmatics of the leaked Carlson email were heavily layered. It was like there was something for everyone. Carlson was distancing himself from his wanting to see the Antifa kid killed but perhaps only because the White Trump supporters were not doing it right. Fox News was severing its ties with Carlson but perhaps only because he made explicit that his racism included a desire for mob violence.

This kind of duplicity actually lies at the heart of Trumpism's relationship to Fox News from the very beginning. Fox News was founded in 1996 by

[48] "Fox News and Dominion Voting Systems Reach Settlement," *Fox News*, April 18, 2023, https://press.foxnews.com/2023/04/fox-news-and-dominion-voting-systems-reach-settlement.

[49] Kristen Holmes and Jon Passantino, "Tucker Carlson Sent a Racist Text to a Producer: 'It's Not How White Men Fight,'" *CNN*, May 3, 2023, https://www.cnn.com/2023/05/03/media/tucker-carlson-text-message/index.html.

its owner Rupert Murdoch and the first chief executive Roger Ailes to be a news channel for the Republican Party, and by the time it became a loyal, if at times wary, ally of Trump, it was heavily invested in spreading lies on his behalf.[50] Actually, as Eric Alterman has emphasized, Fox News from its inception was not really primarily a news organization but more of a propaganda machine that specialized in gaslighting its audience, especially by disputing what was being said by the "mainstream media," as Fox News called it. Fox News was primarily a trolling operation, focusing primarily on rebutting the mainstream media.[51] Trump and others who would come to be aligned with him were long-time viewers of Fox News and learned a lot about trolling from it.[52] This trolling operation served political purposes. It was practicing Trumpism as a discourse in service of Trumpism as a movement.

Yet Fox News also, at times, wanted to be taken seriously as a news organization. When Fox News reported first before other networks that the vote tally in the critical swing state of Arizona was indicating that Biden was likely to win the presidency in 2020, it began to lose Trump viewers who started to turn to upstart channels, like One American News Network and Newsmax, which were willing to lie even more for Trump and refuse to admit defeat. Fox News was in a bind; it wanted to report news, but it also wanted to provide the emotional comfort that lies gave to the Trump base.[53] As a result, Fox switched not votes, but gears, and began to help publicize Trump's lies that the 2020 election was stolen. The defamation lawsuit revealed that this was the dynamic that led Fox to knowingly help smear Dominion by accusing it of helping the Democrats steal votes. Eventually, Fox was called to account, but by not apologizing, it seemed like it was holding out hope that Trump supporters would understand its predicament of being caught between politics and commerce (if you can call it that).[54]

Fox News was held hostage to its audience as much as Trump had come to be to his base; and these were very much the same people who insisted on their Fox News information bubble that insulated them from the real world. Fox News had for years helped its audience come to believe that the

[50] Eric Alterman, "Fox News Has Always Been Propaganda," *The Nation*, April 1, 2019, https://www.thenation.com/article/archive/fox-news-propaganda-eric-alterman/.

[51] Ibid. Also see Brian Stelter, *Network of Lies: The Epic Saga of Fox News, Donald Trump, and the Battle for American Democracy* (Simon and Schuster, 2023), 217–18.

[52] Brian Stelter, *Hoax: Donald Trump, Fox News, and the Dangerous Distortion of Truth* (Simon and Schuster, 2020); and Eric Alterman, "The World of Cable News Is Trump's Reality," *BillMoyers.com*, August 17, 2017, https://billmoyers.com/story/world-cable-news-trumps-reality/.

[53] James Poniewozik, "Everybody Knows What Fox News Is Now," *New York Times*, April 19, 2023, www.nytimes.com/2023/04/19/arts/television/fox-news-settlement.html?smid=nytcore-ios-share&referringSource=articleShare.

[54] Ibid.

Democratic Party, liberals, elites, and the federal government were against them and wanted them replaced. But now it could not turn against Trump, who himself, as an avid viewer of Fox, had learned that this is what the audience/base had come to be committed to believing. Fox was being hoisted with its own petard of lies. And if it wanted to survive now in an increasingly competitive market of liars on cable news shows, then it could not fully apologize even when caught red-handed. Instead, it needed scapegoats like Carlson, whose real crime was getting too good at spreading the lies of White Nationalists.

During the run-up to the trial, Fox News was basically never mentioning that there even was a defamation case.[55] They were gaslighting yet again by diverting attention to focus on issues of immigration and alleged abuses by the FBI in investigating Trump for stealing documents and conspiring to prevent Biden from taking office. They also projected their failures in press reporting onto the "mainstream media," whom they claimed refused to investigate the alleged crimes of Hunter Biden, son of the President, or the failures of Democratic-run cities like New York.[56]

The Fox News' approach to the news as exemplified in the paradigmatic case of Tucker Carlson shows that duplicity when effectively challenged ultimately deconstructs (all on its own). Fox scapegoated Carlson for the smears and lies the network had been pushing. Nonetheless, Fox News, much like Trump himself, was still likely to see how far it could continue to go in stoking hate among its base for both political and economic reasons. The corporation had made hate profitable; and once it shed itself of someone who did its bidding too explicitly, it would likely find its way back to making its economic and political interests synonymous. Firing Carlson was Fox News once again saying it was sorry, not sorry.

The story of Carlson and Fox News shows how Trumpism as a discourse must operate at two levels. First, it must feed the base the demonizations, lies, and contrived grievances that energize and mobilize Right-Wing political

[55] There is one exception to Fox never mentioning the Dominion lawsuit and it is highly ironic. On his Fox News weekly show, media critic Howard Kurtz stated: "Some of you have been asking why I'm not covering the Dominion voting machines case against Fox involving the unproven claims of election fraud in 2020. It's absolutely a fair question. I believe I should be covering it, it's a major media story, given my role here at Fox. The company has decided that as part of the organization being sued, I can't talk about it or write about it, at least for now. I strongly disagree with that decision. But as an employee, I have to abide by it." See Jeff Zymeri, "'I Can't Talk about It': Fox News Media Columnist Says Company Won't Let Him Cover Dominion Voting Case," *National Review*, February 27, 2023, https://www.nationalreview.com/news/i-cant-talk-about-it-fox-news-media-columnist-says-company-wont-let-him-cover-dominion-voting-case/.

[56] Adam Gabbatt, "Hunter Biden and 'Dirty' New York: Fox News Back to Basics after Lawsuit," *The Guardian*, April 22, 2023, www.theguardian.com/us-news/2023/apr/22/fox-news-dominion-lawsuit-tucker-carlson.

action in general and Trumpism in particular. Second, it must resort to metapragmatic discursive moves in order to rationalize its pronouncements to the broader public for fear of condemnation (inside as well as outside the courts). Fox News tries to have it both ways—to have its cake and eat it too. It tries to be both sorry and not sorry, in order to keep its license, remain on cable TV, not get sued out of existence, and still get to spread its disinformation.

Your Monster Requires Care and Feeding

Mary Shelley's *Frankenstein* is a famous story about a monster.[57] Yet, Frankenstein is the name of the monster's creator (first name Victor), and the monster actually remains unnamed as the not fully human being, if feeling and caring creature that it is.[58] It raises the question of who the real Frankenstein monster is: Was it the creature that the scientist created but then, it turns out, abandoned, or was it the scientist who we find out irresponsibly created the creature for his own selfish reasons? One moral of the story is that monsters are not natural but are created, and we need to take responsibility for our creations, or they can wreak havoc on the world. Such is the case with Fox News and Trumpism. After feeding the red meat of racial hatred to the audience and Trump's base for years, we increasingly see this in today's parlance as "stochastic terrorism," which can result in surging efforts of Trump supporters to cling to power any way they can, including by way of making terrorist threats, or even going on to commit violent acts, both of which, as noted, continue to increase dramatically.

The vicious cycle between the leader and the followers has in fact at times turned violent. A number of the White racist attacks in churches, synagogues, mosques, and even supermarkets and shopping malls have been reported as being executed by White males who had published manifestos or left behind writings noting The Great Replacement Theory as a concern that led them to execute their attacks.[59] Fox News, Tucker Carlson, and Trump remain

[57] *Frankenstein: Or, the Modern Prometheus* was originally published in 1818 without attribution, but the 1831 edition identified the author as Mary Shelley. See Mary Shelley, *Frankenstein: Or the Modern Prometheus* (Henry Colburn and Richard Bentley, 1831).

[58] Anne O'Malley, "Frankenstein: The True Monster," *Owlcation*, July 20, 2022, https://owlcation.com/humanities/Frankenstein-Invention-vs-Inventor; and Helena Nicholson, "The Modern Prometheus: The Relevance of *Frankenstein* 200 Years on," *OUPblog*, April 11, 2018, https://blog.oup.com/2018/04/modern-prometheus-relevance-frankenstein-200-years/.

[59] David Bauder, "White 'Replacement Theory' Fuels Racist Attacks," *AP News*, May 16, 2022, https://apnews.com/article/great-white-replacement-theory-explainer-.

unapologetic, and they leave open the door to continue to stoke White resentment for political gain and profit too. It is now woven into the very fabric of Trumpism, and it is not likely to be removed simply by trying to whitewash it with metapragmatic moves that gaslight it, project it by boomeranging it onto enemies, or co-opt their anti-elitism. Instead, it is an indelible stain on both Trumpism and Fox News, but one that Trump's supporters still find alluring.

Whites as the New Victims

For Trumpism then, the ultimate discursive move regarding race just might be the emergence of the idea that Whites are the new victims.[60] Claiming that the tables have turned and now Whites are the new victims of discrimination became a popular Trumpist theme in recent years. It is perhaps Trumpism's greatest example of co-optation, where Whites steal the status of victimhood from non-Whites and boomerang the charges of discrimination and privilege back at non-Whites. It is what is at the core of what is being called "White Identity Politics" and its relationship to Trumpism.[61] Yet, whether this move to co-opt victimhood into being an issue for Whites has effectively moved public opinion is another matter that requires empirical examination.

Evidence of the effect of this inversion in making Whites out to be the victims of discrimination began appearing with the presidency of Barack Obama, who was seen as a threat for simply being the first non-White president in history.[62] The Tea Party was particularly effective in stirring up this kind of sentiment about Whites being the new victims of discrimination during the Obama presidency.[63] The sudden burst of furor over how Whites were

[60] See Richard C. Fording and Sanford F. Schram, "Pride or Prejudice? Clarifying the Role of White Racial Identity in Recent Presidential Elections," *Polity* 55, no. 1 (January 2023): 106–36.

[61] See Ashley Jardina, *White Identity Politics* (Cambridge University Press, 2019), Chapter 2.

[62] For survey research supporting the idea that there had been an increase in Whites who saw themselves as the new victims of discrimination, see Samuel R. Sommers and Michael I. Norton, "Whites See Racism as a Zero-Sum Game that They Are Now Losing," *Perspectives on Psychological Science* 6, no. 3 (May 2011): 215–18, journals.sagepub.com/doi/abs/10.1177/1745691611406922; and Media Relations, "Whites Believe They Are Victims of Racism More Often Than Blacks: In Zero Sum Game: Reverse Racism Seen as Bigger Problem than Anti-Black Racism," *Tufts Now*, May 23, 2011, https://now.tufts.edu/2011/05/23/whites-believe-they-are-victims-racism-more-often-blacks.

[63] Max Brantley, "The New Victims of Discrimination," *Arkansas Times*, November 20, 2019, https://arktimes.com/arkansas-blog/2010/11/20/the-new-victims-of-discrimination; Charles M. Blow, "Let's Recuse the Race Debate," *New York Times*, November 19, 2010, https://www.nytimes.com/2010/11/20/opinion/20blow.html?hp; Robb Willer, Matthew Feinberg, and Rachel Wetts, "Threats to Racial Status Promote Tea Party Support Among White Americans," Stanford Graduate School of Business, Working Paper No. 3422, May 4, 2016, https://www.gsb.stanford.edu/faculty-research/working-papers/threats-racial-status-promote-tea-party-support-among-white; and Christopher S. Parker and Matt A. Barreto, *Change They Can't Believe In: The Tea Party and Reactionary Politics in America* (Princeton University Press, 2013).

the new victims continued to promote animosity toward non-Whites with the rise of Trump and his hateful rhetoric.[64]

A popular metapragmatic move among Trumpists who were keen to emphasize that Whites were the real victims was to implicitly accuse the Black Lives Matter Movement of being discriminatory toward Whites. Black Lives Matter formed after the killing of Trayvon Martin in 2013 by a self-appointed security guard and then gained greater visibility with mass protests after the police killings of Micheal Brown and Eric Garner in 2014 and most dramatically George Floyd in 2020. The response to "black lives matter" from some resentful Whites was "all lives matter." "All lives matter" was an implicit move to accuse those who wanted to champion the slogan "black lives matter" as being anti-White by excluding them from the category of who mattered. "Black lives matter" was however meant to be inclusionary, that the lives of Black people mattered just as much as the lives of White people. Yet, the White metapragmatic move was to invert that and claim that "black lives matter" was exclusionary, only about Blacks and therefore was discriminatory against Whites. Only by saying "all lives matter" could the situation be rectified. Until then, Whites were the new victims of discrimination. It was a powerful retort, a metapragmatic move co-opting the concern about Black lives and simultaneously boomeranging it back at the Black Lives Matter activists. This metapragmatic move helped legitimate the idea that Whites were the new victims that we all needed to be concerned about, especially since they were supposedly selectively being ignored by the prominent Black Lives Matter Movement.[65]

Metapragmatics Solidifies Only the Base

The metapragmatics of Trumpism on race have not always been successful in mainstreaming, normalizing, and legitimating its extremist claims, whether they are about The Great Replacement or other racial threat narratives. Below, I examine recent data that span the trajectory of Trumpism

[64] Michael Scherer, "White Identity Politics Drives Trump, and the Republican Party under Him," *Washington Post*, July 16, 2019, https://www.washingtonpost.com/politics/white-identity-politics-drives-trump-and-the-republican-party-under-him/2019/07/16/a5ff5710-a733-11e9-a3a6-ab670962db05_story.html.

[65] Thanks to Phoebe Cohen for recommending "all lives matter" as a metapragmatic move among Trumpists. See Jessica Keiser, "The 'All Lives Matter' Response: QUD-Shifting as Epistemic Injustice," *Synthese* 199 (2021): 8465–83, https://philpapers.org/archive/KEITAL.pdf.

and show an increase in the partisan divide among Whites on this issue of White Victimhood. It seems that during the time when Trumpism had become ascendant, there was a widening partisan gap in attitudes on the status and treatment of White people.[66] Findings like those shown below are entirely consistent with earlier research, suggesting that Trumpist discourse enables the base to stay put in its resentment, but it turns off others.[67]

For this analysis, I use the American National Election Studies (ANES) presidential election year surveys for 2012 and 2020. The ANES are nationally representative surveys of US citizens, conducted before and after every presidential election since 1948.[68] These data can be used to examine the partisan gap among Whites on attitudes concerning the treatment of Whites by society in general and the federal government in particular.

Table 3.1 presents tabulations for Whites whose partisan identification is either Democrat or Republican for 2012 and 2020. First, the table indicates that in 2012, while Obama was running for reelection against John McCain, 11 percent of Republican Whites perceived there to be a great deal of discrimination in society against Whites, while only 5 percent of White Democrats felt similarly. Fourteen percent of White Republicans perceived no discrimination against Whites at all, while 25 percent of White Democrats felt that way. These differences between the parties are relatively small but noticeable (and statistically significant) in the expected direction where White Republicans compared to White Democrats were more likely to perceive discrimination against Whites in society overall.[69]

By 2020, things had shifted. At that time, when Trump was running for reelection against Joe Biden, 15 percent of White Republicans perceived that there was a great deal of discrimination against Whites, while only 3 percent of White Democrats agreed. The White Republicans who perceived a great deal of discrimination against Whites had ticked up 4 percentage points from 2012, while the percentage for White Democrats that was already very low declined 2 percentage points further. But what was really dramatic was the widening partisan gap in the percent who perceived no discrimination at all.

[66] See Philip Bump, "Scott Adams and the Right-Wing Insistence on White Victimhood," *Washington Post*, February 27, 2023, www.washingtonpost.com/politics/2023/02/27/dilbert-scott-adams-racism/.

[67] See Fording and Schram, *Hard White*, 174–78.

[68] American National Election Studies: https://electionstudies.org/. The ANES is a collaboration of Stanford University and the University of Michigan, with funding by the National Science Foundation.

[69] Statistical significance means that there is a low probability that the difference (i.e., the partisan gap in responses about discrimination against Whites) found in the sample of people who were surveyed would not also be found in the population overall. I used a proportion of differences (*Z* score) test to determine statistical significance: https://www.socscistatistics.com/tests/ztest/default2.aspx.

Table 3.1 Increase in partisan gap for Whites: Discrimination against Whites, 2012–2020

Perceived discrimination	Republicans		Democrats	
	2012	2020	2012	2020
Great deal	11%	15%	5%	3%
Moderate	24%	27%	19%	9%
Little	51%	45%	51%	37%
None	14%	13%	25%	51%
	100%	100%	100%	100%
	N = 1,305	N = 1,934	N = 1,306	N = 1,273

Source: ANES: https://sda.berkeley.edu/archive.htm.

Thirteen percent of White Republicans in 2020 perceived no discrimination at all in society against Whites (about the same percentage as in 2012), but now a whopping 51 percent of the White Democrats surveyed said that there was no discrimination against Whites. The already statistically significant gap between the parties widened dramatically.

That is a big change. The partisan gap in the percent of Whites perceiving no discrimination at all had increased from 14 percent for Republicans versus 25 percent for Democrats in 2012 to 13 percent for White Republicans compared to 51 percent for White Democrats. That is an increase in the gap in perceiving no discrimination from 11 to 38 percent.

According to these data, the increase in the partisan gap among Whites on the issue of perceived discrimination against Whites is driven by the dramatic rise in White Democrats who indicated that they perceived no discrimination at all in society against Whites. The increase in White Republicans perceiving a great deal of discrimination against Whites is itself noticeable, but the increase in White Democrats perceiving no discrimination is most dramatic. While Trumpism has been successful in preaching to the choir, it simultaneously was alienating the other side and at what seemed to be an accelerating rate. People not enamored with Trump's bluster were offering a rejection of Trumpism's efforts to co-opt the status of victimhood for White people. Perhaps, that discursive move may have been motivating the base; it was evidently turning off White Democrats in a big way. The data suggest that if Trumpism was trying to co-opt victimhood for its White Nationalist cause, its effects on public opinion seem only positive with its loyal base but not with the opposition.

These findings are corroborated by data from a nationally representative sample of the Critical Issues Survey, whose respondents were interviewed in

2022.[70] Respondents were asked whether they thought there was "a lot more" discrimination against various groups compared to five years ago. While only 5 percent of White Democrats agreed that there was "a lot more" discrimination against White people, 51 percent of White Republicans did. That is a large partisan gap of 46 percent more White Republicans compared to White Democrats saying they saw this kind of increase over the last five years in discrimination against Whites. It is hard to reconcile this gap with factual evidence about discrimination. It is as if a non-trivial proportion of Republicans are living in a different world. This different world is one where they have become convinced that Whites are the new victims.

Much of the argument about Whites as the new victims involves growing animosity toward the federal government as acting in ways that are prejudiced against Whites. Undoubtedly, prior federal policies like affirmative action, which are particularly unpopular with Trump's White base, are part of this trend. Previous research has shown that White declining trust in government and growing hostility toward the federal government have been growing for some time.[71] This research shows that these trends continued when Trump was campaigning on behalf of Whites as the "forgotten Americans."[72] This research also indicates that growing White hostility toward the federal government is strongest among those with high levels of racial resentment (as measured in the ANES).

We can provide relevant findings from the 2020 ANES sample that White Republicans are much more likely than White Democrats to believe that the federal government treats Blacks better than Whites (see Table 3.2). We do not have comparable tabulations for 2012 as we did in Table 3.1 because the ANES had never asked this question before. That itself is noteworthy, suggesting the very idea that it might be worth asking if the federal government discriminated against White people was not something researchers

[70] The Critical Issues Survey is not well-known like the ANES surveys, but it is competently designed and professionally executed, nonetheless. This installment was carried out from May 6–16, 2022, online, from a nationally representative sample of Nielsen Scarborough's probability-based panel, originally recruited by mail and telephone using a random sample of adults. The national poll was conducted among 2,091 respondents, with a margin of error of +/− 2.14 percent. Overall, the sample was adjusted to reflect population estimates (Scarborough USA+/Gallup) for Americans. The survey variables balanced through weighting were: age, gender, race/ethnicity, household income, level of education, census regional division, and political party affiliation. See Stella Rouse and Shibley Telhami, "Polling Suggests that White and Black Americans Are Coming from Different Positions on Discrimination," *The Conversation*, July 1, 2022, https://theconversation.com/poll-reveals-white-americans-see-an-increase-in-discrimination-against-other-white-people-and-less-against-other-racial-groups-185278.

[71] Alexandra Filindra, Noah J. Kaplan, and Beyza E. Buyuker, "Beyond Performance: Racial Prejudice and Whites' Mistrust of Government," *Political Behavior* 44, no. 2 (2022): 961–79, https://www.ncbi.nlm.nih.gov/pmc/articles/PMC8794735/.

[72] Isabel Sawhill, "What the Forgotten Americans Really Want—and How to Give It to Them," *Brookings Institution*, October 2018, https://www.brookings.edu/longform/what-the-forgotten-americans-really-want-and-how-to-give-it-to-them/.

Table 3.2 Partisan gap for Whites on treatment by the federal government, 2020

Federal government bias	Republicans	Democrats
Treats Whites better	15%	72%
Treats both the same	58%	26%
Treats Blacks better	27%	2%
	100%	100%
	(*N* = 1,278)	(*N* =1,920)

Source: ANES: https://sda.berkeley.edu/archive.htm.

had thought to ask until the rise of Trumpism. It is also important to keep in mind that these responses were given in the last year of Trump's presidency, which many Whites supported. In fact, there is research that shows trust in government, as measured in national surveys, has become a thoroughly partisan issue and Republican trust, which had been falling in the Obama years, rose a bit under Trump.[73] Nonetheless, Table 3.2 shows that there was a wide and probably now what seems to be a persistent gap between White Republicans and Democrats on the issue of racial bias in the federal government.

Table 3.2 shows that in 2020 while Trump was still president, only 15 percent of White Republicans thought that the federal government treated Whites better than Blacks; however, 72 percent of White Democrats felt that way. In comparison, 27 percent of White Republicans indicated that they thought Blacks were treated better than Whites, while only a mere 2 percent of Democrats agreed that the federal government favored Blacks over Whites. These differences are statistically significant and strikingly large.

Regardless of Trump being in the White House, White Republicans were much more likely to see the federal government treating Blacks much better than Whites. One interpretation is that in a post–Civil Rights era, especially since Trumpism furthered the co-opting of the status of victimhood for Whites, a nontrivial proportion of White Republicans became convinced that the federal government had it out for them, whereas hardly any White Democrats saw that happening. Instead, almost three-quarters of White Democrats indicated that the federal government was biased in favor of Whites. This is a dramatic development since at least the Civil Rights Movement of the 1960s, when the federal government had developed the reputation as the champion of civil rights and committed to battling racial

[73] John Halpin, Navin Nayak, and Ruy Teixeira, "Trust in Government in the Trump Era," *CAP*, May 24, 2018, https://www.americanprogress.org/article/trust-government-trump-era/.

discrimination. Evidently, that reputation has been turned on its head by a sizeable minority of White Republicans who have taken that to mean the federal government as an agent of discrimination (against Whites). Also, it is noteworthy that the large percentage of White Democrats who thought the federal government continued to be biased in favor of Whites suggests that they felt the Civil Rights struggle was not over, something most White Republicans would probably disagree with.

An additional consideration is that Trump had added the issue of the "Deep State," referring to an entrenched federal bureaucracy that acted on its own against the wishes of White Americans, regardless of who was president.[74] Therefore, these data seem to indicate that even with Trump in the White House, many White Republicans were likely to assume that the Deep State was still out to act at the expense of White Americans.

Yet, the idea that Whites are the new victims is based on not just the belief that the federal government has turned against White people. It is often now assumed also to be the product of a conscious electoral strategy of the Democrats. A popular idea among Trump supporters is that they are not the ones out to undermine democracy, but instead it is the Democratic Party.[75] This boomerang suggests that these Democrats are intentionally encouraging more immigration of non-White immigrants, especially Latinos, to come to the United States and vote against the largely White Republican Party. For instance, Rep. Elise Stefanik (R-NY), Chair of the House Republican Conference, agreed with people like Gov. Noem and spoke for many in her Party when she ran a Facebook advertisement in 2022 that said, "Radical Democrats" were planning "a PERMANENT ELECTION INSURRECTION." "Their plan to grant amnesty to 11 MILLION illegal immigrants will overthrow our current electorate and create a permanent liberal majority in Washington."[76] When she said "Radical Democrats," she meant all Democrats, since this is how Republicans speak now, given the increasingly desperate trajectory of Trumpism.

Table 3.3 presents data from 2022 that show this type of boomerang continues to resonate with the base.[77] In a sample survey conducted by the Chicago

[74] George Packer, "The President Is Winning His War on American Institutions," *The Atlantic*, April 2020, https://www.theatlantic.com/magazine/archive/2020/04/how-to-destroy-a-government/606793/.

[75] Zack Beauchamp, "The Republican Revolt against Democracy, Explained in 13 Charts," *Vox*, March 1, 2021, https://www.vox.com/policy-and-politics/22274429/republicans-anti-democracy-13-charts.

[76] Kaleigh Rogers, "The Twisted Logic behind the Right's 'Great Replacement' Arguments," *FiveThirtyEight*, May 26, 2022, https://fivethirtyeight.com/features/the-twisted-logic-behind-the-rights-great-replacement-arguments/.

[77] These data are from the Chicago Project on Security and Threats (CPOST) Omnibus Survey September Wave 1 2022, conducted by National Opinion Research Center at the University of Chicago for CPOST. The interviews were conducted from September 90 to September

Table 3.3 Democrats are trying to replace the current electorate, 2022
"The Democratic Party is trying to replace the current electorate—the voters now casting ballots—with new people, more obedient voters from the Third World"

	Democrats	Republicans
Strongly agree	2%	21%
Agree	6%	23%
Neither agree nor disagree	27%	29%
Disagree	20%	14%
Strongly disagree	43%	11%
Don't know	2%	2%
Total	100%	100%
N =	1,532	1,132

Source: CPOST.

Project on Security and Threats (CPOST), a nationally representative sample of US adults were asked if they agreed with the following statement: "The Democratic Party is trying to replace the current electorate—the voters now casting ballots—with new people, more obedient voters from the Third World." Forty-four percent of Republicans agreed or strongly agreed, while only 8 percent of Democrats indicated they felt the same way. (This is a statistically significant difference.) In other words, a substantial proportion of the Republican Party has bought into the idea that the real threat to democracy is not their Party's support for Trumpism but the Democratic Party's plan to encourage immigration to replace the current electorate with one that will vote against Republicans. These public opinion data strongly suggest that the boomerang about which Party is the real threat to democracy resonates with Republicans to believe that the Great Replacement is a Democratic conspiracy.

The results in Table 3.3 encapsulate what racism looks like in the age of Trump. Racism today gets justified by saying your actions are really just a form of self-defense (by White people). Whites get to deny they are racist and instead get to claim they are the victims of other people's racism. In the end, this co-optation of victimhood justifies people acting out against non-Whites, in a variety of ways, including some that, at times, are violent. This type of duplicitous posturing is central to Trumpism as it has evolved (as subsequent chapters will demonstrate).

12, 2022 with 3,145 adults aged 18+: https://d3qi0qp55mx5f5.cloudfront.net/cpost/i/docs/CPOST-NORC_Support_for_Political_Violence_Survey_0922_Topline.pdf?mtime=1663783186.

Polarizing the Party: Racializing the Base

Trumpism is associated with growing numbers of Republican assuming that Whites are the new victims, and the federal government is responsible. Yet it has been a long slide toward becoming a party where growing racial anxiety dominates.[78] While playing the race card was for decades a Republican ploy, the extreme racists in the Party were not in charge, but now it seemed they were.[79] Stuart Stevens has noted that leaders of the Republican Party for years knew that racists were part of their coalition, and they were accommodated. But now they were the leading faction. "A lot of us in the party liked to believe the dark side was a recessive gene, but it's a dominant theme. And it's all about race. The Republican Party is a white party ... [And] I tell my GOP friends, 'It's crazy to say it's 1934 in Germany ... when it's clearly 1936.'"[80]

Today, the Republican Party is not even the same party that nominated John McCain in 2008 or Mitt Romney in 2012. For much of its history in the post–Civil Rights era, there was a definite racist, anti-immigrant, and anti-democratic strain in the Republican Party, represented by people like Patrick Buchanan and his failed 1992 bid for the presidential nomination. Yet, the fact that that wing of the Party did not call the shots was frustrating for hatemongers like Rush Limbaugh even as recently as when McCain and Romney were nominated.

Things started to change with the Tea Party Movement that arose in opposition to the presidency of Barack Obama.[81] While that movement was ostensibly in opposition to Obama's economic policies, it quickly began expressing the racism of many of its members. The Tea Party would eventually become a key coalition in the Republican Party represented as it was by the Tea Party Caucus in the House of Representatives. The transformation of the Republican Party in reaction to Obama's presidency, however, was not able to ensure an extreme Right-Wing presidential nominee would emerge. This is where Trump comes in and takes over the anti-Obama Movement. Trump's gateway was the birther conspiracy claim that Obama was an illegal president because he was not born in the United States but instead was actually born in Kenya (and possibly was also not really a Christian, but a closeted

[78] Peter Wehner, "The Party of Malice," *The Atlantic*, January 21, 2024, https://www.theatlantic.com/ideas/archive/2024/01/haley-trump-gop/677212/.

[79] Stuart Stevens, *It Was All a Lie: How the Republican Party Became Donald Trump* (Knopf, 2020).

[80] Stuart Stevens as quoted in David Corn, "The Republican Party Is Racist and Soulless. Just Ask This Veteran GOP Strategist," *Mother Jones*, September/October 2020, https://www.motherjones.com/politics/2020/08/racism-republican-party-stuart-stevens/.

[81] Christopher S. Parker and Matt A. Barreto, *Change They Can't Believe In: The Tea Party and Reactionary Politics in America* (Princeton University Press, 2013).

Muslim).[82] Trump's birtherism was not necessarily bald-faced racism as much as it exploited the more generalized White ethnocentrism of outgroup hostility. Trump rose through the ranks as a potential presidential nominee by leading the charge to get Obama to release his birth certificate (which he eventually did).

Birtherism made explicit the newer racism in the changing the Republican Party. Over time, the Party's rank-in-file was now shifting, as a significant number of economic and cultural conservatives, turned off by the race-baiting, left. In their place were new Republicans who came in, drawn by the hatemongering of Trump. Other Republicans who had not expressed their racism so explicitly were now emboldened by Trump. The result was the transformation of the Republican Party where the extremist fringe now dominated.[83]

In fact, the rapid transformation of the Republican rank-and-file in recent years is stark and measurable, especially on the critical issue of racial attitudes, and opposition toward continuing trends of the past few decades of increased racial liberalism. Instead, the Republican Party has gone in the other direction, regressing on the issues of race in particular. That transformation is depicted in Table 3.4. In this table, we can see a sustained increase from 2004 to 2016 in the percent of Republicans who can be classified, as Richard Fording and I did in 2020, as Racial Extremists or Racial Conservatives (not quite as extreme) regarding their attitudes toward non-Whites.[84] The percent of Republican voters who could be classified as Racial Extremists increased from 13 to 22 percent from 2004 to 2016, while the percent of less extremist Racial Conservatives increased over that time period from 11 to 16 percent. Combining Racial Extremists and Racial Conservatives creates an increase from 24 to 38 percent. The Party went from about a quarter to well over a third being categorized as extremists or conservative in their attitudes toward non-Whites.

What became Trumpism undoubtedly had helped transform the GOP especially by appealing to White people's growing anger about a changing America, one that could now actually elect a Black man as president. The anger Trump and his allies had stoked still intensifies the partisan polarization and has heightened resentment toward the Democratic Party having power in Washington, DC.

[82] Adam Serwer, "Birtherism of a Nation," *The Atlantic*, May 13, 2020, https://www.theatlantic.com/ideas/archive/2020/05/birtherism-and-trump/610978/.

[83] Stuart Stevens, *It Was All a Lie: How the Republican Party Became Donald Trump* (Knopf, 2020).

[84] These estimates are from Fording and Schram, *Hard White*, 178, where the method for determining who is a Racial Extremist or Racial Conservative is specified. The data are from the American National Election Studies (ANES).

Table 3.4 The transformation of the Republican rank-and-file
The percent of Republican voters, 2004–2016

	Racial extremists	Racial conservatives
2004 (N = 678)	13%	11%
2008 (N = 1,154)	19%	13%
2012 (N = 3,817)	23%	17%
2016 (N = 2,524)	22%	16%

While Trump's Republican Party has drawn in some former Democrats including Obama voters, this is around the margins.[85] Instead, the more likely factor producing this rapid shift in the growing numbers of Republicans with racially extreme and conservative attitudes is that the Republican Party had become the Party of Trump and Trumpism's commitment to standing up for White America.

Don't Be Woke: The Zero Sum of Race Relations

The findings in the preceding section when taken together highlight how many Whites see race relations as zero sum, or, in other words, if one group gains in position, privilege, or power, that must necessarily mean that another group loses.[86] This kind of thinking is very Trumpian, starting with Trump himself.[87] So the gains of the Civil Rights era, and the gains for non-Whites overall, mean that Whites are dropping down in the social hierarchy. Given that there have not been widely publicized developments in society, the economy, or politics that could serve as evidence of widespread discrimination against Whites, the growing tendency of some Whites to feel this way must be due to something else. The something else that is perhaps making Whites increasingly feel like they are losing out is not Whites being pushed down, but non-Whites getting opportunities to move up.

In fact, across a wide variety of venues, there have been concerted efforts to improve the position of non-Whites in society, whether it is the broad trends

[85] See Fording and Schram, *Hard White*, Chapter 9.

[86] Sommers and Norton, "Whites See Racism as a Zero-Sum Game that They Are Now Losing," *Perspectives on Psychological Science*, 215–18. For a critique of the idea that race relations are zero sum, see Heather McGhee, *The Sum of Us: What Racism Costs Everyone and How We Can Prosper Together* (One World, 2021).

[87] See Jamelle Bouie, "The Tariff Saga Is About One Thing," *New York Times*, April 9, 2025, https://www.nytimes.com/2025/04/09/opinion/trump-tariffs-rationale-power.html.

like increases in minority appointments to positions of authority in business or government, or specific changes in federal policies like the attempt at reparations for African American farmers who were discriminated against in seeking assistance for decades.[88] It is true that the federal government under the leadership of both Barack Obama and Joe Biden, as Democratic presidents, has at times made notable but less than concerted efforts to move the Country down the road to achieving racial justice and attack discrimination against minorities more generally. This is what DEI (diversity, equity, and inclusion) initiatives are all about.

Yet, these developments have been met with a White resistance that has served to become a major part of Trumpism. The Trumpist colloquialism for efforts to make society more inclusive is that those DEI policies and practices are just "too woke."[89] This term is yet another example of co-optation. "Woke" started out as a positive appellation used by people encouraging others to wake up to the embedded racial biases built into our society, institutions, and structures of power.[90] One of its earliest uses came in a Lead Belly song about the Scottsboro Boys being falsely accused of raping two White women.[91] Over time, it gained a wider currency often invoked in Black vernacular regarding the need to "stay woke." In recent years, it gained the most prominence through the Black Lives Matter Movement in response to the police killing of George Floyd. We started to see White progressives saying they were on board with trying to be "woke" to the embedded racial biases of society.[92]

Yet, in response, it got co-opted by the Right. Rather than a positive term, it has increasingly come to be deployed metapragmatically as a sarcastic characterization of someone who is too insistent in getting White society to unfairly accept blame for the disadvantages non-Whites endure.[93] For the

[88] Phil McCausland, "Federal Government Taken to Court for Reworking Black Farmers Debt Relief Program," *NBC News*, October 12, 2022, https://www.nbcnews.com/news/us-news/us-government-court-black-farmer-relief-program-rcna5191n an6.

[89] Glenn C. Altschuler and David Wippman, "The Myth of 'Woke' Indoctrination of Students," *The Hill*, April 9, 2023, https://thehill.com/opinion/education/3941143-the-myth-of-woke-indoctrination-of-students/.

[90] Marcyliena Morgan, "'We Don't Play': Black Women's Linguistic Authority Across Race, Class, and Gender," *The Oxford Handbook of Language and Race*, ed. Samy H. Alim, Angela Reyes, Paul V. Kroskrity (Oxford University Press, 2020), 276–77.

[91] Bart Cammaerts, "The Abnormalisation of Social Justice: The 'Anti-Woke Culture War' Discourse in the UK," *Discourse and Society* 33, no. 6 (November 2022): 730–43.

[92] Greg Jaffe, "After Killing of George Floyd, White Liberals Embrace Ideas That Once Seemed Radical," *Washington Post*, June 9, 2020, https://www.washingtonpost.com/national/after-killing-of-george-floyd-looting-and-rage-leads-white-liberals-to-embrace-ideas-that-once-seemed-radical/2020/06/09/63382090-a720-11ea-b619-3f9133bbb482_story.html.

[93] Ishena Robinson, "How Woke Went From 'Black' to 'Bad,'" *NAACP Legal Defense Fund*, August 22, 2022, https://www.naacpldf.org/woke-black-bad/. Robinson provides a thorough timeline of the use of the term "woke."

Right, co-opting "woke" becomes part of the metapragmatic move to cancel "cancel culture," as an overly politically correct insistence against people being able to express themselves freely on issues of racial differences. Co-opting "woke," and inverting its meaning from positive to negative, has proven for the Right to be very successful as an ironic co-optation, thereby contributing to the cause of White resistance to efforts to promote racial justice.

Given the extreme polarization of politics these days, anti-woke Trumpists see race relations as zero sum in a friend/enemy relationship.[94] Therefore, improvements for non-Whites must be resisted as evidence of Whites being threatened with losing their position, privilege, and power. With this kind of thinking, Whites are encouraged to co-opt the victim status that had been reserved for non-Whites in the Civil Rights era. Trumpism is a post–Civil Rights era movement that seeks to have the cycle swing back now to standing up for the rights of Whites (even when they are actually not under assault). Zero-sum thinking makes racial realism ever more insistent on resisting efforts aimed at increasing racial diversity, equity, and inclusion. Zero-sum thinking makes racial realists adamantly opposed to DEI.

White Nationalism vs. White Supremacy

A recent gaslight is to attempt to distinguish White Nationalism (good) from White Supremacy (not necessarily good). This distinction was made by Sen. Tommy Tuberville (R-AL). Remember, Tuberville made news when he said: "Democrats are attacking our military, saying we need to get out the White extremists, the White nationalists ... Well, they call them that. I call them Americans."[95] Tuberville denied he supported racial extremists in the military but also suggested that White nationalists were just good Americans. The Senator added: "You think a white nationalist is a Nazi? I don't look at it like that. I look at a white nationalist as a Trump Republican. That's what we're called all the time. A MAGA person."[96] Tuberville expressed his support for White Nationalists in the military after the Country had just learned that Jack Teixeira, the member of the Massachusetts Air National Guard, had

[94] Cammaerts, "The Abnormalisation of Social Justice: The 'Anti-Woke Culture War' Discourse in the UK," 730–43.

[95] Azi Paybarah, "GOP Senator Says of White Nationalists in the Military, 'I Call Them Americans,'" *Washington Post*, May 11, 2023, www.washingtonpost.com/politics/2023/05/10/tuberville-military-extremists/.

[96] Ibid.

been arrested for leaking top secret documents about Ukraine while posting online about his desire for a race war.

It is true that once White Supremacy was something Southern members of Congress were proud to say on the floor of the House or the Senate that it was something they believed in.[97] Now most members of Congress are hesitant to say they embrace White Nationalism. There are a few like Sen. Josh Hawley (R-MO) who explicitly indicate they support Christian Nationalism, which is a bit different and implies putting emphasis on seeing the United States as a country founded on Christianity and that it needs to remain committed to stressing Christianity as the dominant religion of the Country.[98] While Senator Tuberville embraces White Nationalism, even he is keen to distinguish it from White Supremacy. Based on his admittedly obscure comments, we can venture a guess that Tuberville would likely appreciate the distinction that some researchers have made that White Nationalism is about being proud of your White identity without the racial prejudice of White Supremacy.[99] It would be a sign of progress, but the distinction ends when used by Tuberville as being just another Trumpist gaslight deflecting attention away from the White bias that slides into White prejudice even when people swap out Supremacy for Nationalism.

When campaigning for Texas Senator Ted Cruz's reelection in 2018, Trump said he was a "Nationalist," as if to leave to the side how he courted White Nationalists when running for office.[100] He said this right after talking about how we needed to resist the "Globalists," a term often used to question the loyalty of Jews. The next day, when asked if he was dog-whistling to White Nationalist supporters, Trump boomeranged that it was racist to ask that question. Without the White designation in front of Nationalism, who could tell? But it sure seemed like the dog-whistle people thought it was. While White Supremacy may be now verboten, it seems White Nationalism is something you can at least intimate. With Tuberville, we may get to the point where dog-whistling is no longer needed and having White Nationalists in the military is something to celebrate.

[97] Katznelson, *Fear Itself: The New Deal and the Origins of Our Time*, Chapter 5.

[98] Steve Benen, "Why Josh Hawley's Ahistorical 'Christian Nation' Nonsense Matters," *MSNBC*, July 10, 2024, https://www.msnbc.com/rachel-maddow-show/maddowblog/josh-hawleys-ahistorical-christian-nation-nonsense-matters-rcna161078.

[99] See Amanda Graham, Francis T. Cullen, Leah C. Butler, Alexzander L. Burton, and Velmer S. Burton, Jr., "Who Wears the MAGA Hat? Racial Beliefs and Faith in Trump," *Socius* 7 (2021), https://journals.sagepub.com/doi/10.1177/2378023121992600.

[100] Quint Forgey, "Trump: 'I'm a Nationalist,'" *Politico*, October 22, 2018, https://www.politico.com/story/2018/10/22/trump-nationalist-926745.

Racialized Metapragmatics in Trumpism Today

Trumpism is heavily invested in these discursive moves that reflect the post–Civil Rights era context. Trumpism does not just co-opt victimhood; it also boomerangs and projects cries of racism. It inverts the meaning of being "woke." It disingenuously distinguishes White Nationalism from White Supremacy. Trumpism attempts to push the idea that Whites have a legitimate grievance against how they are now being discriminated against and parries back at the critics as racist for even suggesting that Whites harbor resistance to moving toward a more inclusive society. Racial realism is the implicit fall-back position that is buttressed by zero-sum thinking, and both reinforce the idea that Whites who have legitimate concerns about how multiculturalism are not necessarily racists.

Trumpism's resistance to non-White groups getting opportunities they once were denied might not be racism in the sense of believing in White Supremacy or White superiority, but it is without question some form of racial resentment, where improvements for other groups are seen as threatening to the social dominance of White people.[101] Trump and his allies have turned public opinion with his base, increasing White anxiety about losing position, privilege, and power. It has been less successful in legitimating these concerns with the rest of the electorate. Therefore, the two-step of Trumpism as a discourse that relies on metapragmatics to mainstream, normalize, and legitimate its claims can backfire, when not practiced competently, creating more marginalization than mainstreaming. This is especially the case for Tucker Carlson when his private emails ended up revealing more racism than even his inflammatory television show had intimated. He got replaced, and it would fall to others to continue the dissemination of The Great Replacement Theory.

Yet, such failures in trying to convince everyone that Trumpism is not about racism have proven recurrent, given that racism is so prevalent among Trumpists. Recurrent failure, however, does increase frustration among base supporters. In desperation, leaders reach for what Rick Pearlstein calls the "authoritarian ratchet" to double down on stoking these resentments in order to continue to hold sway with the base by getting them to feel even more

[101] See Felicia Pratto, Jim Sidanius, and Shana Levin, "Social Dominance Theory and the Dynamics of Intergroup Relations: Taking Stock and Looking Forward," *European Review of Social Psychology* 17 (2006): 271–320, www.tandfonline.com/doi/abs/10.1080/10463280601055772.

grievance toward mainstream society and the government.[102] We saw this dramatically in the 2024 presidential campaign where Trump's increased desperation led him to up the ante promising to use the military for mass deportation immigrants he claimed were in the Country illegally. The demands for more radical policy change inevitably intensify when the base gets more resentful about the leadership's inability to enact promised change. This vicious cycle can also become its own form of stochastic terrorism. The process of marginalization can further intensify the hatred of selected fringe actors. It inspires violence along the way (is we show in the next chapter). Trumpism is a discourse with real consequences producing material harm, whether it is through nonviolent policymaking or sometimes even violent terror attacks.

[102] Rick Perlstein, "My Political Depression Problem—and Ours," *The American Prospect*, May 29, 2024, https://prospect.org/politics/2024-05-29-my-political-depression-problem/.

4
Fascism

At the September 29, 2020, presidential debate with Joe Biden, then-President Donald Trump waffled when asked by moderator Chris Wallace from Fox News to tell White Supremacists and Militia groups to "stand down" in response to their violence that year in cities like Kenosha and Portland.[1] Trump said he needed the name of a group; Biden then suggested the Proud Boys. In response, Trump employed the metapragmatic discourse of Trumpism when he said: "Proud Boys, stand back and stand by." He was calling them to be ready to come to his defense but also then suggesting that it was not something that was imminent. If he had simply agreed to tell them to stand down, that would have been perhaps a bit reassuring. Yet, it would then not be Trumpism. Instead, Trump voiced classic Trumpism that was simultaneously threatening but also normalizing as if the threat would only be made real if somehow subsequently justified. Then Trump immediately boomeranged the suggestion that it was the other side that was the problem: "But I'll tell you what, I'll tell you what, somebody's got to do something about ANTIFA and the Left because this is not a Right-Wing problem." Trump claimed he "wanted to see peace" but the Left did not.

This metapragmatic exchange would prove eerily prophetic for Trump because the Proud Boys would soon stand out among those of his supporters who engaged in acts of violence in response to Trump's call for them to march to the Capitol on January 6, 2021, and stop the certification of Biden's victory in that election. The leaders of the Proud Boys and Oath Keepers were ultimately convicted of seditious conspiracy to prevent Biden being installed as president.[2]

Trump never has been shown to have had direct contact with either of these groups who stood at the forefront of the Militia Movement as it became committed to using violence to keep Trump in power. In fact, Trump claimed the

[1] Kathleen Ronayne and Michael Kunzelman, "Trump to Far-Right Extremists: 'Stand Back and Stand By,'" *AP News*, September 30, 2020, https://apnews.com/article/election-2020-joe-biden-race-and-ethnicity-donald-trump-chris-wallace-0b32339da25fbc9e8b7c7c7066a1db0f.

[2] Michael Kunzelman and Alanna Durkin Richer, "Four Oath Keepers Convicted of Jan. 6 Seditious Conspiracy," *Portland Press Herald*, January 23, 2023, www.pressherald.com/2023/01/23/four-oath-keepers-convicted-of-jan-6-seditious-conspiracy/.

The Trajectory of Trumpism. Sanford F. Schram, Oxford University Press. © Oxford University Press (2026).
DOI: 10.1093/9780197827437.003.0004

day after the September 29, 2020 presidential debate when he told the Proud Boys to "stand by" that he actually did not know who they were.[3] Trump's attempt to minimize the threat of the Militia Movement was, however, itself quite disconcerting since just two weeks before the debate, the Director of the FBI (Federal Bureau of Investigation) had testified before Congress saying that violence by domestic groups (on both the Left and the Right) was a growing concern.[4] At the trial for Proud Boys leader Enrique Tarrio on multiple charges that included seditious conspiracy, a witness testified that he had been an informant for the FBI since 2008 and had joined the Proud Boys in 2019.[5] He supplied information about them to the FBI from then on, including his participation in the march to the Capitol where at one point as the storming of the Capitol commenced he texted to his handler: "emergency situation."[6] Evidently, the FBI was concerned about the Proud Boys for some time before the protest turned into a riot that ultimately was part of an insurrection, all on behalf of Trump's attempt to undermine the rule of law and stay in power. But Trump never heard of them even as president. He seemed not to care other than that they supported him.

Trump's insouciance is baked into his personality. His willingness to align himself with the most extreme White Nationalists is perhaps often better seen in strictly transactional terms rather than something that comes from a deep-seated ideological commitment to White Supremacy. Trump's willingness to align himself with the Militia Movement (which includes many members who do hold White Supremacists views) should be seen similarly. He is arguably gaslighting them as much as anybody else. He is using them for his own personal political gain. His willingness to encourage the Militia Movement and others to threaten or actually engage in violence is in that sense strictly transactional. Trump is transactional all the way down. He seems to have no limit in that regard. He will play with fire if it enables him to come out on top. Yet the threat to the rule of law and liberal democracy in the United States remains the same. Perhaps, we should call Trump an "Opportunistic Fascist."

In this chapter, I trace what amounts to an authoritarian turn in the trajectory of Trumpism. I show in detail how that authoritarian turn qualifies as a

[3] Claire Hansen, "Trump: 'I Don't Know Who the Proud Boys Are,'" *U.S. News & World Report*, September 30, 2020, https://www.usnews.com/news/national-news/articles/2020-09-30/trump-i-dont-know-who-the-proud-boys-are.

[4] Olivia Beavers, "Wray: Racially Motivated Violent Extremism Makes Up Most of FBI's Domestic Terrorism Cases, *The Hill*, September 17, 2020, https://thehill.com/policy/national-security/516888-wray-says-racially-motivated-violent-extremism-makes-up-most-of-fbis/.

[5] Michael Kunzelman, "Capitol Riot: FBI Informant Testifies for Proud Boys Defense," *AP News*, March 29, 2023, https://apnews.com/article/proud-boys-capitol-riot-jan-6-informant-3324d58c9f7ba9b3c2f4b2fe7743c920.

[6] Ibid.

fascist movement. It might not be based on a full-throated fascism grounded in some explicit ideology, but it is a real threat to the rule of law, the constitutional order, and democracy in the United States.[7] Not everyone aligned with Trumpism as a movement may be a "fascist to his core," as former Chairman of the Joint Chiefs of Staff Mark Milley said of Trump,[8] yet the champions of Trumpism are willing to engage in metapragmatics that amount to "sanewashing" (i.e., normalizing) even Trump's most outrageous fascistic statements.[9]

While authoritarianism can be defined as a political orientation that favors autocratic state rule, fascism historically is specifically related to the rise of totalitarian rule under first Mussolini's fascists in Italy and then subsequently Hitler's Nazis in Germany, where extreme violence and terror were employed to seize and maintain power, and in the case of the Nazis to seek global domination that involved genocide to eliminate inferior people, Jews in particular. In this light, fascism could be seen as an extreme variant of authoritarianism.[10] Trumpism is however about denying it is either, while encouraging people with authoritarian and even fascist leanings to support Trumpism's quest for unconstrained power. Consistent with my focus in this book, I again examine how Trump and Trumpism seek to have their cake and eat it too, to metapragmatically preserve deniability while stoking the flames of what others call "authoritarian populism," which has attracted extremists to Trumpism as a movement.[11]

This chapter shows how gaslighting, boomeranging, and co-opting get deployed in the fascist gestures of Trumpism in the hopes of trying to have it both ways, mobilizing extremists while denying it so as to normalize the calls for people to be against the law, the constitution, and democracy. These rhetorical moves almost always lack substance and are instead baseless smears and denunciations designed to rationalize extra-legal efforts to gain and cling to power. I will show how the trajectory of Trumpism involves these vacuous discursive moves that, regardless of ideological commitments, aim to mainstream, normalize, and legitimate authoritarian rhetoric so as to energize

[7] Andrew Marantz, "Why We Can't Stop Arguing About Whether Trump Is a Fascist," *New Yorker*, March 27, 2024, https://www.newyorker.com/books/under-review/why-we-cant-stop-arguing-about-whether-trump-is-a-fascist. Marantz dryly notes: "As the old Internet joke goes, it's only true fascism if it comes from Italy; otherwise, it's just sparkling authoritarianism."

[8] Ruby Cramer, "Trump is 'Fascist to the Core,' Milley Says in Woodward Book," *Washington Post*, October 12, 2024, https://www.washingtonpost.com/nation/2024/10/12/mark-milley-donald-trump-fascist/.

[9] Austin Sarat, "Laundering Lies: Glenn Youngkin Shows How Easily Media Is Manipulated to Sanewash Donald Trump," *Salon*, October 16, 2024, https://www.salon.com/2024/10/16/laundering-lies-glenn-youngkin-shows-how-easily-media-is-manipulated-to-sanewash-donald/.

[10] Jason Stanley, *How Fascism Works: The Politics of Us and Them* (Random House, 2015).

[11] Jan-Werner Muller, *What Is Populism?* (University of Pennsylvania Press, 2016).

supporters and thereby ride to power as a minority movement that wins by undermining democracy.

This chapter therefore does not seek to prove whether Trump deep down in his heart is a fascist or if Trumpism is explicitly committed to fascism as a governing philosophy whatever that might be. Yet, Trump and his acolytes are willing to encourage fascist-minded elements of the Movement and those adjacent while trying to maintain deniability. They use metapragmatics to do so.

This encouraging of extremists however has led to Trumpism now being trapped in an "authoritarian ratchet" where there is a felt need to intensify the rhetoric after prior gestures promising extremist actions have failed to fully satisfy resentful supporters.[12] The Movement, including its leader and his key acolytes, are now trapped into making increasingly extreme promises about seizing power even as they still seek to deny it. The result is that the US political system faces the real prospect of what at least amounts to an authoritarian regime being installed at the top of the US government. The vicious cycle of Trumpism where the leaders end up having to deliver to the followers after ratcheting up the rhetoric leads to perhaps what we can call an "American Fascism," which might be more talk than action but dangerous, nonetheless. Nothing shows Trump's commitment to keeping the White Nationalists and others close more than his pardoning almost all the January 6th insurrectionists, including the charged or convicted members of the Patriot Movement, so as not to just reward them but arguably to keep them ready to act illegally on Trump's behalf. Trump's gaslighting about the insurrection in particular helped him gain support for this rogue action. His metapragmatics about the unconstitutional actions he and his administration are taking in his second term as president also dramatically demonstrate how Trumpism operates as a discourse to normalize its authoritarian threat to the US political system. Highlighting how metapragmatics has gotten Trumpism to this point is the goal of this chapter.

Trump's Militia

Less than two weeks after the September 29, 2020, presidential debate, when Trump metapragmatically told the Proud Boys to "stand by," the FBI announced arrests for a group of people who were ultimately convicted for

[12] Rick Perlstein, "My Political Depression Problem—and Ours," *The American Prospect*, May 29, 2024, https://prospect.org/politics/2024-05-29-my-political-depression-problem/.

plotting to kidnap and kill Michigan Governor Gretchen Whitmer. According to Michigan officials involved in the arrests, the plotters were hoping to do more than just take out Whitmer and that they in fact were planning other actions while texting that they hoped their efforts would promote a "civil war leading to societal collapse."[13] At the time, Whitmer criticized Trump for not speaking out forcefully against the Militia Movement. She stated: "When our leaders encourage domestic terrorists, they legitimize their actions. When they stoke and contribute to hate speech, they are complicit."[14] Trump fell back to gaslighting by saying that Whitmer was an ingrate for failing to thank him for getting the kidnappers arrested. At a rally in Lansing, Michigan, later in October 2020, Trump responded, "Your governor, I don't think she likes me too much. ... Hey, hey, hey hey, I'm the one, it was our people that helped her out with her problem. I mean, we'll have to see if it's a problem. Right? People are entitled to say maybe it was a problem, maybe it wasn't. ... It was our people—my people, our people that helped her out. And then she blamed me for it. She blamed me and it was our people that helped her. I don't get it. How did you put her there?"[15]

Trump was gaslighting yet again so that he could have his cake and eat it too. He wanted credit for the arrests of the people who were trying to kidnap and kill Gov. Whitmer, but he also wanted not to say whether there was a "problem," ambiguously implying either the kidnappers were innocent or that the kidnapping was justified. He was trying to get credit for upholding the law while not explicitly condemning his supporters who were actively seeking to violently undermine it.

One connection to Trump was that one of the groups involved in the kidnapping was the Militia group, the Wolverine Watchmen.[16] This group had first gotten some attention as being "regulars" at the pandemic protests against Michigan's COVID-19 restrictions.[17] These and other protests against the pandemic restrictions would prove pivotal for Trump. Up to that point, Trump was both unsure about how to respond to the pandemic and not

[13] Hannah Knowles, "Wolverine Watchmen, Extremist Group Implicated in Michigan Kidnapping Plot, Trained for 'Civil War,'" *Washington Post*, October 9, 2020, https://www.washingtonpost.com/nation/2020/10/08/wolverine-watchmen-michigan-militia/.

[14] Gretchen Whitmer, "I Will Hold the President Accountable for Endangering and Dividing America," *Washington Post*, October 9, 2020, https://www.washingtonpost.com/opinions/2020/10/09/gretchen-whitmer-hold-trump-accountable/.

[15] Maegan Vazquez and Nikki Carvajal, "Trump Appears to Give a Pass to the Domestic Kidnapping Plot against Whitmer," *CNN*, October 27, 2020, https://www.cnn.com/2020/10/27/politics/trump-gretchen-whitmer-kidnapping-michigan/index.html.

[16] Graham Macklin, "The Conspiracy to Kidnap Governor Gretchen Whitmer," *Combating Terrorism at West Point*, 14, no. 6 (July/August 2021), https://ctc.westpoint.edu/the-conspiracy-to-kidnap-governor-gretchen-whitmer/.

[17] Ibid.

interested in recruiting the Militia Movement into his camp of active supporters. These both changed when the pandemic protests took off. Trump became a supporter of the protests, including when armed militia members joined with others, and by association that brought the Militia Movement more into the Trump camp.[18]

While the Militia Movement for a long time had been leery of alliances with government officials, in the case of Trump, this started to change when he pardoned the Bundy ranchers for their squatting on federal land in 2018.[19] Trump's railing against the Deep State going back to his 2016 campaign had already moved some Militia members to be supportive. But with his embrace of the armed protests against the pandemic lockdowns at state capitols around the country, militia organizations moved solidly into the Trump camp. Lawrence Rosenthal, an expert on Right-Wing extremism, noted: "With Trump, the fringe entered the mainstream. Donald Trump has succeeded in being at once the head of government and the head of anti-government. It's a remarkable thing, actually."[20]

At the height of the pandemic protests, the armed protests spread to state capitals where there were Democratic governors. Trump was now in, fully committed to the protests, and on April 17, 2020, he tweeted "LIBERATE MINNESOTA!" (caps in the original tweet). He followed that with "LIBERATE MICHIGAN!" and "LIBERATE VIRGINIA!" Trump was not expressing traditional conservative law and order rhetoric but co-opting liberatory rhetoric from the Left to signal his support for the protests. When asked about the tweets and whether they would encourage protesters to disobey government officials, Trump deflected: "They seem to be protesters that like me and respect this opinion and my opinion is the same as just about all of the governors. They all want to open. Nobody wants to stay shut, but they want to open safely. So do I."[21] Yet others immediately saw the tweets as incendiary, and possibly unconstitutional and illegal because as president,

[18] Anne Gearan and John Wagner, "Trump Expresses Support for Angry Anti-Shutdown Protesters as More States Lift Coronavirus Lockdowns," *Washington Post*, May 1, 2020, https://www.washingtonpost.com/politics/trump-expresses-support-for-angry-anti-shutdown-protesters-as-more-states-lift-coronavirus-lockdowns/2020/05/01/25570dbe-8b9f-11ea-8ac1-bfb250876b7a_story.html.

[19] Amy Cooter, "Militia Expert Explains Trump's Complex Relationship To Jan. 6 Rioters," The Conversation, *Mississippi Free Press*, July 21, 2022, https://www.mississippifreepress.org/25880/militia-expert-explains-trumps-complex-relationship-to-jan-6-rioters.

[20] Amelia Thomson-DeVeaux and Maggie Koerth, "How Trump and COVID-19 have Reshaped the Modern Militia Movement: Researchers Warn There May Be More Violence," *FiveThirtyEight*, September 4, 2020, https://fivethirtyeight.com/features/how-trump-and-covid-19-have-reshaped-the-modern-militia-movement/.

[21] Craig Mauger and Beth LeBlanc, "Trump Tweets 'Liberate' Michigan, Two Other States with Dem Governors," *The Detroit News*, April 17, 2020, https://www.detroitnews.com/story/news/politics/2020/04/17/trump-tweets-liberate-michigan-other-states-democratic-governors/5152037002/.

it could be interpreted that he was encouraging people to stage an insurrection (which eventually in fact happened concerning Trump's 2020 failed reelection bid). Mary McCord, the former US Assistant Attorney General for National Security from 2016 to 2017, responded:

> "Liberate"—particularly when it's declared by the chief executive of our republic—isn't some sort of cheeky throwaway. Its definition is "to set at liberty," specifically "to free (something, such as a country) from domination by a foreign power." We historically associate it with the armed defeat of hostile forces during war, such as the liberation of Western Europe from Nazi Germany's control during World War II. Just over a year ago, Trump himself announced that "the United States has liberated all ISIS-controlled territory in Syria and Iraq." In that context, it's not at all unreasonable to consider Trump's tweets about "liberation" as at least tacit encouragement to citizens to take up arms against duly elected state officials of the party opposite his own, in response to sometimes unpopular but legally issued stay-at-home orders.[22]

Trump was now aligning himself with the Militia Movement and eventually would be toying with the idea that it could help him stay popular and stay in power. The leaders of the Militia Movement in fact were already lining up behind Trump. McCord noted that the day before Trump tweeted LIBERATE, "[T]he Oath Keepers Twitter account tweeted, in an apparent reference to the president, that 'All he has to do is call us up. We WILL answer the call.' Months before, vigilante groups responded to Trump's frequent rhetoric about an 'invasion' on America's southern border by deploying to the border and illegally detaining migrants while heavily armed, dressed in military fatigues and calling themselves the 'United Constitutional Patriots'."[23]

Over time, the fraught ties between Trump and the Militia Movement grew more ominous. Groups like the Proud Boys and the Oath Keepers started to envision themselves as "Trump's Militia."[24] Ultimately, Trump's Militia would go on to publicly display how they were a violent force to undermine US democracy. The trajectory of Trumpism was turning to add a more explicit,

[22] Mary McCord, "Trump's 'LIBERATE MICHIGAN!' Tweets Incite Insurrection. That's Illegal. Federal Law Bans Advocating the Overthrow of Government," *Washington Post*, April 17, 2020, https://www.washingtonpost.com/outlook/2020/04/17/liberate-michigan-trump-constitution/. Also see Jeffrey Isaac, "Trump's Tweets Incite Civil War and Public Health Disaster," *Democracy in Dark Times*, April 17, 2020, https://jeffreycisaacdesign.wordpress.com/2020/04/17/trumps-tweets-incite-civil-war-and-public-health-disaster/.

[23] McCord, "Trump's 'LIBERATE MICHIGAN!' Tweets Incite Insurrection."

[24] Caleb Newton, "Jamie Raskin Hits Trump with Reveal of Jan. 6 Evidence," *Bipartisan Report*, April 18, 2022, https://bipartisanreport.com/2022/04/18/jamie-raskin-hits-trump-with-reveal-of-jan-6-evidence/.

violent, anti-democratic dimension. By implication, Trumpism was becoming more explicitly anti-democratic. It was becoming something close to fascistic, but when that was pointed out, the boomerang got sent out that the critics were the fascists who were locking down the Country. At the height of the pandemic, Trump held rallies against medical-expert advice to celebrate freedom and call out "far-left fascism":

> This attack on our liberty, our magnificent liberty, must be stopped, and it will be stopped very quickly. In our schools, our newsrooms, even our corporate boardrooms, there is a new far-left fascism that demands absolute allegiance ... If you do not speak its language, perform its rituals, recite its mantras and follow its commandments, then you will be censored, banished, blacklisted, persecuted and punished. Not going to happen to us ... Make no mistake, this leftwing cultural revolution is designed to overthrow the American revolution.[25]

Trumpism as Fascism

There had always been a long-standing reluctance among scholars and journalists to use the F-word for fear of being accused of expressing hyperbole or at least anachronism.[26] Early in Trump's ascent to the presidency, William Connolly carefully characterized Trump as only an "aspirational fascist."[27] Connolly noted:

> Trump, I want to say, is not a Nazi. He is, rather, an aspirational fascist who pursues crowd adulation, hyperaggressive nationalism, white triumphalism, a law-and-order regime giving unaccountable power to the police, a militarist, and a practitioner of a rhetorical style that regularly creates fake news and smears opponents to mobilize support for the Big Lies he advances. His internal targets of vilification and intimidation include Muslims, Mexicans, the media, the judiciary, independent women, the professoriate, and (at least early on) the intelligence services. The affinities across real differences between Hitler and Trump allow us to

[25] David Smith, "US Under Siege from 'Far-Left Fascism', Says Trump in Mount Rushmore Speech," *The Guardian*, July 4, 2020, https://www.theguardian.com/us-news/2020/jul/04/us-under-siege-from-far-left-fascism-says-trump-in-mount-rushmore-speech.

[26] On American Fascism, see Jason Stanley, "Tucker Carlson Is Not an Anti-War Populist Rebel. He Is a Fascist," *Guardian*, April 28, 2023, www.theguardian.com/commentisfree/2023/apr/28/tucker-carlson-politics-fascism. Also see Robert Reich, "The Modern Republican Party Is Hurtling towards Fascism," *Guardian*, April 15, 2023, https://www.theguardian.com/commentisfree/2023/apr/15/the-modern-republican-party-fascism-robert-reich.

[27] See William E. Connolly, *Aspirational Fascism: The Struggle for Multifaceted Democracy under Trumpism* (University of Minnesota Press, 2017), 7–8.

> explore patterns of insistence advanced by Hitler in the early days of his movement to help illuminate the Trump phenomenon today.[28]

Yet, Fascism, as many people insist, belongs to another time and place, namely the interwar years in Italy and Germany, when Mussolini's (self-named) Fascists joined forces with Hitler's Nazis to use violence in undermining constitutional democracy and eventually seizing power. Mussolini and Hitler were undoubtedly what we today call fascists. Others have however proven deserving of the title, especially if we define fascism as the Merriam-Webster dictionary does as "a political philosophy, movement, or regime (such as that of the *Fascisti*) that exalts nation and often race above the individual and that stands for a centralized autocratic government headed by a dictatorial leader, severe economic and social regimentation, and forcible suppression of opposition."[29]

For scholars like Ruth Ben-Ghiat, fascism is less an explicit ideology than a method for seizing and holding onto power. Ben-Ghiat notes that the historian Robert Paxton in *The Anatomy of Fascism* gives perhaps the most comprehensive definition, "Fascism may be defined as a form of political behavior marked by obsessive preoccupation with community decline, humiliation, or victimhood and by compensatory cults of unity, energy, and purity, in which a mass-based party of committed nationalist militants, working in uneasy but effective collaboration with traditional elites, abandons democratic liberties and pursues with redemptive violence and without ethical or legal restraints goals of internal cleansing and external expansion."[30]

Ben-Ghiat says that the January 6th coup brought Paxton into line with people like philosopher Jason Stanley about whether Donald Trump and Trumpism can be called fascist. Ben-Ghiat notes that for Stanley, fascism is a "political method" that "can appear anytime, anywhere, if conditions are right. This line of thought risks emptying the term of its historical specificity but is essential for understanding our new authoritarian age and the risks we face in America today."[31] Ben-Ghiat puts Hungary's Viktor Orban with his "illiberal democracy" and other "strongmen" in the same fascist camp as Trump.[32] From the perspective of people like Ben-Ghiat and Stanley, different countries over time can each have their own form of fascism that

[28] Ibid.

[29] https://www.merriam-webster.com/dictionary/fascism.

[30] Robert Paxton, *The Anatomy of Fascism* (Vintage, 2005), 218.

[31] Ruth Ben-Ghiat, "What Is Fascism? A Century of Attempts to Define and Whitewash Fascism," *Lucid*, December 7, 2022, https://lucid.substack.com/p/what-is-fascism. Jason Stanley, *How Fascism Works: The Politics of Us and Them* (Random House, 2018).

[32] Ruth Ben-Ghiat, *Strongmen: Mussolini to the Present* (W. W. Norton, 2020).

takes the shape as called for by that political culture. Trumpism is arguably America's fascism today.

Historian Timothy Snyder sees Trump's outrageous lying about just about anything that affects him and his ability to stay in power as laying the basis for a post-truth politics that constitutes a "pre-fascism."[33] Snyder writes:

> Like historical fascist leaders, Trump has presented himself as the single source of truth. His use of the term "fake news" echoed the Nazi smear *Lügenpresse* ("lying press"); like the Nazis, he referred to reporters as "enemies of the people." Like Adolf Hitler, he came to power at a moment when the conventional press had taken a beating; the financial crisis of 2008 did to American newspapers what the Great Depression did to German ones. The Nazis thought that they could use radio to replace the old pluralism of the newspaper; Trump tried to do the same with Twitter.[34]

Joe Biden has said he decided to run against Trump because of the Charlottesville race riot and Trump's defense of people who participated in it. Biden continued to say throughout his presidency that Americans were in a battle for the "soul of America."[35] Biden gave a major speech as president calling out Trumpism as "semi-fascism."[36] By then, the F-word had at least "semi-" entered the mainstream.

Robert Kagan adds:

> People are wisely reluctant to throw words like "fascism" around loosely, but it is hard to find a better word for the relationship between Trump the leader and his devoted following. Fascism is the malady to which modern democracies are particularly susceptible, and in an age of mass politics—the age we have been living in for the better part of the last two centuries—various forms of fascism have been the likeliest alternative to democracy. Modern nations are not about to establish monarchies. To have any legitimacy beyond the exercise of brute force, modern leaders must at least appear to speak for the masses. In democracies, they must create mass followings that allow them to win within the democratic system and then transform it into a system they can dominate. Hitler came to power in Germany first

[33] Timothy Snyder, "The American Abyss," *New York Times*, January 9, 2021, https://www.nytimes.com/2021/01/09/magazine/trump-coup.html; also see Sanford F. Schram, "Size Matters," *Public Seminar*, January 17, 2017, https://publicseminar.org/2017/01/size-matters/.

[34] Ibid.

[35] David Brooks, "Joe Biden and the Struggle for America's Soul," *New York Times*, April 27, 2023, https://www.nytimes.com/2023/04/27/opinion/biden-trump-soul-america-election-2024.html.

[36] Alex Gangitano, "Biden Says 'Extreme MAGA Philosophy' Is Like 'Semi-Fascism,'" *The Hill*, August 25, 2022, https://thehill.com/homenews/administration/3616105-biden-says-extreme-maga-philosophy-is-like-semi-fascism/.

> by winning democratic elections, by inspiring loyalty among normal middle-class Germans, by offering an alternative to the messy and often gridlocked democracy of Weimar Germany. Only then did he cement his position in power by doing away with democratic forms. Trump's appeal to the masses propelled him into a position of national power that he barely sought. But, once having gained it, he has not been willing to give it up. His narcissism became megalomania, which in turn has made him a would-be tyrant. Trump's assault on American democracy arguably began in 2020, when he refused to accept his defeat at the polls. His rolling coup attempt has continued and grown since, and along with it the determination of millions of his followers to see him returned to power by whatever means necessary.[37]

Given Trump's persistently threatening behavior, it actually is not surprising that people are increasingly alarmed enough that he needs to be labeled a fascist. As his efforts to return to power intensified in the run-up to the 2024 presidential election, Trump increasingly used metapragmatics as if he were prepared to undermine the rule of law and US democracy overall if it meant he could get back in power that way. Trump persists in saying he beat Biden in 2020, that the election was stolen, and that the mainstream press is lying about it, while using dog-whistles to suggest Jews like the philanthropist George Soros paid for Blacks in key cities to steal votes from Trump and give them to Biden.[38] He calls those imprisoned for their participation in the insurrection "hostages."[39] His refusal to renounce the January 6th insurrectionists and even to promise them pardons when he is reelected was but further evidence of his willingness to undermine US law and democratic norms.[40] With the eventual pardoning of almost all the insurrectionists, Trump proved he condones and even celebrates the violence that was enacted to keep him in power.

Trump's inclination to glorify violence is profoundly fascist, especially in appealing to supporters who have grown frustrated with the existing social order. A good example is Trump's having his fellow reality-TV star Dr. Phil film and broadcast ICE (Immigration Control and Enforcement) raids to

[37] Robert Kagan, *Rebellion: How Anti-Liberalism Is Tearing America Apart-Again* (Penguin Random House, 2024), 150–51.

[38] References about George Soros funding the stealing of the 2020 election built off a well-established practice by Trump and his supporters to blame the Jewish philanthropist as the power behind the throne when it comes to American politics. Associated Press, "'Too Crazy' for Trump: Fact-checking the President's Legal Team's Wild Conspiracy Theory," *Haaretz*, November 23, 2020, https://www.haaretz.com/us-news/2020-11-23/ty-article/trump-powell-dominion-biden-election-2020/0000017f-dfa0-db5a-a57f-dfeac5b70000.

[39] Adam Gabbatt, "Trump's Novel Take on January 6: Calling Convicted Rioters 'Hostages,'" *The Guardian*, January 13, 2024, https://www.theguardian.com/us-news/2024/jan/13/trump-january-6-rioters-hostages.

[40] Sam Levine, "Donald Trump Says He Plans to Pardon US Capitol Attack Participants if Elected," *Guardian*, September 1, 2022, https://www.theguardian.com/us-news/2022/sep/01/donald-trump-pardons-january-6-us-capitol-attack.

round up immigrants who increasingly were being detained in barbaric facilities while waiting to be deported.[41] Hitler had Leni Riefenstahl to film his rallies and Trump in his quintessential shlock way has Dr. Phil. Shlock or not, this glorification of violence as spectacle resonates deeply with what Georges Bataille called the "psychological structure of fascism" that provides "common consciousness of increasingly violent and excessive energies and powers that accumulate in the person of the leader and through him become widely available."[42] Trump may not have an explicit fascist ideology, only an American shlock version, but his penchant to mobilize supporters by way of inflaming their most violent desires for expressing frustrations with the limitations of democratic politics is profoundly consistent with that psychological structure of fascism where the leader gave people the "freedom to be your worst self" (as Sherrilyn Ifill said of Trump).[43] Regardless of the extent he has been able to impose his will on the government or society more generally, Trump enacts his own fascist sensibility and often to quite deleterious effect.

American Fascism Today

Trumpism has offered us a new, made-for-TV, distinctively American kind of fascism retrofitted for the post–Civil Rights era.[44] In spite of how much Trump himself liked to sing the praises of foreign autocrats, whether it is Orban or Putin or the others, his expressions of fascist rhetoric have come wrapped in Americanisms, like his appeal to the intentions of the Founding Fathers, who he says supposedly insisted the American President must have "absolute immunity."[45] It does not matter that this is not true; what matters is that Trump feels obligated to justify his calls to put himself above the rule of law by blatantly gaslighting that is what the framers wanted. In fact, he eventually succeeded in getting the six conservative justices on the US Supreme Court to support, if not absolute immunity in all instances, then absolute immunity from prosecution for his "official acts."[46] The normalization of his quest for authoritarian power was by then complete.

[41] Luke Chinman, "Dr. Phil Participated in the Chicago ICE Raids. Why?" *People*, January 31, 2025, https://people.com/dr-phil-chicago-immigration-raid-8783953.

[42] George Bataille, "The Psychological Structure of Fascism," in *Visions of Excess. Selected Writings, 1927-1938*, ed. Allan Stoekl (University of Minnesota Press, 1985), 143.

[43] https://twitter.com/SIfill_/status/1427998307608059904.

[44] Rick Perlstein, "American Fascism," *The American Prospect*, January 24, 2024, https://prospect.org/politics/2024-01-24-american-fascism-john-ganz/.

[45] Paul Blumenthal, "Donald Trump's Bid for 'Absolute Immunity' Is His Most Dangerous Argument Yet," *Huffington Post*, January 9, 2024, https://www.huffpost.com/entry/trump-absolute-immunity_n_65982d98e4b075f4cfd23e78.

[46] *Trump v. U.S. (2024)*, https://www.nytimes.com/interactive/2024/07/01/us/scotus-immunity.html.

Trump himself could be seen as America's Juan Perón, the dictatorial president of Argentina in the 1940s and 1950s, who like Trump relied heavily on a populist rhetoric that reinscribed an "us vs. them" divide.[47] Charles Homans has quoted historian Frederico Finchelstein as saying: "Perón was a fascist who wanted to reformulate himself in democratic terms, whereas Trump seems to be doing the opposite." Both seemingly recognized the impossibility of recreating the fascism of Mussolini or Hitler, who rose to power in a democratic system but then overthrew it. Instead, both Perón and Trump attempted to work within the democratic system to consolidate dictatorial power.

Yet, Trump distinctively used a metapragmatic discourse to suggest he was standing up for democracy against his opponents who were the real fascist threat to democracy. Trump repeatedly in the 2024 campaign said things like this: "Joe Biden and the fascists that control him are really the true threat to democracy. They use the D.O.J., the F.B.I., our election systems. They rigged our elections and attacked free speech. It is amazing all the people that go get investigated, all of them, all of them—they don't go after the people that rigged the election. They go after the people that want to find out who it was that rigged it."[48]

Trump remained the "edgelord of strategic irony" trying to have it both ways when he boomeranged "fascist" back at his adversaries who called him a fascist, thereby making it seem as if fascist leanings were commonplace or that calling your opponents fascists is a normal part of the agonistics of democratic politics. Everybody was vulnerable to being called a fascist was the implication. He made jokes as if to seemingly embrace being a fascist in response to his supporters call for him to be a dictator.[49] Trump's equivocations used gaslighting, boomeranging, and even co-opting the fascist label to make it seem there was nothing un-American about giving the people what they wanted, i.e., a dictator.[50] This kind of double-talk only helped facilitate the injection of fascist rhetoric into the mainstream of American discourse.

What also makes this so American is that it is not based on some well-developed philosophical perspective about the need to seize power to

[47] Charles Homans, "Donald Trump Has Never Sounded Like This," *New York Times*, April 27, 2024, https://www.nytimes.com/2024/04/27/magazine/trump-rallies-rhetoric.html?smid=nytcore-ios-share&referringSource=articleShare&sgrp=c-cb.

[48] Ibid.

[49] Miranda Nazzaro, "'You're Right,' Trump Tells Supporter Calling for '12 Years of Trump,'" *The Hill*, January, 23, 2024, https://thehill.com/homenews/campaign/4424171-2024-election-trump-tells-supporter-calling-for-12-years-youre-right/.

[50] Zeynep Tufekci, "A Strongman President? These Voters Crave It," *New York Times*, January 14, 2024, https://www.nytimes.com/2024/01/14/opinion/trump-voters-iowa-caucus.html. "[Trump supporters] are not turned off by Trump's extreme, authoritarian rhetoric—they are attracted to it," said political scientist Stanley Feldman as quoted in Thomas B. Edsall, "We Are Normalizing Trump-Again," *New York Times*, January 24, 2024, https://www.nytimes.com/2024/01/24/opinion/trump-republican-nomination-coalition.html.

maintain White Supremacy. Instead, it is an unfortunate result of the American tendency to rely on what is taken to be the common sense of US culture.[51] That common sense tends to accept uncritically a number of things like White privilege. It is also consistent with the American common sense in that it is more about Trump himself assuming that naturally he is authorized to be doing this for his own personal benefit in our highly individualistic society where politicians are assumed to be very much focused on their own success (like everyone else). In this way, there is no need for an explicit ideological statement or justification. In both these ways, Trumpism is an American Fascism, where, without explicit philosophical justification for its cynical power grab, Trump can boomerang cries of fascism back at his critics, gaslight the broader public, and co-opt the claim that he is saving democracy from those who are trying to undermine it.

There were many seemingly required metapragmatic denials that were designed to deflect attention away from the fascist sources of what was being said and to alternatively suggest there was nothing un-American about the fascist rhetoric. For instance, Trump's saying that immigrants were "poisoning the blood" of the country was dismissed by then-Sen. J. D. Vance (R-OH) as not repeating a Hitlerism but only referring to immigrants bringing fentanyl or COVID and other infectious diseases over the border.[52] These gaslighting moves got repeatedly deployed by Vance when running in the 2024 campaign as Trump's vice presidential candidate. As Trump's gaslighter-in-chief, Vance repeatedly sought to defuse opposition to Trump's extremist calls for a strongman to lead the US government and stand up for the American people against foreign threats.[53]

Jason Stanley has effectively noted that not only does fascism vary by place and time, but the United States has its own well-established history of American Fascism.[54] He notes, as others have, that Hitler himself drew inspiration from the American South's Jim Crow system of apartheid between the races. Further, Stanley writes:

[51] The American tendency to privilege instrumental thinking, to emphasize pragmatic experimentalism and assume an unquestioned commonsense for action, is examined in a variety of literatures. For instance, see Louis Hartz, *The Liberal Tradition in America: An Interpretation of American Political Thought since the Revolution* (Harcourt Brace and Co., 1955); and Richard Rorty, *Achieving Our Country: Leftist Thought in Twentieth Century America* (Harvard University Press, 1998).

[52] Brett Samuels, "Harris: Trump's 'Poisoning the Blood' Comment 'Rightly' Being Compared to Hitler," *The Hill*, December 19, 2023, https://thehill.com/homenews/administration/4368459-harris-trumps-poisoning-the-blood-comment-rightly-being-compared-to-hitler/.

[53] Neil Vigdor, "Vance Complains About Democrats Using 'Fascist.' Trump Uses It Often," *New York Times*, September 18, 2024, https://www.nytimes.com/2024/09/18/us/politics/vance-trump-fascist.html.

[54] Jason Stanley, "Tucker Carlson Is Not an Anti-War Populist Rebel. He Is a Fascist," *Guardian*, April 28, 2023, https://www.theguardian.com/commentisfree/2023/apr/28/tucker-carlson-politics-fascism.

> We should look to history as our guide here. But the history that best informs us in this case is not European history, but *American* history. Before the beginning of World War II, all of America's pro-fascist parties opposed U.S. intervention on the side of its allies against Nazi Germany. Often, the opposition to the U.S. supporting Britain against Nazi Germany was represented as "isolationism." There were openly fascist organizations during this time, such as the German American Bund. Somewhat more ambiguous was the America First Committee where in a packed America First rally in Madison Square Garden in 1941, Sen. Burton K Wheeler (R-MT) denounced "jingoistic journalists and saber-rattling bankers" who were pushing the nation into war against Germany. While the agenda of *some* members of the America First Movement at the time might have genuinely been pacifist, it's quite clear that the main agenda was in fact support for Hitler. The America First movement had strong support from American fascist movements of various stripes.[55]

The original America First Committee's most prominent spokesperson was the aviation hero, Charles Lindbergh, who just before the United States entered World War II said the following:

> It is now two years since this latest European war began. From that day in September, 1939, until the present moment, there has been an over-increasing effort to force the United States into the conflict. ... The three most important groups who have been pressing this country toward war are the British, the Jewish and the Roosevelt administration. ... In selecting these three groups as the major agitators for war, I have included only those whose support is essential to the war party. If any one of these groups—the British, the Jewish, or the administration—stops agitating for war, I believe there will be little danger of our involvement.[56]

Lindbergh had tried to clarify that he opposed the persecution of German Jews, but subsequently he indicated he was concerned about the future of the White race. He might not have been a Nazi himself, but he partnered with Americans who were Nazi sympathizers.[57]

According to Stanley, Trumpism with its own America First sloganeering follows the traditions of American Fascism more generally, demonizing outgroups, non-Whites in particular, opposing immigration, leaning toward

[55] Ibid.

[56] "Lindbergh Accuses Jews of Pushing U.S. to War, Jewish," *Jewish Virtual Library* (Speech given by Charles Lindbergh, Des Moines Iowa, September 11, 1941), https://www.jewishvirtuallibrary.org/lindbergh-accuses-jews-of-pushing-u-s-to-war.

[57] Kevin Duchschere, "Was Charles Lindbergh a Nazi Sympathizer?" *Minneapolis Star Tribune*, June 3, 2022, https://www.startribune.com/charles-lindbergh-little-falls-world-war-2-nazi-germany/600178871/.

isolationism, resisting cultural diversity, denouncing the media, intellectuals, blaming Jews and cosmopolitan elites for the country's troubles, and glorifying violence to impose anti-democratic rule.[58] There is good reason to put the fascist label on the apartheid regime of Jim Crow in the South that emerged after the Civil War and Reconstruction. Hitler was inspired by it as a model for dealing with the Jews of Germany. The Ku Klux Klan was essentially a paramilitary fascist force aimed at using violence to enforce racial subordination. The Second Klan in the 1920s spread widely beyond the South in the face of growing opposition to immigration and vied for influence in the Democratic Party.[59] The American First Committee formed to oppose US entry into World War II and as indicated above, it indeed was populated with Fascist and Nazi sympathizers.

After partnering with the National Rifle Association, the German American Bund in February 1939 held a Pro-American Rally at Madison Square Garden with over 22,000 in attendance. Speeches supported creating an American Fascist government.[60] Even after World War II and the defeat of Fascism and Nazism, homegrown fascists and Nazis continued to seek to mobilize supporters to undo liberal democracy. They rallied around Sen. Joe McCarthy (R-WI) in the early 1950s. Trump himself held a Madison Square Garden rally near the end of his 2024 campaign. By then, Trump was widely being called a fascist and the rally did not undermine that characterization. Yet, one difference is that the Trump campaign tried to metapragmatically dismiss that label, saying the incendiary racism that was expressed was only in jokes by a comedian.[61] That gaslighting might not have persuaded anyone, but it marked the metapragmatic distinctiveness of the Trump approach to not fully embracing the label.

In other words, there is a long lineage of American Fascism preceding the American First Committee's opposition to US involvement in World War II running through to McCarthyism after the war, right through to Trumpism today.[62] Along the way, prominent among these efforts, there were such

[58] See Richard Steigmann-Gall, "Star-Spangled Fascism: American Interwar Political Extremism in Comparative Perspective," *Social History*, 42, no. 1 (2017): 94–119.

[59] See Linda Gordon, *The Second Coming of the KKK: The Ku Klux Klan of the 1920s and the American Political Tradition* (Liveright, 2017).

[60] Linda Gordon, "The American Fascists," in *Fascism in America: Past and Present*, ed. Gavriel D. Rosenfeld and Janet Ward (Cambridge University Press, 2023), 141–69.

[61] "Trump Tries to Limit Damage of Rally Comedian's Puerto Rico 'Joke,'" *The Telegraph*, October 28, 2024, https://www.telegraph.co.uk/us/news/2024/10/28/us-election-latest-donald-trump-kamala-harris/.

[62] Larry Tye, "When Senator Joe McCarthy Defended Nazis," *Smithsonian Magazine*, July 2020, https://www.smithsonianmag.com/history/senator-mccarthys-nazi-problem-180975174/.

characters as George Lincoln Rockwell, the long-time head of the American Nazi Party.[63] Since then, in recent decades, fascist militia and related extremist groups have populated the fringes of society in growing numbers and have added to the increases in incidents of domestic terrorism.[64] Their tactics to normalize extremism by appealing to the White majority have always been the same. Trumpism is just the latest and perhaps most duplicitous, and therefore ambivalent, installment of that thoughtless American Fascism that assumes it is appropriate to undermine democracy to keep Trump and his White allies on top.

The Psychological Structure of American Fascism Today

Trumpism has risen up during a time of increased "negative partisanship" and "affective polarization." Negative partisanship, as it is called by political scientists, was now playing a major role.[65] Negative partisanship is where if Democrats say the election was not stolen, that means Trump's Republicans must, of necessity, say yes it was, given how polarized politics cues up positions people feel obligated to take. This kind of mysideism relates to affective polarization,[66] where you so strongly emotionally identify with your side against the other side, and raises the question of how far loyal Trump supporters will go in insisting on the need to have Trump's back. Affective polarization opens the door to blind loyalty to someone like Trump. It need not lead to affective party attachments that create the emotional intensity that underwrites committing acts of political violence, but it seems that that is what is happening in selected instances.

In an era of growing affective polarization, the newly transformed Trump-aligned Republican Party sounds ever more hateful and cruel in its opposition to the established order. Adam Serwer argues that increased expressions of

[63] Lois Beckett, "George Lincoln Rockwell, Father of American Nazis, Still in Vogue for Some," *The Guardian*, August 27, 2017, https://www.theguardian.com/world/2017/aug/27/george-lincoln-rockwell-american-nazi-party-alt-right-charlottesville.

[64] See Richard C. Fording and Sanford F. Schram, *Hard White: The Mainstreaming of Racism in American Politics* (Oxford University Press, 2020), Chapter 3.

[65] See Alan I. Abramowitz and Steven W. Webster, "Negative Partisanship: Why Americans Dislike Parties But Behave Like Rabid Partisans," *Advances in Political Psychology* 39, no. S1 (February 2018): 119–35.

[66] Thomas J. Rudolph and Marc J. Hetherington, "Affective Polarization in Political and Nonpolitical Settings," *International Journal of Public Opinion Research*, 33, no. 3 (2021): 591–606, https://doi.org/10.1093/ijpor/edaa040. "Affective polarization" was originally coined as an analytical term in Shanto Iyengar and Sean J. Westwood, "Fear and Loathing Across Party Lines: New Evidence on Group Polarization," *American Journal of Political Science* 59, no. 3 (2015): 690–707. Also see Lilliana Mason, *Uncivil Agreement: How Politics Became Our Identity* (University of Chicago Press, 2018).

cruelty among Trumpists are not an accidental byproduct of Trump and his allies pushing the boundaries of normal political contestation. Instead, it is an intentional result:

> It is that cruelty, and the delight it brings them, that binds his most ardent supporters to him, in shared scorn for those they hate and fear: immigrants, black voters, feminists, and treasonous white men who empathize with any of those who would steal their birthright. The President's ability to execute that cruelty through word and deed makes them euphoric. It makes them feel good, it makes them feel proud, it makes them feel happy, it makes them feel united. And as long as he makes them feel that way, they will let him get away with anything, no matter what it costs them.[67]

Bataille's "psychological structure of fascism" resonates with Serwer's emphasis on the importance of cruelty in Trumpism. Yet, it is not clear just how prevalent in today's Trumpified Republican Party is the thirst for inflicting pain on opponents. Further, it is not clear whether Trump's exploitation of affective polarization has transformed the Republican Party all by itself or whether other factors like the changing composition of who identifies with the Republican Party has played a role.[68] Yet, it is clear that Trumpism has become ascendant in the current Republican Party, and it leads that Party in a profoundly racist, xenophobic, and anti-democratic direction with an intensity so hot that it includes a tendency toward violence. At a minimum, the dramatic actions during Trump's second term as president suggest that the Republican Party is too intimidated to cross him. More broadly, the cruelty is about intimidating and silencing the opposition.[69] As a result, those silenced become complicit in furthering Trump's transitioning his presidency toward promoting an "illiberal democracy" much like what we find today in Orban's Hungary. Trump's authoritarianism includes no small amount of retribution against his opponents, and cruel policies against various groups who he seeks to demonize like people of color, immigrants in general and not just the undocumented, members of the LGBTQ+ community, and many others.

[67] Adam Serwer, *Cruelty Is the Point: Why Trump's America Endures* (One World, 2020), 62, 103–04.
[68] See Mason, *Uncivil Agreement*, Chapter 8.
[69] Corey Robin, "The Cruelty Is Not the Point: On Muskism and McCarthyism," March 8, 2025, https://coreyrobin.com/2025/03/08/the-cruelty-is-not-the-point-on-muskism-and-mccarthyism/. After being skeptical of calling Trumpism a fascist movement, with the early actions of the second term for Trump as president, Robin said he was wrong about being reluctant to call Trump a fascist.

Gaslighting the Insurrection

The most dramatic eruption of anti-democratic, authoritarian, and even fascist behavior came when Trump lost the 2020 election to Joe Biden, but he refused to accept it and got his transformed party to back him on that denial. Gaslighting the American public helped. Trump said he did not lose, but instead Biden stole the election. Trump followed Hitler's playbook and told a Big Lie. For Hitler, it was that the Jews undermined Germany's efforts in World War I and they should be blamed for the country's problems.[70] Trump's gaslighting paralleled Hitler's by demonizing Blacks in central cities as actively working to illegally flip the election from Trump to Biden. He even called out African American election staff and showed videos that allegedly proved they were discarding votes for Trump. Trump accused Ruby Freeman, a Fulton County Georgia election worker, of being a "vote scammer." In his pleading on the phone with Georgia Secretary of State Brad Raffensperger to find enough votes so that Trump could be declared the winner in that state, Trump said, "And they had a post office box number and that's not allowed. We had at least 18,000, that's on tape, we had them counted very painstakingly. 18,000 voters having to do with Ruby Freeman. She's a vote scammer, a professional vote scammer and hustler Ruby Freeman. That was the tape that's been shown all over the world that makes everybody look bad, you, me and everybody else, where they got number one, they said very clearly."[71]

Ruby Freeman and her daughter Shaye Moss, another election worker, got so many death threats and people coming to their door at home that they had to move. Ruby Freeman stopped working as an election officer. This was a highly publicized case that included Freeman and Moss testifying before the January 6th Committee that investigated the insurrection. But many other poll workers all across the country were also being threatened with death.[72]

Yet not one of Trump's claims about election fraud was true. Trump however never backed down. In fact, he insists to this day that he did not lose the 2020 election. And he continues to demand that the federal government should investigate the Democrats for their undermining democracy.

[70] Zachary Jonathan Jacobson, "Many Are Worried about the Return of the 'Big Lie,'" *Washington Post*, May 21, 2018, https://www.washingtonpost.com/news/made-by-history/wp/2018/05/21/many-are-worried-about-the-return-of-the-big-lie-theyre-worried-about-the-wrong-thing/.

[71] "Donald Trump Georgia Phone Call Transcript with Sec. of State Brad Raffensperger: Says He Wants to 'Find' Votes," *@rev*, January 4, 2021, https:www.rev.com/blog/transcripts/donald-trump-georgia-phone-call-transcript-brad-raffensperger-recording.

[72] Linda So and Jason Szep, "U.S. Election Workers Get Little Help from Law Enforcement as Terror Threats Mount," *Reuters*, September 8, 2021, https://www.reuters.com/investigates/special-report/usa-election-threats-law-enforcement/.

Trump's metapragmatic move was to claim that he was standing up for the law rather than trying to undermine it.

Trump's Big Lie that the 2020 election was stolen was nothing less than audacious gaslighting that sought to mainstream its claim by using a demonized "other" group to legitimate it.[73] This gaslighting however had unleashed a mob who felt they were the ones standing up for democracy, not trying to undermine it. It all reached a pinnacle on January 6. After trying a variety of tactics, some legal and many others not, Trump called for his supporters to come to Washington, DC, on January 6 to stop Congress' certification of Joe Biden to be the next president of the United States. In front of the assembled crowd, which included armed militia members, Trump implored them to march on the Capitol to stop the certification. Trump reiterated that he had actually won the election, noting it was actually by a landslide. Then he said: "We fight like hell. And if you don't fight like hell, you're not going to have a country anymore."[74] He continued: "I know that everyone here will soon be marching over to the Capitol building to peacefully and patriotically make your voices heard." Trump was still always trying to have it both ways. That's just his style and the Militia members there knew to ignore that part about being peaceful.

When the January 6th protests turned into an insurrection to stop the peaceful transfer of power, Trump delayed for hours in saying people should stop. His inaction was a dangerous form of action.[75] As a president charged by the Constitution to "take care that the laws are faithfully executed," this dereliction of duty was its own stochastic terrorism of silence. His not commenting on the insurrection while it was happening was a *sotto voce* metapragmatic move, endorsing what was happening without publicly saying so. He was legitimating the insurrection with his silence, and he was complicit via his inaction to allow it to continue. When he finally issued a video for people to stand down, he said the insurrectionists were "very special" and they should "remember this day forever." So even his acting to end the turmoil included an endorsement.[76] And his justification was the Big Lie that the

[73] On how metapragmatic moves like gaslighting often implicitly assume that the criticism that necessitated the gaslighting comes from a deviant "other," see Bart Cammaerts, "The Abnormalisation of Social Justice: The 'Anti-Woke Culture War' Discourse in the UK," *Discourse and Society*, 33, no. 6 (November 2022): 730–43.

[74] Brian Naylor, "Read Trump's Jan. 6 Speech, A Key Part of Impeachment Trial," *NPR*, February 10, 2021, https://www.npr.org/2021/02/10/966396848/read-trumps-jan-6-speech-a-key-part-of-impeachment-trial.

[75] Elise Berman, "Avoiding Sharing How People Help Each Other Get out of Giving," *Current Anthropology*, 61, no. 2 (April 2020): 141–282.

[76] Brian Naylor, "Trump Downplays Insurrection but Tells Supporters to 'Go Home,'" *NPR*, January 6, 2021, https://www.npr.org/sections/congress-electoral-college-tally-live-updates/2021/01/06/954098712/in-video-trump-sympathizes-with-protesters-but-tells-them-to-go-home.

election had indeed been stolen and people were in their right to rise up and stop the steal by blocking the peaceful transfer of power. In Trump's inverted world, not only was inaction a form of action but violently storming the Capitol was a way of standing up for the Constitution, the rule of law, and democracy.

Trump's Big Lie arguably constituted gaslighting like never before in presidential electoral discourse. He was telling the biggest of lies to provoke an armed mob to use violence to keep himself in power, and he justified it by claiming the insurrectionists were patriots who were actually trying to save democracy, not overthrow it. Maybe he did this only for his own personal reasons to never admit losing, but the result was that he was instigating a violent attack by armed militia on the members of Congress just so he could stay in power. This, I would argue, makes his gaslighting fascistic. At that point, Trump was not just an aspirational fascist, but a real one. He was willing to lie to justify using violence to cling to power.

Trump's Big Lie that the 2020 election was stolen remained influential among Republicans. A March 2023 poll indicated that 63 percent of Republicans and Independents who lean toward the Republican Party still thought the election had been stolen.[77] After all that time and all the failed attempts to produce any evidence of election fraud, Trump supporters persisted in agreeing with the Big Lie. Whether they really believed it or just said it out of loyalty to Trump, i.e., whether it was a substantive political stance or just an artifact of affective polarization, either way it is disturbing. By the time we reached the third anniversary of the insurrection, Trump's gaslighting had succeeded in getting a significant proportion of the Republican Party to join with him in saying the people incarcerated for participating in the insurrection were not prisoners but "hostages" who had simply been peacefully protesting a rigged election.[78]

Years ago, Stanley Milgram conducted experiments that showed that ordinary Americans were prone to defer to leaders to the point of being willing to inflict pain on others for things as innocuous as failing to answer test questions correctly.[79] Milgram warned that someday a Hitler-like politician could come along and get people to follow them just about anywhere down that

[77] Alison Durkee, "Republicans Increasingly Realize There's No Evidence of Election Fraud—But Most Still Think 2020 Election Was Stolen Anyway, Poll Finds," *CNN*, March, https://www.forbes.com/sites/alisondurkee/2023/03/14/republicans-increasingly-realize-theres-no-evidence-of-election-fraud-but-most-still-think-2020-election-was-stolen-anyway-poll-finds/?sh=6877003828ec.

[78] Hayes Brown, "A New Poll Shows the Consequences of the GOP's Lies about Jan. 6," MSNBC, https://www.msnbc.com/opinion/msnbc-opinion/poll-january-6-republicans-peaceful-protest-rcna131935.

[79] Stanley Milgram, "Behavioral Study of Obedience," *Journal of Abnormal and Social Psychology* 67 (1963): 371–78.

road of cruelty. While people have disputed Milgram's work, Trump's ability to continue to inflame his base to support acts of violence suggests Milgram was on to something. While Milgram's experimental subjects were shown to be reluctantly deferring to persons in positions of authority, Trump's followers include people who seem more than willing in taking their cues from Trump's "stochastic terrorism" and thereby making political violence all the more likely.

The Violence Preference

A disbarred lawyer who had defended members of the Oath Keepers used an innovative gaslight to call the charges against them for seditious conspiracy "thought crimes."[80] The Oath Keepers attorney was trying to make the case that Stewart Rhodes, their leader, and others were only talking about using violence to stop Biden's certification as President, but they never committed acts of violence, which were done by others. The jury did not buy into this gaslighting. Stewart Rhodes was convicted and sentenced to eighteen years in prison. The attempt to recast the crime as mere talk was a failed whitewashing that tried unsuccessfully to reframe illegal activity as something protected by the free speech clause of the First Amendment. This thoroughly Trumpist discursive move did not in the end keep Stewart Rhodes and other members of the Oath Keepers, and the Proud Boys as well, out of prison. Their expressed preference for using violence to undermine democracy and thereby keep Donald Trump in power was a contributing factor in their convictions for seditious conspiracy.

Seditious conspiracy is a serious federal crime whether the planning of seditious act or acts actually resulted in violence or not. But Rhodes and his conspirators are not alone in embracing the Big Lie. Many people, probably millions, say they believe Trump's Big Lie that the 2020 election was stolen by Biden and the Democrats, especially in cities in swing states where African Americans govern.[81] For many Trump supporters, this proclaimed stealing of the election justifies engaging in acts of violence in order to keep Trump in power. Many of the January 6th insurrectionists who were not part of the

[80] Adam Klasfeld, "Disbarred Lawyer for the Oath Keepers Tries to Dismiss Seditious Conspiracy and Other Charges, Calls Them 'Thought Crimes,'" *Law & Crime*, April 11, 2022, https://lawandcrime.com/u-s-capitol-breach/disbarred-lawyer-for-the-oath-keepers-tries-to-dismiss-seditious-conspiracy-and-other-charges-calls-them-thought-crimes/.

[81] Sarah Longwell, "Trump Supporters Explain Why They Believe the Big Lie," *The Atlantic*, April 18, 2022, https://www.theatlantic.com/ideas/archive/2022/04/trump-voters-big-lie-stolen-election/629572/.

Militia Movement felt that way.[82] Many of them and others who did not participate in the insurrection still think violence is justified to return Trump to power.[83] Their rationale is that the Democrats stole the election, and they are the ones who are undermining democracy. This justifies using violence to restore democracy. This boomerang continues to fuel the crisis US democracy confronts in the face of Trumpism and his allies' continuing efforts to claim the mantle as the vanguard of "Real Americans" who are being denied their rightful leader from staying in power.

The Big Lie boomerang shows how deep "affective polarization" can go. Just the idea of Democrats displacing Trump is enough for some to justify violence in the name of saving the Country from Democratic rule. It is "negative partisanship" on steroids. Some Trump supporters are at that point where violence is necessary to save democracy from the Democratic Party. Unfortunately, given the intensification of the partisan battle, there is evidence that a smaller but not insignificant number of Democrats feel that same way.[84]

Robert Pape and the Chicago Project on Security and Threats (CPOST) amassed impressive empirical evidence on the insurrectionists and the larger movement that supports their efforts to overturn the 2020 election. Pape and his associates have found that the insurrectionists were part of an ongoing national movement coming from forty-two different states. Many were not poor and were from areas that voted for Biden and from areas where the White population was declining and being replaced by non-Whites.[85] For Pape, this is initial but significant evidence that the Great Replacement Theory along with the Big Lie that the election was stolen were key concerns stoked by Trump and others leading the Movement that inspired participation in the insurrection.

Pape also studied the broader population who were associated with the Movement but did not participate in the insurrection. His findings about

[82] Greg Miller, Greg Jaffe, and Razzan Nakhlawi, "A Mob Insurrection Stoked by False Claims of Election Fraud and Promises of Violent Restoration," *Washington Post*, January 9, 2021, https://www.washingtonpost.com/national-security/trump-capitol-mob-attack-origins/2021/01/09/0cb2cf5e-51d4-11eb-83e3-322644d82356_story.html.

[83] Robert A. Pape, "Deep, Divisive, Disturbing and Continuing: New Survey Shows Mainstream Support for Violence to Restore Trump Remains Strong Chicago Project on Security and Threats," Chicago Project on Security and Threats, January 2, 2022, https://cpost.uchicago.edu/publications/deep_divisive_disturbing_and_continuing_new_survey_shows_maintream_support_for_violence_to_restore_trump_remains_strong/.

[84] Alan Feuer, "As Right-Wing Rhetoric Escalates, So Do Threats and Violence," *New York Times*, August 22, 2022, https://www.nytimes.com/2022/08/13/nyregion/Right-Wing-rhetoric-threats-violence.html. Also see Nathan P. Kalmoe and Lilliana Mason, *Radical American Partisanship: Mapping Violent Hostility, Its Causes, and the Consequences for Democracy* (University of Chicago Press, 2022).

[85] Robert A. Pape, "Why We Cannot Afford to Ignore the American Insurrectionist Movement," *Chicago Project on Security and Threats*, August 6, 2021, https://cpost.uchicago.edu/publications/why_we_cannot_afford_to_ignore_the_american_insurrectionist_movement/.

the Trumpist Movement in general are probably even more disconcerting than those about the insurrectionists. In a series of national surveys conducted in the spring and fall of 2021 and 2022, Pape and associates find a large proportion of Americans not only feel the 2020 election was stolen by the Democrats but also that it justifies using violence to reclaim power and thereby ironically claim they are the ones who are saving democracy. This is the big boomerang for Trumpism that has pushed many over the edge to supporting illegal, unconstitutional, and even violent actions in the name of standing up for the Real Americans and democracy as they see it.

Figure 4.1 shows for the four CPSOT surveys conducted in 2021 and 2022 the estimated number of Americans supporting the use of violence to restore Trump to power. The initial June 2021 survey estimated 23 million Americans supported using violence to put Trump back in power. The September 2021 survey reported an increase to an estimated 26 million, but after that there had been a bit of a decline to 21 million in April 2022 and then all the way down to 13 million in September 2022. Pape attributes much of the decline to the January 6th Congressional Hearings that sent a signal out that the federal government was serious about holding people accountable for turning to violence on Trump's behalf.[86]

But 13 million Americans supporting using violence to return Trump to power is nothing to scoff at. Other studies have confirmed Pape's startling findings.[87] Based on his research, Pape has sought to sound the alarm. When interviewed by Margaret Brennan on CBS's "Face the Nation" on September 16, 2022, immediately after CPOST tabulated the last of their surveys on support for violence for Trump, Pape was very explicit:

> We have not just a political threat to our democracy, we have a violent threat to our democracy. Today, it's quite clear. And the problem that we face is that over and over in tweets by the former president, he is deliberately stoking not just the fires of anger getting him political support. And that is really the heart of our problem that we face as a threat to democracy. Because if it's just a political threat, well, then we can have elections, but once it's not just denying an election, but using

[86] Robert A. Pape, "The Jan 6th Hearings Are Reducing the Violent Threat to Democracy," *CPOST*, September 25, 2022, cpost.uchicago.edu/publications/the_jan_6th_hearings_are_reducing_the_violent_threat.

[87] See Lilliana Mason and Nathan P. Kalmoe, "What You Need to Know about How Many Americans Condone Political Violence—and Why," *Washington Post*, January 11, 2021, https://www.washingtonpost.com/politics/2021/01/11/what-you-need-know-about-how-many-americans-condone-political-violence-why/; William A. Galston and Elaine Kamarck, Is Democracy Failing and Putting Our Economic System at Risk? *Brookings*, January 4, 2022, https://www.brookings.edu/research/is-democracy-failing-and-putting-our-economic-system-at-risk/.

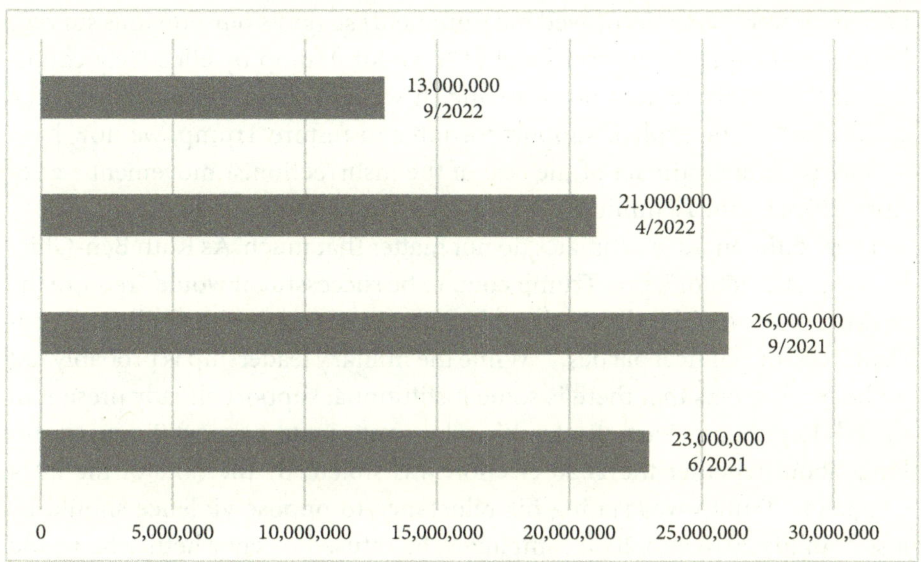

Figure 4.1 Estimated number of Americans supporting the use of violence to return Trump to power

Estimated number of US adults

Source: CPOST, Understanding Support for Political Violence in America, https://cpost.uchicago.edu/research/apv/surveys/.

> violence as the response to an election denial, now we're in a new game. And that's why it's so important we have this conversation.[88]

The decline in the number of Americans willing to use violence to return Trump to power is therefore not necessarily reassuring. As Pape and others have indicated, there is still a sizeable proportion of the population that supports using violence to put Trump back in the White House. In comparison to successful coups in the past around the world, this is more than enough people to help make it happen.[89] Beyond that sizeable population of supporters, we need to emphasize that many of the supporters of violence are mainstream middle-class people, not fringe skinheads or survivalists. Further, Pape and his research team have refined their estimates to say that by 2023, there were 4 million more than the estimated 13 million supporting violence to put Trump

[88] "Transcript: Robert Pape on 'Face the Nation,'" *CBS News*, September 18, 2022, https://www.cbsnews.com/news/robert-pape-transcript-face-the-nation-09-18-2022/.

[89] Barton Gellman, "Trump's Next Coup Has Already Begun," *The Atlantic*, December 6, 2021, https://www.theatlantic.com/magazine/archive/2022/01/january-6-insurrection-trump-coup-2024-election/620843/,

back in power. "This [improved measurement] suggests our previous surveys have underestimated the true level of force for Trump by effectively counting all the ambivalent as not agreeing. If we add these 4 million from the ambivalent to the explicit support for force to restore Trump, we now have a more accurate estimate of the size of the insurrectionist movement—as of April 2023, about 17 million."[90]

These differences in estimates do not matter that much. As Ruth Ben-Ghiat has emphasized, for a pro-Trump coup to be successful, it would "require the backing of powerful individuals and institutions, whether the military, security forces, or political parties."[91] While the military leadership is probably not on board, it seems that there is some institutional support already present in today's Republican Party leadership who continue to support Trump in his lying about whether the 2020 election was stolen. By the time of the 2024 campaign, Trump was stating his reluctance to oppose violence should he lose.[92] In his 2016 and 2020 campaigns, he refused to say whether he would accept the results. Even after the failed assassination attempt on his life the week before, Trump did not state in his presidential nomination acceptance speech that political violence is wrong.

Regardless of whether Trumpism would ever lead to another coup attempt after he has returned to power, there is still a dangerous level of support for political violence among mainstream Americans. In 2024, there persisted indications in polling data that showed there had been a trend of growing support among Republicans for a coup to depose a "corrupt" government.[93] There has been a rapid polarization on this issue since Trump became president. In fact, once Trump was indicted for stealing classified documents and while he was rumored to be soon indicted for his attempts to stop the peaceful transfer of power (which soon followed), the support among Republicans for the use of violence to return him to power began increasing again.[94]

[90] Robert A. Pape, "Introducing CPOST's New 'Political and Violent Dangers to Democracy: April 2023 Survey Report," *Chicago Project on Security and Threats*, April 30, 2023, https://cpost.uchicago.edu/publications/april_2023_survey_report_introducing_cposts_new_political_and_violent_dangers_to_democracy_tracker/.

[91] Ruth Ben-Ghiat, "Coups Make a Comeback as GOP Elites Declare 'Total War' on US Democracy," *Lucid*, December 14, 2022, https://lucid.substack.com/p/coups-make-a-comeback-as-gop-elites.

[92] Eric Cortellessa, "How Far Trump Will Go" *Time*, April 30, 2024, https://time.com/6972021/donald-trump-2024-election-interview/.

[93] Noam Lupu, Luke Plutowski, and Elizabeth J. Zechmeister, "Would Americans Ever Support a Coup? 40 Percent Now Say Yes," *Washington Post*, January 6, 2022, https://www.washingtonpost.com/politics/2022/01/06/us-coup-republican-support/.

[94] Tara Suter, "More Say Violence Could Be Necessary to Restore Trump to White House: Survey," *The Hill*, July 25, 2023, https://thehill.com/homenews/campaign/4119386-more-say-violence-could-be-necessary-to-restore-trump-to-white-house-survey/.

What will happen if Trump's second term efforts to consolidate power are blocked? Will the preference for violence reassert itself?

The trend is ominous, especially with Trump's promises of revenge and retribution once back in power. The rank-in-file Trumpers had evidently become significantly more willing to support him in this endeavor, considering their persistent support across several years for the use of violence to overthrow a government they do not support. In 2017, for both Democrats and Republicans, about 30 percent believed a military coup would be justified if there were a lot of government corruption, but by 2021, that had increased for Democrats to 40 percent while the increase for Republicans was much larger, growing to 54 percent supporting a military coup. Extreme polarization was setting in. While these data are about a hypothetical situation, the fact that Republicans much more than Democrats had become more favorable toward a coup is highly suggestive. Yet, the support for violence is not just among Trump's supporters but among increasingly polarized adversaries in both parties.[95] Negative partisanship is fueling increases in affective polarization with a very fraught intensity about who gets to rule and by what means.

Beyond the expressed attitudes of the mass public, there are the actions of extremists. For some time, researchers have been reporting that there has been a sharp increase in Far-Right domestic terror attacks (see Figure 4.2).[96] Far-Right domestic terror attacks were almost nonexistent in recent years until 2013 when they began sharply increasing during the presidency of Barack Obama. By 2017, they became the most common form of terror attack in the United States and have only continued to rise sharply since. Most of these attacks were executed by White males acting along. At first, many reporters often characterized the assailant in any one case as a "lone wolf" and frequently emphasized mental health issues as being involved in influencing the attacker, as was arguably the case in the two assassination attempts on Trump.[97] This was at times a mischaracterization, and it has become less

[95] See Feuer, "As Right-Wing Rhetoric Escalates, So Do Threats and Violence"; and Kalmoe and Mason, *Radical American Partisanship*.

[96] See Rachel Kleinfeld, "The Rise of Political Violence in the United States, *Journal of Democracy*, 32, no. 4 (October 2021): 160–76. Kleinfeld reports on data from the Global Terrorism Database maintained by the National Consortium for the Study of Terrorism and Responses to Terrorism at the University of Maryland.

[97] One gruesome case was of a son decapitating his father for being a federal civil servant and therefore a "traitor." Jo Ciavaglia, J. D. Mullane, and Christopher Cann, "A Recent Dramatic Example of a Mentally Unstable Person Spouting Trumpist Fears and Hate Was the Pennsylvania Man in Custody after Posting Bideo of Father's Decapitated Head on YouTube," *USA Today*, January 31, 2024, https://www.usatoday.com/story/news/nation/2024/01/31/pennsylvania-man-justin-mohn-charged-after-beheading-father/72418454007/.

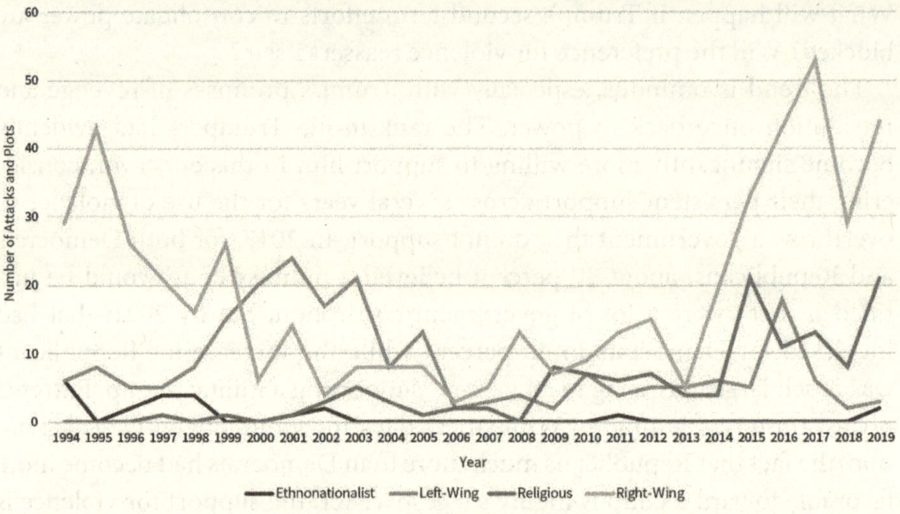

Figure 4.2 Far-Right terror attacks increasing, 2013–2019

Source: Seth G. Jones, Catrina Doxsee, and Nicholas Harrington, "The Escalating Terrorism Problem in the United States," *CSIS Briefs*, June 17, 2020, https://www.csis.org/analysis/escalating-terrorism-problem-united-states.

common in recent years to say the attacker was a lone wolf even if they were acting alone.[98] Instead, over time, more of the attacks get reported, noting that a lone assailant was involved in White Supremacists or neo-Nazi networks, connecting online with similar minded White extremists who were also not averse to promoting, if not actually engaging in, terror attacks.[99]

Some of the deadliest mass shootings in recent years were committed by White Supremacists who posted manifestos citing the Great Replacement Theory and restating talking points of Trump and his fellow hatemongers. Prominent examples include: the Tree of Life Synagogue, Pittsburgh, PA, shootings that occurred on October 27, 2018, that killed eleven and injured two other members of the combined congregations and five law enforcement officers; the Cielo Vista Walmart mass killing in El Paso, TX, on August 3, 2019, killing twenty-three people; the Tops Grocery Store, Buffalo, NY, attack on May 14, 2022, that killed ten people as well as injured three others; and the Allen Premium Outlets, Allen, TX, May 6, 2023, shootings that killed eight

[98] The Editorial Board, "There Are No Lone Wolves," *New York Times*, November 19, 2022, https://www.nytimes.com/2022/11/19/opinion/us-white-supremacy-violence.html; and Adele M. Stan, "White Nationalist Does Massacre. Now the Gaslighting Begins," *The American Prospect*, August 5, 2019, https://prospect.org/justice/white-nationalist-massacre.-now-gaslighting-begins./.

[99] Catrina Doxsee, Seth G. Jones, Jared Thompson, Kateryna Halstead, and Grace Hwang "Pushed to Extremes: Domestic Terrorism amid Polarization and Protest," *Center for Strategic and International Studies*, May 17, 2022, https://www.csis.org/analysis/pushed-extremes-domestic-terrorism-amid-polarization-and-protest.

and wounded seven people. All these domestic terror attacks were committed by White Nationalists who had posted their hate online, often mentioning the Great Replacement Theory and other sources for the desire to kill people they saw as a threat to America's White population.[100]

The context is important, and it shows that political violence on the Right has been increasing. While we might want to see these developments as just a momentary eruption of extreme beliefs and behaviors, there is evidence that these trends are likely to persist as long as leaders like Trump keep inflaming their supporters with hateful anti-democratic rhetoric.

Normalizing Fascism

The eruption of Far-Right violence in recent years was profoundly disturbing, but we should not lose sight of how Trumpism's style of expression played a key part in inciting that violence. This is especially the case with the January 6th insurrection. There was the gaslighting about the 2020 election, suggesting Trump's loss was due not to his unpopularity but cheating by the Democrats (especially those living in the Black "inner cities"). There was the boomeranging of claims about who was trying to undermine democracy, with Democrats being accused of a long-running coup, starting with Trump's two impeachments while being president. Trump repeatedly claimed he was not an insurrectionist, but instead then-Speaker of the House of Representatives Nancy Pelosi was. "I think it was an insurrection caused by Nancy Pelosi," Trump stated at a press conference while the US Supreme Court heard oral arguments over whether he should be removed from the 2024 presidential ballot due to his participation in the insurrection.[101] There was along the way also the constant suggestion that ANTIFA and Black Lives Matter protesters were the real insurrectionists and violent extremists who were trying to overturn democracy. There was the co-opting of the claim as to who were the real constitutionalists standing up for the rule of law.

All this Trumpist bluster by the "edgelord of strategic irony" himself can make things very confusing if you are not paying close attention. And it can

[100] U.S. Department of Justice, "Hate Crimes Case Examples," www.justice.gov/hatecrimes/hate-crimes-case-examples. Also see "Shooter in Allen, Texas, Embraced Antisemitism, Misogyny and White Supremacy," *ADL*, May 8, 2023, https://www.adl.org/resources/blog/shooter-allen-texas-embraced-antisemitism-misogyny-and-white-supremacy.

[101] "Colorado Ballot: Supreme Court Justices Appear Skeptical of Arguments to Kick Trump Off State Ballots," *New York Times*, February 8, 2024, https://www.nytimes.com/live/2024/02/08/us/trump-supreme-court-colorado-ballot?action=click&pgtype=Article&module=&state=default®ion=footer&context=breakout_link_back_to_briefing#in-remarks-during-the-arguments-trump-argues-he-did-nothing-wrong-on-jan-6.

provide cover to justify a person's affective political attachments and how they are expressed via negative partisanship. It is however classic Trumpism. Ivanka Trump once liked to deflect criticism of her father's pugilistic tendencies by saying he was a counterpuncher.[102] She was saying that Trump only punched after being attacked. But the counterpunching of Trumpists had become largely one big boomerang to deny how they were moving in highly undemocratic ways to preserve their hold on power.

Even attempts by Democrats to end the filibuster have been said to be anti-democratic. Yet, the filibuster was long a tool used by segregationists that allows a minority to prevent a majority in the US Senate from passing legislation.[103] Republicans get accused of being anti-democratic and their response is like them saying: "no, actually it is the Democratic critics who are the real threat to democracy for trying to make our institutions more consistent with principles of majority rule."[104] We could say this is actually boomeranging in the name of gaslighting. In the process, the facts of the matter get obscured, and the outrageous anti-democratic maneuvers of the Republicans get normalized as just healthy democratic agonistic politics. Many Republican-leaning voters end up going along.[105] Unfortunately, in our hyper-polarized politics in the age of Trumpism, negative partisanship wins the day, where just being against the opposition is always the correct position.[106] These discursive moves continue to be the Republicans' *modus operandi* whether it is about reducing access to the ballot, gerrymandering state legislative and congressional districts, claiming the 2020 election was stolen, or a myriad of other anti-democratic moves by Republicans. The common refrain is the boomerang that they were not the ones threatening democracy; instead, they were taking those anti-democratic actions in order to protect their version of democracy from attacks by Democrats.

As already noted, the counterpunching extends to who is the fascist.[107] Trump's use of the term is not surprising since, as indicated earlier, he likes

[102] "Ivanka Trump Defends Her Father's Campaign Style," *CBS Evening News*, May 12, 2016, https://www.cbsnews.com/news/ivanka-trump-defends-her-fathers-campaign-style/.

[103] Rick Scott, "Biden and Schumer's Shameless Filibuster Hypocrisy," *Fox News*, January 13, 2022, https://www.foxnews.com/opinion/biden-and-schumers-shameless-filibuster-hypocrisy-sen-rick-scott.

[104] Ross Pomeroy, "Democrats or Republicans: Who Is More Anti-Democratic?" *Real Clear Science*, September 30, 2022, https://www.realclearscience.com/articles/2022/09/30/democrats_or_republicans_who_is_more_undemocratic_856350.html.

[105] Steve Benen, *Ministry of Truth: Democracy, Reality, and the Republicans' War on the Recent Past* (Mariner Books, 2024).

[106] See Abramowitz and Webster, "Negative Partisanship: Why Americans Dislike Parties But Behave Like Rabid Partisans," 119–35.

[107] Bethany Dawson, "2020 Video of Trump Calling Democrats 'Fascists' Resurfaces after Republicans Slammed President Biden for Saying MAGA Ideology Was 'Semi-Fascism,'" *Insider*, September 4, 2022, https://www.businessinsider.com/video-of-trump-calling-democrats-fascists-resurfaces-goes-viral-2022-9.

to boomerang the epithet when it is used against him. It is all part of his preference to smear people rather than debate substance. Democrats have felt increasingly obligated to use the term, given Trump's increasingly hostile rhetoric and promises to act on it once back in office. As time has gone by, more and more people are willing to say that Trump and Trumpism are fascistic. In light of the constant anti-democratic maneuvering by Republicans under Trump's leadership, Robert Reich has highlighted a major problem:

> Without two parties committed to democratic means to resolve differences in ends, the party committed to democracy is at a tactical disadvantage. If it is to survive, eventually it, too, will sacrifice democratic means to its own ends.
>
> In these circumstances, partisanship turns to enmity and political divisions morph into hatred. In warfare there are no principles, only wins and losses. America experienced this 160 years ago, when the civil war tore us apart. Donald Trump is not singularly responsible for this dangerous trend, but he has legitimized and encouraged the ends-justify-the-means viciousness now pushing the GOP toward becoming the American fascist party.[108]

As discussed earlier, there is precedent for designating Right-Wing racist movements in the United States as fascist. Hitler's approach to the Jews of Germany was inspired by America's treatment of African Americans. The America First Committee that opposed US entry into World War II was led by fascist and Nazi sympathizers. Trump's second installment of a movement with the slogan "America First" suggests that Trumpists embrace the comparison to a group that was led by fascists. Yet, despite this brazenness, there is still reticence to call Trumpism fascism. Some say "authoritarian populism" is the more appropriate term to characterize Trumpism as an anti-democratic movement led by a power-hungry demagogue.[109]

Whether Trumpism is better described as fascist than say an authoritarian-populist movement is perhaps no longer worth debating. Joe Lowndes put it well:

> Scholars have long debated the issue, with some insisting that Trump is better understood as an authoritarian populist. But particularly since he became the Martyr of Butler County, Trump has undergone a kind of apotheosis. He is now

[108] Robert Reich, "The Modern Republican Party Is Hurtling towards Fascism," *The Guardian*, April 15, 2023, https://www.theguardian.com/commentisfree/2023/apr/15/the-modern-republican-party-fascism-robert-reich.

[109] Pippa Norris, "It's Not Just Trump: Authoritarian Populism Is Rising Across the West," *Washington Post*, March 11, 2016, https://www.washingtonpost.com/news/monkey-cage/wp/2016/03/11/its-not-just-trump-authoritarian-populism-is-rising-across-the-west-heres-why/.

> described in almost superhuman terms as indestructible, as always rising. The qualities projected onto Trump are politically formidable precisely because they enact the story of national renewal captured by the phrase "Make America Great Again." The air of inevitable triumph, of Trumpist victory as a sacred Telos, moves us somewhere closer to fascism. For his people, Trump is both the essence of national vitality, and a perfect instrument of God's will.[110]

Toward the end of the 2024 campaign, Trump showed a growing willingness to take on the role as the symbolic embodiment of his movement in ways that reinforced its fascistic elan. His willingness to use fascist terminology in characterizing his opposition as "vermin" just as Hitler did added support to the argument that Trump was posturing as a fascist and doing so because he knows many of his supporters leaned that way as well. They increasingly wanted to crush the opposition on behalf of their leader, literally not just figuratively. Trump's candidacy had passed from body to spirit. It did not matter anymore that he increasingly made no sense when talking. The babble reinforced his deified status. Yet, whatever term is most appropriate for Trumpism as it had evolved, its metapragmatic discourse obscured the commitment to undermine democracy, including by force, and suggests that the fascist vs. authoritarian distinction itself in the case of Trumpism is somewhat moot.

The Legal Coup: Anti-Democratic Lawfare

Trumpism has pursued a strategy to exploit weaknesses in the constitutional order so as to be able to undermine democracy and cling to power. Thomas Edsall has quoted political scientist Rogers Smith as saying: "There is no doubt that democratic processes and judicial decisions can be used to limit the power of the people, restructuring governments and institutions to make them less representative, more undemocratic. The classic examples are partisan gerrymandering and barriers to voting, but in recent years Republicans have gone further than ever before in using their overrepresentation in state legislatures to shift power to those legislatures, away from officeholders in Democratic-led cities, from officials elected statewide and from voters."[111] Under cover of Trumpist discourse, be it via boomeranging, gaslighting, or

[110] Joseph Lowndes, "The Apotheosis of Donald Trump," *Logos*, 23, no. 3 (2024), https://logosjournal.com/issue/2024-vol-23-no-3/.

[111] Rogers Smith, as quoted in Thomas Edsall, "What Republicans Are Doing Is 'One of the Odd and Scary Things About American Politics,'" *New York Times*, April 19, 2023, https://www.nytimes.com/2023/04/19/opinion/democracy-authoritarianism-trump.html.

even co-opting the Left's critiques, the less-than-covert maneuvers to undermine democracy have intensified, giving us a new form of lawfare, i.e., trying to make illegal power grabs seem to be perfectly legal.

Trump's most dramatic legalistic maneuver to undermine the 2020 election was the fake electors scheme.[112] The project involved getting supporters to meet in state capitals and pretend to be authorized alternative slates of electors for the Electoral College. These slates were then to be submitted to Vice President Pence to be used on January 6 as a pretext for not certifying Joe Biden as the winner of the 2020 presidential election. Pence refused in the end to go along, and the plot failed, leading to Trump encouraging his supporters to go to the Capitol not just to urge Pence to change his mind but also to try to get Congress to delay or stop the certification. Instead, the protest morphed into a sacking of the Capitol that constituted a full-blown insurrection. At that point, the legalistic maneuvering phase of Trumpism merged with the violent overthrow of the government phase. In Timothy Snyder's phrasing, the "gamers" and "breakers" became one.[113] This merging was vividly depicted once a photo of Trump lawyer Kenneth Chesebro (the key proponent of the fake electors plot) and incendiary Right-Wing propagandist Alex Jones of Infowars was shown to be marching together among the protesters on January 6. Chesebro would eventually plead guilty for his involvement in plotting the fake electors scheme and Jones would go bankrupt over his profligate lying about school shootings.[114]

The fake electors scheme was essentially an attempt at a "legal coup" (i.e., an illegal coup executed via using legal procedures). No coup is strictly speaking legal; instead, a legal coup is a coup executed by means of using the law against itself. It is a quintessentially metapragmatic move. It recategorized illegality making it seem legal. This contradiction once enacted in the case of the fake electors scheme fomented a "constitutional crisis," where the issue of what was or was not constitutional about seeking to gain power was thrown into doubt, opening the door for Trump to snatch victory from the jaws of defeat.[115] The fake electors scheme involved getting Pence to renounce what states had already determined. Therefore, any proclamation by Pence along

[112] Alan Feuer and Katie Benner, "The Fake Electors Scheme, Explained," *New York Times*, July 27, 2022, https://www.nytimes.com/2022/07/27/us/politics/fake-electors-explained-trump-jan-6.html.

[113] Timothy Snyder, "The American Abyss," *New York Times*, January 9, 2021, https://www.nytimes.com/2021/01/09/magazine/trump-coup.html.

[114] Alan Feuer and Maggie Haberman, "Architect of Fake Electors Scheme Appeared to Be Outside Capitol on Jan. 6," *New York Times*, August 18, 2023, https://www.nytimes.com/2023/08/18/us/politics/kenneth-chesebro-jan-6-trump.html.

[115] Josh Kovensky, "The Legal Coup: New Documents Reveal How Trump Lawyers Sought 'Chaos' to Force SCOTUS, or Whoever Else, to Anoint Trump," *TPM*, February 12, 2024, https://talkingpointsmemo.com/feature/intro-chesebro-docs.

those lines would be entirely consistent with the metapragmatics of Trumpism as a discourse. It was an explicit reference to the real electors who had been certified. The fake electors claim suggested the real electors were fake and the fake Trump electors were the real ones. It was performative gaslighting done in service of an anti-democratic agenda that sought legitimation via what was asserted without credible legal justification to be a legal maneuver. Some of the electors in multiple states were charged with the crime of seeking to obstruct an official government proceeding (i.e., the certification of Biden as president). It was classic Trumpism trying to undermine democracy while denying it was actually doing that. It exploited deficiencies in the Constitution and the laws governing presidential elections in order to achieve its anti-democratic ends without resorting to violence. It ended up however being part of a larger anti-democratic strategy that eventually led to a violent attempt to stop the peaceful transfer of power.

The fake electors scheme shows that the US constitutional system, even as it has been reformed over time, remains less than fully democratic and people who oppose democracy and greater inclusion, can exploit the system's deficiencies.[116] This type of anti-democratic maneuvering need not be fascistic. In my mind, for anti-democratic maneuvering to be fascistic, it needs to be done in the name of marginalizing minorities, via using lies, while demonizing the defenders of a democratic society, including the press and intellectuals, and backing up those efforts with threats of violence. That would make the anti-democratic maneuvering fascistic. After the January 6th insurrection, it has become harder to say that the ongoing anti-democratic lawfare, like legislating ballot restrictions and gerrymandering, is not part of a fascistic movement aimed to undermine liberal democracy in the United States. As Jamelle Bouie has written:

> The fact of the matter is that there *are* forces that are trying to break the stasis of American politics. There's the Supreme Court, which has used its iron grip on constitutional meaning to accumulate power in its chambers, to the detriment of other institutions of American governance. There's the Republican Party, which has used the counter-majoritarian features of our system to build redoubts of power, insulated from the voters themselves. And there is an authoritarian movement, led and animated by Trump, that wants to renounce constitutional government in favor of an authoritarian patronage regime, with his family at its center.[117]

[116] Suzanne Mettler and Robert C. Lieberman, *Four Threats: The Recurring Crises of American Democracy* (St. Martin's Press, 2020).

[117] Jamelle Bouie, "Something's Got to Give," *New York Times*, May 5, 2023, https://www.nytimes.com/2023/05/05/opinion/constitutional-amendments-supreme-court.html?smid=nytcore-ios-share&referringSource=articleShare.

This too increasingly is a global phenomenon of which Trumpism is just one prominent example of using the rules of an electoral democracy against itself to facilitate a legal coup. It has become a more frequent occurrence to see elected leaders like Hungary's Orban practice what is called "autocratic legalism," where they ascend to office with the support of disenchanted voters and act on promises to undo the existing constitutional order and thereby consolidate their own power.[118] Yet, we could go further and say that the anti-democratic maneuvering via deficiencies and weaknesses in the existing US constitutional system could arguably be said to be a phase in Trumpism as a fascist movement.

This is Jason Stanley's argument.[119] He notes that Toni Morrison, in her 1995 Howard University speech on "Fascism and Racism," made the point that fascism does not come to power all at once. Instead, there are stages.[120] For Trumpism, the United States is in the legal phase, where the Far-Right has overtaken the Republican Party, runs candidates in elections, passes laws to restrict the opposition from participating, and redraws district boundaries to magnify its power and reduce the representation of its opponents, while stacking the courts to impose anti-democratic rulings and does many other things within the law to undermine democracy. We could call this authoritarian populism but that would not capture all that is Trumpism. While many observers persist in suggesting that using the F-word to describe Trumpism is hyperbole or an anachronism, increasingly it seems to be historically accurate.

When the Gloves Come Off

For too long, people had been reluctant to call out the increasingly clear fascist turn in Trumpism. The mass media unfortunately were well-established prime culprits in this complicity in allowing the gaslighting and boomeranging to normalize, mainstream, and even to some extent legitimate this authoritarian turn in Trumpism.[121] Yet as the 2024 presidential campaign was peaking, Democrats increasingly called out Trump as a fascist, given

[118] Kim Lane Scheppele, "Autocratic Legalism," *The University of Chicago Law Review* 85, no. 2 (March 2018): 545–84.

[119] Jason Stanley, "America Is Now in Fascism's Legal Phase," *The Guardian*, December 22, 2021, https://www.theguardian.com/world/2021/dec/22/america-fascism-legal-phase/.

[120] Toni Morrison, "Racism and Fascism," *The Journal of Negro Education* 64, no. 3 (Summer, 1995): 384–85, https://doi.org/10.2307/2967217.

[121] Chris Lehmann, "The 'Is Donald Trump a Fascist?' Debate Has Been Ended—by Donald Trump," *The Nation*, November 14, 2023, https://www.thenation.com/article/politics/donald-trump-fascist-vermin/.

his increasingly extreme rhetoric including using the military against his enemies.[122] Even Trump's former Chief of Staff John Kelly agreed.[123]

Nonetheless, Trumpism was still largely operating according to the metapragmatics of deniability. Gov. Christopher Sununu (R-NH), who had previously opposed Trump's 2024 candidacy in favor of Nikki Haley's bid for the Republican Party presidential nomination, had come around to supporting Trump even after the fascist label was getting put on him by an increasing number of people. Sununu stated that despite the evidence that Trump was noted for appreciating dictators and even Hitler that it was "kind of baked into the vote" with "a guy like that."[124] Sununu had said dismissive things like this before and his constantly insouciant smiling face whenever he did made it seem as if it were just a "friendly fascism" we could learn to love.[125]

As the 2024 campaign swung into its final two weeks, Vice President Kamala Harris focused her campaign on this issue and joined the growing chorus of people who now were rushing to try to stop Trump from returning to power by naming him a fascist. A major poll was then released that estimated half the Country thought Trump was a fascist (though one in eight of those people thought that was a good thing).[126]

At that point, with election day looming, the Country had to confront, despite all the prevaricating, what was staring them in their face, what we can call a modern American form of fascism that uses the metapragmatic discursive moves that are needed maintain the deniability that is needed in the post–Civil Rights society. It was working the legal system to undermine democracy and was now something that the Country had to recognize as also backed by violence or its threats (on January 6 in particular, but at other times as well). Remember all the poll workers who now regularly receive death threats.

The fascist posturing of Trump and his allies was becoming ever more controversial once Trump and his acolytes began to explicitly promise his return to office would lead to a strongman government that concentrated power in

[122] Jonathan Weisman, "Harris and Democrats Lose Their Reluctance to Call Trump a Fascist," *New York Times*, October 17, 2024, https://www.nytimes.com/2024/10/17/us/politics/harris-trump-fascism.html?smid=nytcore-ios-share&referringSource=articleShare&tgrp=cnt&pvid=44C9589A-8EA0-41E0-AB67-FE446A1D22F9.

[123] Jeffrey Goldberg, "Trump: 'I Need the Kind of Generals That Hitler Had'," *The Atlantic*, October 22, 2024, https://www.theatlantic.com/politics/archive/2024/10/trump-military-generals-hitler/680327/.

[124] Dana Wormald, "Editor's Notebook: Chris Sununu and the 'Baked-in' Trump Vote," *New Hampshire Bulletin*, October 24, 2024, https://newhampshirebulletin.com/2024/10/24/editors-notebook-chris-sununu-and-the-baked-in-trump-vote/.

[125] On "friendly fascism" from an earlier era in US politics, see Bertram Gross, *Friendly Fascism: The New Face of Power in America* (M. Evans and Co., 1980).

[126] Gary Langer and Steven Sparks, "Half of Americans See Donald Trump as a Fascist: Poll," *ABC News*, October 25, 2024, https://abcnews.go.com/Politics/donald-trump-fascist-concerns-poll/story?id=115083795.

his presidency and used claims of "absolute immunity" to extract retribution when seeking revenge on his opponents (backed by the military power of the state as authorized under the Insurrection Act).[127] Six conservative justices of the US Supreme Court had granted Trump a big victory on this front when, on July 1, 2024, they ruled that the president did indeed have absolute immunity when conducting "official acts" as president. This decision only furthered emboldened Trump who now could see his quest to become an authoritarian strongman becoming normalized. By then, Trump had already refused to dismiss the necessity of violence if he loses in his attempts to regain power.[128] When his pronouncements led to increased enthusiasm among his supporters for a Trump presidency aimed at extracting retribution, the alarm bells were finally ringing just about everywhere.[129]

Trump increasingly invoked Nazi rhetoric on defeating the "enemy within,"[130] by deploying the US military against American citizens.[131] It was at that point frightening to think that perhaps we were moving to where the metapragmatic moves were less needed to legitimate what was becoming popular with so many Trump supporters staying with him no matter how fascistic his rhetoric became. The 2024 Trump presidential campaign was slow to disavow veiled references to creating an American "unified Reich," and Trump's staff came to be increasingly populated with young people with White Nationalist and neo-Nazi ties.[132] Increasingly, it was accepted that Trump was not joking, but instead his pronouncements were resulting in his inevitably leading to what we can call a new American Fascist Movement.

With Trump back in the White House, we might have to witness the extent to which Trump's rhetorical gestures toward authoritarian and even fascistic rule have become the Country's reality. The fact that he pardoned over 1,500 charged or convicted insurrectionists while issuing numerous executive orders that abrogated civil rights, free speech, funding for education and research, and much more all on his first day back in the White House was a harbinger of subsequent events that we had already gotten to that point.

[127] John Knefel, "Bannon's 'War Room' Is the Media Home of Project 2025 and Trump's Retribution Plans," *Media Matters for America*, November 9, 2023, https://www.mediamatters.org/steve-bannon/bannons-war-room-media-home-project-2025-and-trumps-retribution-plans.5.

[128] See Cortellessa, "How Far Trump Will Go."

[129] Tufekci, "A Strongman President? These Voters Crave It"; and Lehmann, "The 'Is Donald Trump a Fascist?' Debate Has Been Ended—by Donald Trump."

[130] Alice Herman, "Trump Warns of Enemies "Within our Country" to Christian Media Gathering," *The Guardian*, February 23, 2024, https://www.theguardian.com/us-news/2024/feb/23/trump-national-religious-broadcasters-enemies-within-country.

[131] Ellie Quinlan, "Even Team Trump Is Panicking Over His Fascist Military Threat," *The New Republic*, October 15, 2024, https://newrepublic.com/post/187178/donald-trump-team-freaking-enemy-within-military.

[132] David Austin Walsh, "Do You Want a 'Unified Reich' Mind-Set in the White House?" *New York Times*, May 24, 2024, https://www.nytimes.com/2024/05/23/opinion/trump-unified-reich.html.

5

Civil War

After she tweeted on February 20, 2023, that "we need a national divorce,"[1] US Rep. Marjorie Taylor Greene (R-GA) went on Sean Hannity's Fox News show the next night to state that her critics were wrong to say that she was calling for civil war.[2] Instead, she boomeranged that it was the Democrats who were pushing for civil war. Greene said: "The last thing I ever want to see in America is a civil war. No one wants that—at least everyone I know would never want that—but it's going that direction, and we have to do something about it." She added: "In my life and my world, all of my friends are regular Americans. Everyone I talk to is sick and tired and fed up with being bullied by the left, abused by the left, and disrespected by the left. ... Our ideas, our policies and our ways of life have become so far apart that it's just coming to that point."

Greene then stated what she seemed to think was a clarification of her original tweet that it was meant only to suggest "a legal agreement to separate our ideological and political disagreements by states while maintaining our legal union." Greene emphasized that the country had a "divide so deep" that her proposed separation was increasingly likely and that the movement for separation was "much bigger than most people in Washington even realize. ... The amount of likes and retweets that those tweets got should tell people a lot." She was again boomeranging the criticism about her calling for civil war back at the Democrats, while still insisting we could no longer work together and needed to separate. Her call for no civil war but separation was somehow an attempt to have her cake and eat it too. She wanted separation but not civil war—this was her way to be inflammatory but still maintain deniability. The two-step metapragmatic move of Trumpism as a discourse was once again on full display with her continuing to recharacterize her incendiary initial comments.

[1] https://twitter.com/mtgreenee/status/1627665203398688768.

[2] Sinéad Baker, "MTG Defends Her Call to Split Up the US by Saying the Country Is Moving towards Another Civil War: 'We Have to do Something about It,'" *Insider*, February 22, 2023, https://www.businessinsider.com/mtg-defends-call-split-up-us-says-civil-war-looming-2023-2.

The Trajectory of Trumpism. Sanford F. Schram, Oxford University Press. © Oxford University Press (2026).
DOI: 10.1093/9780197827437.003.0005

In this chapter, I highlight what is driving the increased talk among Trumpists about civil war, how they use metapragmatics to justify it, and how serious the situation has become. While the theme is different, the metapragmatics of Trumpism remain the consistent approach to legitimating their extremist claims, pushing the Country inevitably that much closer to the breaking point.

From Culture War to Civil War

If there is a logic to Greene's civil war pronouncement, it is cultural not economic. The Red states where Republicans hold most of the government offices are much more dependent on the federal government than the Blue states dominated by the Democratic Party. Eight of the ten most federally dependent states are Republican, while seven of the ten least federally dependent states are Democratic, which suggests that, overall, Republican states are more dependent upon federal assistance than Democratic ones.[3] Breaking up the union, letting states go their own way or some other kind of "divorce" would be very costly economically for the Red states.

But Greene and her supporters do not care about those economic facts. She was not complaining about who was benefiting economically from the current arrangement. Instead, Greene was pointing to the intensification of the Culture War that had been brewing for decades, perhaps stretching as far back as the sixties and maybe even before.[4] For a long time, Right-Wing hatemongers have been exploiting simmering resentments to the cultural changes overtaking the Country. Whether it was about the decline of religion, the changes in sexual mores, women's rights, gun control, educational reform, and of course civil rights, the Right-Wingers could stir people in the Heartland to fear the liberal cosmopolitan, bi-coastal elites who were changing America into a more open, pluralistic, diverse, and secular society.[5]

For James Davidson Hunter, who popularized the term Culture War several decades ago, the Culture War, as it has evolved, is about more than issues. For

[3] Zoe Manzanetti, "Are Republican States More Federally Dependent?" *Governing*, March 22, 2021, https://www.governing.com/finance/are-republican-states-more-federally-dependent.html.

[4] See James Davidson Hunter, *Culture Wars: The Struggle to Define America* (Basic Books, 1991); and Zach Stanton, "How the 'Culture War' Could Break Democracy," *Politico*, May 20, 2021, https://www.politico.com/news/magazine/2021/05/20/culture-war-politics-2021-democracy-analysis-489900.

[5] Jeff Sharlet, *The Undertow: Scenes from a Slow Civil War* (W.W. Norton, 2023); Katherine J. Cramer, *The Politics of Resentment: Rural Consciousness in Wisconsin and the Rise of Scott Walker* (University of Chicago Press, 2016); and Lawrence Rosenthal, *Empire of Resentment: Populism's Toxic Embrace of Nationalism* (New Press, 2020).

Hunter, the Culture War is about how "the culture underwrites our politics." He states:

> [T]he *bigger* story is about the cultures that underwrite our politics, and the ways in which our politics become reflections of deeper cultural dispositions—not just attitudes and values—that go beyond our ability to reason about them. In simpler terms, I would make the distinction between the weather and the climate. Almost all journalists and most academics focus on what's happening in the weather: "Today, it's cold. Tomorrow, it's going to be warm. The next day, it's going to rain." I find the *climatological* changes that are taking place to be much more interesting. And it's those that are really animating our politics and polarization, animating dynamics within democracy right now.[6]

Greene was expressing a view consistent with Hunter's perspective. Yes, her politics are very different and her relationship to facts has always been suspect, but she shares with Hunter an appreciation that what is really going on is not just solitary policy disagreements between groups, like evangelical Christians and secular feminists over abortion, but something much larger. The Culture War is about the battle over the way the dominant culture, as it evolves, will get to frame and influence not just what values will be hegemonic but how those values will influence the political struggle for power in society overall.[7] The culture war is about the underlying core values that get to ascend in society. If you get to implant those in society, isolated policy differences will be framed in terms of those core values. The Culture War is about who gets to set the basic rules we all are expected to live by.

Relatedly, today's polarization is cultural more than it is economic.[8] The evidence that White voters with less than a college degree are increasingly voting Republican can be misleading us into thinking the battle lines are drawn along economic lines. But this is misleading for a variety of reasons. First, not everyone without a college degree is working class or poor. Over 60 percent of American workers do not have a four-year degree, making that group far wider than the working class or below based on income. Second, many non-Whites without a college degree continue to vote Democratic. Third, it also is important to recognize the long-established fact that many people on the lower ends of the socioeconomic ladder, whether they have a college degree or not, frequently emphasize cultural over economic issues when voting. Last, the divide is increasingly racialized with the Democratic Party pushing for

[6] Hunter as quoted in Stanton, "How the 'Culture War' Could Break Democracy."
[7] Ibid.
[8] See Fording and Schram, *Hard White*, Chapter 10.

more racial inclusion and the Republican Party seeking to limit the political influence of African Americans and other non-Whites. For all these reasons, it makes sense that even though the Republicans are capturing a growing percentage of the non-college-educated White vote, they do not emphasize economic policies that would benefit the lower classes over those who are of higher incomes.[9]

Nonetheless, the cultural divide is real, with college education being an important dividing line at least among Whites. It is also regional, with bicoastal liberalism not quite a gross oversimplification. The Northeastern and New England states are Blue as is the West Coast and the heartland is disproportionately Red. But there is also an urban–rural divide, with central cities being very Blue, liberal Democratic bastions, and the outlying areas more likely to be trending Red in favor of the Republicans. For years, we have known that people's residential choices have been influenced by class and race, but now there is research that people also choose where to live based on partisanship.[10]

The country is pulling apart into competing camps about what it means to be an American. The Culture War has made politics much more fraught; it becomes a battle that ultimately puts the viability of democracy in doubt. The Culture War has led to the growing negative partisanship we have witnessed in recent decades where in the extreme you vote for whomever and whatever if it leads to the defeat of your opponents.[11] Negative partisanship is associated with that affective polarization (discussed in the last chapter), where your partisan identity becomes a critical component of your overall personal identity.[12] Your party identification becomes more than an affiliation; it becomes an emotional attachment that is fundamental to your personality. Under these conditions, issues matter less, opposing the opposition, and staying loyal to your political tribe matters more. Rational disputation over the facts associated with key policy issues moves to the background or becomes irrelevant. In its place, the partisan emotional attachment to your side and resentment of the other side become paramount. The opposition

[9] Ibid. Also see Thomas Frank, *What's the Matter with Kansas?: How Conservatives Won the Heart of America* (Picador, 2005) and many other books and research papers that followed Frank's analysis.

[10] W. Ben McCartney, John Orellana, and Calvin Zhang, "'Sort Selling': Political Polarization and Residential Choice," *Reserve Bank of Philadelphia*, March 2, 2021, https://www.philadelphiafed.org/-/media/frbp/assets/working-papers/2021/wp21-14.pdf.

[11] Alan Abramowitz and Steven Webster, "'Negative Partisanship' Explains Everything," *Politico Magazine*, September/October 2017, www.politico.com/magazine/story/2017/09/05/negative-partisanship-explains-everything-215534/.

[12] Thomas J. Rudolph and Marc J. Hetherington, "Affective Polarization in Political and Nonpolitical Settings," *International Journal of Public Opinion Research* 33, no. 3 (2021): 591–606. https://doi.org/10.1093/ijpor/edaa040.

comes to be seen as not just adversaries in a contest over who wins an election or which issue positions will win out. Instead, under affective polarization, the members of the opposition are no longer adversaries but now enemies.

With the rise of negative partisanship and the resulting increased affective polarization, political combat becomes like war. You must defeat the other side because they represent an existential threat to your very being. With growing levels of affective polarizations, researchers have started to investigate whether people with high levels of affective polarization end up supporting acts of violence against the opposition.[13] If it gets to that point, then democratic political contestation is not sustainable and instead using force, even violent force, to defeat the other side becomes more likely.

When interviewed about how the Culture War had evolved since he wrote about it several decades ago, Hunter poignantly noted that under today's conditions, the Culture War is encouraging civil war and represents a real threat to the sustainability of democracy:

> [T]he argument I [originally] made was that culture wars always precede shooting wars. They don't *necessarily* lead to a shooting war, but you never have a shooting war without a culture war prior to it, because culture provides the justifications for violence. And I think that's where we are. . . . Not to hope—to give in to despair—is never an option, in my opinion. That's an ethical position I think one has to take. But I also don't think that you tell a patient that they have a bad cold when, in fact, they have a life-threatening disease.[14]

Gaslighting Tops Boomeranging

There is in fact increasing discussion among political observers, including scholars, about how the United States is moving toward a new civil war.[15]

[13] See James Druckman and Jeremy Levy, "Affective Polarization in the American Public," Working Paper WP-21-27, Northwestern Institute for Policy Research, https://www.ipr.northwestern.edu/our-work/working-papers/2021/wp-21-27.html; See Lilliana Mason, *Uncivil Agreement: How Politics Became Our Identity* (University of Chicago Press, 2018); and Nathan P. Kalmoe and Lilliana Mason, *Radical American Partisanship: Mapping Violent Hostility, Its Causes, and the Consequences for Democracy* (University of Chicago Press, 2022).

[14] Hunter as quoted in Stanton, "How the 'Culture War' Could Break Democracy."

[15] Steven Simon and Jonathan Stevenson, "The Threat of Civil Breakdown Is Real," *Politico*, April 21, 2023, https://www.politico.com/news/magazine/2023/04/21/political-violence-2024-magazine-00093028.

Books are written about it,[16] commentators publish essays debating it,[17] and increasingly ordinary Americans talk about it as reported in surveys.[18] It is a fraught situation. The divisions exist and may be increasing, even if they do not break down neatly by regions. Nonetheless, there is reason to pause to reconsider how we got here. There is evidence that political elites, the likes of Marjorie Taylor Greene, are doing the most to make this happen.[19] And it is primarily something coming from the Right. And it is largely a product of gaslighting and the related metapragmatic discursive moves.

When Greene and other Right-Wingers talk about civil war, they are gaslighting us just by using the term civil war. A civil war is where there are two combating sides. Both sides are involved in producing the conflict. While the Culture War might be arguably seen in this way, the new civil war misleadingly suggests that both sides are equally involved in pulling the Country apart to the point of dissolving the Republic. There may be, these days, increased negative partisanship and affective polarization, but it is more extreme on one side than the other. And that is largely, if not entirely, due to political leadership in today's radicalized Republican Party.[20]

There is some truth to the idea that the two major political parties are more firmly entrenched in highly polarized positions on the political spectrum to an unprecedented degree. Political commentator Ron Brownstein has noted: "The parties now represent coalitions with such divergent visions of America's future, particularly whether it welcomes or resists racial and cultural change, that it's unclear what could allow one side to break out from the close competition between them. And that includes the prospect of Republicans choosing a presidential nominee who could be shuttling between the campaign trail and the courtroom."[21] Political Scientist Lynn Vavreck has noted that: "The two political parties are farther apart on average than they have been in our

[16] Stephane Marche, *The Next Civil War: Dispatches from the American Future* (Avid Reader Press/Simon and Shuster, 2022); and Barbara F. Walter, *How Civil Wars Start: And How to Stop Them* (Viking, 2022).

[17] Jamelle Bouie and Tim Alberta, "Is the U.S. Headed for Another Civil War?" *New York Times*, October 12, 2022, https://www.nytimes.com/2022/10/12/opinion/the-argument-america-civil-war.html?smid=nytcore-ios-share&referringSource=articleShare.

[18] Martin Pengelly, "More than 40% of Americans Think Civil War Likely within a Decade," *Guardian*, August 30, 2022, https://www.theguardian.com/us-news/2022/aug/29/us-civil-war-fears-poll.

[19] Big Brains Podcast, "Is the U.S. Headed toward Another Civil War? with William Howell," *UChicago News*, January 5, 2023, https://news.uchicago.edu/us-headed-toward-another-civil-war-william-howell.

[20] Jeffrey Isaac, "Reflections on the New Anarchy and the Real Danger of MAGA Republicans," *Common Dreams*, April 4, 2023, https://www.commondreams.org/opinion/anarchy-and-the-real-danger-of-maga-republicans.

[21] Ronald Brownstein, "Even Trump's Indictments Haven't Shattered the Deadlock between the Parties," *CNN Politics*, August 1, 2023, https://www.cnn.com/2023/08/01/politics/trump-indictments-deadlock-democrats-republicans-fault-lines/index.html?fbclid=IwAR1SGBnJDA4pQkqOfnOPwVD2kla6_Z-BwjVDa3C9knTh25J2wxcD4dawEkc.

lifetime."[22] Yet some of the best research available also suggests that polarization is not simply a case where the rank-and-file of both parties are pulling apart all on their own and in equal amounts.[23]

First, there is strong evidence that for years now, it is the Republicans political elites who are becoming much more extremist in their views compared to the Democratic political leadership. Take the research on Congress. Figure 5.1 shows that for both the House and the Senate, from the 92nd Congress, 1971–72, to the 117th Congress, 2021–22, it was the Republicans who were moving much further to the Right end of the political spectrum, compared to Democrats moving to the Left, based on their roll-call votes for proposed legislation.[24] In fact, Democrats in Congress are hardly any more liberal in their voting than they were fifty years ago, with their scores reported in Figure 5.1 increasing a mere 6 percent in the Senate and only 7 percent in the House. Over the same time period, the average ideological score based on voting for Republicans in the Senate moved to the Right 28 percent, while the average score for House Republicans increased 25 percent in the conservative direction.

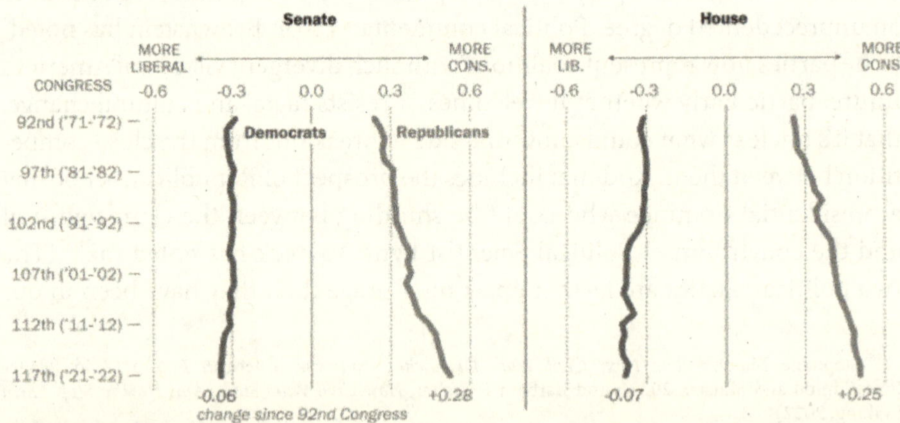

Figure 5.1 Republicans have moved further to the Right than Democrats to the Left: Average ideology for members by Congress

Source: Pew Research Center, https://www.pewresearch.org/short-reads/2022/03/10/the-polarization-in-todays-congress-has-roots-that-go-back-decades/

[22] As quoted in Ibid.

[23] Naomi Ehrich Leonard, Keena Lipsitz, Anastasia Bizyaeva, Alessio Franci, and Yphtach Lelkes, "The Nonlinear Feedback Dynamics of Asymmetric Political Polarization," *Proceedings of the National Academy of Science*, December 14, 2021, doi:10.1073/pnas.2102149118.

[24] "Republicans Have Moved Further to the Right than Democrats have to the Left," *Pew Research Center*, March 9, 2022, https://www.pewresearch.org/ft_22-02-22_congresspolarization_featured_new/.

Second, there is research that shows that this Right-Wing polarization is much more extreme among the Republican Party elites than the rank-and-file.[25] And to the degree the rank-and-file update their views in a more extreme direction, research is showing this is very much contingent upon taking cues from party leaders and responding on the basis of affective polarization.[26] Yet this is perhaps mitigated more than we think by taking the views of the opposing party's leadership into account.[27] Anthony Fowler and William Howell write, "Our results also help explain how mass moderation can persist in the face of widening levels of elite polarization. The effects of elite polarization, of course, are not entirely innocuous. We find that in-party effects tend to exceed out-party effects, which would imply that elite polarization increases public polarization. But because partisans respond positively to both parties, the translation of elite to mass polarization does not proceed seamlessly. Importantly, exposing partisans to positions from the opposition mitigates rather than exacerbates mass polarization."[28]

Therefore, there is reason to think that growing partisan polarization today is driven most significantly by the leaders of Trumpism as a movement and the leaders of the Republican Party that is increasingly dominated by Trump-aligned politicians. There is, however, a simpler reason to doubt the both-siderism implied by invoking "civil war." For the most part, the only people really talking about wanting civil war are the Right.[29] Radical Republicans in Congress like Marjorie Taylor Greene or less prominent Trumpists like Thomas Massie may say they do not really want a civil war, but they add that it is now nonetheless a necessity. This is classic Trumpism, double-speak that provides deniability, while actually pushing the incendiary idea forward.

Invoking civil war is therefore not just a gaslight, but it is a boomerang when people like Greene say it is the Democrats who are the ones who want it the most and that is therefore why we need to consider separation out of necessity. Yet this is a boomerang working in favor of gaslighting, for it reinforces how the term civil war unavoidably implies both sides are pushing the breakup, when it is actually one side pushing to undermine the constitutional order and the other is trying to uphold it (even if not always effectively). Trumpists create a cloud of confusion when talking about how growing polarization is

[25] Anthony Fowler and William G. Howell, "Updating Amidst Disagreement: New Experimental Evidence on Partisan Cues," *Public Opinion Quarterly* 87, no. 1 (Spring 2023): 24–43, https://doi.org/10.1093/poq/nfac053.

[26] Leonard et al., "The Nonlinear Feedback Dynamics of Asymmetric Political Polarization."

[27] Ibid.

[28] Ibid.

[29] Angela McArdle and Zach Weissmueller, "Debate: It's Time for a National Divorce: Are Political Breakups Really as American as Apple Pie?" *Reason*, May 2023, https://reason.com/2023/04/08/proposition-its-time-for-a-national-divorce/.

allegedly caused by the rank-and-file in both parties, when it actually is to a significant degree something caused by the leadership of one party.[30]

Today's Civil War is a metapragmatic mirror world. The original Radical Republicans in Congress during the real Civil War pushed for the abolition of slavery and the creation of a political system where Blacks had equal rights with Whites. The new radical Republicans in Congress today are pushing back against cultural change to prevent the United States from further moving down the road toward an inclusive multicultural society. In their mirror world, they use the metapragmatic discourse of Trumpism to undermine the push for a more inclusive society. Their calling for their own "fake" civil war is designed to obfuscate that it is mostly them pushing back against mainstream society as it evolves. The disingenuous boomeranging, but especially the gaslighting, provides cover for their intensifying resistance. Metapragmatics provide cover and suggest it is both sides becoming implacably resistant, when one side is increasingly becoming extremist.

The Ominous Signs

To be sure, there are others talking about civil war, but most prominently they are academics who themselves are not for civil war but instead are assessing how the Right is pushing for it.[31] What they discuss needs to be taken seriously. Probably the most widely discussed book is by Barbara Walter, *How Civil Wars Start: And How to Stop Them.*[32] Walter is a long-time scholar on civil war around the world, especially in developing countries. She uses that deep knowledge to document how the United States has fallen down slipping into that space between democracy and autocracy, which she reminds us is sometimes referenced as "anocracy." According to Walter, the United States has lost its grip on maintaining a stable democratic system. It has drifted away from democracy due to a confluence of factors that have commonly led countries to slide toward an authoritarian takeover.

As a political scientist, Walter emphasizes statistical measures as well as her first-hand experience studying other countries that lost their democracies. In particular, she relies on the Polity Project at the Center for Systemic Peace started many years ago by the renowned scholar of political violence, Ted Gurr. The main indicator Walter invokes is the Polity Score that varies from −10 (fully authoritarian) to +10 (fully democratic). She indicates that

[30] Isaac, "Reflections on the New Anarchy and the Real Danger of MAGA Republicans."
[31] See Marche, *The Next Civil War*; and Walter, *How Civil Wars Start.*
[32] Barbara Walter, *How Civil Wars Start: And How to Stop Them* (Viking, 2022).

the US score in the era of Trumpism has been declining as the Republicans in Congress and the courts have helped Trump roll back safeguards against the abuse of presidential power; but the US score fell precipitously with the January 6th insurrection, dipping to its lowest level since 1800, when it was not clear that there would be a peaceful transition from the presidency of John Adams to Thomas Jefferson assuming the office.

Walter emphasizes that once a country falls into that gray area of anocracy between democracy and autocracy, that is when it is most likely to be vulnerable to civil war. The Polity Score data confirm this hypothesis. The instability of the situation increases the likelihood (see Figure 5.2). While this unstable situation is most likely when dictatorships get overthrown and are replaced by weak reformist governments, Walter notes that it can happen when countries move away from democracy as with Viktor Orban's Hungary or Donald Trump's America.

Using her experience with other countries and statistical indicators like the Polity Score, Walter provides credible evidence that the United States is losing its grip on democracy. She explains why our grip on democracy has weakened due to a number of factors, including the perhaps most significant factor of the dominant ethnic or religious group seeing its status decline. And then another common factor is when demagogues are making the most of the changing status of the dominant group to stir up people's resentments while targeting outgroups for demonization. These two important factors in fact hold in the United States today with the rise of Trumpism continuing to agitate people's resentments in just this way. Walter says Marjorie Taylor Greene is the most

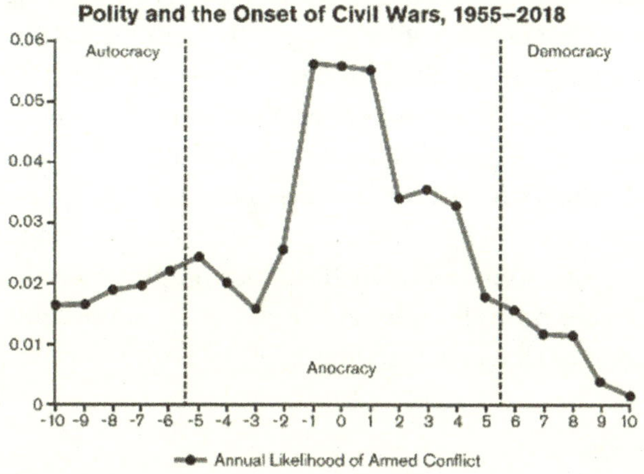

Figure 5.2 Polity and onset of civil wars, 1955–2018

Source: Barbara F. Walter, *How Civil Wars Start: And How to Stop Them* (Viking, 2022), 22.

prominent political leader whose polarizing rhetoric against the Democratic opposition includes endorsing civil war. She quotes Greene as saying: "the only way you get your freedoms back is it's earned with the price of blood."[33]

Yet the prospects for a civil war like the one we had over slavery are very low. The United States has a military now that is much stronger than that of 1860. Also, the geographic division is not as neat as when there was the battle between the North and the South. Instead, Walter says: "Those who wage war against their governments in the twenty-first century tend to avoid the battlefield entirely; they know they will almost certainly lose in a conventional war against a powerful government. Instead, they choose the strategy of the weak: guerrilla warfare and terrorism. And, increasingly, domestic terror campaigns are aimed at democratic governments."[34] This too is what we see in the United States today.

In fact, other scholars think that the new civil war has already started (something that Walter tends to agree with). This is the position of Stephen Marche who says: "Two things are happening at the same time. Most of the American right have abandoned faith in government as such. Their politics is, increasingly, the politics of the gun. The American left is slower on the uptake, but they are starting to figure out that the system which they give the name of democracy is less deserving of the name every year."[35]

Neither Walter nor Marche however give enough attention to the way Trumpism has operated as a discourse that helps legitimate its anti-democratic and authoritarian moves that only sometimes lead to gun violence. Trumpism does operate to vilify the opposition, the government, the press, and outgroups, but often features metapragmatic moves to make its outrageous statements acceptable. In the process, Trumpist discourse is proving successful with its base, legitimating their feelings that they are the real victims in our changing society. This emboldens their claim that they are the real proponents of liberal democracy and the individual rights it accords its citizens. Yet this pattern is not limited to terrorist manifestos or electoral campaign rhetoric. The Trumpist kind of discourse has also proven effective in enacting increasingly cruel public policies, by both states and the federal government. As a result, democratic institutions and practices as well as people and their rights are now all under attack ironically supposedly for failing to uphold a democracy that privileges the rights of Trump supporters. This kind

[33] Ibid., 172.

[34] Walter, *How Civil Wars Start*, 167–68.

[35] Stephen March, "The Next US Civil War is Already Here—We Just Refuse to See It," *Guardian*, January 4, 2022, https://www.theguardian.com/world/2022/jan/04/next-us-civil-war-already-here-we-refuse-to-see-it. Also, see Marche, *The Next Civil War*.

of linguistic jujitsu has proven dangerously effective. Three examples from the states confirm this analysis.

Greg Abbott Gaslights Gun Violence as Mental Illness

The United States has gone gun crazy. There has been a dramatic rise in gun ownership in recent decades, including owning assault rifles like the AR-15, which has become the most popular gun to buy in recent years.[36] About 6 percent of Americans now own an AR-15.[37] The most popular reason for buying one that people give is "self-defense." It is referred to as the "modern-day musket."[38] It also seems increasingly to be the preferred gun of the perpetrators of mass killings, including White Supremacists.[39] An AR-15 type gun was used in the failed assassination attempt of Donald Trump at a 2024 campaign rally.

Texas leads the country in gun sales.[40] Texas is also near the top in the country in mass shootings and deaths.[41] Yet, Texas Governor Greg Abbott refuses to support legislation that would limit access to guns of any kind, including the AR-15. Instead, since 2021, Texas has had a permitless carry law that allows a gun owner to openly carry a gun in public without a permit.[42] All the while, the mass shootings in Texas have become more frequent.[43]

Abbott's response is to avoid talking about banning assault weapons or limiting access to guns in any way. Instead, he wants to harden "soft targets" with more armed security guards and to investigate mental illness as the supposed

[36] Emily Guskin, Aadit Tambe, and Jon Gerberg, "Why Do Americans Own AR-15s?" *Washington Post*, March 27, 2023, https://www.washingtonpost.com/nation/interactive/2023/american-ar-15-gun-owners/.

[37] Jake Fogleman, "Poll: One in Twenty Americans Own an AR-15," *The Reload*, March 29, 2023, https://thereload.com/poll-one-in-twenty-americans-own-an-ar-15/.

[38] Todd C. Frankel, Shawn Boburg, Josh Dawsey, Ashley Parker, and Alex Horton, "The Gun that Divides a Nation," *Washington Post*, March 27, 2023, https://www.washingtonpost.com/nation/interactive/2023/ar-15-america-gun-culture-politics/.

[39] Solcyre Burga, "How the AR-15 Rifle Became America's Most Dangerous Weapon," *Time*, May 10, 2023, https://time.com/6278608/ar-15-rifle-assault-weapons-uvalde/.

[40] Caroline Covington, "Texas' Complex Relationship with Firearms: Len Gun Sales, but with a Declining Gun Ownership Rate," *The Texas Tribune*, July 28, 2022, https://www.texastribune.org/2022/07/28/texas-gun-stats/.

[41] Arianna Johnson, "Texas Has the Second Most Mass Shootings in 2023: How Its Other Gun Violence Crimes Measure Up," *Forbes*, May 8, 2023, www.forbes.com/sites/ariannajohnson/2023/05/08/texas-has-the-second-most-mass-shootings-in-2023-how-its-other-gun-violence-crimes-measure-up/?sh=240eb41e54b0.

[42] Mandi Cai and Chris Essig, "Texas has had Nine Mass Shootings in the Past 14 Years, while Lawmakers have Steadily Loosened Restrictions on Carrying Firearms," *The Texas Tribune*, May 8, 2023, https://apps.texastribune.org/features/2019/texas-10-years-of-mass-shootings-timeline/.

[43] Ibid.

cause for many attacks.[44] This is pure gaslighting, thoroughly consonant with the way Trumpism talks about a whole panoply of issues the Movement refuses to address. This subterfuge amounts to lying about the causes of gun violence today. This is of necessity as Trumpists seek to maintain the support of gun owners. Yet, they then must turn a blind eye to doing anything about the increases in gun deaths, even when there are more mass shootings popping up at schools, churches, shopping malls, and grocery stores.

Although mental illness is a factor in leading to some mass shootings, most shootings in fact, including mass shootings, do not clearly involve issues of mental illness per se. While it is clear that most mass shootings are conducted by people who are angry and have issues of hate toward others, most of these people have not been shown to have diagnosable conditions beyond that.[45] Then there is the issue of "soft targets." Jamelle Bouie has asked an important question that takes on growing importance with the rise in the number of mass shootings. He has asked:

> What is a "soft target"? It is a school or a mall or a church or a gym. It is a library, a movie theater, a grocery store or anywhere people gather to live their lives. What would it mean to "harden" those targets, most of which have already been targeted at one point or another? It would mean additional police officers and armed security; metal detectors and reinforced doors designed to bar entry; heightened scrutiny for visitors and even mandatory checks for identification.
>
> To harden our soft targets is, in other words, to turn the entire country into an airport security line. And far from a free society, this hardened America would be a continental version of Baghdad's Green Zone, each checkpoint or guard a visible reminder that we've organized our entire lives around the prospect of instant death by lethal violence.[46]

Governor Abbott's invocation of mental illness is an established fallback position on the Right. Immediately following the mass shooting at a school in Nashville, Tennessee, in March 2023, Rep. Andy Ogles (R-TN) said: "Ultimately I think what this does is highlight some of the mental health issues, the mental health crisis we have in this country that needs to be the real

[44] David Nakamura and Karin Brulliard, "Weakened Gun Laws Put Texas Gov. Greg Abbott on the Defensive," *Washington Post*, May 25, 2022, www.washingtonpost.com/nation/2022/05/25/uvalde-shooting-laws/.

[45] James Silver, Andre Simons, and Sarah Craun, *A Study of the Pre-Attack Behaviors of Active Shooters in the United States between 2000 and 2013* (U.S. Department of Justice, Federal Bureau of Investigation, 2018).

[46] Jamelle Bouie, "A Gun-Filled America Is a World of Fear and Alienation," *New York Times*, May 9, 2023, https://www.nytimes.com/2023/05/09/opinion/allen-texas-shooting-guns.html.

conversation we're having right now."[47] Yet right after that, Ogles and other House Republicans voted against more federal funding for mental health services, sending that bill down to defeat.[48] The concern for mental health is as hollow as offering "thoughts and prayers" after each mass shooting. "Thoughts and prayers" is but just another way of trying to show you are concerned about growing gun violence but then not having to do anything about it. It is classic Trumpism of "sorry, not sorry."

Invoking "mental health" is a co-optation of the Left's concern about the government's failure to address the lack of mental health services in the country. Yet, in the hands of the Right, "mental health" is mostly a dodge. It is yet another way of saying "guns don't kill people, people do." When co-opting the concern about mental health, Right-Wing elected officials like Abbott are often only interested in taking certain actions, and then often reluctantly. They can be pressed to support "red flags" that bar people with a history of mental illness from getting a gun. Yet Trumpism generally opposes even that. One of Trump's first actions as President after getting elected in 2016 was to sign into law a repeal of an Obama-era check on access to guns by people with documented mental health problems.[49]

Another old saw for opponents of gun control was: "The only thing that stops a bad guy with a gun is a good guy with a gun." For a while, the call for more armed personnel on site was the response to mass killings around the country, and especially in Texas after the horrific mass shooting at the Robb elementary school in Uvalde, Texas, in 2022 that left nineteen young children and two teachers dead.[50] After Uvalde, Texas Attorney General Ken Paxton called for arming teachers and Sen. Ted Cruz (R-TX) said: "We know from past experience that the most effective tool for keeping kids safe is armed law enforcement on the campus."[51] But then the videos leaked showing the full squadron of armed local and state law enforcement officers hanging back in the hallway while the Uvalde shooter was still doing his killing. There is no evidence that shows this is an effective solution, especially as mass shootings are almost always unanticipated; and with AR-15s being the gun of choice

[47] See U.S. Congressman Mike Thompson, Press Release: "Thompson Releases Statement on Republicans Refusing to Save Lives," March 28, 2023, mikethompson.house.gov/newsroom/press-releases/thompson-releases-statement-republicans-refusing-save-lives.

[48] Ibid.

[49] Ali Vitali, "Trump Signs Bill Revoking Obama-Era Gun Checks for People with Mental Illnesses," *NBC News*, February 28, 2017, https://www.nbcnews.com/news/us-news/trump-signs-bill-revoking-obama-era-gun-checks-people-mental-n727221.

[50] Susan Milligan, "Uvalde, Buffalo Shootings Expose the Myth of the 'Good Guy with a Gun,'" *U.S. New and World Report*, May 27, 2022, https://www.usnews.com/news/the-report/articles/2022-05-27/uvalde-buffalo-shootings-expose-the-myth-of-the-good-guy-with-a-gun.

[51] Ibid.

for these killers, the killing happens so fast with the use of a semi-automatic weapon that was originally designed for use on the battlefield. Whether guns or people kill people, arming others is not an effective deterrent to stop the killing and suggesting that it is amounts to just more gaslighting.

The metapragmatics is a way to gaslight a populace when there is overwhelming support even in Texas for "common sense" gun reforms such as raising the minimum age to eighteen for a gun purchase.[52] Greg Abbott's desperation to avoid having to enact those reforms in the face of growing mass killings in his state is itself very much consistent with the trajectory of Trumpism. For years, Right-Wing political leaders like Abbott gained support by telling Republicans that the opposition was coming for their guns and was going to take away "our freedoms."[53] They have been aided greatly in this gaslighting by the National Rifle Association operating as a well-heeled lobby to fund campaigns of legislators and members of Congress, as well as governors and presidents who are willing to oppose gun reform. After a certain point in this concerted campaign to resist reform despite public demand for action, there is no turning back, even when it means you will be seen as indifferent to people, including young children, getting slaughtered. Your only alternatives, short of switching sides, is to boomerang and gaslight, or even co-opt the Left's concern for providing more assistance for treatment of mental illness. The result is more gobbledygook that tries to resist doing what needs to be done.

The gun culture is strong in Texas, but its ability to resist criticism from other parts of the country is not quite as strong as it could be if a civil war led to a new constitutional system. Intense commitment to protecting gun rights can lead to growing interest in revising the current constitutional system, where increased state rights about issues regarding guns would be less subject to attack. Abbott's Texas would then be better able to avoid criticism coming from Washington and more liberal corners of the country with increased separation. The idea of separating in some way, as Marjorie Taylor Greene insinuates, gains increased credibility and fuels support for an Article V convention to revise the current constitution. And if that is not enough, there is the possibility that the people with guns will use them to force the separation.

[52] Texas Democrats, "Texas Democrats Demand Gun Safety Reforms Before the Adjournment of the 88th Legislative Session," May 7, 2024, https://www.texasdemocrats.org/media/texas-democrats-demand-gun-safety-reforms-before-the-adjournment-of-the-88th-legislative-session.

[53] Rep. Jim Jordan (R-OH), Chair of the House Judiciary, frequently complains about Americans losing their freedoms but only about selected issues, including gun rights. See U.S. Congress, House of Representatives, Judiciary Committee, Press Release Announcement, "Jim Jordan: Dems 'Coming Directly After Your Second Amendment Liberties,'" July 19, 2022, https://judiciary.house.gov/media/press-releases/jim-jordan-dems-coming-directly-after-your-second-amendment-liberties.

As outrageous as that seems, there are people on the Right who openly express such views.[54] This is where the trajectory of Trumpism has pointed for some of the more extreme Trumpers.

The New States' Rights: Prosecuting Women Who Travel Out-of-State

Marjorie Taylor Greene backed down from calling for civil war, boomeranging that it was the Left that wants civil war. She stepped back further saying somewhat murkily that we need a "national divorce." And then she almost immediately rephrased it as "a legal agreement to separate our ideological and political disagreements by states while maintaining our legal union."[55] So ultimately her call for civil war was actually intoning the South's call for states' rights, now in a different idiom. Yet, the trajectory of Trumpism has bent "states' rights" into a hideous perversion, where states get to deny their citizens basic rights, except when it comes to gun rights, as in letting them brandish guns in public without permits. Under Trumpism, states' rights come to include the right to abrogate US citizens' constitutional rights, like the right to travel out-of-state to get an abortion.[56]

That might be Idaho, where, in May 2023, Republican Governor Brad Little signed into law legislation that prohibits citizens from assisting females under eighteen to cross state lines to get an abortion, with criminal penalties that could include two to five years in prison. Is this the new states' rights where states are authorized to override the federal government, ignore Supreme Court precedent, and deny citizens constitutional rights? States had only recently gained the leeway to ban abortion outright when in 2022 in the case *Dobbs v. Jackson Women's Health Organization (2022)* the US Supreme Court overturned *Roe v. Wade (1973)*, which established the constitutional right to abortion that had stood for almost fifty years.[57] Now Idaho was flexing its new-found muscles to not just ban abortion. It was going further to

[54] "Pushing Election Lies, TPUSA Audience Member Asks Charlie Kirk When They Can 'Use the Guns' and 'Kill These People,'" *Media Matters*, October 26, 2021, https://www.mediamatters.org/charlie-kirk/pushing-election-lies-tpusa-audience-member-asks-charlie-kirk-when-they-can-use-guns; and "'When Do We Get to Use the Guns?': Attendee Shut Down at Right-Wing Event," *CNN Politics*, www.cnn.com/videos/politics/2021/10/27/charlie-kirk-denounces-violence-mh-orig.cnn.

[55] Baker, "MTG Defends Her Call to Split Up the US by Saying the Country Is Moving towards Another Civil War."

[56] PBS News Hour, "Transcript: Idaho Criminalizes Helping Minors Travel Out of State to Get an Abortion," May 5, 2023, https://www.pbs.org/newshour/show/idaho-criminalizes-helping-minors-travel-out-of-state-to-get-an-abortion.

[57] *Dobbs v. Jackson Women's Health Organization*, No. 19-1392, 597 U.S. (2022); and *Roe v. Wade*, 410 U.S. 113 (1973).

assert that its powers as a state in the federal system extended to limiting the rights of its citizens to be assisted in traveling out-of-state. At a minimum, this brazen attempt to extend the state's power to ban abortion suggested a new federalism where states could criminalize the actions of their citizens for simply assisting a minor in traveling out-of-state and seeking health services that were available in another state.

This was, it seems, a significant change in US federalism. A number of states require minors to have parental permission in order to get an abortion. But this is a restriction of a different order. It criminalizes anyone who helps a minor go out-of-state to access abortion services even if the parents approve. Further, you could conceivably argue that Idaho's ban violated the "Full Faith and Credit Clause" of Article IV, Section 1, of the US Constitution that states: "Full Faith and Credit shall be given in each State to the public Acts, Records, and judicial Proceedings of every other State." In other words, if a young woman went to another state to get an abortion, where that state had offered that service, the state from where the woman came had no business saying that the other state's services were legally suspect, even if they banned that service (abortion) in their own state. I guess Idaho could say they were not questioning the other state's right to offer abortion services, but instead it was only imposing criminal penalties on those who helped the young woman travel out-of-state to access those legal services.

Yet, the Idaho ban was a perversion of federalism in another perhaps more frightening way. The Idaho law arguably contravenes the federal right to travel as established by the US Supreme Court. The right to travel is a well-established constitutional right, affirmed in a welfare-rights case in the late 1960s. It was reaffirmed in the welfare rights case *Saenz v. Roe (1999)*.[58] Therefore, when Idaho enacted its anti-assist in traveling for abortion law, it was putting states' rights above federal power to enforce individual rights. Therefore, not only was the ban abrogating a fundamental constitutional right, it was acting in a way that contravened the Supremacy Clause of the Constitution (Article VI, Clause 2) that states: "This Constitution, and the Laws of the United States which shall be made in Pursuance thereof; and all Treaties made, or which shall be made, under the Authority of the United States, shall be the *supreme Law of the Land*; and the Judges in every State shall be bound thereby, any Thing in the Constitution or Laws of any State to the Contrary notwithstanding."[59] In other words, states are bound to uphold federal law, including the right to travel out-of-state to access services in another state.

[58] 526 U.S. 489. The decision was 7–2 with even Justice Antonin Scalia joining in the majority. Justice Clarence Thomas was one of the two who did not.

[59] Italics added.

This is no minor transgression. States defying federal law is at the core of the original Civil War.

Idaho was so keen to prevent its citizens from getting abortions that it enacted a subterranean law that put state power above federal power in contravention of the Constitution. It inverted federalism while indirectly denying its citizens a basic right enshrined in the US Constitution. I do not see how this is consistent with Marjorie Taylor Greene's statement that we needed a new "legal agreement to separate our ideological and political disagreements by states while maintaining our legal union." This is not maintaining the union. It is undermining the Constitution, its principles, and the rights accorded citizens. If Greene and other Trumpists support Idaho in this endeavor, then they are not asking for a legal agreement that gives states new rights under "our legal union." They are seeking to empower states in ways that would eventually dissolve the union and the constitutional system that supports it. No amount of bad-mouthing the federal government as undermining their rights could justify supporting states taking away individual rights granted by the Constitution. This is boomeranging and co-opting with flagrant disregard for the basic rules of the US Constitution.

The Idaho law was challenged.[60] Yet, the Supreme Court would not prevent it from going into effect while the case works its way through the courts. In the interim, other states enacted similar bans regarding out-of-state travel. A threat by the Alabama Attorney General to prosecute people aiding out-of-state travel for getting an abortion was explicitly rejected by a federal judge for violating the constitutional right to travel.[61] These attempts at hindering out-of-state travel for abortion will likely end up before the US Supreme Court. Yet a 6–3 majority of Republican appointees (three by Trump) on the Court makes the final outcome uncertain. They are not the same justices who specified the constitutional right to travel in the welfare cases. The conservative jurists who dominate the Court today have already repealed the constitutional right to abortion, but whether they are ready to repeal significant dimensions of the federal system or to undermine the constitutional right to travel is another matter. How far are they willing to go to allow Marjorie Taylor Greene's "national divorce" to go into effect? If they uphold the Idaho law, then they are authorizing each state to go very far down the

[60] Megan Burbank, "Activists Sue Idaho Over 'Abortion Trafficking' Travel Ban," *Crosscut Cascade PBS*, August 3, 2023, https://crosscut.com/news/2023/08/activists-sue-idaho-over-abortion-trafficking-travel-ban.

[61] John Fritze, "Federal Judge Blasts Threat by Alabama to Prosecute Groups Aiding Out-of-State Abortions," *CNN*, May 7, 2024, https://ktvz.com/politics/cnn-us-politics/2024/05/07/federal-judge-blasts-threat-by-alabama-to-prosecute-groups-aiding-out-of-state-abortions/.

road to becoming more than a police state. They are authorizing states to ignore their relationship to other states and the US Constitution as well. States will be authorized to become rouge actors in an extra-constitutional system. The "national divorce" will indeed be closer to "civil war" than it might sound at first. That would be a remarkable discursive move, a gaslighting of extra-constitutional proportions.

There is indeed an "inverted federalism" that is making Marjorie Taylor Greene's idea of a "national divorce" more plausible. For years, the federal government was the engine of innovation in the federal system using both the "carrots" of federal grants-in-aid and the "sticks" of regulation and mandates to get states to adopt advances in public policy.[62] In recent years, the federal government has been mired in policy paralysis wrought by polarization.[63] As a result, states have come to take actions on their own across a number of policy areas. State initiative can even take the form of a progressive "activist form of bottom-up federalism," where citizens in the states approve referenda to change public policy on any number of issues where the federal government has failed to act.[64] This activist bottom-up federalism sometimes occurs where there is extreme gerrymandering and the legislature is not representative of the state's citizenry overall act, and the legislature acts independently to make policy that moves the state further away from what most people support.[65] Referenda initiatives can counter the unrepresentativeness of state legislatures as well as respond to policy paralysis at the federal level.

Some states have made major advances in social and economic policy.[66] Other states, often via legislatures enacting new laws, have used their powers to impose conservative policy on guns, abortion, the schools, gender identity, and other cultural issues.[67] The differences in states in practicing this new inverted federalism have widened preexisting state disparities based on differing political cultures and partisan alignments. This inverted federalism is pulling the states apart, making living in one or another state a very

[62] Susan Welch and Kay Thompson, "The Impact of Federal Incentives on State Policy Innovation," *American Journal of Political Science* 24, no. 4 (November 1980): 715–29.

[63] Cynthia R. Farina, "Congressional Polarization: Terminal Constitutional Dysfunction?" *Columbia Law Review* 115 (2015): 1689. Also see Jacob M. Grumbach, *Laboratories Against Democracy: How National Parties Transformed State Politics* (Princeton University Press, 2022).

[64] Kathleen Ferraiolo, "State Policy Activism via Direct Democracy in Response to Federal Partisan Polarization," *Publius: The Journal of Federalism* 47, no. 3 (Summer 2017): 378–402, https://doi.org/10.1093/publius/pjx032.

[65] Jane Mayer, "State Legislatures Are Torching Democracy," *New Yorker*, August 15, 2022, https://www.newyorker.com/magazine/2022/08/15/state-legislatures-are-torching-democracy.

[66] See Ryan Cooper, "The New Minnesota Vikings," *The American Prospect*, May 22, 2023.

[67] David Pepper, *Laboratories of Autocracy: A Wake-Up Call from Behind the Lines* (St. Helena Press, 2021).

different experience for ordinary citizens, especially for the most disadvantaged.[68] Idaho's controversial abortion travel ban is but an extreme example of how a state legislature can intensify states pulling apart in an age of inverted federalism.

There is tremendous variation among the states on the right to abortion. According to the Guttmacher Institute, four states have passed a constitutional amendment explicitly declaring that their constitution does not secure or protect the right to abortion or allow the use of public funds for abortion, while seventeen states and the District of Columbia have laws that protect the right to abortion.[69] Three of these states have protections for the right to abortion in their state constitutions. But since the *Dobbs* decision, twelve states have imposed total or near-total bans on abortion (some of which were pre-existing bans, only reactivated once *Roe* was overturned).[70] Several additional states have no clinics to perform abortions. A number of other states have gestational bans, with the abortion bans beginning as early as six weeks in the case of Georgia and twelve or fifteen weeks in a few other states. As many as twenty-four states were expected to have total or partial bans in place during 2023. The ground is shifting radically, putting women's health in jeopardy in some states more than others.[71]

The issue of having to go out-of-state to get an abortion had been increasing in intensity before the *Dobbs* decision. Yet, immediately after *Dobbs*, it burst on the headlines when a ten-year-old girl from Ohio, who had been raped, went to Indiana to get an abortion. The Ohio Attorney General David Yost initially stated publicly he doubted the girl's story though eventually someone was charged with her rape.[72] In response, women's groups worked with others in a broad coalition to get a referendum initiative on the ballot to revise the State's Constitution to guarantee women (and girls) the right to abortion. Yet the Republican-dominated state legislature responded by calling for a referendum to require an extra-majority 60 percent of those voting to approve

[68] Jacob M. Grumbach, "From Backwaters to Major Policymakers: Policy Polarization in the States, 1970–2014," *Perspectives on Politics* 16, no. 2 (2018): 416–35; and Jacob M. Grumbach and Jamila Michener, "American Federalism, Political Inequality, and Democratic Erosion," *The ANNALS* 699, no. 1 (2022): 143–55, https://doi.org/10.1177/00027162211070885.

[69] "Abortion Policy in the Absence of Roe," *Guttmacher Institute*, April 24, 2023, https://www.guttmacher.org/state-policy/explore/abortion-policy-absence-roe.

[70] Elizabeth Nash and Isabel Guarnieri, "Six Months Post-Roe, 24 US States Have Banned Abortion or Are Likely to Do So: A Roundup," *Guttmacher Institute*, January 2023, https://www.guttmacher.org/2023/01/six-months-post-roe-24-us-states-have-banned-abortion-or-are-likely-do-so-roundup.

[71] Tanya Albert Henry, "Access to Abortion and Women's Health: What the Research Shows, *American Medical Association*, July 5, 2022, https://www.ama-assn.org/delivering-care/population-care/access-abortion-and-women-s-health-what-research-shows.

[72] Marty Schladen, "Affidavits: 2 More Pregnant Minors Who Were Raped Were Denied Ohio Abortions," *Ohio Capital Journal*, September 26, 2022, https://www.cincinnati.com/story/news/2022/09/27/affidavits-2-more-raped-minors-were-denied-ohio-abortions/69520380007/.

any constitutional amendments.[73] The Republicans were not giving up, even if it meant they were at risk of being seen as anti-democratic or at least anti-majority rule. In the end, the Republicans lost both the 60 percent and the right to abortion referenda.

When testifying before the Ohio Legislature about the controversy, Ohio anti-abortion activist Laura Strietmann addressed the rape of the ten-year-old girl by saying that, while the child's pregnancy "might have been difficult, [...] a woman's body is designed to carry life. That is a biological fact."[74] When anti-abortion activists say, "that's a fact," there is reason to suspect they doth protest too much. These days, it seems to be a common refrain among Trumpists who want to assert as fact unsubstantiated nonfacts, rumors, lies, and conspiracy theories. It is akin to what Trump said regarding his infamous claim about the Charlottesville race riot that there were "fine people on both sides," to which he added: "I have no doubt about it, and you don't have any doubt about it either."[75] It remains a mystery how Trump knew nobody had any doubts about his outrageous statement. To say "that's a fact" about something controversial is a tell that you are straining to make a claim that really is not well-supported by facts.

But there was something worse in the anti-abortion activist Strietmann's testimony: She called the ten-year-old child who had been raped "a woman." While some states require minors to get parental permission for an abortion, here the ten-year-old girl is being assumed to be "a woman" (who incidentally had received permission and assistance in traveling out-of-state from her parents to get an abortion).[76] The gaslighting contradictorily treats girls as too young to decide to have an abortion but old enough to bear a child. The deflection here was conveniently adultifying the victim so as to make it seem plausible that she could easily endure childbirth, which actually, it turns out, is not true.[77] Actually, pregnancy and childbirth complications are the leading killer of girls aged fifteen to nineteen worldwide, according to the World

[73] Ian Cross and Morgan Trau, "Ohio Lawmakers Pass Resolution to Ask Voters to Require 60% Vote to Amend Constitution Ahead of Abortion Vote," *News 5 Cleveland*, May 10, 2023, https://www.news5cleveland.com/news/politics/ohio-politics/house-passes-resolution-to-require-60-supermajority-to-amend-ohio-constitution-ahead-of-nov-abortion-vote.

[74] Giulia Carbonaro, "Young Girls' Bodies 'Designed' to Carry Babies—Anti-Abortion Activist," *Newsweek*, April 21, 2023, https://www.newsweek.com/young-girls-bodies-carry-babies-anti-abortion-activist-1795813.

[75] "President Donald Trump on Charlottesville: You Had Very Fine People, on Both Sides," *CNBC*, *YouTube*, https://www.youtube.com/watch?v=JmaZR8E12bs.

[76] Ava Sasani, "Suspect Is Arrested in Ohio after Rape of 10-Year-Old Girl," *New York Times*, July 16, 2022, https://www.nytimes.com/2022/07/13/us/ohio-arrest-rape-abortion.html.

[77] See Nicoletta Lanese, "What's the Youngest Age that a Person Can Get Pregnant and Give Birth?" *Live Science*, August 2, 2022, https://www.livescience.com/youngest-age-give-birth-pregnancy.

Health Organization.[78] In this context, gaslighting girls as women capable of bearing children can be lethal. It is much more than mere talk, especially when testifying before a congressional committee.

At the time, US Senator J. D. Vance (R-OH) was a candidate and he wanted to remind everyone that the rapist was an "illegal immigrant." This was a rather desperate instance of gaslighting. Vance had previously said questions about the health of the mother were "inconvenient," adding "the question to me is really about the baby."[79] Vance has once been critical of Trump, but then sought his endorsement and eventually became an ardent defender. (Vance eventually was chosen by Trump to be his vice presidential candidate in 2024). Here he was practicing pure Trumpism gaslighting, deflecting attention away from the girl who had been raped to focus on the rapist and reminding everyone about the supposed threat immigrants posed.

For a long time, the major gaslight on the abortion issue was that anti-abortion activists claimed they were "pro-life." The Pro-Life Movement has for decades demonstrated its lack of concern about the lives of pregnant women or, now we see quite clearly, girls. It is not a fact that life begins with insemination or that any fetus should be considered a life that must be saved. Rather than admitting that the question of when life begins is subject to debate, the Pro-Life Movement asserts they know the answer. Like Trump, they are saying "[We] don't have any doubt about it and you don't have any doubt about it either." The pro-fetus, anti-pregnant women and girls movement would be a more appropriate name. But I would settle just for the gaslighting to stop. In the meantime, the anti-abortion movement is still pushing the country apart and leading states to act outside the bounds of the Constitution. The national divorce that Marjorie Taylor Greene hopes for seems ever closer.

The American public however increasingly was supporting abortion rights and states began to increasingly support legal changes granting the right to abortion after the Dobbs decision. Trump himself was forced to modify his position in a desperate move to maintain electability. "This is why he has tried the two-step of celebrating his appointments to the (U.S. Supreme) Court but distancing himself from the consequences, both practical and political, of his anti-abortion accomplishments," noted Jamelle Bouie.[80] Trump's classic

[78] Jill Filipovic, "Opinion: Cruel GOP Rhetoric about Rape Survivors and Abortion Is Far More than Words," *CNN*, June 28, 2022, https://www.cnn.com/2022/06/28/opinions/abortion-ban-rape-exception-republicans-filipovic/index.html.

[79] Ibid.

[80] Jamelle Bouie, "Donald Trump Is Stuck," *New York Times*, September 6, 2024, https://www.nytimes.com/2024/09/06/opinion/trump-dobbs-abortion.html.

metapragmatic two-step got invoked when he announced at the height of the 2024 campaign that he was proud to appoint the justices that overturned the constitutional right to abortion, but he supported states deciding what to do about that. Further, as the campaign reached its zenith, Melania Trump, who had been silent for most of it, announced she supported a national right to abortion.[81] This was yet again the classic metapragmatic move of Trumpism with Trump's initial push to crack down on abortion getting softened by his wife. The discourse of Trumpism was forever seeking to normalize its extremism with contradictory statements designed to gaslight the public.

Where Woke Goes to Die: Co-opting "Critical Race Theory"

We can see the metapragmatics of Trumpism operating on other cultural clashes. The Right-Wing publicist Christopher Rufo rose to prominence in the pantheon of Trump propagandists when he succeeded in making "critical race theory" a popular Trumpist meme. Rufo says he liked the term because it sounded like something he could use as a "political battering ram." "I basically took that body of criticism ... and made it political. Turned it into a salient political issue with a clear villain."[82] In other words, he did not really care what the term actually referred to but how it could become a target of demonization.

Critical Race Theory was originally a school of thought, first developed by progressive law professors in the 1980s to examine the structural causes of racism.[83] Rufo however co-opted the term, using it to demonize first diversity training and then just about any teaching about America's racial history. It was his way of pushing back against nascent progressive efforts to teach more honestly about the history of race relations, inspired in part by the killing of George Floyd by a Minneapolis police officer in 2020. The highjacking of Critical Race Theory helped create a moral panic among parents with children in elementary school to oppose their children having to learn what they were

[81] Aaron Blake, "Why is Melania Trump Coming Out for Abortion Rights?" *Washington Post*, October 3, 2024, https://www.washingtonpost.com/politics/2024/10/03/why-is-melania-trump-coming-out-abortion-rights/.

[82] David Theo Goldberg, "Meet Christopher Rufo—Leader of the Incoherent Right-Wing Attack on 'Critical Race Theory,'" *Salon*, August 1, 2021, www.salon.com/2021/08/01/meet-christopher-rufo—leader-of-the-incoherent-right-wing-attack-on-critical-race-theory/?fbclid=IwAR388ek1SIB1y1l8Xnjr-wTEL9xRFuyZYQcx4hjA2N0D7OTy9wDxPtIar3o.

[83] Richard Delgado and Jean Stefancic, *Critical Race Theory: An Introduction* (New York University Press, 2001). Kimberlé Crenshaw is widely credited with coining the term and she and others, such as Derrick Bell, published the initial analyses that employed Critical Race Theory.

told was Critical Race Theory, even though schoolteachers were not actually teaching it. Trump saw Rufo on Fox News, invited him to the White House, and then issued an executive order repealing diversity training for federal bureaucrats. States passed laws banning the teaching of Critical Race Theory even though it was still not being taught in most cases, especially at an elementary school. Rufo would eventually say, "We have successfully frozen their brand—'critical race theory'—into the public conversation and are steadily driving up negative perceptions. We will eventually turn it toxic, as we put all of the various cultural insanities under that brand category. The goal is to have the public read something crazy in the newspaper and immediately think 'critical race theory.' We have decodified the term and will recodify it to annex the entire range of cultural constructions that are unpopular with Americans."[84]

The Rufo-caused moral panic helped swing the Virginia gubernatorial election to Glenn Youngkin in 2021, and it eventually made Rufo a top advisor to Gov. Ron DeSantis (R-FL). DeSantis used this panic to get books banned from school libraries, textbooks rewritten, and the curriculum in public schools restricted when it came to teaching about race. Even college courses were scrutinized and restricted as to what they should say about race. The Individual Freedom Act, also known as the "Stop Woke Act," was signed into law by DeSantis in 2022. "It bans teaching that one race or gender is morally superior to another and prohibits teachers from making students feel guilty for past discrimination by members of their race. And it specifically bars portraying racial colorblindness—which the law labels a virtue—as racist."[85]

Today, learning about the history of race relations in the United States is very different in states like Florida in comparison to New York or California. Alabama and other states have followed Florida in prohibiting the teaching of "divisive concepts" in public schools, including colleges, and universities, an evident attempt to ban teaching about the history of White racism.[86] The country is seemingly pulling apart not just on guns and abortion but also what the generations coming up get to learn. In the states where Trumpism is ascendant, young students are sheltered from the truth, clearly an ominous sign of what the future might bring.

[84] Victor Ray, "Critical Race Theory's Merchants of Doubt," *Time*, August 1, 2022, https://time.com/6202664/critical-race-theorys-merchants-of-doubt/.

[85] Daniel Golden, "Muzzled by DeSantis, Critical Race Theory Professors Cancel Courses or Modify Their Teaching," *ProPublica*, January 3, 2023, https://www.propublica.org/article/desantis-critical-race-theory-florida-college-professors.

[86] Ryan Quinn, "Alabama Governor Signs Bill Targeting DEI, 'Divisive Concepts,'" *Inside Higher Education*, March 22, 2024, https://www.insidehighered.com/news/quick-takes/2024/03/22/alabama-governor-oks-bill-targeting-dei-divisive-concepts.

Once again co-opting for purposes of denigrating an idea like "Critical Race Theory" can be an effective strategy. And co-opting the term "woke" for sensitivity to instances of racial injustice to make it sound bad follows the same insidious metapragmatic path. These discursive moves make progressive politics look bad, just by perverting the meaning of the terms in question. Such metapragmatic moves reference what the other side is saying in ways that are designed to repudiate them. The campaign against Critical Race Theory as being "too woke" is making a statement about the discourse of the other side, recharacterizing it in ways that are denigrating. It is using the Left's words against itself.

This type of double-speak about the simple, honest teaching of US history at all levels so as to tell a fuller story about race relations is made out to be an insidious plot to make White people, young students in particular, to hate themselves for being White. Nobody, however, was even trying to do that, and Critical Race Theory was never about shaming people, young students or adults. No one actually was trying to do that. Rufo's propaganda was outrageous in lying about the efforts to teach the history of race relations. Yet, it came to be outrageously successful, proving once again the extent to which Trumpism as a metapragmatic discourse frequently was about demonizing the opposition, just to get votes and stay in power. And as Fox News and the rest of the Right-Wing media outlets and social media threads were quick to get on board, the propaganda could spread quickly, and the demonization could go viral.

Another related example of metapragmatic co-optation for purposes of denigration is "social justice warriors," once strictly a positive appellation on the Left has over time become an epithet among Trumpers who want to excoriate people for being too earnest in trying to change society for the better.[87] Critical Race Theory is however the most dramatic example of co-optation in today's installment of the ongoing Culture War. It co-opted a relatively uncontroversial school of scholarship among a limited group of social and legal theorists, falsely implied it was a public-school curricular effort and ended up scaring parents and gaining their votes for Trump-aligned candidates. This accelerated to the point where teaching about race in some states is now profoundly hampered or perverted, while other states work to enlighten young minds as best they can.

[87] See Phoebe Cohen, *Populism, Framing, and the Alt-Right: How the Social Justice Warrior Became a Symbol of Rightwing Resentment* (Senior Thesis Submitted to the Political Science Department, Hunter College, CUNY, December 21, 2022).

The success of co-opting Critical Race Theory and boomeranging it into an epithet eventually laid the groundwork for a wider assault on educational institutions and diversity, equity, and inclusion (DEI) initiatives more broadly. Rufo ultimately was at the forefront in the successful effort to force Harvard University President Claudine Gay (the first Black president of Harvard) to resign due to flimsy plagiarism charges first lodged by Rufo himself. After Gay resigned, Rufo declared: "We launched the Claudine Gay plagiarism story from the Right. The next step is to smuggle it into the media apparatus of the Left, legitimizing the narrative to center-left actors who have the power to topple her. Then squeeze."[88]

His demonizing strategy of boomeranging and co-opting terms to be used as epithets against his opponents could not be clearer. In the process, propagandistic uses of lying and spreading misinformation to normalize his demonizations as legitimate criticisms have proven outstandingly effective. In response, Gay wrote poignantly the day after resigning:

> As I depart, I must offer a few words of warning. The campaign against me was about more than one university and one leader. This was merely a single skirmish in a broader war to unravel public faith in pillars of American society. Campaigns of this kind often start with attacks on education and expertise, because these are the tools that best equip communities to see through propaganda. But such campaigns don't end there. Trusted institutions of all types—from public health agencies to news organizations—will continue to fall victim to coordinated attempts to undermine their legitimacy and ruin their leaders' credibility. For the opportunists driving cynicism about our institutions, no single victory or toppled leader exhausts their zeal.[89]

A Smoldering Civil War

These examples of the use of gaslighting, boomeranging, and co-opting highlight that much of the growing division that Marjorie Taylor Greene and other Trumpists are calling a civil war is visible even if there is no armed conflict. Today, we have something less than a hot civil war. There are no armies

[88] Christopher F. Rufo, "How We Squeezed Harvard to Push Claudine Gay Out," *Wall Street Journal*, January 3, 2024, https://www.wsj.com/articles/how-we-squeezed-harvard-claudine-gay-firing-dei-antisemitism-culture-war-a6843c4c.

[89] Claudine Gay, "What Just Happened at Harvard Is Bigger Than Me," *New York Times*, January 3, 2024, https://www.nytimes.com/2024/01/03/opinion/claudine-gay-harvard-president.html.

engaging the US military. Nonetheless, it seems that that is increasingly a real possibility. Today there is on the Right what Jamelle Bouie has called a new "thirst for vigilantism."[90]

An extreme example is Texas where officers from the Texas Military Department blocked federal Border Patrol agents from responding to help a family that was crossing the Rio Grande into Texas from Mexico. The two children and their mother drowned.[91] Texas insisted on keeping up the razor-wire it had installed at the border, in spite of a US Supreme Court ruling that the Biden Administration's Department of Homeland Security was authorized as a matter of federalism to take down the fencing and maintain its authority for policing the border.[92] All other Republican governors except for Phil Scott of Vermont quickly said they stood with Texas Governor Abbott. Donald Trump added he wanted all the Republican governors to send their states' National Guard to stand with Texas in defending the border.[93]

The gaslight that Trump, Abbott, and several of the supporting Republican governors used to legitimate their subversion of the law was that supposedly the US Constitution empowered states to take action against an "invasion" (in this case against allegedly being inundated by drug dealers, terrorists, and unspecified threatening "others" who were assumed to predominate among the immigrants crossing the border).[94] In his second term in office, Trump would lean heavily on this reinterpretation to justify mass detention, extraordinary renditions and deportations under the guise of saying that was authorized by the Alien Enemies Act of 1798 for removing people from the country during wartime.[95] Yet there are two major problems with this assertion associated with the two times the Constitution specifically talks about "invasion."

First, the initial "invasion clause" Abbott referred to in the written statement he released to justify his actions actually specifies that it is the federal

[90] Jamelle Bouie, "The Republican Embrace of Vigilantism Is No Accident," *New York Times*, May 16, 2023, https://www.nytimes.com/2023/05/16/opinion/neely-penny-perry-rittenhouse-desantis.html.

[91] Eduardo Cuevas, "2 Children, Woman Die in Rio Grande as Feds, Texas Debate Border Control," *USA Today*, January 13, 2024, https://www.u,"satoday.com/story/news/nation/2024/01/13/children-woman-die-texas-mexico-border/72219807007/.

[92] John Moritz, "Abbott Keeps up Border Security Fight after Supreme Court Rules Feds Can Cut Razor Wire," *USA Today*, January 24, 2024, https://www.usatoday.com/story/news/nation/2024/01/24/supreme-court-razor-wire-texas-biden-border/72330906007/.

[93] Lauren Irwin, "Trump Calls for States to Deploy National Guard to Texas Amid Border Feud," *The Hill*, January 25, 2024, https://thehill.com/homenews/state-watch/4430262-trump-calls-states-deploy-national-guard-to-texas-amid-border-feud/.

[94] Olivia Rosane, "25 GOP Governors 'Stand with Texas' in Defying Supreme Court at Border," *Truthout*, January 25, 2024, https://www.commondreams.org/news/25-gop-govs-texas-border.

[95] U.S. Office of the President, "Invocation of the Alien Enemies Act Regarding the Invasion of the United States by Tren De Aragua," March 25, 2025, https://www.whitehouse.gov/presidential-actions/2025/03/invocation-of-the-alien-enemies-act-regarding-the-invasion-of-the-united-states-by-tren-de-aragua/.

government that is empowered to defend the states from invasion, not the other way around.[96] Abbott noted that Article IV, Section 4, of the Constitution states: "The United States shall guarantee to every State in this Union a Republican Form of Government, and shall protect each of them against Invasion; and on Application of the Legislature, or of the Executive (when the Legislature cannot be convened) against domestic Violence."[97] Abbott however claimed that since the federal government was not defending Texas from "invasion," another part of the Constitution, Article I, authorized Texas to take action to repel the invasion. According to Article I, states are denied the right to wage war "unless actually invaded, or in such imminent danger as will not admit of delay" (US Constitution, Article I, Section 10). But this is where the second problem arises. The idea that immigrants can constitute an invasion was rejected by the framers of the Constitution and it has never received any support in the courts.[98]

Abbott claimed in his written statement that the federal government had broken its "compact with the states," and his most aggressive form of inverted federalism was therefore justified. This was seen by some commentators as referencing the long ago repudiated successionist theory that the Constitution created a federal government based on a compact between the states. This theory allowed for southerners like John C. Calhoun pre-Civil War (i.e., antebellum) to argue for the states having the power to nullify federal law. Yet, Daniel Webster, the prominent Senator from Massachusetts, had long ago famously repudiated Calhoun's theory by arguing that the Constitution was not created by the states but by the people of the United States independent of the states.[99] Ever since the Civil War, Webster's view has become the predominant one.[100]

So, all told, Abbott, Trump, and the other Trumpists were essentially gaslighting the public about how Texas had constitutional authority to repel an invasion of immigrants. Nonetheless, by contorting the meaning of the Constitution to undermine the authority of the federal government, the

[96] See Governor Greg Abbott, January 24, 2024, https://gov.texas.gov/uploads/files/press/Border_Statement_1.24.2024.pdf.

[97] U.S. Congress, *Constitution Annotated: Analysis and Interpretation of the U.S. Constitution*, https://constitution.congress.gov/browse/essay/artIV-S4-1/ALDE_00013635/.

[98] Lauren Camera, "Abbott Escalates Border Dispute from Political Crisis to Constitutional Crisis," *U.S. News & World Report*, January 26, 2024, https://www.usnews.com/news/national-news/articles/2024-01-26/abbott-escalates-border-dispute-from-political-crisis-to-constitutional-crisis.

[99] Daniel Webster, "The Constitution is not a Compact," *National Constitutional Center* (1833), https://constitutioncenter.org/the-constitution/historic-document-library/detail/daniel-webster-the-constitution-is-not-a-compact-1833.

[100] Ronald Reagan was roundly criticized for pushing the compact theory of the Constitution. See Samuel H. Beer, *To Make a Nation: The Rediscovery of American Federalism* (Harvard University Press, 1993).

obfuscating discourse of Trumpism was dangerously edging the country closer to a hot civil war. As of late spring 2024, as part of "Operation Lone Star," Texas continued to construct facilities for its National Guard and the Texas Department of Public Safety to police the border while infringing on the authority of the federal government's Department of Homeland Security. Texas insists that it has the right to do this in spite of court rulings that have not said that. Yet, it continues to celebrate its questionable actions: "Since the launch of Operation Lone Star, the multi-agency effort has led to over 509,500 illegal immigrant apprehensions and more than 42,100 criminal arrests, with more than 37,400 felony charges. In the fight against the fentanyl crisis, Texas law enforcement has seized over 476 million lethal doses of fentanyl during this border mission."[101]

While this kind of state vigilantism is associated with other instances of vigilantism about the border, it is taking it to another level because it is sanctioned by the state. The private militia are still relevant, posturing in the background as saber-rattling by extremists. Further, there are extremists going beyond the nonviolent vigilantism of the "Take Our Border Back" convoy and other vigilante groups who have responded to the Texas Military Department's calls for volunteers to help police the border.[102] The trajectory of Trumpism is getting to the point where there is growing support for committing terrorist acts of violence, and not just aimed at immigrants. This is not just deranged "lone wolves" who engage in mass killings. Instead, it is a manifestation of the same thirst for cruelty among Trumpists that has led to the draconian state policies highlighted in this chapter.[103] For Adam Serwer, this streak of cruelty that runs through Trumpism is not a "bug" but rather a "feature."[104]

Then Trump won reelection in 2024, and Texas switched to cooperating with the federal border enforcement.[105] Talk of a civil war dissipated with Trump reclaiming the White House and promising to begin mass deportations of undocumented immigrants. Metapragmatic posturing had contributed to bringing the Country to this perilous point.

[101] "Operation Lone Star Continues Construction for Forward Operating Base," April 24, 2024.

[102] Charles P. Pierce, "God, Save Me from Your Followers Heading to the Border Calling Themselves 'Patriots,'" *Esquire*, January 26, 2024, https://www.esquire.com/news-politics/politics/a46556503/border-trucker-convoy-gods-army/.

[103] Adam Serwer, *Cruelty Is the Point: Why Trump's America Endures* (One World, 2020), 100.

[104] Cynthia Tucker, "Cruelty Isn't a Bug, It's a Feature," *Albany Times-Union*, June 24, 2019, https://www.timesunion.com/opinion/article/Cynthia-Tucker-Cruelty-It-isn-t-a-bug-it-s-a-14038717.php.

[105] Priscilla Alvarez, Ashley Killough, and Tierney Sneed, "Texas Pivots from Feuding with Biden over the Border to Providing the Blueprint for Trump," *CNN*, November 26, 2024, https://www.cnn.com/2024/11/26/politics/donald-trump-texas-border/index.html.

Many of Trump's followers were there for the civil war that allowed them to act out their cruelty, one way or another. That's how much they hate the opposition. And that is why they rush to defend the rogue actors like Kyle Rittenhouse, Daniel Perry, or Daniel Penny, when they engage in vigilante violence against people who can possibly be accused of just standing up for the other side or are seen as representing the other side. Rittenhouse traveled across state lines with an assault rifle to go to war, in 2020, against protesters in Kenosha, Wisconsin, who were protesting a police-killing of a Black man. Daniel Perry killed a Black Lives Matter protester in Austin, Texas, without provocation in 2020. Daniel Penny choked to death a homeless man who was acting out on a New York subway in 2023. Regardless of the evidence against them, all three were heralded as heroes by Trumpists, and still are. They were seen as standing up for order over chaos, a convenient way to characterize the widening division in the United States. It was a tendentious framing that justified vigilante violence.

As Bouie notes, these rogue actors are now called "Good Samaritans," not for being charitable or exhibiting mercy but for simply committing acts of violence against people who could be seen as being part of the opposition. Killing for Trumpism makes you a Good Samaritan. To suggest that is just gaslighting done in the name of rewarding and encouraging violence on behalf of Trumpism. Once again, Trumpism operates as a legitimating discourse that makes the bad good and those who use violence to undermine the rule of law to be the real patriots. Trumpism has us pulling apart by creating an alternative upside-down universe for its supporters to inhabit.

Yet, as this chapter has shown, Trumpism's legitimating practices also embolden policymakers at the state level to exploit deficiencies in our liberal democratic institutions to undermine democracy while claiming they are the real defenders of democracy. Promoting disunion between the states, while exploiting the porousness of the federal system becomes allegedly acting in service of preserving the union. This is how the new civil war is getting promoted both via violent acts and extremely regressive state policies that go against the Constitution, majoritarian principles, and individual rights. With Trumpism, these anti-democratic developments, violent and nonviolent, are getting mainstreamed via a discourse of denialism. Gaslighting lies, boomeranging criticisms, and co-opting progressive ideas have helped with this mainstreaming. In this upside-down world, civil war talk becomes another way to promote the dissolution of the constitutional system. In the process, the January 6th insurrectionists become heroic patriots who are political prisoners, or as Trump calls them "hostages." Today, that is Trumpism as a dangerous metapragmatic discourse.

Yet, the clash between the federal government and the states is not over with Trump winning reelection. Now it is governors and mayors who are saying they will not cooperate with federal efforts to enlist local law enforcement in the massive deportation program that Trump has announced. Some officials have said they would actively encourage protests and resistance to block federal removal of people living in their communities.[106] The looming clashes could extend the talk of civil war rhetoric as yet another sign of how polarized the Country has become.[107]

[106] Robert Tate, "Trump Border Chief Threatens Jail for Denver Mayor Amid Deportation Dispute," *The Guardian*, November 26, 2024, https://www.theguardian.com/us-news/2024/nov/26/trump-tom-homan-border-denver.

[107] David Dayen, "The Cold Civil War," *The American Prospect*, October 7, 2024, https://prospect.org/politics/2024-10-07-cold-civil-war/.

6

Prosecutions as Persecutions

Trumpism as a Cult

At the trial where Donald Trump was found liable for defamation and sexual abuse against E. Jean Carroll, in May 2023, Carroll's lawyers showed a video of Trump's deposition. The video showed his answer to a question about another video, the infamous *Access Hollywood* recording where Trump lets on that women allowed him to "grab them by the pussy." Trump asserted in the deposition: "Historically, that's true with stars. ... If you look over the last million years, I guess that's been largely true. Not always, but largely true. Unfortunately or fortunately."[1] It was classic Trump, defiant, boastful, lying, and still trying to have it both ways. Trump's claim was that women let him do it, and that was something that you could say was unfortunate or fortunate, depending on your point of view. In other words, he did not deny assaulting women; instead, he saw it as a badge of honor, though suggesting that maybe given how attitudes had changed, he must admit it is an unfortunate feature associated with the history of patriarchy.

He then went on to his usual gaslighting, saying that neither Carroll nor her attorney Roberta Kaplan was his "type," as if that really mattered all that much when it came to his assaulting women. He called them both "nasty," his favorite term when he sought to simultaneously sexualize and demonize a woman.

Even as he was at risk of losing millions of dollars in a defamation suit, Trump continued to defame both Carroll and Kaplan after the jury found for Carroll and the judge ordered Trump to pay $5 million in damages and penalties. Trump continued to defame Carroll even during a second trial that ended in a verdict ruling that Trump had to pay her an additional $83.3 million.[2]

Why would Trump say what he said in his deposition since it probably sealed his fate in this case? Why did he keep it up after the verdict put him

[1] Abigail Weinberg, "What Was Trump Thinking?," *Mother Jones*, May 5, 2023, https://www.motherjones.com/politics/2023/05/trump-deposition-e-jean-carroll-access-hollywood-thats-true/.

[2] "Trump Ordered to Pay E. Jean Carroll $83.3M in Defamation Damages Trial," *Washington Post*, January 26, 2024, https://www.washingtonpost.com/politics/2024/01/26/trump-verdict-e-jean-carroll-defamation-trial/.

The Trajectory of Trumpism. Sanford F. Schram, Oxford University Press. © Oxford University Press (2026).
DOI: 10.1093/9780197827437.003.0006

at risk of having to pay more damages for his defamatory statements? Was he playing to the misogynists in his base but then still trying to claim he recognized groping women is wrong? Was staying politically popular more important than winning a lawsuit even at the cost of millions of dollars?

Trump seems just not to be able to stop himself from railing about what he sees as attacks on him as a person. Trump followed the DARVO playbook of sex offenders: Deny, Attack, Reverse Victim and Offender.[3] Trump engaged in the metapragmatics of Trumpism to gaslight, boomerang, and co-opt his way to dismiss the charges against him. Trump's gaslighting included his claim that he did not sexually molest Carroll because she is not his type. He claimed he does not even know who she is even though there was a picture of him talking to her at some reception. He boomeranged that those going after him with lawsuits like this were doing it for political reasons and they are the ones guilty of crimes, not him. Last, he co-opted the status of the victim from Carroll to claim he was being unfairly tried for doing what he was saying was normal or mainstream (at least for "stars"). The metapragmatics of Trumpism were on full display in this trial as they were in others before and since.

Regarding this case, Trump was not alone in invoking what had become standard metapragmatic moves for Trumpism. Following the $83 million verdict, when asked about it on the ABC's "This Week" by host Martha Raddatz, Trump supporter Sen. Tim Scott (R-SC) first gaslighted, then boomeranged, and ultimately co-opted the other side's talking points in rapid fashion:

RADDATZ: I want to start with the breaking news on Friday, and that was that your candidate, former President Trump, was ordered by a jury to pay $83 million for defaming writer E. Jean Carroll. He was also found before, as you know, liable for sexual abuse. Does that give you any pause in your support?

SCOTT: You know, myself and all the voters that support Donald Trump, support a return to normalcy, as it relates to what affects their kitchen table. The average person in our country, Martha, isn't – they're not talking about lawsuits. As a matter of fact, what I have seen, however, is that the perception that the legal system is being weaponized against Donald Trump is actually increasing his poll numbers.

RADDATZ: I understand that, but this was—they were jury trials. They were jury trials. They started when Donald Trump was president. You—that does—that gives you no pause whatsoever?

[3] Sidney Blumenthal, "Deny, Attack, Reverse—Trump Has Perfected the Art of Inverted Victimhood," *The Guardian*, February 1, 2024, https://amp.theguardian.com/commentisfree/2024/feb/01/trump-victim-political-strategy-manipulation.

SCOTT: I don't have a—the Democrats don't pause when they think about Hunter Biden and the challenges that—that he brings to his father. The one thing I think the electorate is thinking about most often is how in the world will the next president impact my quality of life? How will America regain its standing in this world? They were better off under Trump, and they're looking for four more years of low inflation, low crime, low unemployment, and high enthusiasm for our country. We haven't had that in the last four years.[4]

Scott deflected answering about the verdict by gaslighting that people were more interested in a "return to normalcy" and when pressed again to answer, he boomeranged a whataboutism concerning Hunter Biden (President Joe Biden's son), while ending with co-opting democratic talking points regarding the success of Biden's economic policies as if they were what Trump had done but Biden had not.

It seemed that Trumpism as a discourse was inscribed in a memo all his supporters were given to stay on point to gaslight, boomerang, and eventually co-opt their way into defending their leader. This kind of blatant refusal to answer journalists' questions has become commonplace among Trumpers. It is possible they are being coached to display disdain for the press as part of an explicit metapragmatic strategy. Metapragmatics work better when they are used against a demonized other.[5]

During the early stages of his 2024 reelection campaign, Trump was increasingly distracted with additional legal troubles regarding the January 6th insurrection, his mishandling of top secret documents, his various campaign finance violations, his hush money payments to cover-up affairs, his tax and insurance scheming in the millions of dollars, and sundry other alleged illegalities. As a result, the trajectory of Trumpism turned yet again and Trump's woes seemed to become a threat that could separate him from the Movement. It was starting to look like Trump would forever be busy fighting for his own personal freedom in court, while the Movement could go on railing against those who they see as threatening theirs. Then again, with a base of support that was verging on becoming an authoritarian personality cult, it was no stretch in seeing their adored leader as someone who needs to be protected at all costs. In that case, Trump was able to mix his legal difficulties and political challenges and achieve success in both arenas. Eventually,

[4] "'This Week' Transcript 1-28-24: Sen. Tim Scott, Gov. Gavin Newsom & Gen. CQ Brown," *ABC News*, January 28, 2024, https://abcnews.go.com/amp/Politics/week-transcript-1-28-24-sen-tim-scott/story?id=106743064.

[5] See Bart Cammaerts, "The Abnormalisation of Social Justice: The 'Anti-Woke Culture War' Discourse in the UK," *Discourse and Society* 33, no. 6 (2022): 730–43.

Trump was convicted only in the hush money trial and there he was sentenced with no fine or jail time, while winning the presidency once again. When allocuting at his sentencing hearing, Trump declared his trial a fraud and said: "It was done to damage my reputation so I would lose the election and obviously that didn't work."[6] Instead, it was his strategy that had worked.

This chapter examines how this remarkable turn of events allowed Trump to use metapragmatics to solidify his Movement as an authoritarian personality cult that had come to focus on fighting for its leader everywhere—inside and outside the courtroom, on the campaign trail, and in social media, no matter how humiliating it all could be. Trump sought to blur the boundary between his political campaign and personal legal battles in court, seeking to have each help him win the other. The Movement became caught in defending Trump from legal accountability, arguing that his prosecutions are political persecutions. An authoritarian personality cult should be quite comfortable with that formulation for fighting for the well-being of the leader is everything for the Trumpist Movement under these circumstances. Metapragmatics played a central role in articulating the relationship between legal and political challenges Trump faced and, in the process, cemented the Trumpist Movement as an authoritarian personality cult.

Trump Embodies His Movement and His Followers Commit to Saving Him

When Trump announced his third consecutive run for the presidency as a major party candidate in March 2023, he ended his speech dramatically stating: "In 2016, I declared: I am your voice. Today, I add: I am your warrior. I am your justice. And for those who have been wronged and betrayed: I am your retribution."[7] Trump was running to seek retribution for what he saw was a stolen 2020 election. His retribution was the Movement's. His fate and the Movement were in his mind, it seems, synonymous. And so, it was for many of his followers; Trump personally embodied the Movement, much like a medieval king embodied his kingdom.[8] For many of Trump's followers,

[6] "Trump Spared Jail at Hush Money Sentencing, Days before Inauguration," *CNA*, January 10, 2025, https://www.channelnewsasia.com/world/trump-spared-jail-hush-money-sentencing-days-inauguration-4850336.

[7] David Smith, "'I am Your Retribution': Trump Rules Supreme at CPAC as He Relaunches Bid for White House," *The Guardian*, March 4, 2023, https://www.theguardian.com/us-sdnews/2023/mar/05/i-am-your-retribution-trump-rules-supreme-at-cpac-as-he-relaunches-bid-for-white-house.

[8] Ernst Kantorowicz, *The King's Two Bodies: A Study in Medieval Political Theology* (Princeton University Press, 1957).

he was the Movement. For some he was their god.[9] From the perspective of his most devoted followers, the entire fate of Trumpism as a movement was inextricably entangled with Trump's. For them, without Trump there was no Trumpism. His personal travails did not take away from the Movement; they personified its struggle.

Even Trump's allies in Congress intimated that if Trump suffered losses in court on one or another of his legal scandals, his base would rise up in violent protest. Even the prosecution of Trump for tax fraud was affected by the possibility of supporters attacking judges and lawyers.[10] A judge warned Donald Trump not to publicly share evidence from pre-trial discovery in his criminal prosecution for alleged falsification of business records to pay hush money to "catch-and-kill" a story about Trump having had sex with the porn star Stormy Daniels.[11] The fear was that supporters would be encouraged by Trump to threaten court officials or even the jury. Lindsey Graham suggested as much regarding another case when he said in August 2022: "If they try to prosecute President Trump for mishandling classified information after Hillary Clinton set up a server in her basement, there literally will be riots in the street. I worry about our country."[12]

The Metapragmatics of Mixing Politics and Law

When arraigned on June 13, 2023, in Miami, Florida, having been at that point indicted on thirty-seven counts, most regarding his illegally withholding classified documents, some including highly sensitive military secrets, Trump later that night boomeranged: "This day will go down in infamy and Joe Biden will forever be remembered as not only the most corrupt president in the history of our country but, perhaps even more importantly, as the president who, together with a band of his closest thugs, misfits and Marxists, tried to destroy American democracy."[13] Trump gaslighted: "Under the

[9] David Ramsey, "How Donald Trump Became God," *Baptist News Global*, January 27, 2022, https://baptistnews.com/article/how-donald-trump-became-god/.

[10] Adam Reiss and Rebecca Shabad, "Judge Threatens to Imprison Trump for Violating Gag Order in New York Fraud Trial," *NBC News*, October 20, 2023, https://www.nbcnews.com/politics/donald-trump/judge-threats-imprison-trump-biolat-rcna121403.

[11] See Shayna Jacobs, "Trump to Appear Remotely in N.Y. Criminal Court to Hear Judge's Warnings," *Washington Post*, March 23, 2023, www.washingtonpost.com/national-security/2023/05/23/trump-court-hearing-share-evidence/.

[12] Jonathan Weisman, "Graham Predicts 'Riots in the Streets' if Trump Is Prosecuted," *New York Times*, August 29, 2022, https://www.nytimes.com/2022/08/29/us/politics/lindsey-graham-trump-riots.html.

[13] Katie Sobko, "Donald Trump Makes Return to NJ after Arraignment in Miami, Calls Charges 'Fake,'" *NorthJersey.com*, June 13, 2023, https://www.northjersey.com/story/news/politics/2023/06/13/trump-speech-nj-indictment-return-arraignment-fake/70315827007/.

Presidential Records Act—which is civil, not criminal—I had every right to have these documents. The crucial legal precedent is laid out in the most important case ever on this subject, known as the Clinton socks case."[14] His indictment, however, referenced the Espionage Act but made no mention of the Presidential Records Act, which Trump had mischaracterized and seemed in no way relevant to his indictment. The "Clinton socks" case involved recordings historian Taylor Branch had made and were kept in a sock drawer by Clinton, who won the right to keep them. Since the Supreme Court decided in that case that those were private recordings and not official presidential records, Clinton did not need to turn them over to the federal government's National Archives for safekeeping. The relevance of the Clinton case to Trump's indictment for withholding top secret government documents was not apparent to most observers. But as always, Trump continued to gaslight this lie while insisting that he was unfairly subject to selective prosecution.

The false equivalence with the Clinton socks case was a desperate attempt to claim selective prosecution and thereby co-opt the status of the victim. This contrast allowed Trump to boomerang that it was his opponents who were undermining the rule of law, not him. Instead, what Trump had done was something qualitatively different than what Clinton did and was glaringly clear to many observers illegal. Trump took documents important to national security that he was not allowed to possess, stubbornly refused to return them, and then actively conspired with others to keep the federal government from retrieving them. No ex-president had ever done anything like that. No amount of gaslighting, boomeranging, and co-opting to smear his opponents and normalize his actions could make the claim of selective prosecution plausible.

Trump nonetheless was defiant in his desperation and added to his torrent of misleading statements that sought to demonize his opponents by flinging back characterizations and criticisms that were used against him.[15] He boomeranged saying those who were persecuting him were the real "fascists," and Biden was the one who had illegally taken documents not him. He also reminded everyone that Hillary Clinton had improperly stored government communications on a private computer server and that she should have been prosecuted for holding classified information, not him. Last, he co-opted the

[14] Philip Marcelo and Angelo Fichera, "FACT FOCUS: Trump Twists Presidential Records Act, Clinton 'Sock Drawer' Case to Mount Defense," *AP News*, June 13, 2023, https://apnews.com/article/trump-indictment-presidential-records-act-1df64502d1640076690fac52638daebf.

[15] Jeff Zymeri, "In Post-Arraignment Speech, Trump Slams Jack Smith and the 'Corrupt Sitting President'," *National Review*, June 13, 2023 https://www.nationalreview.com/news/in-post-arraignment-speech-trump-slams-jack-smith-and-the-corrupt-sitting-president/.

claim that it was he who was upholding the law and not the corrupt thugs of the Justice Department. For Trump, it was tit for tat all the way down.

This was Trumpism in its most personally petulant form being expressed by the Movement's leader and the Republican Party's 2024 presidential nominee all to save himself from imprisonment and go on to win reelection. Trump did not take care to speak carefully about the law; he did not speak legalese (even if it sounded that way to supporters). He was instead speaking the discourse of Trumpism, gaslighting, boomeranging, and co-opting to deflect accusations against him. As personally perilous as his indictment was, when Trump spoke about it, it was all about politics regardless of whether what he said risked getting him into more legal trouble.

Yet, the ultimate metapragmatic move in mixing up politics and the law in the classified documents indictment came when the Trump-appointed judge Aileen Cannon dismissed the case saying that Special Prosecutor Jack Smith's appointment was unconstitutional.[16] Trumpists had originally insisted that Attorney General Merritt Garland appoint a special prosecutor, so the investigation was independent from political officials in the Biden Administration. The law was not to be contaminated by politics. Then, when Garland did exactly what they wanted, Trump moved to sue him for acting unconstitutionally on the hypocritical grounds that the prosecutor was required to be a political appointee nominated by the president and approved by the senate.

In this sense, Cannon's ruling in the classified documents case was about what was the proper mixing of politics and law when it came to appointing a special prosecutor. It was appealed. Yet that appeal would put the documents case on hold and allowed Trump to run for reelection without that case being resolved. The indeterminate status of the case was an important political reprieve for Trump, while he conducted his political campaign to get back into power where he could cancel the case when he became the president. The law and politics were not separate, and Trump knew that. That was his long game. Legal justice delayed would produce political justice denied. Trump could mix politics and the law to win at both. Recategorizing legal proceedings as political and using them for political effect was profoundly hypocritical but they also were quintessential metapragmatic moves that made Trump's mixing of law and politics so Trumpian and so successful.

Across any number of prosecutions, for Trump there was no dividing line between politics and law, and in fact, legal battles were best fought in the

[16] "Judge Dismisses Classified Documents Case against Trump," *New York Times*, July 15, 2024, https://www.nytimes.com/live/2024/07/15/us/trump-documents-case-dismissed.

political arena. He not only tried to fight his legal battles in the political arena but also increasingly used his struggles in court to win increased political support as someone who was being unfairly persecuted.[17] The legal and political battles served to support each other. Trumpian metapragmatics helped make that happen. Trump played the victim card again and again as when he said that his indictment by Jack Smith for the January 6th insurrection to stop Biden from becoming president proved that President Biden had now "weaponized" the law to take down Trump as his opponent in the 2024 presidential election. This was also Trump boomeranging back at prosecutors as he was being indicted in part for politicizing the Justice Department to use the law to give him a what he insisted was his deserved political victory.

Trump went on to claim that he had "absolute immunity" from prosecution as president and his prosecutions not only were persecuting him but also undermining the constitutional system that accords presidents wide political powers. When the US Supreme Court largely agreed with Trump, it was a dramatic normalization of his hypocritical quest to become an authoritarian strongman, while calling his opponents fascist. More than expected, the prosecutions were aiding the politics and vice versa. The irony was palpable since the Supreme Court ruling basically said that presidents could exercise political control over the Justice Department, which is what Trump had been accusing Biden of doing. The Supreme Court's immunity ruling ironically concluded that the president had the power to essentially politically commandeer the Justice Department.

Trumpism had become a Mobius Strip: if you looked on one side, politicizing the law was wrong as when Trump got indicted for trying to block the peaceful transfer of power or for stealing classified documents. Yet, on the other side, it was right when Trump claimed absolute immunity from being charged with politicizing the Justice Department to initiate legal proceedings to keep him in power. But the law and politics were interrelated and one could be twisted to be the other. Learning when you could or could not mix law and politics was essentially a partisan decision, justified metapragmatically. Fortified now by a Supreme Court ruling, Trumpism was operating to normalize its extremism and its blatant power grabs by politically using the law against itself. Trumpist discourse was operating so they get to have their cake and eat it too, being for and against the law simultaneously, using the law to legitimate illegality.

[17] Sarah Smith, "Donald Trump Turns His Legal Battles into Campaign Spectacle," *BBC*, January 11, 2024, https://www.bbc.com/news/world-us-canada-67953895.

The discourse was mainstreaming what is essentially their own Schmittean power politics as practiced under Trumpism.[18] For Carl Schmitt, Nazi theoretician as he was, the head of state can fulfill his responsibility to the people to decide to put himself as needed above the law in a "state of exception," even to the point of imposing a dictatorship allegedly in the name of saving democracy from the inadequacies of weak-kneed liberalism. Under these conditions, there is no law, just metapragmatic power moves where dictatorship is reframed as democratic all to justify power grabs as legal. Even political violence could be justified as necessary to rise above the limitations of the liberal legal order that vitiated attempts to realize the will of the people.[19]

In fact, Trump's vice presidential nominee, Sen. J. D. Vance (R-OH), went so far to fling his own Ivy-League boomerang (being the Yale Law School graduate that he was) in a barely concealed projection when he said (without irony) that it was liberal Democrats who were consciously using Schmitt's claim that politics is where there is no law just the quest for power.[20] According to Vance, it was the Democrats who were using Schmitt to justify their politicizing the law. Vance went on to claim liberals were demonizing Trump as the dictatorial threat to liberal democracy when in fact the liberals were the real anti-democratic threat. Yet, Vance defended Trump's promise to be a dictator "only for one day" without mentioning Schmitt's controversial claim that dictatorship could be the ultimate realization of real democracy. For Vance, it was the liberals who were the dangerous practitioners of Schmittean logic and Trump was only appropriately using constitutional law to question the legality of an election. Vance seemed to be saying it was only Trump who was legitimately going above the liberal limitations of the law to fulfill its democratic promise.

It was at this point that Trumpian metapragmatics about law and politics, and democracy and dictatorship, were transparently contradictory and profoundly self-serving. When it was Trump, it was okay to politicize the law, but when liberals did it, that was wrong. When Trump acted like a threat to democracy, he was actually realizing it, but that would not be true if liberals used such Schmittean logic. This was partisan boomeranging of the highest order.

[18] Jennifer Szalai, "The Nazi Jurist Who Haunts Our Broken Politics," *New York Times*, July 13, 2024, https://www.nytimes.com/2024/07/13/books/review/carl-schmitt-jd-vance.html.

[19] Robyn Marasco, "The Real Possibility of Physical Killing: A Feminist Critique of Carl Schmitt," *American Journal of Political Science* 67, 3 (2023): 1067–79.

[20] Szalai, "The Nazi Jurist Who Haunts Our Broken Politics."

I Lie for You and You Stand for Me

Trump is his own "one-trick pony."[21] Trumpism is metapragmatics all the way down. As a campaign advisor to the then candidate Bill Clinton back in 1992, James Carville successfully championed the slogan: "It's the economy, stupid!" Keep it simple, stay focused, emphasize the material issue of people's economic well-being. It worked. Clinton won and became a president who stuck to that slogan to much political success (despite other controversies that marred his personal reputation). Understanding Trump is sometimes just as simple: "It's the lie, stupid!" Trump only knows one way to behave: counterpunch, as Ivanka liked to call Trump's attempts to vanish his opponents (as if he would be nice were they not to bring up his misbehavior). Whether attacked in court or in an election campaign or while flailing about as president, Trump only knew how to practice metapragmatics: gaslight, boomerang, co-opt, and seek to smear his opponents, thereby making the metapragmatics all the more convincing. He always turned away from substance and facts and resorted to inflammatory rhetoric, lies, demonizations, and anything else that would enable him to evade actually engaging the criticisms or charges made against him. Now with the prospect of facing years in prison, he only knew how to do the same. His limited repertoire meant that he had to resort to polluting public discourse while undermining the rule of law. His obsession with his own status at the expense of everything else meant he could not afford to care about what he was doing to both our politics and the constitutional order. If there ever were a political bull in the US constitutional china shop, he was it. And as Bannon continually emphasized: "Go back and just look at how he pounds it. Wash, rinse, repeat. Wash, rinse, repeat. It's very powerful."[22]

Trump continued to "flood the zone," drown out bad news with a torrent of lies, in other words, did as he always does, and as authoritarian leaders often do. Whether it was about who was acting unconstitutionally, or who was fomenting violence, or even whether inflation was cooling, Trump piled one lie upon another. Like other authoritarians, Trump insisted people express their loyalty by committing with him to insisting on the most outrageous lies. In this way, they proved their fealty, especially if they continued to repeat the leader's lies even if they did not believe those lies themselves.[23]

[21] Jonathan Swan and Maggie Haberman, "One of Trump's Oldest Tactics in Business and Politics: I'm Rubber. You're Glue," *New York Times*, January 10, 2024, https://www.nytimes.com/2024/01/10/us/politics/trump-court-campaign-tactic.html.

[22] Swan and Haberman, "One of Trump's Oldest Tactics in Business and Politics: I'm Rubber. You're Glue."

[23] Sarah E. Parkinson, "Acting 'as if' during Pandemic: Information and Authoritarian Practice in White House," *Items*. June 25, 2020, https://items.ssrc.org/covid-19-and-the-social-sciences/democracy-and-pandemics/acting-as-if-during-pandemic-information-and-authoritarian-practice-in-white-house/.

Politically, Trump's approach to his legal woes seemed to be working far beyond what his opponents ever expected. Almost all his competitors for the 2024 Republican nomination had rallied around him, frequently repeating Trump's charge concerning one case or another that it all was a witch hunt.[24] Most rank-in-file Republicans agreed that Trump's indictments were partisan. According to the first national poll reported after Trump's January 6 indictment, the vast majority of self-identified Republicans, not just Trump supporters, said politics was driving the case.[25] Trump backers like Tucker Carlson paved the way for Trump's followers to say that the case in particular was a political witch hunt. Carlson and others had repeatedly gaslit the January 6 insurrection as an inside job concocted by the FBI to disqualify Trump from getting back into office.[26] It was unsettling then when polling indicated more than three in ten Republicans had come to agree with Carlson and believed that January 6 was in fact an inside job concocted by the FBI to make Trump look bad.[27] And even after Trump had for several years obstructed the government's efforts to reclaim his stolen classified documents, by 2023, 81 percent of Republicans still responded when polled that the documents indictment was also politically motivated.[28]

In the process, Trump was also succeeding in doing something else that is likely to prove to be the ultimate verdict on Trumpism as a distinctive movement. As Trump had done a number of times before, he implicated his followers by emphasizing that whatever happened to him personally would have critical consequences for his followers. His personal legal difficulties were their political challenge. As the 2024 presidential race for the White House unfolded, Trump continued to implicate his supporters in his prosecutions: "In the end, they're not coming after me. They're coming after you—and I'm just standing in their way." Back in March of 2023, when Trump had originally announced his campaign to run again for the White House, he had said: "In 2016, I declared: I am your voice. Today, I add: I am your warrior. I am your justice. And for those who have been wronged and betrayed: I am your

[24] David Charter, "Republicans United Over 'Witch-Hunt' against Donald Trump," *The Times*, June 15, 2023, https://www.thetimes.co.uk/article/donald-trump-ron-desantis-poll-us-presidential-election-florida-2023-n0s00mvp6.

[25] Jason Lange, "Trump Indictment: Reuters/Ipsos Poll Shows Most Republicans Think Charges Are Politically Motivated," *Reuters*, June 14, 2023, https://www.reuters.com/world/us/poll-trump-holds-double-digit-lead-after-federal-indictment-reutersipsos-2023-06-12/.

[26] Sophia Ankel, "Trump Supporter Who Went into Hiding over a Jan. 6 Conspiracy Theory Says Tucker Carlson is 'Obsessed' with Him," *Business Insider*, April 24, 2023, https://www.businessinsider.com/jan-6-ray-epps-tucker-carlson-trying-to-destroy-life-2023-4.

[27] Tom Jackman, Scott Clement, Emily Guskin, and Spencer S. Hsu, "A Quarter of Americans Believe FBI Instigated Jan. 6, Post-UMD Poll Finds," *Washington Post*, January 4, 2024, https://www.washingtonpost.com/dc-md-va/2024/01/04/fbi-conspiracy-jan-6-attack-misinformation/.

[28] Lange, "Trump Indictment: Reuters/Ipsos Poll Shows Most Republicans Think Charges Are Politically Motivated."

retribution."[29] But now, Trump turned the tables, and he was not his followers' retribution as much as they were now to be his protection. The law was serving politics and vice versa. It was building the Movement while leading it to rally around Trump.

Trump Is a Charismatic Leader (For His Base)

Trump could get away with suggesting any attack on him was an attack on his supporters, because as much as many people do not want to admit it, Trump is a charismatic leader. His use of the failed assassination attempt against him eventually became the paradigmatic example. Trump thrilled the crowd immediately after surviving the attack, with his face bloodied pumping his fist and shouting "fight, fight, fight."[30] He was inspiring his followers to believe he was the chosen one to lead them to "Make America Great Again."

Charismatic leaders can occasionally be found across the political spectrum, especially leading movements pushing for dramatic change.[31] Charismatic leaders stand out for having the ability to inspire people to join in one or another ambitious project by dint of their personal appeal. Trump fits that mold.[32] Trump's charisma has led an intensely mobilized political movement demanding an overturning of mainstream institutions and politics. Many of his followers deeply identify with him as a distinctively different political leader who rejects political norms and conventions and speaks in unvarnished "truths" that many of his followers had for a long time wished their leaders would say to give voice to their grievances against the mainstream.

Trump's charisma also inspires them to follow his lead in how they act and how they talk. As Sherrilyn Ifill has noted: "What Donald Trump offered was the freedom to be your worst self. And it turns out many Americans have been waiting for the opportunity."[33] This commitment to Trump the person has not diminished among his base of supporters who join with him in spreading lies, misinformation, and demonizations, all to advance Trump's cause of seizing and keeping power. One implication of Trump's charismatic hold on

[29] David Smith, "'I am Your Retribution': Trump Rules Supreme at CPAC as He Relaunches Bid for White House," *The Guardian*, March 4, 2023, https://www.theguardian.com/us-news/2023/mar/05/i-am-your-retribution-trump-rules-supreme-at-cpac-as-he-relaunches-bid-for-white-house.

[30] David Smith, "'Fight! Fight! Fight!': Trump Emerges as an American Messiah with Swagger," *The Guardian*, July 19, 2024, https://www.theguardian.com/us-news/article/2024/jul/19/donald-trump-rnc-speech-american-messiah-with-swagger.

[31] See Jan Willem Stutje, ed., *Charismatic Leadership and Social Movements: The Revolutionary Power of Ordinary Men and Women* (Berghahn, 2012).

[32] Sidney M. Milkis, "Review Essay: Donald Trump, Charismatic Leadership and the "Deep State," *Political Science Quarterly* 140, 2 (2024): 309–325, https://doi.org/10.1093/psquar/qqae018.

[33] https://twitter.com/SIfill_/status/1427998307608059904.

his followers is that if the elections or courts repudiate Trump, many people are prepared to take it personally. His base is appreciative of Trump's opening the door for them to be their "worst selves." His "honesty" is such a breath of fresh air for them; it is like they will not be able to breathe without Trump's leadership. While for many of Trump's nonsupporters he is a vile and disgusting person, his human frailties further endear him to his supporters because he seems to be one of us, not one of them, the elites who present themselves as without flaws.

If fact, Trump's charismatic hold on his supporters remarkably parallels the dynamic outlined by the prominent German sociologist Max Weber in the early twentieth century. Given his work in the comparative study of religions, Weber adopted the idea of charisma from the Christian religion and applied it to other social movements. A long time ago, the sociologist Thomas Dow dramatically extracted from Weber's writing what he meant by charisma:

> In Weber's original formulation, charismatic authority is said to exist when an individual's claim to "specific gifts of body and mind" is acknowledged by others as a valid basis for their participation in an extraordinary program of action. The leader's authority and program are thus specifically "outside the realm of everyday routine and ... [therefore] sharply opposed both to rational ... and to traditional authority .... Both ... are ... forms of everyday routine control ... while charismatic authority ... is ... a specifically revolutionary force." In this sense, "charisma is self-determined and sets its own limits."[34]

Trump's demagoguery invalidates him for what Weber idealized as a charismatic leader who would responsibly lead people beyond the nihilism that engulfs modern society.[35] For Wendy Brown, Weber believed that a real charismatic leader would "renew, and redeem, the distinctly human capacity to shape or direct common life in accordance with the capacity to create value."[36] Nonetheless, it is nothing less than stunning how Weber's initial characterization of the charismatic leader describes at least Trump's relationship to many of his followers. For them, if not for Weber, Trump represents a quintessential charismatic leader who inspires people to "release" themselves from "custom, law and tradition," and "all notions of sanctity," or even one's own "conscience."[37] As a charismatic leader who can inspire people in

[34] Thomas E. Dow, Jnr., "An Analysis of Weber's Work on Charisma," *The British Journal of Sociology* 29, 1 (1978): 83–93.
[35] Wendy Brown, *Nihilistic Times: Thinking with Max Weber* (Harvard University Press, 2023), 36–57.
[36] Ibid., p. 36.
[37] See Dow, "An Analysis of Weber's Work on Charisma."

this way, Trump's leadership of his Movement will be something not easily dismissed or left behind. It is also what makes Trumpism so volatile.

Trump's version of charismatic leadership has "offered people the freedom to be their worst selves."[38] Then again, Trumpers have at times celebrated the opportunity to express their cruelty on any number of issues.[39] It is entirely consistent with the "psychological structure of fascism."[40] This is the heart of Trumpism, and Trump's everlasting allure stems from his blithefully making this possible. He is like a rock star. People follow him from rally to rally just to be there at the moment when he says something outrageously hateful.[41] "Donald Trump allows us to be free," said one of his serial rally attendees in 2020. "He's never stopped fighting for us, so we are here fighting for him," she added. Another who attended his fourth rally in 2020, said: "It's like a festival." His supporters may feel they are upholding the true values of the country by violating basic legal and political principles. But Trump's charisma largely serves his selfish ends, inspiring followers to even go so far as to break the law and violate social norms when necessary, largely it seems only for his own personal benefit.

While the surveys of Trump rally goers do not provide much insight, they are likely mostly peaceful people (even if it is highly likely most own guns). But they are also likely to support others using violence to keep Trump in power, as the data we reviewed in Chapter 5 indicates. Chapter 4 reported that more than thirteen million Americans in 2022 indicated they supported the use of violence to return Trump to power (see Figure 4.1). It is not clear how far that support will go should it come to that. Were Trump supporters just saying this because they were so mad (about things that pre-date Trump's loss, but also the 2020 election in particular)? Or are they now really ready to man the barricades? I suspect it is not the latter. Instead, the real danger here is that they will support others committing selected act of violence on behalf of Trump and Trumpism. That is itself quite disconcerting.

When the failed assassination attempt occurred, Trump was railing against immigrants. After cowering from the shots fired, Trump stood back up and it was at that point that he pumped his fist saying fight, fight, fight. It did not matter that the shooter was a conservative, twenty-year old, gun enthusiast, fresh out of high school, using his father's semiautomatic rifle. At the

[38] See Sherrilyn Ifill, https://twitter.com/SIfill_/status/1427998307608059904.

[39] Adam Serwer, *Cruelty Is the Point: Why Trump's America Endures* (One World, 2020).

[40] George Bataille, "The Psychological Structure of Fascism," in *Visions of Excess: Selected Writings, 1927–1938*, ed. Allan Stoekl (University of Minnesota Press, 1985), 143.

[41] Katie Surma and Jen Fifield, "Meet the MAGA Diehards Who Travel the Country for Trump Rallies," *The Republic—azcentral.com*, February 19, 2020, www.azcentral.com/story/news/local/phoenix/2020/02/19/phoenix-supporters-president-donald-trump-campaign-rally/4809568002/.

Republican nomination convention the next week, Trump called for unity but not commonsense gun reform. He continued to complain that it was not him but the "Democrat Party" that was weaponizing prosecutions against political opponents. His supporters went along with the lie. The metapragmatics were all part of the campaign to vilify the opposition. Regardless of the calls for unity, Trump did not waver in his political campaign. In the hands of a charismatic leader, the boomerangs could inspire a loyal base to not question what was really happening.

Prosecution as Persecution: An Electoral Strategy

The dividing line between what is political and legal is always somewhat blurry.[42] Many legal decisions are informed by politics, and using the law to achieve political advantage is an everyday occurrence. Yet, Trump's mixing law and politics, his prosecutions and electoral campaigns, was not only blatantly based on lies and disinformation but also involved exploiting his charismatic hold on his followers to serve his selfish ends of evading legal accountability.

Trump had already arranged for his daughter-in-law Lara Trump, Eric's wife, to be installed as cochair of the Republican National Committee, where she completed a deal where donations to the party would be shared with a super-PAC (Save America) and those donations would go to paying Trump's legal bills. The Republican Party was at that point basically broke and would continue to be so from that point on as it devoted a good portion of its contributions to covering Trump's personal legal costs.[43] In the process, these moves, along with others, reduced Trumpism as a Movement to be singularly about Trump's own personal political and legal precarity.

If this were most other political movements, getting caught up in the leader's petty squabbling with the legal system would be a most inappropriate strategy for political success. And it might have been originally easy to imagine that supporters were to tire of diverting all their political energy just to try to save Trump from his legal difficulties. Yet, it is Trump's charisma that has allowed him to parlay the mixing of law and politics to combine the Movement's mobilization with his legal strategy and vice versa. He has used the

[42] Jedediah Britton-Purdy, "No Law without Politics (No Politics without Law)," *LPE Project*, October 2, 2018, https://lpeproject.org/blog/no-law-without-politics-no-politics-without-law/.

[43] Shane Goldmacher and Maggie Haberman, "Trump's Deal with R.N.C. Prioritizes PAC Paying His Lawyers," *New York Times*, March 21, 2024, https://www.nytimes.com/2024/03/21/us/politics/trump-legal-bills-rnc.html.

Movement to gain control of the Republican Party. The Movement's members have never had such an influential spokesman for their causes: White Nationalism, gun rights, anti-abortion efforts, and so on. And in response, Trump has been able to get people to express their outrage at his prosecutions as political persecutions.

Throughout it all, even in his criminal prosecutions, the metapragmatics of the MAGA Movement were starkly evident. As Trump's hush money trial was moving toward completion, a number of Republican members of Congress traveled to New York on several occasions and assembled en masse outside the courtroom, with Rep. Matt Gaetz (R-FL) later on a pivotal day posting a photo of them that was captioned: "Standing back, and standing by, Mr. President."[44] Trump had previously employed that metapragmatic phrasing in a debate when refusing to plainly denounce the saber-rattling of the Proud Boys who subsequently came to be part of his militia during the January 6th insurrection. Gaetz was gesturing that the MAGA Caucus in Congress was similarly positioning itself to do what it could to ensure Trump's return to the White House this time by opposing his criminal prosecution. Once again, "standing by" was the threatening part, and "standing back" was the metapragmatic reinterpretation reassuring that a full assault was not imminent just yet. Trumpists were now using metapragmatics to mix politics and law to try to influence Trump's criminal prosecution to protect their leader while simultaneously moving the Movement forward in what was increasingly looking like an authoritarian personality cult.

Trumpism Is a Cult

The transformation of Trumpism to being so thoroughly focused on Trump's personal legal peril was a pivotal moment. Trumpism was at risk of turning from a political movement into a personality cult. In fact, right after Trump's indictment in the documents case, former Republican vice presidential nominee Sarah Palin was asked on the Newsmax cable channel if she thought Trump supporters were a cult. She said they did not fit the definition of a cult because "[t]he definition of a cult is a group of people who are excessively supporting one another and a cause. [It's] all about conformity and compliance

[44] Martin Pengelly, "Gaetz Invokes Trump's Call to Far-Right Proud Boys at Hush-Money Trial," *The Guardian*, May 16, 2024, https://www.theguardian.com/us-news/article/2024/may/16/trump-hush-money-trial-matt-gaetz-proud-boys.

and intolerance of anyone who doesn't agree with what their mission is."[45] She seemed to forget the part where she needed to point out how Trump supporters do not insist on conformity and compliance and intolerance to those who do not agree with them, when in fact they do. She did however go on to say it was good that Trump is being persecuted because it fires him up and stirs up his base to mobilize on his behalf. Palin stated:

> This two-tier system of justice is—Well, you know what it's doing—it's adding fuel to the fire. And when you look at President Trump and how fired up he is, well, when you go through the fire, he comes out lit and that's exactly what we want and what we need today in order to take back our country, get government off our backs, on our side, and make America great again. I'm thankful that President Trump is so fired up.[46]

Palin's reference to a "two-tier system of justice" is but a sad attempt at a Trumpian co-optation of the Black Lives Matter meme regarding the police's treatment of Blacks but also Whites. Yet, if Trumpism as a movement is reduced to being singularly focused on defending Trump from prosecution so that he can become president again and use his political power to shield himself from legal accountability, it would make Trumpism a political movement look ever more like a personality cult. The shift from a movement to a cult would further the push for Trump to move from aspiring to be president again to go on to become an extra-constitutional strongman.

Trump had worked long and hard to build up welding of his fate with that of his followers. When indicted for trying to obstruct the peaceful transfer of power on January 6, 2021, so that he could prevent Joe Biden from replacing him as president, Trump could not resist speaking out. He stated on the day of his arraignment as posted in desperate ALL CAPS on his Twitter knock-off network Truth Social: "I AM NOW GOING TO WASHINGTON, D.C., TO BE ARRESTED FOR HAVING CHALLENGED A CORRUPT, RIGGED, & STOLEN ELECTION. IT IS A GREAT HONOR, BECAUSE I AM BEING ARRESTED FOR YOU."[47] Trump was inverting reality. He was not a criminal but a heroic martyr sacrificing himself for his Movement.

[45] Martin Pengelly, "Sarah Palin Denies Then Seems to Confirm That Trumpism Is a Cult," *The Guardian*, June 15, 2023, https://amp.theguardian.com/us-news/2023/jun/15/sarah-palin-trumpism-cult-confirmation.

[46] Ibid.

[47] Isaac Arnsdorf, Josh Dawsey, and Michael Scherer, "Trump Plans to Use Charges to Revisit 2020 Election, a Fraught Topic for GOP," *Washington Post*, August 3, 2023, https://www.washingtonpost.com/politics/2023/08/03/donald-trump-charges-election-republicans/.

Once Trump was hit with a warning from Judge Tanya S. Chutkan who was overseeing the January 6 case to not say derogatory things about people involved in the case, he resorted to ventriloquizing his smears through sycophants like Rep. Matt Gaetz (R-FL). It was classic Trumpism now the result of a judicial order forcing Trump to limit his statements. He was maintaining deniability by having someone standing next to him make threats for him. At the Iowa State Fair on August 12, 2023, with Trump standing at his side, nodding in agreement, Gaetz said:

> We are having a great time at the fair. We love standing with you. But we know that only through force do we make any change in a corrupt town like Washington, DC. And so, to all my friends here in Iowa, when you see them come for this man, know that they are coming for our movement and they are coming for all of us. And as hard as you see him work, I need you working ten times harder, a hundred times harder. We're going to win Iowa, we're going to march to the nomination and we're going to save the greatest country.[48]

Gaetz was the kind of congressman who would never be elected before Trump. The increased use of hyper-gerrymandering intensified the political polarization of recent years that allowed extremists like Gaetz to come to Congress to represent an uber-Right Wing enclave and slavishly work to support Trump's efforts to undermine the constitutional order. Gaetz did little else as a congressman. His resume largely is blind loyalty to Trump with almost nothing else to show. With Trump's tacit backing, he personally led the effort in the Republican House Conference to block Kevin McCarthy from becoming Speaker in early 2023. Gaetz eventually succeeded in leading the push among Trumpists in the House to have McCarthy removed as Speaker. Gaetz had his own self-serving reasons for pushing McCarthy out: he was seeking to undermine a House Ethics Committee investigation into his having had sex with underage girls (and he eventually resigned from Congress). Yet Gaetz's slavish loyalty to Trump solidified his standing with the MAGAs among the House Republicans, including Marjorie Taylor Greene (even as she continued to support McCarthy to the bitter end if only for transparently transactional reasons of gaining more influence in the Republican Caucus). The one thing that binds these extremists is their commitment to Trump. These people were leading the GOP down a dark path to becoming an authoritarian party blindly loyal to a candidate who faced prosecution for trying to

[48] Caleb Howe, "Matt Gaetz Shouts That 'Only Through Force Do We Make Any Change' While Standing Beside Trump in Iowa," *Mediate*, August 12, 2023, https://www.mediaite.com/politics/matt-gaetz-shouts-that-only-through-force-do-we-make-any-change-while-standing-beside-trump-in-iowa/.

subvert the peaceful transfer of power after the 2020 election. Their loyalty is to an authoritarian leader not the US constitutional system.

Trump continued to rely on loyal surrogates to maintain deniability so he could continue to ramp up his stochastic terrorism to intimidate those involved in his trials. This was starkly represented during his New York City election interference case that involved hush money payments to the porn star Stormy Daniels. Once the jury began to be selected, Jesse Watters on Fox News basically outed Juror 2 and suggested she was part of a liberal conspiracy to get Trump convicted. Trump then posted on Truth Social: "They are catching undercover Liberal Activists lying to the Judge in order to get on the Trump Jury—Jesse Watters."[49] When the prosecution claimed the next day in court that Trump was violating his gag order in that trial, his lawyers claimed he was only "reposting" [*sic*] what someone else was saying. Yet, it was then noted that Trump was actually typing out a revised version of what Watters said, and it technically was not what people call a retweet. This pitiful attempt to distance Trump from the act of jury tampering was to no avail and Trump eventually got sanctioned for violating his gag order in that trial. Yet, this retweeting gambit is an old tried-and-true Trump practice designed to shelter himself from direct liability for endorsing other people's inflammatory statements. In this case, it was in mob-like fashion to encourage terrorizing a juror while still denying trying to do so. In any case, it worked, and Juror 2 responded in court, after the back forth between the lawyers, that she did not feel safe, and the judge allowed her to step off the jury. For this trial, Jesse Watters was Trump's new Matt Gaetz who gave Trump cover while he practiced more stochastic terrorism, this time to successfully intimidate a juror to step off the jury.

Using loyal surrogates to speak on his behalf, Trump was once again engaging in metapragmatic discourse, where the referencing of other people's words created a way to maintain deniability while advancing the threats. It was at this point more than a persistent pattern. It showed how deep Trumpism as a discourse had come to be embedded in Trump's whole political approach, and it was one that given his loyal following he could continue to invoke and even expect others to emulate. A metapragmatic discourse of deniability is more easily advanced when you have a loyal following of diehard supporters who are willing to say and do the most inflammatory things on your behalf. You only need to encourage them and to help disseminate their statements while still getting to metapragmatically deny that you actually said or did

[49] Connor Summate, "'Not Permissible': Donald Trump Accused of Violating Judge's Gag Order by Citing Fox News 'Liberal Activist' Jury Conspiracy," *Radar*, April 18, 2024, https://radaronline.com/p/donald-trump-violate-gag-order-fox-news-liberal-activist-conspiracy/.

those things. It also helps when the other side has been thoroughly demonized to the point of losing credibility. Metapragmatic demonization had become a constant for Trumpism in defending their leader.

The Trump Davidians

Evidence of the ongoing transformation of Trumpism as a cult was actually available much earlier than Trump's prosecutions. Early signs were visible when Trump consciously chose to make a statement by holding the first rally of his presidential campaign for the 2024 election in Waco, Texas, the home of the Branch Davidian compound where David Koresh and his followers died in a standoff with law enforcement.[50] It was reminiscent of Ronald Reagan kicking off his 1980 presidential campaign at the Neshoba County Fair in Philadelphia, Mississippi, which was the site where three civil rights activists, James Chaney, Andrew Goodman, and Michael Schwerner, were murdered by members of the Ku Klux Klan in 1964.[51] At the fair, Reagan signaled his support for "states' rights" (code for White opposition to integration). At the beginning of Trump's campaign there was the question: what was Trump signaling by going to Waco? Could this have been an accident that Trump was mistaken in choosing to have his reelection kickoff associated with an anti-government cult? Instead, Trump most likely did want to associate himself with Koresh's cult. He was playing to his anti-government base and that was all that mattered to him. Again, Trumpism operated with a wink and a nod.

Trump, ever the performer, saw his campaign as a series of performances, often designed to symbolize what he was about. At the end of his campaign, he staged a rally at Madison Square Garden, just when he was leaning into fascism as his orientation to governing. Trump had no chance of winning New York State's electoral votes, but he still held a rally on the site where in 1939 American Nazis Movement staged a rally against the United States entering World War II against Hitler's Nazi government. The symbolic significance was visible to anyone who cared to look.

The signals however had to be nuanced to simultaneously show support to the extremists but not openly embrace their deeds, whether it was fascists, racists, or religious zealots. At the beginning, Trump's campaign was glossing over the fact that Koresh's cult was at the time of the raid under suspicion for

[50] Charles Homans, "A Trump Rally, a Right-Wing Cause and the Enduring Legacy of Waco," *New York Times*, March 24, 2023, https://www.nytimes.com/2023/03/24/us/politics/donald-trump-waco-branch-davidians.html.

[51] Bob Herbert, "Righting Reagan's Wrongs?," *New York Times*, November 13, 2007, https://www.nytimes.com/2007/11/13/opinion/13herbert.html.

child sexual abuse among other charges.[52] The siege at the Branch Davidian compound led to a fire that saw seventy-nine deaths, including twenty-one children. What matters to Trump is that Waco became basically a shrine to the Militia Movement for it symbolized the abusive power of the federal government. Waco is not a big city. It is not a transportation hub. It is not the first place a presidential candidate would choose for his first rally to kick off his presidential campaign. Trump probably chose to hold his first rally there to tip his hat (while maintaining deniability) to the Militia Movement, who were still a key part of his base of supporters. As Trumpism verged on becoming better seen as a personality cult more than anything else, the tie to Waco seems more appropriate given its connection to Koresh and the Branch Davidians. It is unlikely that Trump and his Movement will end similarly as the Branch Davidians going down in flames were still loyal to their leader, but that too, I would argue, is not to be totally dismissed.

Kicking off the presidential campaign in Waco was a symbolic gesture designed to appeal to supporters who had resentment toward the federal government. By itself it did not suggest in and of itself that Trumpism as a Movement was shifting into becoming a personality cult. Yet, the relationship might have been more than accidental. Trump seemed to be increasingly working to create slavish devotion by his base if he could stay true to their resentments, and they to his. Trump's metapragmatic moves frequently seemed to be designed to help solidify the Movement into becoming a cult.[53] A cult requires unquestioning loyalty. Sometimes the loyalty test comes in the form of a willingness to agree with the leader's most outrageous lies even when it is widely known they are not true. The gaslighting, boomeranging, and co-opting had helped normalize, mainstream, and legitimate the worst lies about Trump's legal difficulties about stealing documents, elections, and other things. Insisting on his followers embracing the lies at times seemed to be a loyalty test of the kind an authoritarian leader of a personality cult might impose.

Therefore, the threat Trump has posed exceeded his outrageous lying as was indicated by Special Prosecutor Jack Smith's filing evidence on behalf of the superseding indictment of Trump for his actions associated with trying to stop confirmation of Joe Biden as president on January 6, 2021. In the middle of the 2024 campaign, Jamelle Bouie wrote: "[T]he basic problem with

[52] Sarah Rimer with Sam Howe Verhovek, "Growing Up under Koresh: Cult Children Tell of Abuses," *New York Times*, May 4, 1993, https://www.nytimes.com/1993/05/04/us/growing-up-under-koresh-cult-children-tell-of-abuses.html.

[53] James Pfiffner, "The Lies of Donald Trump: A Taxonomy," *SSRN*, November 28, 2018; and Andrew Sullivan, "The Madness of King Donald," *New York Magazine*, February 10, 2017, https://nymag.com/intelligencer/2017/02/andrew-sullivan-the-madness-of-king-donald.html.

Donald Trump runs deeper than a contempt for the truth. Trump rejects the very basis of democracy or republicanism or whatever you want to call it—that the people are sovereign, and the people decide. And if there is a single reason to keep him out of office, it's that the kind of person who rejects the right of the people to choose their leaders is the kind of person who will not give up power when his term ends and the people say his time is past."[54]

Normalizing Blind Loyalty

Yet, as we were to see, blind loyalty to an anti-democratic leader can get normalized when mainstream political actors go along. This was most dramatically demonstrated when the US Supreme Court surprisingly was willing to entertain Trump's argument that he had "absolute immunity" from prosecution as president. While none of the nine justices expressed support for *absolute* immunity, the six conservative justices were eventually to rule that "official acts" as president were granted absolute immunity. This was a huge step in the direction of normalizing Trump's outrageous claims to the right to be all-powerful leader of the government.[55] The Court sacrificed its legitimacy to help normalize Trump's outrageous behavior and his over-the-top constitutional interpretation. In the end, the constitutional presidency, as we had come to know it, was destroyed and a type of president-king was created, all in the very partisan effort to shield Trump from prosecution and being held legally accountable for the many crimes he committed during his presidency.

Some of the justices had already been quoted from private conversations as admitting there was a partisan civil war ongoing in the country and one side or the other would have to win.[56] These secret recordings show the extent to which Trumpism as a discourse was already at work in normalizing the dangerous anti-democratic and authoritarian power seeking that Trump and his acolytes were obsessed with. Mainstream political officials end up going along out of fear of retribution but also because partisan attachments that have become so deeply held in an age of extreme polarization.[57] It will be

[54] Jamelle Bouie, "Trump Did Nothing to Stop the Mob," *New York Times*, October 5, 2024, https://www.nytimes.com/2024/10/05/opinion/jan-6-trump-jack-smith.html.

[55] Ruth Ben-Ghiat: https://twitter.com/ruthbenghiat/status/1783516548184826319. Jamelle Bouie, "This Whole King Trump Thing Is Getting Awfully Literal," *New York Times*, April 26, 2024, https://www.nytimes.com/2024/04/26/opinion/trump-immunity-supreme-court.html.

[56] Joan Biskupic, "Samuel Alito, Caught on Tape, Reinforces Why People Are Skeptical of the Supreme Court," *CNN*, June 12, 2024, https://www.cnn.com/2024/06/12/politics/alito-supreme-court-tape-analysis/index.html.

[57] Lilliana Mason, *Uncivil Agreement: How Politics Became Our Identity* (University of Chicago Press, 2018).

difficult to put the genie of liberal democracy back in the constitutional bottle given the successes of Trumpism as a normalizing discourse.

Trumpism had gotten to this place by using metapragmatics to normalize what had become its intensifying focus on an authoritarian takeover of the government. The Supreme Court's decision was like an official stamp of approval. It opened the door to saying Trump's actions to stop the peaceful transfer of power were legal and therefore should be considered normal (if actually unprecedented). Trump and his allies had taken to constantly calling Joe Biden a "dictator" in a pre-emptory move to defang accusations that Trump was openly pursuing becoming a dictator when reelected.[58] Trumpism was at work using metapragmatics to normalize it by gaslighting what was happening was not what it seemed, or by boomeranging it was no different than what the other side had been doing, or was justified by co-opting liberal rhetoric. We might wake up one day and finally see it for what it was but perhaps when it was too late. The trajectory of Trumpism, however, was not guaranteed. He did win reelection and the attempts to prosecute him for his crimes had failed miserably.[59] Trump then proceeded to seek to install a second-term administration comprised of questionable appointees whose loyalty to Trump was their major qualification. That was followed with a series of dramatic actions that included Trump threatening to pursue criminal prosecutions of his political opponents, as well as dramatic cutbacks in staffing and funding of the federal bureaucracy. Trump went on to threaten lawyers and the media with lawsuits and to cut funding and impose other restrictions on the universities. Denying due process to those facing deportation was matched by attempts to get around checks imposed by the courts. It was all very much part of the Orban playbook on how to transition a liberal democracy to an authoritarian regime. How far Trump would all go in undermining the Constitution, the rule of law, and even basic human rights remained an open question.

[58] Jamelle Bouie, "Why Republicans Are Talking about Biden's 'Dictatorship,'" *New York Times*, June 25, 2024, https://www.nytimes.com/2024/06/25/opinion/biden-burgum-trump-dictatorship.html?smid=nytcore-ios-share&referringSource=articleShare&sgrp=c-cb.

[59] Samuel Moyn, "Liberals Bet They Could Beat Trump with the Law: They Lost," *New York Times*, November 22, 2024, https://www.nytimes.com/2024/11/22/opinion/trump-legalism-trials.html.

7

Alternative Futures of Trumpism

As the preceding chapters have demonstrated, different inflection points in the trajectory of Trumpism have had a distinctive consistency in using metapragmatic speech, where gaslighting, boomeranging, and co-opting got deployed to rationalize what is being said. The different inflection points also bleed into each other, at times overlapping and reinforcing each other. Many White Nationalists were active in the Militia Movement whose members were identified at trial for calling for civil war. Nonetheless, the consistency of invoking the same metapragmatic moves across the different inflection points highlights how Trumpism was operating as a coherent discourse that worked to mainstream, normalize, and legitimate its outrageous lies, smears, and contrived grievances. This coherency helped sustain Trumpism as a force to be reckoned with, right up to Trump being reelected.

With Trump once again back in the White House, it has become clear that Trumpism as a Movement has moved further rightward to go so far as to support the toppling of US democracy and installing an authoritarian regime. Still, the discourse of Trumpism persists even in the initial efforts to legitimate this transformation Trump has claimed the validation for this power grab on the basis of his achieving a narrow popular vote victory, using the gaslighting of Trumpism to recharacterize his slim popular vote victory as giving him a mandate for a variety of extremist policies, including a mass detention and deportation program, massive tax cuts to the wealthy, radically slashing government assistance programs especially for the needy, eliminating most programs of foreign assistance as well as repealing civil rights initiatives, especially Diversity, Equity and Inclusion (DEI) efforts, and a full-on assault on scientific and health research and guidance. Trumpism had been previously more about inflaming grievances than actually making policy but morphing into something more was always possible.

The first weeks of Trump's second term suggested Trump himself still was very much focused on fanning the flames of resentment to seek retribution on his enemies.[1] His followers continued to stay with him in the process,

[1] Jamelle Bouie, "Trump Promised Retribution. Turns Out He Had a Very Big Target in Mind," *New York Times*, March 5, 2025, https://www.nytimes.com/2025/03/05/opinion/trump-revenge-american-people.html.

The Trajectory of Trumpism. Sanford F. Schram, Oxford University Press. © Oxford University Press (2026).
DOI: 10.1093/9780197827437.003.0007

though less than impressive poll numbers suggested that Trump's focus on revenge might work more with his base but not with others. Yet, for Trump, it seems to matter. Extracting retribution and fanning the flames of resentment became now the basis for policymaking, especially in working with Elon Musk's DOGE (Department of Government Efficiency) to take unconstitutional actions to decimate the federal government, undermine the rule of law and free his presidency from any sort of legal accountability. Creating a massive effort to detain and deport undocumented immigrants moved forward dramatically including the use of flagrant racial profiling. And old became new with demonizing those receiving government aid so as to enact a massive transfer of wealth from the poor to the rich via tax cuts once again took center stage. Trumpism as a discourse however had operated most significantly to legitimate and normalize this latest version of Trump's extremism including the move to topple liberal democracy and move the United States toward a more authoritarian-style "illiberal democracy."[2] Yet, slim hope remained regarding what happens if the courts were to ever get around to ruling against him. How far down the road of what people euphemistically call "democratic erosion" remained an open question.

In fact, there are alternative futures for Trumpism as a movement overall that deserve serious contemplation. In what follows, I begin the process of examining Trumpism's trajectory going forward. I conclude with considerations on how people should respond.

A Cautionary Note

I begin with a cautionary note: Making predictions lately has been a dicey affair. Too often when it comes to Trumpism, there has been the tendency to prematurely dismiss it as an abnormality when in fact it has now created a new normal. One important group of observers, professional political scientists, often approached the rise of Trumpism as an aberration that did not merit serious consideration. That would have been nice. But when that was proven wrong, then there was a pronounced tendency to write about Trumpism as something that was a short-term spasm of hate that would blow over and pass away like bad weather. Sunny days would return soon seemed to be a common perspective. I sensed a strong reticence to take Trumpism seriously,

[2] Ryan D. Enos and Steven Levisky, "Harvard Must Take a Stand for Democracy," *The Harvard Crimson*, March 6, 2025, https://www.thecrimson.com/article/2025/3/6/enos-levitsky-harvard-trump-democracy-fight/.

perhaps out of a desire to resist having to revise one's understanding of mainstream politics. The hope persisted that the spasms of hate would fade and their ability to overtake electoral politics would be proven unsustainable.

Established research had shown that in the post–Civil Rights era, playing the race card had to be done with dog-whistles because voters were turned off by explicit racism.[3] Trump's race-baiting was expected to sink his 2016 candidacy. But it did not. Trump ushered in a new era where his explicit race-baiting attracted a larger than expected following of voters even as it turned off others. Significantly, many experts on the study of elections were just not prepared intellectually and methodologically to grasp how an extremist political movement, like Trumpism, could commandeer the Republican Party and go on to overtake conventional electoral politics. Political Scientist Peter Levine put his finger on this limitation in the approach of many political scientists, one week after Trump had won the 2016 election:

> Last March, I argued that mainstream—empirical or positivist—political science research on "American government" (as the specialty is called) has a vulnerability. Aiming to be a science, it uses data that can be amalgamated to produce models and predictions, such as data from modern US elections. The main method of prediction is to run trend lines from the past into the near future. Although normative assessment is always marginal in positivist social science, most of this research has an implied value-stance: our system works, it follows rules and norms, it's fairly durable, the players are reasonably competent professionals who support the regime, and you should understand and respect it even if you want to reform it. Any reform proposals should be informed by empirical evidence, because otherwise the reforms will have unintended consequences that are likely to be bad. As the great Theodore Lowi wrote: "Realistic political science is a rationalization of the present. The political scientist is not necessarily a defender of the status quo, but the result is too often the same, because those who are trying to describe reality tend to reaffirm it."[4]

From Levine's perspective, many political scientists, especially many who studied elections, were not ready to examine Trumpism as a movement that had overturned conventional electoral politics. They were set up to study elections in a more routine fashion. Perhaps subconsciously there was a tendency to disbelieve that it was necessary to have to approach what was happening

[3] Tali Mendelberg, *The Race Card: Campaign Strategy, Implicit Messages, and the Norm of The Race Card: Campaign Strategy, Implicit Messages, and the Norm of Equality* (Princeton University Press, 2001).

[4] Peter Levine, "Why Political Science Dismissed Trump and Political Theory Predicted Him, Revisited," *Blog for Civic Renewal*, November 10, 2016, https://peterlevine.ws/?p=17668.

using a different theoretical and methodological perspective. It was as if, having invested in a certain understanding of American elections, they were hoping not to have to change. I was one of those political scientists.

A good, related example is the issue of the "shy Trump voter" confounding pollsters to the point that the polls became very confusing as the 2016 election approached.[5] Many commentators suggested that the polls were wrong in 2016 because Trump voters were reluctant to admit to pollsters who they were supporting. It turns out that was probably not that much of a problem. Instead, the polls were often not wrong except in critical swing states, leading to too many wrong predictions about who would win the Electoral College. One reason for this mistake was indeed nonresponse bias introduced by Republicans not responding to requests from pollsters to complete a survey.[6] Yet, Michael Bocian, a pollster, indicated that the most significant problem was that the major polling firms had incorrect models for converting their polling results into voting estimates. In particular, the pollsters stuck with their established models that underestimated the surge in non-college-educated voters for Trump. The reluctance to adjust the established models doomed the predictions in key swing states. In refuting the "shy Trump voter" myth, Bocian noted:

> The more likely explanation is that pollsters underrepresented non-college educated voters in 2016—which meant most of the political class failed to notice the magnitude of Trump's surge. The Midwest states where polling was off have particularly large populations of White voters without a college education. The Pew Research Center estimates that 60 percent of voters in 2016 lacked a four-year college degree, but that number was even higher in Pennsylvania (64 percent), Wisconsin (63 percent), Michigan (62 percent), Iowa (65 percent) and Ohio (66 percent). White voters without a college education vote Republican at higher rates than White voters with a college degree. This education gap was much larger in the 2016 election than it had been before, so the underrepresentation of non-college voters caused a larger error. In Michigan, for example, the final polling average showed [Hillary] Clinton leading by 3.4 percentage points, but Trump won by 0.3 points. In Wisconsin, Trump won by 0.7 points, but the polling suggested Clinton would win by 6.5. And in Pennsylvania, the polling average showed Clinton leading by 1.9, while Trump won by 0.7.[7]

[5] Michael Bocian, "There's No Such Thing as a Shy Trump Voter," *Washington Post*, November 2, 2020, https://www.washingtonpost.com/outlook/2020/11/02/shy-trump-voters-myth/.

[6] Nate Cohn, "A Worrisome Pattern Re-emerges in Seeking Response from Republicans," *New York Times*, November 1, 2022, https://www.nytimes.com/2022/11/01/upshot/polling-2022-midterms.html.

[7] Ibid.

The "shy Trump voter" nonresponse problem in 2016 was not, strictly speaking, as much of the problem as bad polling estimation models. The larger issue is that it is an example of how people allow preexisting assumptions to infiltrate their attempts to judge what is happening (and not just in elections). In the field of social psychology, it is called "confirmation bias."[8] Already assuming the worst about Trump voters' alienation from the mainstream led some observers to assume they were willing to lie to pollsters. That is an understandable assumption, so was the possibility that they were ashamed to be voting for a hatemonger like Trump. Yet, it seems that there were not that many liars responding to pollsters. Instead, it was the pollsters who were the problem. They were too committed to sticking to their outdated models and were reluctant to accept the necessity that they had to change how they researched the electorate, given the rise of Trumpism. Trump mobilized many previously nonvoting, less-than-college-educated members of the electorate that the models assumed would not be voting.[9] That assumption about how to model the electorate according to established prior research was simply wrong. The models have since been adjusted.

Perhaps, Political Science more generally needs to adjust its perspective on American politics overall, especially now that Trump's hatemongering has helped return him to the White House. This is now the new reality: Blatant hatemongering is a winning strategy. American politics is now on a new terrain. There were always hatemongers but none as successful as Trump. This is further surprising due to the fact that Trump and Trumpism are not universally popular. According to an April 2023 national survey conducted by NBC News, while an estimated two-thirds of Republicans stood behind Trump in his 2024 presidential campaign and indicated they were unbothered by his legal difficulties, still only about one-quarter of Americans overall had a positive image of Trump's MAGA (Make America Great Again) Movement.[10] A slightly higher percentage of the Americans (34 percent) had a positive image of Trump himself while over half (54 percent) had a negative image of Trump. Most Americans did not want Trump to run again for the presidency and most did not want to see another Biden–Trump rematch. But, run he did; and he eventually won reelection despite all his legal difficulties that had haunted him.

[8] Scott Plous, *The Psychology of Judgment and Decision Making* (McGraw-Hill, 1993).

[9] See Richard C. Fording and Sanford F. Schram, *Hard White: The Mainstreaming of Racism in American Politics* (Oxford University Press, 2020), Chapter 9.

[10] Bridget Bowman, "'MAGA Movement' Widely Unpopular, New Poll Finds," *NBC News*, April 25, 2023, https://www.nbcnews.com/meet-the-press/meetthepressblog/maga-movement-widely-unpopular-new-poll-finds-rcna81200.

We all have been repeatedly getting surprised. John Harris, the founding editor of *Politico*, had envisioned Trump fading fast after the 2020 election when he wrote that December, after Trump lost the election but before the January 6 insurrection occurred:

> It is not just in American history but American imagination that self-invented, outsized outsiders don't have staying power. Willie Stark, modeled after Huey Long, was shot at the end of "All the King's Men." F. Scott Fitzgerald delivered the same fate to Jay Gatsby. Not long after the Wizard of Oz is exposed as an amiable fraud ("Pay no attention to that man behind the curtain!"), Dorothy awakens to discover it was all just a dream. The Trump years were not just a hallucination. But chances are they will soon enough come to feel like they were—which won't leave much opportunity to return to real power.[11]

Harris' prediction was ill-timed given that the very next month, Trump incited an insurrection to stop the peaceful transfer of power and then remained atop his Movement and the Republican Party. Predicting which alternative future of Trumpism is something to be done with caution and humility.

Movement vs. Party: Grievance Politics vs. Policymaking

A major factor determining the path forward for Trumpism involves whether it becomes more about the Republican Party, making public policy as opposed to remaining a movement that is more focused on expressing grievances irrespective of whether there are any substantive policy accomplishments. From its inception, Trumpism has been most prominently about expressing rage at the mainstream society, culture, and political system. In this way, for some people, the Movement is more important than the Party because it allows the emphasis to be on the airing of grievances over the relatively more boring process of electing candidates and making public policy.[12] Yet, for others, working with the Republican Party is critical because their primary goals are to elect candidates who will make public policy consistent with their deeply felt convictions about abortion, guns, the border,

[11] John F. Harris, "Relax, a Trump Comeback in 2024 Is Not Going to Happen," *Politico*, December 10, 2020, https://www.politico.com/news/magazine/2020/12/10/trump-comeback-2024-not-happening-444135.

[12] For a review of literature on the relationship of movements to parties, see Sanford F. Schram and Richard C. Fording, "Racial Liberalism Resurgent: Connecting Multi-Racial Protests and Electoral Politics Today," *Journal of Race, Ethnicity and Politics* 6, no. 1 (2021): 97–119.

Political Organization	Political Emphasis Grievance Politics	Policymaking
Movement	White Nationalists	Anti-Abortion Activists
Party	Marjorie Taylor Greene	Lindsey Graham

Figure 7.1 Tensions in Trumpism Movement vs. Party—grievance politics vs. policymaking

taxes, regulation, race relations, etc. Having said that, it is also possible that some Movement activists are thoroughly committed to achieving major policy change, but they do not trust the Republican Party to provide it because Party leaders seemed in the past too willing to compromise. There are then multiple positions Trumpists may have on whether to emphasize either the Movement or Party and policymaking over grievance stoking.[13]

Figure 7.1 presents a taxonomy of possible positions people can take on emphasizing the Movement versus the Party as the primary organizational vehicle for Trumpism and whether the primary political emphasis is on expressing grievances versus influencing the public policymaking process. Each of the four quadrants shows an example of Trumpists who emphasize either the Movement or the Party while primarily focusing on grievance politics or policymaking. Movement activists who are more interested in building the Movement and emphasize grievance politics are well-represented by White Nationalists who often have no explicit policy agenda and are more interested in just mobilizing more White people to take action, sometimes violently, to stand up for the United States being a White Christian country. Movement activists who emphasize working to get policy change are well-represented by anti-abortion activists who sometimes feel the need to go around the Republican Party and work to push it to embrace more radical policy proposals like a national abortion ban. Trumpists who emphasize working within the Republican Party but more for the purposes of amplifying extremist views rather than getting policies enacted are well-represented by someone like Marjorie Taylor Greene, who uses her position in Congress to talk about civil war. The last quadrant is for Trumpists who are part of the Republican establishment, and are focused on policymaking, as is Lindsey Graham. There are therefore real-life examples of these theoretically possible positions within Trumpism that vary in the degree to which they emphasize the Movement or the Party and grievance politics versus policymaking.

[13] Azari, "Trump's Dominance in the GOP Isn't What It Seems."

Figure 7.1 suggests that there are multiple factions within the Trump coalition—some are more interested in building the Movement, others more interested in working within the Republican Party. Some are more interested in pushing grievance politics and others in achieving policy change. The divisions between the factions can lead to splintering of the Trump coalition and its eventual dissipation as a force in American politics. For now, however, the coalition remains intact. My bet is on the Movement persisting for some time going forward with its focus remaining on grievance politics more than public policymaking even with Trump in the White House and the enactment of a budget bill that imposed a massive transfer of wealth from the poor to the rich via demonizations of those who received needed government assistance. The prospect for more extremist politics that sometimes leads to extremist policies is strong.[14]

Transactional Chaos: The Grievance Politics/Policymaking Compound Solution

Taking this analysis a step further, we must consider that the policymaking/grievance dichotomy is helpful only up to a point. If you look at how Trump has practiced policymaking in the past, we can see it as a fuzzy dichotomy at best. This is especially the case with Trump at the head of the Movement. His personality and personal goals complicate any diagnosis and influence any responses. We may be in for a time of what I call "transactional chaos."

Steve Bannon originally got involved with Trump via interviews for a series of podcasts. He was effective in tutoring Trump on being aggressive in attacking the mainstream institutions, practices, and policies so as to mobilize the disaffected, while still promising to stand up for the "real" America. Trump liked both the aggressiveness and the coyness. Trump was in the process of becoming a newly minted out-and-out radical extremist who had previously held many liberal positions. But Bannon's tutoring was something Trump could warm to since he had spent a career in business being entirely untrustworthy and always purely transactional. Trump's approach to dealmaking in fact made him even more transactional than most people in the real estate

[14] Nella Van Dyke, Kyle Dodson, Paul Almeida, and Jaqueline Novoa, "Social Movement Partyism and Congressional Opposition to Certifying the 2020 Presidential Election Results in the United States," *American Behavioral Scientist* 68 (November 2024): 1761–81, https://journals.sagepub.com/doi/epub/10.1177/00027642241267933.

business.[15] Trump's transactional approach to life in general seems baked into his narcissistic personality. Everything is open to transactional wheeling and dealing for Trump, including whether he should be held accountable for his abuses of power. This type of transactional approach to life has shaped everything he has done as a politician, including balancing his relationship with his Movement and the Republican Party.

The transactional approach is at the core of his relationship with Elon Musk, who Trump authorized to go beyond Project 2025 plans to take control of the data for all federal agencies in the hopes of eliminating programs and slashing costs.[16] Trump wants to succeed as the Great Disrupter and so does Musk. Trump wants to be seen as the successful leader of a Movement based on resentment of the established order, and Musk wants to succeed as the great techno guru who can make everything run more efficiently than the established ways of doing things would have it. Yet, this melding of grievance politics and policymaking almost immediately confronted massive opposition for being conducted illegally and in blatant violation of the Constitution. The Trump–Bannon assault on the federal agencies and federal bureaucrats was quickly proving to be too much for Trumpist discourse to normalize as anything remotely legitimate.

Further storm clouds emerge with Trump continuing to try to have it both ways in combining grievance politics and policymaking as with his "One Big Beautiful Bill" that massively transferred wealth from the poor to the rich via tax cuts for the wealthy and cuts in assistance to the needy. Ultimately, Musk opposed the bill's tax cuts as massively increasing the Debt and Bannon opposed the cutbacks in needed health insurance that many MAGA supporters relied on.

The path forward could be one that features policymaking but primarily only for political effect. Using policy to influence politics is not specific to Trump. Political scientists study it when examining what they call "policy feedback."[17] Yet, Trump has taken this phenomenon to a whole other level where he is really not interested in making policy just scoring political points. Trump sees policymaking more as a dramaturgical activity designed to just stir up supporters making him more popular, powerful, and increasing his

[15] Andrea Bernstein, "Where Trump Learned the Art of the Quid Pro Quo," *The Atlantic*, January 20, 2020, https://www.theatlantic.com/ideas/archive/2020/01/trumps-brand-of-transactional-politics/604978/.

[16] Jonathan Swan, Theodore Schleifer, Maggie Haberman, Kate Conger, Ryan Mac, and Madeleine Ngo, "Inside Musk's Aggressive Incursion Into the Federal Government," *New York Times*, February 3, 2025, https://www.nytimes.com/2025/02/03/us/politics/musk-federal-government.html?unlocked_article_code=1.uU4.4kBG.yLEDSmSd9rOr&smid=url-share.

[17] See Daniel Béland, Andrea Louise Campbell, and R. Kent Weaver, *Policy Feedback How Policies Shape Politics* (Cambridge University Press: 2022).

chances of making more money. We see this disingenuous approach to policymaking most starkly when Trump started to move toward focusing on the 2024 campaign. Since leaving the presidency in 2020 but still leading the Movement, Trump actually insisted that his followers in Congress not try to govern but instead create more and more chaos to create more support for him coming back to power. He prefers that to getting things accomplished, especially with Joe Biden as president and Trump was always keen to make his adversaries look bad. In this regard, it seems Trump's attempt to work both sides of the street and be a leader of both a Movement and a Party was bound to come into tension.[18] As the saying goes: "watch out for what you wish for, you just might get it."

Populist movements involve the mobilization of ordinary people to band together to challenge established institutions. Rarely do they overtake those institutions. Instead, their influence is more episodic and disruptive.[19] Trumpism had been like the proverbial dog that chases and finally catches the car. Now what? Trumpism was more about railing against the established order on behalf of White people who feel threatened by how liberal democracy increasingly means sharing power with outgroups. In his first term, Trump himself was not really prepared to govern. The disastrous mismanagement of the response to the COVID pandemic that arguably resulted in hundreds of thousands of avoidable deaths is a stark example.[20] At times, the rhetoric from Trump and other Movement leaders seemed more designed to keep the base of supporters agitated rather than implement a policy agenda.

Remember that Trump ran for reelection in 2020 without a Party platform, reserving the right to not be explicit about many promises he only vaguely alluded to.[21] After the Republican Party 2020 Presidential Nomination Convention had nominated Trump, the Republican Party posted its decision that stated: "*RESOLVED*, That the Republican National Convention will adjourn without adopting a new platform until the 2024 Republican National Convention."[22] This declaration suggested that Trumpism was self-evident; Trump did not need a platform. It seemed as if Trump was running

[18] Julia Azari, "Trump's Dominance in the GOP Isn't What It Seems," *Politico*, May 18, 2023, https://www.politico.com/news/magazine/2023/05/18/donald-trump-paradox-gop-00097458.

[19] Herbert G. Blumer, "Collective Behavior," in *Principles of Sociology*, ed. Alfred McClung Lee (Barnes and Noble Books, 1969), 65–121, and many other sources. In particular, see Frances Fox Piven and Richard A. Cloward, *Poor People's Movements: Why They Succeed, How They Fail* (Vintage Books, 1977), 65–68.

[20] David Corn, "New Revelations Emerge on How Donald Trump Killed 400000 (or More) Americans," *Mother Jones*, November 17, 2021, https://www.motherjones.com/politics/2021/11/new-revelations-emerge-on-how-donald-trump-killed-400000-coronavirus-pandemic/.

[21] Tom Wheeler, "The 2020 Republican Party Platform: 'L'etat, c'est moi,'" *Brookings*, August 25, 2020, https://www.brookings.edu/blog/up-front/2020/08/25/the-2020-republican-party-platform-letat-cest-moi/.

[22] Ibid.

to stay in office to do what he does, to stir up people's resentments, in good part for his own personal glory and to give people the opportunity to see their lingering resentments get publicized.

This time, however, there was Project 2025 that had been touted as a blueprint for governing, even if it is a radical approach that seems keen to please extremists first and foremost. During the 2024 campaign, Trump insisted that he was not committed to enacting that blueprint, though leaders in the Movement like Bannon right after the election suggested otherwise.[23] But then Trump unleashed Musk on the federal agencies, taking the Project 2025 to dismantling the federal government on still another level.

The retribution-as-policymaking compound solution was now on steroids. It is actually well-established in Trumpism. We can also see the preoccupation for using policy to achieve personal and political success in Trump's past efforts to juggle being both head of the Movement and the Party. At the height of the Debt Ceiling impasse between President Biden and House Speaker Kevin McCarthy (R-CA) in the spring of 2023, Trump appeared at a CNN Town Hall meeting where he was the sole politician taking questions from his handpicked audience. When asked about the impasse and whether the possibility of the US government defaulting on its debts was potentially devastating for the global economy, Trump stated: "You don't know. It's psychological. It's really psychological more than anything else. And it could be very bad. It could be, maybe, nothing. Maybe it's—you have a bad week or a bad day, but, look, you have to cut your costs. We're—we're spending $7 trillion on—much of it on nonsense—$7 trillion on nonsense."[24] Evidently, Social Security and National Defense are nonsense. Yes, Social Security could be reformed, and the Defense budget is bloated with waste and corruption. But the solution is to propose reforms not just keep railing about these problems. As Trump returns to the White House and he appoints oligarchic billionaires to oversee the cutting of key government programs, there is the danger that Trump might have to support policy changes that could seriously jeopardize the coalition he built based on metapragmatic double-talk.

Trump's double-talk had conveniently failed to mention that he had major responsibility for creating a disproportionate amount of the government's

[23] Rhian Lubin, "MAGA Allies Say They Can Finally Admit Project 2025 'is the Agenda' for Trump's Second Term," *Independent*, November 6, 2024, https://www.independent.co.uk/news/world/americas/us-politics/trump-project-2025-steve-bannon-election-b2642968.html.

[24] "READ: Transcript of CNN's Town Hall with Former President Donald Trump," *CNN*, May 11, 2023, https://www.cnn.com/2023/05/11/politics/transcript-cnn-town-hall-trump/index.html. Also see John Cassidy, "Don't Believe Donald Trump: A Failure to Raise the Debt Ceiling Would Be Disastrous," *New Yorker*, May 15, 2023, https://www.newyorker.com/news/our-columnists/dont-believe-donald-trump-a-failure-to-raise-the-debt-ceiling-would-be-disastrous.

shortfall with massive tax cuts he got enacted in 2017.[25] He also neglected to admit to his successfully getting bipartisan support without any real opposition for raising the Debt Ceiling three times as president.[26] But Trump never deals in details; he is all about saying outrageous things his base loves. He likes to be seen as someone who can go against conventional wisdom and offer a unique alternative perspective. It is often just a fantasy that what he says has any merit. His talk about defaulting on the debt was widely condemned as irresponsible.[27]

Trump had strong support among House Republicans. McCarthy remained indebted politically to Trump in backing him in his bid to become Speaker until the extremists like Matt Gaetz pushed him out. His replacement, Mike Johnson, who was chosen because McCarthy was seen as an unreliable Trumpist, followed suit. The threat of default was something Republicans had done before with Democratic presidents. The worst standoff was between Newt Gingrich as Speaker and Bill Clinton as President back in 1995.[28] This sort of political posturing is what Trump does best, not actual budgeting. This was consistently the case, much like with his allowing there to be the longest government shutdown in US history without any real policy changes ultimately occurring in 2018.[29] His goal in 2023 was to get the Republicans in the House to make Biden look bad at budgeting by pushing for allowing the government to default on loans due to not raising the Debt Ceiling. Trump's approach to the Debt Ceiling was more political theater. This perennial partisan move persists as a way to demonize the Democrats as spendthrifts giving away "our" money to those "other" people who do not really need the assistance they get from the government.

The Debt Ceiling gambit would return when Trump as Presidential-Elect joined with Elon Musk, who had risen to become something like the oligarch-behind-the-presidential-throne, to very publicly on social media work to block the late-2024 bipartisan agreement to continue funding the

[25] Bobby Kogan, "Tax Cuts Are Primarily Responsible for the Increasing Debt Ratio," *Center for American Progress*, March 27, 2023, https://www.americanprogress.org/article/tax-cuts-are-primarily-responsible-for-the-increasing-debt-ratio/.

[26] Damakant Jayshi, "Did GOP Vote to Raise Debt Ceiling 3 Times with No Preconditions During Trump Era?" *Snopes*, May 3, 2023, https://www.snopes.com/fact-check/gop-debt-ceiling-trump-presidency/.

[27] John Cassidy, "Don't Believe Donald Trump: A Failure to Raise the Debt Ceiling Would Be Disastrous," *New Yorker*, May 15, 2023, https://www.newyorker.com/news/our-columnists/dont-believe-donald-trump-a-failure-to-raise-the-debt-ceiling-would-be-disastrous.

[28] Clay Chandler, "Gingrich Vows No Retreat on Debt Ceiling Increase," *Washington Post*, September 22, 1995, https://www.washingtonpost.com/archive/politics/1995/09/22/gingrich-vows-no-retreat-on-debt-ceiling-increase/9f7c9620-e6aa-489e-8ace-3ebb27e349bc/.

[29] Maggie Haberman, "Trump Has Used Government Shutdowns as Leverage Before," *New York Times*, December 20, 2024, https://www.nytimes.com/live/2024/12/20/us/trump-government-shutdown-news#trump-government-shutdown-threats-leverage.

government.[30] Yet, this time, rather than using the threat of not raising the Debt Ceiling in order to get budget cuts, the gambit was more the reverse. Now Trump and Musk were withholding support for the spending bill to get the Debt Ceiling put on hold. This time, the effort was to sideline Debt Ceiling so that it could clear the way for massive tax cuts for the rich to be enacted in the first months of the new presidential term. The goal was to undermine the redistributive welfare state that aids the less advantaged and instead redistribute resources ever more upward by extending Trump's first-term massive tax cuts to the wealthy.

Trump had already appointed Musk, the wealthiest person in the world, with the less wealthy, but still very rich, Vivek Ramaswamy to co-direct his informal Department on Government Efficiency. Quickly, Ramaswamy exited and left Musk to do his dirty work all on his own, with the help of a questionable group of young hackers and coders. That informal entity, it seemed, was intended to lay the groundwork for massively restructuring the federal government in ways reminiscent of what Musk did to massively cut and restructure Twitter and turn it to his own purposes. This seemed to be the model Trump had in mind when he allowed Musk to lead the charge on the late-2024 imbroglio on a temporary funding bill being made contingent on putting the Debt Ceiling on hold. Trump seemed more interested in working with Musk to do to the federal government what Musk had done to Twitter: radically disrupt how it operated so that it could be turned to his own purposes. Musk got to use the re-made Twitter as his own personal soapbox that led to his dominating public discourse, and Trump quickly moved once back in office to restructure the federal government to become his own fiefdom.[31]

When Trump seeks to be disruptive, it is often to overturn an established relationship, agreement, or institution that is considered by his opponents to be valued. Trump inevitably invokes the metapragmatic dimension of language when he seeks to be disruptive because he is responding to what others have established by word and deed. The politics of disruption fit perfectly within the metapragmatic discourse of Trumpism. The disruption over funding the government was in fact consistent with Trumpism in both form and function. Throughout this struggle over keeping the government open with a financing extension in late 2024, Trump kept calling his opponents names

[30] Rachel Leingang, "Elon Musk Showcases Grip on Washington by Impeding Spending Bill," *The Guardian*, December 19, 2024, https://www.theguardian.com/technology/2024/dec/19/elon-musk-trump-government-shutdown.

[31] Philip Bump, "Trump Wants Elon Musk to do to the Government What He Did to Twitter," *Washington Post*, September 5, 2024, https://www.washingtonpost.com/politics/2024/09/05/trump-musk-government-commission/.

and threatening them with retribution, all to lay the groundwork for his pending tax cuts.[32] This was for Trump not anything distinctive. That was his style. It was, however, more than hot air. It was his way of stopping people from governing so that he could reward his supporters. Trump's Debt Ceiling politics highlighted how his approach to policymaking was more about solidifying his political standing than anything else.

The Debt Ceiling, however, itself is vulnerable to criticism.[33] In the United States, it emerged from a requirement originally put in place in 1917 in response to the growing use of bonds by Congress. The Public Debt Act of 1939 created one overarching Debt Ceiling for the federal government overall. It can and has been raised many times, making it less than a real limit and more something that can be manipulated for political purposes, as Trump has distinctively shown. Denmark is the only other country with an absolute debt ceiling like the United States. Trump has never really been consistent about whether he supports or opposes it. Trump at times joined others who had long ago latched onto it as a way to invalidate the federal government as a legitimate institution more generally. Now he wanted it to be sidelined so that he could reward supporters with tax cuts.

Trump's position on the Debt Ceiling is like his wavering on many other important policy issues. For instance, Trump has long opposed the Affordable Care and Patient Protection Act of 2010 (aka Obamacare). He probably hates Obamacare first and foremost because he seeks to repudiate his nemesis Obama, and he thinks his fervent base wants to do the same. Trump has been more interested in ginning up his base than actually making public policy. It seemed like he could care less that people's healthcare could be jeopardized if he could score political points in the process. He never put forward his long-promised plan to replace it. He was always just stoking resentment via policymaking. Yet, Obamacare eventually became more popular over time as more people have benefited from it (an example of positive policy feedback).[34] Trump then switched gears and ended up lying about his attempts to repeal Obamacare.

This self-serving posturing about policy just to stay popular, get votes, or reward his supporters had seemed to reach its pinnacle when Trump, as the

[32] Brett Samuels, "Trump Threatens Primary Against Texas Conservative Chip Roy," *The Hill*, December 19, 2024, https://thehill.com/homenews/campaign/5049317-donald-trump-chip-roy-primary-challenge-shutdown-talks/.

[33] Elliot Smith, "The U.S. Isn't the Only Country with a Debt Ceiling. Here's How Denmark Avoids the Drama," *CNBC*, May 23, 2024, https://www.cnbc.com/2023/05/24/the-us-isnt-the-only-country-with-a-debt-ceiling-heres-how-denmark-avoids-the-drama.html.

[34] Zachary B. Wolf, "Obamacare Has Gotten Popular. Trump Doesn't Care," *CNN*, November 29, 2023, https://www.cnn.com/2023/11/29/politics/obamacare-trump-what-matters/index.html.

leader of his party, got Republicans in both houses to refuse to enact bipartisan immigration reform just so that Trump could run in 2024 on the issue of Biden failing to deal with the crisis at the southern border over the influx of immigrants seeking asylum.[35] Trump openly blocked a policy solution just so that he could have a policy problem to campaign on. Trump is not really interested in policymaking but prefers using the issue to demonize his opponent so as to help himself at the ballot box. He even admitted as much, as if that brazen disregard about policymaking also redounded to his advantage with his base of angry supporters.

For years, Trump had frequently demonstrated that he had been more of a movement leader who inflames grievances than the head of a political party that seeks to actually make policy.[36] Then again, he was even more about prioritizing his own political standing over everything else. He was always prioritizing his standing when he was using policymaking strictly for his own political advantage. Transactional chaos was his approach to policymaking. Trump sought to rule like an autocrat. Trump's constant invocation of the metapragmatic dimension of language greatly facilitated that. Trump's penchant to push his autocratic tendencies as far as he could while maintaining deniability was now featured as he began his second term with a keen interest in acting unilaterally, even if it was unconstitutional.[37]

The Trajectory of Trumpism Going Forward: Hot Air vs. White Hot Violent Intensity

Trump's return to the White House this time comes fully staffed with people prepared to enact an extremist agenda, including billionaires keen to just about totally eliminate the welfare state. Grievance politics may well morph into a full-throated neo-fascist set of policy initiatives that go so far as to impose authoritarian rule and basically vitiate the constitutional order as we know it.[38] His initial flurry of executive orders, cabinet nominations, other executive branch appointments, and the mass pardons suggested the latter.

[35] Stef W. Kight, "Trump, House Republicans Plot to Kill Border Deal," *Axios*, January 29, 2024, https://www.axios.com/2024/01/29/trump-republicans-border-deal-senate-immigration.

[36] Azari, "Trump's Dominance in the GOP Isn't What It Seems."

[37] Peter Baker, "'People Will Be Shocked': Trump Tests the Boundaries of the Presidency," *New York Times*, January 26, 2025, https://www.nytimes.com/2025/01/26/us/politics/trump-boundaries-presidency.html.

[38] Shane Goldmacher, Jonathan Swan, Maggie Haberman, and Stephanie Lai, "Trump's Second-Term Goal: Shattering the Norms He Didn't Already Break," *New York Times*, May 11, 2023, https://www.nytimes.com/2023/05/11/us/politics/trump-2024-cnn-town-hall.html.

Trump was consciously turning the government over to resentment politics, where the people who opposed the government and its policies were now running it.

It is this possibility that led many observers to express increasing dread at the prospect of Trump returning to the White House. These commentators took seriously Trump's assertions as to what he would do once he is president again. After Trump appeared on a CNN Town Hall broadcast in May 2023, a somewhat lone voice among Republicans US Senator Mitt Romney (R-UT) warned: "You see what you're going to get, which is a presidency untethered to the truth and untethered to the constitutional order."[39] Trump's second term, many people said, would likely deliver on his promise to seek retribution. In fact, Trump started his first week in office pardoning the insurrectionists. He also continued to seek ways to use the law to investigate and prosecute his opponents. He leaned in on executive actions that would basically destroy the civil service. In the end, it is difficult to avoid the conclusion he was generally seeking to undermine the rule of law. His administration would implement an American version of Viktor Orban's "illiberal democracy," where elections are held, but Trump uses his powers to undermine democratic accountability.[40] In this, he would be joining with Benjamin Netanyahu of Israel and other heads of state who in recent years have used populist backing to try to undermine the rule of law and compromise democratic institutions.[41] Given his consistent pledge to avoid military intervention abroad, Trump is however not likely to follow Netanyahu in waging war in a way that is designed to keep himself in power. But he is likely to allow Netanyahu to continue to do just that. The same for Putin in Ukraine, who Trump had publicly declared to be a friend and ally.

A key issue for assessing the alternative futures of Trumpism is to what extent Trump and his followers mean what they say, especially given his reelection. How far would Trump go in enacting his authoritarian tendencies as government policy or would he allow the courts to stop his unconstitutional illegal attempts to override the system of checks and balances and the rule of law? In 2020, before he lost the presidential election that year but before the insurrection, Trump was rated by historian J. R. McNeill as only having "pronounced fascist leanings," as someone who talked more about

[39] As quoted in Goldmacher, Swan, Haberman, and Lai, "Trump's Second-Term Goal: Shattering the Norms He Didn't Already Break."

[40] Jasper Theodor Kauth and Desmond King, "Illiberalism," *European Journal of Sociology/Archives Européennes de Sociologie* 61, no. 3 (December 2020): 365–405.

[41] Ishaan Tharoor, "Netanyahu's Israel Finds Kindred Spirits in Hungary and Poland," *Washington Post*, March 28, 2023, https://www.washingtonpost.com/world/2023/03/28/netanyahu-israel-hungary-poland-orban-illiberal-nationalist/.

undermining democracy with brute force than actually doing so.[42] As political theorist William Connolly termed him, Trump was an "Aspirational Fascist," someone who admired authoritarian leaders and their use of force to stay in power, but who himself was reluctant to actually do that.[43]

Yet, assessments have changed since the insurrection and then with Trump declaring his second term would be one of retribution.[44] Trump is now arguably facing a Movement that for some time, at least since the failed insurrection, is expecting further moves to take power and use it aggressively.[45] There is a vicious cycle to the growing support that can impel movement in that direction. Trump's base has expressed a growing interest in an authoritarian presidency that can override the rule of law and the checks and balances of the existing constitutional system in order to enact the extremist policies Trump has promised.

The turn to policymaking might lead Trumpism to undergo what Weber called the "routinization of charisma."[46] This normalization of Trumpism is possible if Trump finally decides to take governing seriously. Yet, this would undoubtedly be disappointing to many of his supporters who embraced him as their "different" kind of leader who gave priority to giving voice to their deep-felt grievances rather than compromising to get incremental policy change. Trump risks then being seen as someone who agitated his base for his own political ends, just so that he could mobilize supporters to enable him to win elections and achieve personal glory.

Yet, from the initial phase of his second term, Trump seems to be someone who is about more than blustering for his own advantage independent of everything else. He might have previously been an "aspirational fascist," but only if it got him the power he craved for himself.[47] Trump's Big Lie was, of course, more than bluster when it inspired the insurrection and the violent attempt to keep Trump in power. But it was first and foremost in service of keeping Trump in power, more so than creating a government ruled by White Nationalists or a Trumpist junta. If that is as far as the hateful rhetoric takes us, then it could be that Trumpism will over time become less of a threat to

[42] J. R. McNeill, "How Fascist Is President Trump? There's Still a Formula for That," *Washington Post*, August 21, 2020, https://www.washingtonpost.com/outlook/how-fascist-is-president-trump-theres-still-a-formula-for-that/2020/08/21/aa023aca-e2fc-b0477ed4_story.html.

[43] William E. Connolly, *Aspirational Fascism: The Struggle for Multifaceted Democracy under Trumpism* (University of Minnesota Press, 2017), 7–8.

[44] Robert Reich, "The Modern Republican Party is Hurtling towards Fascism," *The Guardian*, April 15, 2023, https://www.theguardian.com/commentisfree/2023/apr/15/the-modern-republican-party-fascism-robert-reich.

[45] Solnit, "Donald Trump's Power Is Fading: Trumpism Is the Clear and Present Danger Now."

[46] Dow, "An Analysis of Weber's Work on Charisma," 83–93.

[47] Connolly, *Aspirational Fascism.*

the constitutional order and more a Movement that got grifted by a corrupt politician. Of course, these alternatives are not necessarily mutually exclusive.

Yet, two dangerous variants of this possibility have emerged that need serious examination. First, Trump's blustering in the name of his own political success or that of the Movement has already become normalized within the Republican Party. The Republican Party for a long time was already deep into the politics of demonization before Trump, but now that is basically what it does overall just to cling to power.

The second variant of Trumpism as blustering hot air is that the disaffected White supporters who were mobilized to get change by disrupting the status quo become even more disaffected because they feel now not just deserted by the mainstream political system but by Trump and his allies in the Republican Party. It is at this point that the blustering of Trumpism must confront the monster it has created. Bluster that does not deliver on its promised extremist actions risks leading to a desperate effort to continue to keep the base committed. Inevitably, this leads to ever more outrageous bluster or what Rich Perlstein calls the "authoritarian ratchet."[48] Yet, the constant invocation of authoritarian rhetoric and posturing may over time force Trumpism to put up or shut up, leading to the actual enactment of authoritarian policies or even worse.[49] This is a predicament that is fraught with real danger, and it will not matter if Trump is still leading the Movement or not. Further, feeling ever more left behind, the more violent-prone disaffected members of the Trump Movement may increase the number of violent attacks above the even already high numbers of domestic terrorism incidents that have already been increasing with the rise of Trumpism. Under this last scenario, the trajectory of Trumpism turns into even more of a threat to the constitutional order than it already is.

The Trojan Horse: Normalizing Trumpism

Whatever the trajectory of Trumpism going forward, it has been helped to become the insidious force that it is by its discourse. All the gaslighting, boomeranging, and co-opting of terms have helped Trumpism insinuate itself into mainstream politics and perhaps even broaden its coalition. Trumpism has been, from its inception, about making mainstream politics unable

[48] Rick Perlstein, "My Political Depression Problem—and Ours," *The American Prospect*, May 29, 2024, https://prospect.org/politics/2024-05-29-my-political-depression-problem/.

[49] See Barbara McQuade, *Attack from Within: How Disinformation Is Sabotaging America* (Penguin Random House, 2024).

to go forward in ways that could redound to the advantage of most Americans. In spite of its claim that Trumpism would Make America Great Again, that it would stand up for the "real" Americans, Trumpism has not been primarily about winning elections to make public policy that would improve the material well-being of the American people. Instead, it has emphasized making people feel good that they have a leader who can express their disenchantment with the established order. Trumpism has been primarily about expressing white hot rhetoric on behalf of its disenchanted base of White supporters.

Yet, the deniability of metapragmatics is critical here, making grievance politics a successful, if frightening, policy agenda. Trumpism's success in executing this grievance agenda is in no small part due to how Trumpism gaslights people beyond its core of supporters into not seeing the viciousness, how it boomerangs criticisms back at its opponents to suggest that it is just doing what others do, and how it co-opts other people's ideas and perverts them to be used for Trumpist ends. With Trump in the White House, the extremists of the MAGA Movement, and others who are so inclined, can now use the discursive portal established by Trumpism to infect political discourse in ways that are destructive of democracy's need to rely on shared facts necessary for democratic deliberation.[50] At a minimum, Trumpism is profoundly undermining American democracy at a fundamental level, making democratic deliberation at best a fading ideal.[51]

Trumpism has been so successful in polluting public discourse that lying is now more than previously assumed and distrust over what people say is to an unprecedented degree the default position for all political deliberation. Trumpism makes all policy disagreements existential struggles, for which there can be no compromise. Trumpism politicizes everything that could be used to demonize opponents and secure power over adversaries. There becomes less available space for civil discourse and democratic deliberation over even mundane policy differences. The conditions under which ordinary people can effectively participate in democratic deliberation concerning US politics get thoroughly undermined.[52] But, as we have seen in the foregoing analysis, the idea that Trumpism is a threat to democratic deliberation risks being seen as a bit too quaint. Trumpism poses even greater threats for it is not just undermining the conditions for democratic deliberation, but it is also

[50] Steve Benen, *Ministry of Truth: Democracy, Reality, and the Republicans' War on the Recent Past* (Mariner Books, 2024), 187–90.

[51] André Bächtiger, John S. Dryzek, Jane J. Mansbridge, and Mark Warren, eds., *The Oxford Handbook of Deliberative Democracy* (Oxford University Press, 2018).

[52] See Dennis F. Thompson, "Deliberative Democratic Theory and Empirical Political Science," *Annual Review of Political Science* 11 (2008): 497–520.

polarizing the electorate to the extreme, while it amps up anger and hate and even for some encourages a turn to violence.

Trumpism as a discourse is not just dangerous in ramping up polarization and hate of opponents or its blatant incitements to violence. Trumpism is dangerous because it makes those things seem mainstream and acceptable. It is therefore all the more important to study not just what is said, but how. The deniability that gaslighting provides, the both-sideism that boomeranging offers and the claiming of privileged positions from the other side that co-opting secures, all further the legitimating of Trumpism's dangerous rhetoric. It is these discursive moves that make Trumpism so insidious.

To take but one dramatic example, a normalizing metapragmatic move came immediately after the failed attempt to assassinate Trump in July 2024 at a Pennsylvania rally. Trump had finally started to get aggressive push back in the 2024 campaign from Biden himself on his incendiary rhetoric. After the assassination attempt, Trump and his allies began an intense campaign to boomerang those charges, claiming that it was Biden and the Democrats who were practicing their own stochastic terrorism and encouraging the attack on Trump.[53] By making this metapragmatic move, Trump and his followers were normalizing their extremism as if it were something both sides do equally and therefore it was just politics as usual. This was undoubtedly not true in multiple ways, but it was classic Trumpism that would seek to pave the way to Trumpism's extremism getting ever more mainstreamed.

Trumpism as discourse makes everything about which side you are on. If you criticize Trumpists for anything, you are the devil. If you call Trumpism a form of fascism, then you are the fascist. Again and again, gaslighting, boomeranging, and co-opting reign supreme. Everything is about staying loyal to your side and demonizing the other for what they criticize you for. This is schoolyard-level discourse, but that is what Trumpism has made of our politics. Every day, new developments on this front make political discourse ever more polarized and demeaning.[54] It is also very dangerous. Every day, the heightened intensity in rhetoric is matched by increases in threats against election workers, county officials, judges, prosecutors, and others, increasing the potential for violence and the strain it puts on the government to simply

[53] Jeffrey Isaac, "Republican Feigned Outrage About Violence Must Not Be Allowed to Buoy Trump," *Democracy in Dark Times*, July 14, 2024, https://jeffreycisaacdesign.wordpress.com/2024/07/14/republican-feigned-outrage-about-violence-must-not-allowed-to-buoy-trump/?fbclid=IwZXh0bgNhZW0CMTEAAR1U8uYunHUEqJ5nNuMQTb9bt6yVx0YHEmw6GG2ujlTxUZg3KrDIEZrqDg4_aem_9qwXwBoA5w0fWVutxMdAaw.

[54] Trump has regularly taken to calling judges, prosecutors, and other officers of the court "fascists," preferring to spit back the epithet used by his critics against him. See Brett Samuels, "Trump Lashes Out after Lawyers Meet with DOJ," *The Hill*, June 6, 2023, thehill.com/homenews/campaign/4036546-trump-lashes-out-after-lawyers-meet-with-doj/.

enforce the law.[55] It is the new normal bequeathed to us by Trumpism. As the initial actions of Trump upon returning to the White House suggest, the success of the deniability of metapragmatics leads to unconstitutional unilateral policymaking via executive orders that Trump can claim are legal when in fact they are not only illegal but also implementing a profoundly cruel and anti-democratic agenda.

In that sense, Trumpism is like the proverbial Trojan Horse—once inside the walled city of mainstream politics, the hateful rhetoric gets normalized. Trumpism is now a legitimate way to run for office and how to talk and behave once in office. Yet, it is also very unpopular with many people who recognize the danger. There is however a Zen Paradox to Trumpism as discourse.[56] The more the metapragmatics of Trumpism enable its mainstreaming, the more its supporters feel emboldened to actually achieve the implementation of things like the authoritarian agenda of Project 2025. But when that fails to be achieved, the ever-present potential for violence associated with Trumpism implicit can be activated.[57] Either way, Trumpism has brought the United States to a dangerous juncture.

The Looming Threat of a Trump Dictatorship

As the leader of a movement that has sought to undermine the constitutional order, Trump has already indicated that he will ever more thoroughly erase the line between politics and law and act unilaterally to weaponize the Justice Department, in just the way he has falsely claimed Biden had done to him (and this time, Trump will have Supreme Court backing).

Winning reelection has done nothing to diffuse this. Trump's metapragmatic boomeranging about weaponizing the law for political purposes also illustrates how autocrats sometimes get to consolidate power by using the law against itself.[58] The shift away from constitutional democracy grounded in the rule of law can, under the right circumstances, come not so much from a violent overthrow of the government as from a legal coup from within. Aligned with Trump's 2024 campaign, lawyers like Jeffrey Clark worked on arguments to legitimize that weaponization. Clark was an obscure lawyer in the Justice

[55] Adam Rawnsley and Asawin Suebsaeng, "Trump: The Political Threats Will Stop … When You Agree with My Lies," *Rolling Stone*, January 24, 2024, https://www.rollingstone.com/politics/politics-features/trump-threats-2024-election-horror-show-1234953036/.

[56] Chung-ying Cheng, "On Zen (Ch'an) Language and Zen Paradoxes," *Journal of Chinese Philosophy* 1 (1973): 77–102, http://www.thezensite.com/ZenEssays/Philosophical/OnZenLanguage.htm.

[57] See Kam Shapiro, "Violence and Politeness: From Walter Benjamin's 'Critique' to the Streets of Chicago," *Constellations* 27, no. 3 (September 2020): 438–51.

[58] See Ben-Ghiat, *Strongmen*, Part I: Getting to Power.

Department when he became a personality in the January 6th investigations, for working with Trump to arrange for fake electors from key states to give Trump an Electoral College victory in 2020, contrary to what the voters in those states had decided. Clark had invoked the Right-Wing version of the "unitary executive theory" used by Project 2025 to argue Trump as president can seize total control of the Justice Department and use it to prosecute his enemies, something Trump tried to do during his first term but failed to complete.[59] The US Supreme Court would basically embrace this theory when it affirmed the power of the president to include being immune from prosecution for attempting to commandeer the Justice Department for political purposes.[60] It would be another highpoint in Trumpism where Trump gets to do that which he falsely accused his opponents of doing.

Even before Trump won reelection, he suggested that he could, as president, invoke the Insurrection Act to deploy the military as necessary to put down his opposition for their allegedly being the real insurrectionists, not his supporters.[61] Until *Trump v. U.S.*, the Posse Comitatus Act of 1878 as passed by Congress bars military troops from participating in civilian law enforcement. Now that the Supreme Court has granted the president absolute immunity for core constitutional responsibilities, this authoritarian action has actually started to get real.[62] Nothing tops being the commander-in-chief of the military for being a core presidential responsibility according to the Constitution. And the Constitution takes precedence over legislation passed by Congress. This unchecked power now can be used to deploy the military to round up and help deport undocumented immigrants or to repress protest demonstrations. And now it has already happened.

Even if Trump were to waver in following through on his rhetoric, the bluster had already mobilized "constitutional sheriffs" in Arizona and Texas, who have for years preceding argued that they have constitutional power to act to uphold the US Constitution even in contradiction of the federal government.[63] The main "constitutional sheriffs" association issued a statement after

[59] See Jeffrey Bossert Clark, "The U.S. Justice Department Is Not Independent," *Center for Renewing America*, May 17, 2023, https://americarenewing.com/issues/the-u-s-justice-department-is-not-independent/.

[60] *Trump v. U.S. (2024)*, https://www.nytimes.com/interactive/2024/07/01/us/scotus-immunity.html.

[61] Ellie Quinlan, "Even Team Trump Is Panicking Over His Fascist Military Threat," *The New Republic*, October 15, 2024, https://newrepublic.com/post/187178/donald-trump-team-freaking-enemy-within-military.

[62] Felipe De La Hoz, "The Supreme Court Just Supercharged the Scariest Part of Trump's 2025 Agenda," *Slate*, July 19, 2024, https://slate.com/news-and-politics/2024/07/supreme-court-trump-2025-mass-deportation-plan.html.

[63] Ethan Fauré, "Leading 'Constitutional Sheriffs' Organization Announces 'Full Support' for Trump's Mass Deportations," *Religious Dispatches*, December 6, 2024, https://religiondispatches.org/leading-constitutional-sheriffs-org-announces-full-support-for-trumps-mass-deportations/. On "constitutional

Trump was elected that they were prepared to form vigilante posses to assist to make Trump's mass deportation program feasible. This is entirely consistent as yet another Trumpist boomerang where those acting contrary to the law claim to be upholding it. It also would be entirely consistent with Trumpism as a discourse that has persistently expressed ways to justify Trump's autocratic tendencies. In other words, the "constitutional sheriffs" would be lending their own long-standing Orwellian perspective to Trump to justify undermining the rule of law by claiming that is what is necessary to allegedly get justice.

Taking this upside-down logic to the extreme, the authors of Project 2025 had called for an all-powerful president who heads up a "post-constitutional government."[64] Project 2025 included many previously announced Trump campaign plans for what amounted to politicizing the bureaucracy and placing greater emphasis on making politically self-serving appointments to the judiciary. The central Trump tenet was to make all appointments contingent upon promises of loyalty.[65] A full panoply of unconstitutional, antidemocratic, and autocratic moves in fact had already become part of Trump's most boastful promises for his return to power, especially as he unleashed Elon Musk on the federal agencies.

We might still want to conclude that Trump's bluster about becoming a "dictator for one day" is just that and that he can never deliver on his attempts to worm his way around the Constitution, the rule of law, and the democratic impulses of most Americans.[66] Try as they might, the second Trump term has featured the most extravagant lies about almost anything. Yet, Trumpism is more than talk. Like any discourse, its words motivate actions. The level of bluster in Trumpism is high and would be worthy of dismissal were it not that so many people are willing to partake in the bluster and use it to justify many deleterious acts, from Right-Wing terrorist killers to an insurrection to stopping the peaceful transfer of power and ultimately to the efforts to replace democracy with dictatorship.[67] This fraught moment makes all the

sheriffs" as rogue law enforcement officers at the forefront of the MAGA Movement, see Emily M. Farris and Mirya R. Holman, *The Power of the Badge: Sheriffs and Inequality in the United States* (University of Chicago Press, 2024), 143–45.

[64] Will Bunch, "The Scariest Word in America Is 'Post-Constitutional,'" *Philadelphia Inquirer*, https://www.inquirer.com/columnists/attytood/trump-post-constitutional-american-russell-vought-20240611.html.

[65] Ibid.

[66] Marina Pitofsky, "Donald Trump Repeats Comment He Would Be a Dictator 'for One Day' if Reelected in 2024," *USA Today*, December 11, 2023, https://www.usatoday.com/story/news/politics/elections/2023/12/11/donald-trump-dictator-one-day-reelected/71880010007/.

[67] Stuart Stevens, *The Conspiracy to End America: Five Ways My Old Party Is Driving Our Democracy to Autocracy* (Twelve, 2023).

gaslighting, boomeranging, and co-opting by Trump and his acolytes nothing less than incendiary.

The Crisis Is Now

By the time the 2024 presidential campaign was in full swing, Trumpism, both as a movement and as a discourse, had become centered on supporting a personality cult where loyalty to the leader is everything and the law and truth do not matter.[68] Trump received almost no pushback from his Party when he openly suggested that, if elected, he would pardon those convicted regarding the January 6th insurrection, calling those incarcerated "hostages."[69] He promised to go after and prosecute Democrats who cheated and who stole the 2020 election.[70] He also promised to go after Joe Biden for a variety of things, including encouraging illegal immigration to get more votes and various other alleged questionable acts as president. Even after the six conservative justices on the US Supreme Court ruled that Trump had absolute immunity from prosecution for actions taken as part of his "official" duties as president, Trump contradictorily still insisted that, if reelected, he would use his powers to prosecute Biden for alleged illegal acts he had committed as president.[71] Trump was already using authoritarian tactics by making a refusal to accept the 2024 results unless Trump approves to be a prerequisite for anyone gaining the chance to be his vice presidential nominee (including J. D. Vance, who Trump subsequently chose).[72]

Right after the Supreme Court ruled for the most part in favor of Trump's claim that presidents have absolute immunity, Kevin Roberts, President of the Heritage Foundation, said: "We are in the process of the second American Revolution, which will remain bloodless, if the left allows it to be."

[68] See "'American Fascism': Historian Rick Perlstein on Trump's Grip on the GOP & Chances of a Second Jan. 6," *Democracy Now*, January 24, 2024, https://www.democracynow.org/2024/1/22/ron_desantis_drops_out_2024?fbclid=IwAR31sCgPQiTtbJ1RprH4gjfMqS44FYAeWL3jXH4GHf65EloIq2ZRoQ5J7xg.

[69] Adam Gabbatt, "Trump's Novel Take on January 6: Calling Convicted Rioters 'Hostages,'" *The Guardian*, January 13, 2024, https://www.theguardian.com/us-news/2024/jan/13/trump-january-6-rioters-hostages.

[70] Stephen Fowler, "Trump May Get Another Chance to Be President. He's Planning an Aggressive Second Term," *NPR*, April 30, 2024, https://www.npr.org/2024/04/30/1248151906/donald-trump-time-magazine-interview-abortion.

[71] Alan Feuer and Maggie Haberman, "Trump Wants to Prosecute Biden. He Also Thinks Presidents Deserve Immunity," *New York Times*, April 30, 2024, https://www.nytimes.com/2024/04/30/us/politics/trump-biden-president-immunity.html

[72] Patrick Svitek, "Top Republicans, Led by Trump, Refuse to Commit to Accept 2024 Election Results," *Washington Post*, May 8, 2024, https://www.washingtonpost.com/elections/2024/05/08/trump-republicans-2024-election-results/.

This was yet another metapragmatic, preemptive boomerang, anticipating criticism for inciting violence by suggesting it was the violent tendencies of the Left that justified Trumpists engaging in violence.[73]

With less than a week before election day in 2024, Trump implied to Tucker Carlson in an interview before an adoring crowd that his opponents should face a firing squad.[74] Actually, Trump explicitly said about Liz Cheney, his lead Republican opponent: "Let's put her with a rifle standing there with nine barrels shooting at her. Let's see how she feels about it, you know, when the guns are trained on her face." The nine-barrel reference was widely understood to refer to a firing squad. Yet, Rep. Tim Burchett (R-TN), who like Sen. Lindsey Graham (R-SC) is always available to go on news programs to metapragmatically recharacterize Trump's extremist statements as actually harmless and did so the next morning. Burchett denied that the reference was to a firing squad even though he admitted he had no evidence to support that. The Trump campaign followed up and also denied the connection to a firing squad. But, regardless, Trump made a gesture toward using violence, and his supporters were quick to try to deny that. Right to the end, Trumpism was using a metapragmatic two-step to normalize extremism. And then he won reelection.

Trump has landed back in office, where he is preoccupied with concentrating power in the presidency, by claiming that his subversion of the Constitution is actually what is necessary to uphold it. He went ahead and pardoned the insurrectionists, almost all of the over 1,500 who have been convicted or charged for participating in the violence to stop the peaceful transfer of power on January 6, 2021. On his first day back in office, he also took other unilateral actions for things he had promised to do, many of them unconstitutional regarding a number of Project 2025 policy initiatives regarding immigration, civil rights, the federal bureaucracy, international agreements, and much more. These constitutionally questionable executive orders were more about Trump's need for retribution as well as the desire to address the resentments of his base of supporters.[75]

Many of Trump's proclamations are not legally binding, including his claim that only he and the Attorney General get to decide what is legal. Yet his legally

[73] Philip Bump, "The Target of the Right's 'Revolution' Is Pluralistic Democracy Itself," *Washington Post*, July 3, https://www.washingtonpost.com/politics/2024/07/03/heritage-foundation-trump-revolution/.

[74] J. D. Wolf, "Trump Campaign Defends Threatening Firing Squad Comments Aimed at Liz Cheney," *MTN*, November 1, 2024, https://meidasnews.com/news/trump-campaign-defends-threatening-firing-squad-comments-aimed-at-liz-cheney.ent

[75] Erwin Chemerinsky, "Will the Courts Enforce the Constitution Against President Trump?" *The American Prospect*, January 22, 2025, https://prospect.org/justice/2025-01-22-will-courts-enforce-constitution-against-president-trump/.

questionable actions to freeze agency funding and fire thousands of federal civil servants have caused serious harm to individual workers, programs, and their beneficiaries. Most significantly, the Musk-led DOGE funding freezes. And firings are not about eliminating fraud and waste but are the spear of a concerted Trump Administration effort to demonize and discredit the federal bureaucracy and existing public policy. The gaslighting remains the most prominent feature of Trumpism.

Trump's DOGE agency is itself a stark example of Trumpian metapragmatics that are designed to normalize extremism while evading political accountability. During the transition to Trump's second term, DOGE was originally not a real government agency, but only an informal advisory body headed by Elon Musk, who himself would not take a formal government appointment. Then, in an attempt to make it appear more substantial, on the first day in office, Trump's White House announced that DOGE was the acronym for a renamed Department of Digital Services, now DOGE Services, not improving government information processing but instead supposedly searching out waste, abuse, and corruption. Yet, in court papers, the Trump administration denied that it could specify who was the head of the agency and that Musk had no formal role in it. Nonetheless, Musk continued all this time to tweet out orders to the federal bureaucracy, announcing the freezing of funds, the firing of civil servants, and the abolishing of federal agencies, none of which either he or DOGE Services had the power to do. Ostensibly created to weed out waste and abuse in the federal bureaucracy, DOGE instead employed hackers to claim it found wrongdoing but actually was just cutting away at programs that Trump opposed. In questioning the constitutionality of DOGE, a federal judge mutely stated: "It does seem to me if you have people that are not authorized to carry out some of these functions that they're carrying out that does raise an issue."[76] It was all gaslighting all the way down, all the while government agencies, programs, and civil servants were being destroyed. As the controversy around DOGE swirled, it was reminiscent of Sarah Kendzior's cautionary statement that Trump's go-to strategy was to always try to cover up his crimes with scandal, deflecting attention away from his grift.[77]

While it was unclear as to the legal status of DOGE, there was no doubt that the 2024 Supreme Court decision on presidential power has significantly undermined the constitutional guardrails to restrain Trump from abusing

[76] Alan Feuer, "Judge Questions Constitutionality of Musk's Cost-Cutting Operation," *New York Times*, February 24, 2025, https://www.nytimes.com/2025/02/24/us/politics/doge-elon-musk-lawsuits.html.

[77] Sarah Kendzior, *Hidden in Plain Sight: The Invention of Donald Trump and the Erosion of America* (Flatiron Books, 2020), 7.

his reclaimed presidential powers. He was positioned to employ Trumpism's metapragmatic discourse in service of his extremism yet again. Metapragmatics normalize this extremism in a variety of disconcerting ways. Early on in his second term, we say that Trump's threats got anticipated with compliance even before he acts. It seems that no one wanted to get on the wrong side of a vengeful president. "Anticipatory compliance," as Timothy Snyder calls it, had already even before the inauguration become common among corporate leaders. That is a quintessential metapragmatic move where one takes action based on what is already assumed to have been threatened by Trump, thereby trying to defuse the retribution from ever happening. Authoritarian power becomes self-enforcing.[78]

While Trump was gaslighting when he said he was taking action against antisemitism, his arrest of Columbia University graduate student Mahmoud Khalil for protesting the Israeli slaughter of Palestinians was clearly an illegal action designed to intimidate protesters more generally. Most troubling was the fact that Khalil had a green card, so his abduction was threatening the freedom of anyone with legal standing to be in the United States, citizens included. There were almost immediately a number of other deportations of protesters for the supposed crime of harboring antisemitic beliefs. Further, there were the extraordinary renditions of supposed illegal immigrants accused of being members of drug gangs, including Kilmar Abrego Garcia, who was neither a gang member nor an illegal immigrant. When the courts demanded his return, the Trump Administration defied them with gaslighting, saying when the Supreme Court required them to "facilitate" his return, that did not mean they needed to do anything other than allow him back in the Country if he were to be released.[79] It all portended a future where the metapragmatics of Trumpism would usher in a more wide-ranging fascist assault on free speech, political participation, basic civil rights, and the rule of law overall.[80]

For Trump as president, it is metapragmatics all the way down. He is always poking to see how far he can evade the law while still claiming to be acting within it, whether by claiming he can ignore a judge's ruling because a plane deporting Venezuelans to El Salvador was over international waters or that

[78] Timothy Snyder, *On Tyranny: Twenty Lessons from the Twentieth Century* (Crown, 2017), as quoted in Jonathan Last, "The Guardrails Are Already Crumpling," *The Bulwark*, October 25, 2024, https://substack.com/home/post/p-150729926.

[79] Alan Feuer, "U.S. Renews Opposition to Bringing Back Maryland Man Wrongly Deported to El Salvador," *New York Times*, April 13, 2025, https://www.nytimes.com/2025/04/13/us/politics/trump-courts-deportation-el-salvador.html.

[80] Farah Najjar, "Mahmoud Khalil Arrest: Can the US Deport a Green Card Holder?" *Al Jazeera*, March 12, 2025, https://www.aljazeera.com/news/2025/3/12/mahmoud-khalil-arrest-can-the-us-deport-a-green-card-holder.

Joe Biden's preemptory pardons of members of the January 6th Committee were null and void because they were signed using autopen. The idea that immigrants could be classified as part of an "invasion," thereby justifying their expulsion under the Alien Enemies Act of 1798, became a legitimate legal issue. Trump's two-step for justifying placing his presidency above the law was ever present as his second term commenced. In fact, analysts have suggested that the defining feature of the initial phase of Trump's second term is "disinformation overload."[81]

As practiced by an autocrat in the White House, Trumpism becomes more than evanescent metapragmatic bluster. It becomes the rationalization of a coup to install an authoritarian government beyond legal restraint. The federal bureaucracy and the programs it implements have already suffered irreparable material damage. The weaponization of civil and even criminal law to attack political opponents quickly has been made commonplace. The repudiation of science, facts, and truth as the baseline for enacting public policy has been quickly initiated. Ever after Trump leaves the political scene, we may see the routinization of charisma where the effort to remake and then weaponize the federal bureaucracy may prove too difficult to undo, and the imprint of Trump's authoritarianism lingers on for a long while. Trump's charismatic movement may have lasting effects that the country will have to grapple with. This makes it all the more important to combat Trumpism now, rather than hoping it will all blow over. Trumpism as a discourse that normalizes extremism must be continually resisted.

Under these conditions, democracy stands at a precipice verging on being replaced by autocracy emboldened further by the popular-vote coalition that put Trump back in power. Democracy becomes its own undoing. It is true that there has been a growing wave of frustration with democracy that has spread across developed countries. In fact, a decline in support for democracy as a form of government has emerged as a common feature of public opinion in developed countries.[82] Trumpism is a significant manifestation of this surge. The Country's response must be an explicit denunciation that highlights the role of Trumpism as a deleterious discourse that mainstreams the idea of replacing democracy with dictatorship. It must also go beyond that repudiation.

[81] Steven Lee Myers and Stuart A. Thompson, "In His Second Term, Trump Fuels a 'Machinery' of Misinformation," *New York Times*, March 24, 2025, https://www.nytimes.com/2025/03/24/business/trump-misinformation-false-claims.html.

[82] Richard Wike and Janell Fetterolf, "Satisfaction with Democracy has Declined in Recent Years in High-Income Nations," *Pew Research Center*, June 18, 2024, https://www.pewresearch.org/short-reads/2024/06/18/satisfaction-with-democracy-has-declined-in-recent-years-in-high-income-nations/.

As part of the effort to respond effectively, analysts have proposed various reforms of the electoral system as well as constitutional amendments to overcome deficiencies in the US political system to make it more consistent with democratic standards of majority rule.[83] Yet, these needed reforms only will stop a minority from sabotaging democracy in the future. And only then if they are actually enacted and enforced. In the meantime, Trumpism can continue to run roughshod over the far less than perfect political system currently in place, exploiting its anti-majoritarian features, and work at all levels of government to make the system less democratic and perhaps for years to come.[84]

Electoral reform is only effective if elections continue to determine who gains power in the government. Trump's refusal to honor the rule of law or oppose violence in response to his side losing the presidential election is an indicator that the conflict has shifted to a higher level.[85] Now the conflict is about being for or against maintaining electoral democracy in an increasingly diverse society. Rather than waiting for electoral reform, more drastic action is needed in response to the threat posed by the latest bend in the arc of Trumpism.

Yet, the opponents of Trumpism seem unprepared to provide the needed response.[86] The failure to derail Trumpism is exacerbated by the inflection of well-established tendencies among liberals to emphasize reasoned deliberation, facts, and the law while conservatives increasingly stress emotion.[87] The distinction has widened with Trumpism, emphasizing the rhetoric of dominance while their liberal opponents tend to try to emphasize moderation.[88] Increasingly, we see that the liberal approach takes too long and fails to sufficiently inspire enough people to action. We need more than fact-checking—we need leaders who can mobilize the public to resist the normalizing of extremism.

In the United States in particular, liberalism is spent, wasted now on failing to connect to ordinary people's heartfelt disappointments with the

[83] See, for instance, Steven Levitsky and Daniel Ziblatt, *Tyranny of the Minority: Why American Democracy Reached the Breaking Point* (Crown, 2023).

[84] Ari Berman, *Minority Rule: The Right-Wing Attack on the Will of the People—and the Fight to Resist It* (Farrar, Straus and Giroux, 2024).

[85] See Eric Cortellessa, "How Far Trump Will Go" *Time*, April 30, 2024, https://time.com/6972021/donald-trump-2024-election-interview/.

[86] Rick Pearlstein, "A Republic, If We Can Keep It," *The American Prospect*, May 1, 2024, https://americanprospect.bluelena.io/index.php? action=social&chash=a431d70133ef6cf688bc4f6093922b48.2699&s=09aecd2fedb37399022935bd3068c8f2.

[87] Sanford F. Schram, *Welfare Discipline: Discourse, Governance and Globalization* (Temple University Press, 2006), Chapter 7.

[88] M. Steven Fish with Laila M. Aghaie, *Comeback: Routing Trumpism, Reclaiming the Nation, and Restoring Democracy's Edge* (Rivertown Books, 2024).

elite-dominated established order. Trumpism as a movement thrived on these disappointments. If there is to be an effective counter-movement, it must be associated with a thorough-going campaign to connect to the middle and working classes including the many among them that are so disenchanted with the way things are in what they see as an elite-dominated political system.[89] No amount of pointing to positive statistical indicators can substitute for that.[90]

To be successful in this electoral struggle, increasing voter turnout among people opposed to the anti-democratic movement to decrease access to the ballot is essential. Trumpism as a movement is succeeding in good part through voter suppression and other unconstitutional actions focused on undermining democracy. But mobilizing the working class with policies that are geared to addressing their discontent is equally critical. And highlighting how Trumpism as a discourse has misled ordinary people remains very important indeed as this foregoing analysis in this book has demonstrated. Informing voters who have been misled is an imperative, especially as Trumpism targets undermining important government programs that aid the poor and the working class. The evidence persists that Trumpism has exploited "low-information voters" and filled their heads with lies, misinformation, and conspiracy theories.[91] That proved once again to be a factor in the 2024 election as it did the first time Trump won.[92] Young voters are especially important since the youth overwhelmingly oppose Trumpism but misinformation especially via social media could change that.[93] Women, people of color, and other people who have been vilified by Trumpism need to be reached as well. Further, a broad coalition of people who are willing to stand up for democracy and individual rights, even in our less than perfect political system, is part of the solution.

There is no doubt that the bluster of Trumpism risks becoming stochastic terrorism that might incite violence among Trump's base against those inside and outside the government who act to block anti-constitutional actions.

[89] Milan Loewer, "If Harris Loses Today, This Is Why," *Jacobin*, November 5, 2024, https://jacobin.com/2024/11/harris-trump-election-messaging-populism-elites.

[90] Eza Klein, "Where Does This Leave Democrats?" *New York Times*, November 7, 2024, https://www.nytimes.com/2024/11/07/opinion/ezra-klein-podcast-election.html? smid=nytcore-ios-share&referringSource=articleShare.

[91] Charles Bethea, "Among America's 'Low-Information Voters,'" *New Yorker*, August 22, 2024, https://www.newyorker.com/news/letter-from-the-south/among-americas-low-information-voters.

[92] Richard C. Fording and Sanford F. Schram, "'Low Information Voters' Are a Crucial Part of Trump's Support," *Washington Post*, November 7, 2016, https://www.washingtonpost.com/news/monkey-cage/wp/2016/11/07/low-information-voters-are-a-crucial-part-of-trumps-support/.

[93] Greg Sargent, "Striking New Data about Young Voters Should Alarm Trump and the GOP," *Washington Post*, July 25, 2023, https://www.washingtonpost.com/opinions/2023/07/25/voters-progressive-trump-harvard-youth-poll-gop/.

Trump's refusal to address the increased violence, including targeted political assassinations in Minnesota in 2025, does not help. While Trumpist bluster does not always lead to violence, it can nonetheless work to legitimate the efforts to overturn democracy for authoritarian rule that can lead to its own horrifying effects, for immigrants, women, foreign aid recipients and many others. Yet, Trump is greedy, and he is prone to overreaching and then pulling back in order to maintain popularity and to be seen as acting within the law when he is tempted to go beyond it.

Whether this will happen with his willingness to declare national emergencies to justify aggressive unilateral action it unclear on a number of fronts: whether it is federalizing the national guard or deploying troops to squash protests against deportations of immigrants, or, relatedly, the less-than-targeted abductions for removal from the U.S. of a growing number of people seeking asylum on the highly questionable grounds of fighting an "invasion," or even his redefining as antisemitic student protests regarding the cause of the Palestinians. Then there is Trump's questionable assault on the federal bureaucracy to redefine large numbers of civil servants as political appointees, or his unilateral imposition of widely imposed tariffs on fabricated grounds of a national economic emergency, or the attempts to criminally prosecute his political enemies as if they, not him, were undermining the rule of law. There is the persistent abuse of the pardon power to free people who give him money or pledge loyalty, The ongoing assaults on the media, the universities and the legal profession are matched by a full-time grift to amass personal wealth by exploiting his recently unchecked presidential power. All of these are further signs that the U.S. constitutional democracy has been already seriously undermined.

Across all these issues, the constant metapragmatic redefinitions enable Trump to cross the boundaries of the rule of law but have also provoked nationwide backlash. Trump's desire to stay popular at times can override his desire to seek retribution and lead to his stepping back from these transgressive acts. A renewal of the Resistance Movement that formed when Trump was first elected becomes once again important, but it seems this time that it must overcome being bashful in the face of its prior defeats. For there to be an effective response to the threat of Trumpism, this time the coalition needs to be broadened to include the disaffected from various backgrounds. Nothing short of a broad-based campaign must start immediately to alert people to the looming danger of Trumpism now with Trump back in the White House. The resistance begins with an all-out attack on Trumpism as a perfidious discourse of constant lying and associated mystifications.

Index

For the benefit of digital users, indexed terms that span two pages (e.g., 52–53) may, on occasion, appear on only one of those pages.

Note: Tables and figures are indicated by an italic *t* or *f*.

Abbott, Greg, 66, 159–163, 174, 175–176
abortion rights, 14–15, 163–170, 171
Abrego Garcia, Kilmar, 229
accelerationism, 67
Access Hollywood tape, 29–30
Adams, John, 156–157
affective polarization. *See* polarization, affective
affirmative action, 79–80
Affordable Care and Patient Protection Act (2010), 215
African Americans. *See* Black Americans
Ailes, Roger, 91–92
Alien Enemies Act (1798), 174, 230
Allen Premium Outlets shooting, 138–139
Alterman, Eric, 91–92
Alt-Right Movement, 27, 84–85
America First Committee, 3–4, 124–127, 141
America First Movement, 124
"America First" slogan, 3–4, 58, 141
American National Election Studies (ANES), 97, 97*t*, 99–100
American Nazi Party, 126–127, 198–199
anarchism, 49–50
Anatomy of Fascism, The (Paxton), 119
Anglin, Andrew, 80
anocracy, 156
anti-abortion efforts, 193–194, 208, 208*f*, 210
anticapitalist Left, 49
Anti-Defamation League, 63
anti-democracy, 3–4, 12, 15–16, 18, 20–21, 33, 36, 37–38, 39–40, 55, 61–62, 70–71, 73–74, 117–118, 125–126, 129, 139–140, 143–145, 158–159, 177, 222–223, 232
  and lawfare, 142–145
anti-elitism, 94–95
ANTIFA, 88, 91, 111
anti-feminism, 14–15
antiliberalism, 6
antisemitism, 229
anti-vaxxers, 50
Anti-War Movement, 49–50
Argentina, 123
Articles of Confederation, 73
authoritarian ratchet, 17–18, 48, 109–110, 114, 220–221
authoritarianism, 2–3, 11–12, 14–21, 34–35, 37–38, 39–40, 55–56, 112–114, 158–159
autocracy, 156
Azari, Julia, 53–54

Babbitt, Ashli, 66
Bannon, Steve, 27–30, 50, 56–57, 84–85, 188, 209–210, 212
Bataille, Georges, 121–122, 128
Ben-Ghiat, Ruth, 119–120, 136
Biden, Hunter, 93, 180–181
Biden, Joe
  2020 election, 29–30, 45–47, 61–62, 90–92, 97–98, 121, 129–130, 132–133, 143–144, 194, 200
  2024 campaign, 222
  2024 election, 185–186, 206
  and border control, 215–216
  calling Trumpism "semi-fascism," 63, 120
  debating Trump, 76
  DEI initiatives, 105–106
  as president, 210–213, 219
  Trump's boomerangs about, 31–33, 63–64, 81, 84–85
  Trump's criticism of, 123, 183–184, 201, 223–224, 226, 230
Biden Administration, 174, 185
Big Lies, 4, 45–46, 62, 118, 129, 130–131, 132–133, 218–219
  see also lies
birther movement, 2–3, 76–77, 103–104
Black Americans
  America's treatment of, 141
  blamed for election fraud, 129, 139
  demonization of, 129
  equal rights for, 156
Black Lives Matter Movement, 46–47, 87–88, 96, 106, 177, 195
Black Panthers, 49–50
blind loyalty, 127, 197, 200–201
Blumenthal, Sidney, 47

Bocian, Michael, 205
Boebert, Lauren, 34
Boogaloo Bois, 67
boomeranging
  about Biden, 31–33, 63–64, 81, 84–85
  about the Capitol insurrection, 66, 67–68, 133–134
  by Carlson, 88–89
  on civil war rhetoric, 148, 152–156
  about the COVID-19 pandemic, 117–118
  of Critical Race Theory, 172–173
  and fascism, 29–30 n. 129, 113–114, 123–124, 139–140
  metapragmatics of, 29–31, 35–38, 181, 224, 226–227
  about racism, 33, 58, 77, 81, 87, 109
  by Republicans, 140
  about rule of law, 184–186
  about sexual assault, 47, 180
  on support for democracy, 101–102
  and Trumpism, 142–143, 199–200, 202, 221–223
  in Trump's election campaign, 38, 39–40, 63–64
  on Trump's indictments, 68
  Trump's use of, 43–44
  in use of Far Left terminology, 67
  see also metapragmatics
Border Patrol, 174
Both-sideism, 51, 222
Bouie, Jamelle, 144, 160, 169–170, 174, 177, 200
Branch, Taylor, 183–184
Branch Davidians, 62, 198–200
Brennan, Margaret, 134
Brown, Micheal, 96
Brown, Wendy, 191–192
Brownstein, Ron, 153
Buchanan, Pat, 7, 7 n. 26
bullshitting, 34
  see also lies
Bundy ranchers, 116
Burchett, Tim, 227

Calhoun, John C., 175
Camp of the Saints, The (Raspail), 84–85, 87
cancel culture, 50–51, 106–107
Cannon, Aileen, 185
capitalist system, 48–49, 67
Capitol insurrection
  as constitutional crisis, 61–62, 194
  and the fake electors scheme, 143–144, 224
  and the FBI, 189
  gaslighting about, 66–68, 114, 129–132
  implications of, 135–136
  investigation of, 129, 224
  January 6th Committee, 230
  and the Militia Movement, 88, 111–112, 114, 130, 132–133
  Republican response to, 48–49
  and the rule of law, 88, 130–131, 139, 231
  timeline of, 207, 218
  Trump's indictment for, 63–64, 185–186
  Trump's role in, 45–46, 61–62, 111–112, 114, 116–117, 130–131, 139, 143, 200
  undermining democracy, 146
Capitol insurrectionists
  convictions of, 59, 111, 132
  as "hostages," 66, 121, 131, 177, 226
  Militia Movement, 59, 62, 88, 111
  origins of, 133
  pardoning of, 63–64, 66, 226–228
Carlson, Tucker, 25–26 n. 110, 87–91, 93–95, 109, 189, 227
Carroll, E. Jean, 179–180
Carville, James, 188
Catholics, 14–15
Center for Systemic Peace, 156–157
Chaney, James, 198
charisma, 191, 218
  see also Trump, Donald, as charismatic leader
Charlottesville race riot, 56–57, 80–81, 120, 168
checks and balances, 217–218
Cheney, Liz, 227
Chesebro, Kenneth, 143
Chicago Project on Security and Threats (CPOST), 101–102, 133–134, 134*f*
China, 16–17
Chretien, Spencer, 18
Christian culture, 82–84, 85–86
Christian Nationalism, 14–15, 18, 108
Chutkan, Tanya S., 196–197
Cielo Vista Walmart violence, 138–139
civil rights, 147, 149
civil rights activists, 49–50
Civil Rights Movement, 7, 12, 29–31, 33, 53–54, 77–78, 100–101
Civil War (American), 65
civil war ("new")
  and accelerationism, 67
  belief that war has already begun, 158
  boomeranging about, 155–156
  call for, 73
  and culture war, 149–152
  efforts to promote, 114–115
  gaslighting about, 152–156
  Greene's rhetoric about, 65, 149, 152–153, 155–156, 157–158, 173–174, 208
  as inflection point, 66
  and the Militia Movement, 202
  nonviolent, 73

polity and the onset of, 157*f*
and the Right Wing, 155
signs pointing to, 156–159
tied to racism and fascism, 66
and Trumpism, 37–38, 43–44, 45–46, 55, 64–68, 75, 148–149
Clark, Jeffrey, 224
Cleveland, Grover, 5–6
Clinton, Hillary, 29–30, 183–185, 205
Clinton, William "Bill," 29–30, 183–184, 188, 213
Cloward, Richard, 52–53
Cohen, Michael, 68–69
Cointelpro, 49–50
communism, 3–4, 16–17, 49–50
Confederate memorials, 80–81
Confessore, Nick, 88–89
confirmation bias, 206
Connolly, William, 118, 217–218
conspiracy theories, 23–24, 46–47, 51, 60–62, 232
constitutional authority, 24
constitutional convention, 73
constitutional sheriffs, 225
co-optation
and the Capitol insurrection, 67–68
by Carlson, 88–89
of Critical Race Theory, 173
and fascism, 113–114, 123
of Leftist terminology, 142–143, 171, 173
of the Left's liberatory rhetoric, 116–117
metapragmatics of, 29–33, 172, 181
of progressive ideas, 177
about racism, 58, 77, 95
about rule of law, 184–185
and Trumpism, 35–36, 37–40, 47, 87, 199–200, 202, 221–223
of victim status, 180
of victimhood for Whites, 98
of "woke," 106–107
see also metapragmatics
counter-movements, 53
COVID-19 pandemic, 59–61, 115–116, 211, 220
anti-lockdown protests, 59–61, 116
deniers of, 50
Critical Race Theory, 46–47, 170–173
Cruz, Ted, 108, 161–162
Culture Wars, 7, 64, 149–152, 153, 172

Daniels, Stormy, 68–69, 81, 183, 197–198
Dans, Paul, 18
DARVO, 47, 180
Davis, Mike, 18
Debt Ceiling, 212–215
Deep State, 31, 50, 61–62, 65, 68–69, 101, 116
Defense Production Act, 60
DEI (diversity, equity, and inclusion) initiatives, 105–107, 173
democracy
vs. autocracy, 156
constitutional, 224
electoral, 145, 231
erosion of, 39–40
frustration with, 230
illiberal, 39–40, 119–120, 128, 202–203, 217
inclusive, 16–17, 20–21
liberal, 4, 12, 15–16, 112, 126, 158–159, 177, 202–203, 211
movement away from, 157
multiracial, 13, 20–21
saving, 123–124, 130, 133–134
social, 4
threats to, 38–39, 112–113, 123, 134, 152, 183–184, 187, 202, 230
undermining of, 113–114, 121, 129–130, 132–133, 139, 142–145, 217–218, 221, 232
in the US, 156
Democratic Party
accusations against, 29–30, 37, 67, 77–78, 88, 129–130, 132–134, 192–193, 222, 226
accused of replacing the current electorate with immigrants, 87–88, 101–102
demonization of, 37, 46–47, 157–158, 213
extremism in, 154, 154*f*
and the Ku Klux Klan, 12, 125–126
and progressive movements, 53–54
and racial inclusion, 172
resentment toward, 104, 133
Democrats
accusing Trump of fascism, 140–141, 145–146
belief in possible coup, 137
boomeranging about, 31–33, 140, 148, 155–156
in Congress, 67–68
death threats against, 74–75
and filibuster, 140
former, 105
gaslighting about, 62, 107–108, 139
as governors and mayors, 116–117, 142–143, 149, 151
liberal, 187
non-White, 150–151
polarization of, 48
as presidents, 213
Radical, 101
threats against, 67–68, 74–75
denialism, 43–44, 83–84, 87, 177
racist, 84–87
Department of Homeland Security, 174–176

Department of Justice (DOJ), 184–185
  control of, 224
  politicization of, 185–186
  Trump's attack on, 123
  weaponization of, 223–224
  see also justice system
DeSantis, Ron, 58, 65, 171
dictatorship, 69–70, 119, 123, 157, 187, 222–225, 230
  see also Trump, Donald, as dictator
disinformation, 10–11, 28, 93–94, 193, 230
Dobbs v. Jackson Women's Health Organization, 163–164, 167–170
DOGE (Department of Government Efficiency), 202–203, 214, 228–229
Dominion Voting Systems, 46–47, 90–92, 93 n. 55
Dow, Thomas, 191

Edsall, Thomas, 142–143
educational reform, 149
election fraud, 61–62, 93 n. 55, 129–131
Electoral College, 3–4, 9–10, 43, 143, 205, 224
electoral reform, 230–231
enemy within, 5, 74–75, 147
enthymeme, 35
entryism, 56–58
Espionage Act, 183–184
ethnocentrism, 86, 103–104
evangelical Christians, 14–15
executive orders, 19, 147, 216–217, 227–228
extremism
  encouraging of, 114
  legitimation of, 24, 29, 32–33
  mainstreaming of, 21, 26–27
  normalization of, 11–12, 21, 24, 27–29, 126–127, 169–170, 186, 222, 227, 231–232
  political, 209
  religious, 14–15
  in the Republican Party, 154
  Right-Wing, 20–21, 116
  in Trumpism, 4–5, 8–9, 11–12, 47–48, 58–59, 162–163, 202–203
  White, 7, 12, 137–138
  see also terrorism

fake electors scheme, 143–144, 224
fake news, 26, 120
Far Left, 49, 67
  see also Left Wing
Far Right, 3–4, 31
  co-opting Far Left terminology, 67
  domestic terrorism, 137–138*f*, 139
  and the Republican Party, 145
  see also Right Wing
fascism
  American, 21, 114, 122–128
  aspirational, 118, 131, 217–219
  boomeranging of, 29–30 n. 129
  copycat, 37
  defined, 29–30, 119
  far-left, 117–118
  and the MAGA movement, 114
  and the new civil war, 66
  normalization of, 139–142
  psychological structures of, 121–122, 127–128, 192
  Trumpism as, 3–4, 7, 15–17, 33, 36, 37–38, 43–44, 58–64, 75, 112–114, 118–122
Fauci, Anthony, 61
FBI
  attacks on, 63
  and the Capitol insurrection, 67–68, 189
  Cointelpro program, 49–50
  concern for violence from domestic groups, 111–112
  Trump's attack on, 123
fear-mongering, 3–4, 23–24
  see also hatemongering
Federal Reserve, 19
federalism
  and border control, 174
  bottom-up, 166
  changes in, 163–165
  inverted, 165–167, 175
feminism, 14–15
fentanyl crisis, 175–176
filibuster, 140
Finchelstein, Frederico, 123
Fitzgerald, F. Scott, 207
Florida, 171
Floyd, George, 96, 106, 170–171
fluoridation, 50
Fording, Richard, 104
Fowler, Anthony, 155
Fox News
  covering Trump's hush money trial, 197–198
  on Critical Race Theory, 170–172
  defamation lawsuit, 90–91
  firing Carlson, 89–91, 93–94
  gaslighting racism, 87–88, 91–95
  Hannity's show, 148
  Levin from, 67
  Rufo on, 170–171
  Trolling, 27 n. 117
  Trumpism and, 10–11, 29, 34–35, 91–92, 94
  Wallace from, 111
Frankenstein (Shelley), 94
free speech, 20–21, 28, 123, 132, 147, 229
Freeman, Ruby, 129
French, David, 10–11

Freyd, Jennifer, 47

Gaetz, Matt, 194–195, 196–198, 213
Garland, Merritt, 185
Garner, Eric, 96
gaslighting
  about abortion, 168–169
  about the Capitol insurrection, 66–68, 114, 129–132, 189
  by Carlson, 88–89
  about civil war, 152–156
  of criticisms, 177
  defined, 1, 1 n. 3
  and deniability, 222
  about DOGE, 228–229
  about election fraud, 62, 130–131, 139
  and fascism, 113–114, 123, 131
  on gun violence, 159–160
  about immigration issues, 124, 174, 229
  to justify power grab, 69–70
  of lies, 177
  as metapragmatic discourse, 29–33, 181, 199–200, 202, 221–223, 229
  by the NRA, 162
  about racism, 58, 77, 80–81, 84, 87, 126
  rewarding and encouraging violence, 177
  about rule of law, 185
  about sexual assault, 180
  of Trumpism, 35–36, 37–40, 47, 142–143, 202, 228
  by Trump's supporters, 180
  about Trump's trial, 183–184
  by Vance, 124
  of White Nationalism, 107–108
  Gov. Whitmer, 114–115
  see also metapragmatics
Gay, Claudine, 173
Gaza, 81
gender identity, 166–167, 171
gender stereotypes, 1
genocide, 113
German American Bund, 124, 126
gerrymandering, 9–10, 140, 142–144, 197
Gingrich, Newt, 213
Globalists, 108
Good Samaritans, 177
Goodman, Andrew, 198
Graham, Lindsey, 23, 183, 208, 208*f*, 227
Grassley, Chuck, 18
Great Replacement Theory, 84–85, 87–91, 94–97, 109, 133, 138–139
Greene, Marjorie Taylor
  civil war rhetoric, 65, 67, 149, 152–153, 155–156, 157–158, 173–174, 184, 208
  and Culture Wars, 149–150
  and the discourse of Trumpism, 25 n. 110
  and grievance politics, 208, 208*f*
  grievance politics of, 208*f*, 208
  and the MAGA movement, 34, 197
  on need for "national divorce," 91–92, 148, 162–163, 165–166, 169
grievance politics, 14–15, 207–217, 208*f*, 221
gun control/gun rights, 149, 159–163, 171, 192–194
Gun Rights Movement, 53–54, 71–72*f*, 72
gun violence, 158–163
Gurr, Ted, 156–157
Guttmacher Institute, 167

Haley, Nikki, 65, 146
Hampton, Fred, 49–50
Hannity, Sean, 148
Harris, John, 207
Harris, Kamala, 146
Hart, Merwin, 3–4
hate speech, 81–82
hatemongering, 15, 67–68, 79, 103–104, 138–139, 149, 206
Hawley, Josh, 108
Heritage Foundation, 18–19, 226–227
Heyer, Heather, 80
Hitler, Adolf, 62, 113, 119, 121 123, 124–126, 129, 131–132, 142, 146, 198–199
Hitlerism, 124
Hofstadter, Richard, 48
Homans, Charles, 123
horse-shoe theory, 50
How Civil Wars Start: And How to Stop Them (Walter), 156
Howell, William, 155
human rights, 201
Hungary, 16–17, 39–40, 119–120, 128, 145, 157
Hunter, James Davidson, 149–150, 152

ICE (Immigration Control and Enforcement) raids, 121–122
Idaho, 163–166
Ifill, Sherrilyn, 121–122, 190–191
immigrants
  apprehension and deportation of, 121–122
  Black Haitian, 58, 84
  demonization of, 2–3, 5, 23, 27–28, 37, 84–86, 101–102, 102*t*, 124, 127–128, 169
  deportation of, 19, 109–110, 225, 229–230, 232
  illegal/undocumented, 224–226
  Indian, 84–85
  Latino, 83–84, 87–88, 101
  non-White, 84–85, 101
  rights of, 20–21

immigrants (*Continued*)
seeking asylum, 215–216
violence against, 63
immigration
bipartisan reform, 219–220
clashing views on, 67–68
and the fentanyl crisis, 175–176
on Fox News, 93
global, 8
as "invasion," 7 n26, 84–85, 117, 174–176, 230
opposition to, 12, 15–16, 174
Trump and, 76–77, 227–228
in the US, 8
impeachment, 139
Individual Freedom Act, 171
Infowars, 143
insurrection, January 6, 2021. *See* Capitol insurrection
Insurrection Act, 146–147, 224–225
insurrectionism, 12
integration, 77–78
intertextuality, 25–26 n. 113
Islamophobia, 29–30 n. 129
isolationism, 3–4, 7 n. 26, 125–126
Israel, 81, 217, 229

January 6th Committee, 129, 230
Jefferson, Thomas, 156–157
Jews
demonization of, 3–4, 11–12, 80, 121, 125–126
in Hitler's Germany, 62, 113, 125–126, 129, 141
Laura Loomer, 29–30 n. 129
questioning the loyalty of, 108
violence against, 63, 71–72, 80
and World War I, 62, 129
and World War II, 125
Jim Crow system, 124–126
Johnson, Mike, 213
Jones, Alex, 143
Jordan, Jim, 162 n. 53
justice system
weaponization of, 19, 38, 73–74, 180, 185–186, 192–193, 223–224, 230
see also Department of Justice (DOJ)

Kagan, Robert, 6, 120
Kaplan, Roberta, 179
Kelly, John, 145–146
Kendzior, Sarah, 228–229
Kennedy, Robert Jr., 50
Khalil, Mahmoud, 229
King, Martin Luther Jr.l, 49–50
Klein, Naomi, 29, 50
Koresh, David, 198–199
Ku Klux Klan, 12, 125–126, 198
Kurtz, Howard, 93 n. 55

Labor Movement, 49–50
Lead Belly, 106
Lee, Robert E., 80–81
Left Wing
alienation of, 49–50
extreme agitation by, 50–51
Far Left, 48–50, 67, 117–118
fringe Trump supporters, 50
liberatory rhetoric of, 116–117
Levin, Mark, 67
Levine, Peter, 204–205
LGBTQ+ community, 63, 82, 128
see also sexual minorities
liberalism, 6, 15–16, 20, 187, 232
see also democracy, liberal
lies
vs. bullshitting, 34
of Carlson, 90–91
by Fox News, 92–93
in the media, 92
about non-Whites and immigrants, 5, 87–88
propagandistic, 173
Right-Wing, 93–94
by Trump, 8–9, 46–47, 120
of Trumpism, 5, 12, 23–24, 25–28, 51, 188–190, 221–222, 226, 232
White Nationalist, 92–93
see also Big Lies; misinformation
Limbaugh, Rush, 103
Lindbergh, Charles, 125
Little, Brad, 163–164
Loomer, Laura, 29–30 n. 129
Lowndes, Joe, 141

Maddow, Rachel, 29–30 n. 129
MAGA (Make America Great Again) Movement
and the Capitol insurrection, 133–134
coalition partners, 46–47
criticism of, 51
defending Trump from prosecution, 194
evolution of, 15
extremism of, 41–43, 221
and fascism, 114
inspirations for, 7 n. 26
issues ignored by, 159–160
legacy of, 54–55
loyalty of followers, 46–47
mainstreaming, 9–10
metapragmatics of, 194–195
racism in, 58
and the Republican Party, 207–208
resentment of, 44
shifts in, 55–56

support for, 206
support for Trump, 41
supporters in Congress, 67
Trump's role in, 36, 41, 44–45, 46–47, 52–53, 69, 181–183, 189–190, 191–192, 207, 209–216, 220–221
vengeful rhetoric and nostalgia of, 3, 17–18
Marche, Stephen, 158–159
marriage, inter-ethnic and inter-racial, 86–87
Martin, Trayvon, 96
Marxism and Marxists, 15–17, 183–184
mass killings, 71–72, 138–139, 159–160, 162–163, 173–174, 176
see also violence
Massie, Thomas, 67, 71–72*f*, 155
McCain, John, 97, 103
McCarthy, Joe, 3–4, 126
McCarthy, Kevin, 197, 212–213, 219
McCarthyism, 3–4, 126–127
McConnell, Mitch, 48–49
McCord, Mary, 116–117
McEntee, John, 18
McGraw, Dr. Phil, 121–122
McNeill, J. R., 217–218
media
Balkanization of, 10–11
see also social media
megalomania, 120
mental illness, 159–163
metapragmatics
of "all lives matter," 96
boomeranging, 29–31, 35–38, 181, 224, 226–227
and civil war, 156
deniability of, 222–223
of gaslighting, 29–33, 181, 199–200, 202, 221–223, 229
and the grievance agenda, 221
and gun violence, 162
linguistic, 214–215
of the MAGA movement, 194–195
of mixing politics and law, 183–187
origin of term, 30–31 n. 134
racialized, 95–96, 109–110
rationalizing violence, 74–75
of Trump, 63–64, 69, 111, 124, 126, 130–131, 169–170, 187–188, 222, 230
of Trumpism, 31–34, 38–40, 58, 62, 73, 90–91, 96–102, 112–114, 170, 177, 180–182, 185, 202, 223, 229
see also boomeranging; co-optation; gaslighting
Milgram, Stanley, 131–132
militarism, 118
Militia Movement
and the Capitol insurrection, 88, 111–112, 114, 130, 132–133
and civil war, 202
fascism and 58–64
Trump's alignment with, 58–64, 67, 111–112, 114–118, 199
In Waco, Texas, 199
White Nationalists in, 202
see also Oath Keepers; Patriot/Militia Movement; Proud Boys; Wolverine Watchmen
Miller, Stephen, 84–85
Milley, Mark, 112–113
Mirror World, 29
misinformation, 11, 27–28, 173, 190–191, 232
see also lies
misogyny, 47
Morrison, Toni, 145
Moss, Shaye, 129
multiculturalism, 7, 15–16, 17–18, 109, 156
Murdoch, Rupert, 91–92
Musk, Elon, 2–3, 202–203, 210, 212, 213–214, 225–226, 228–229
Mussolini, Benito, 113, 119, 123
Myers, Seth, 31–32

narcissism, 24, 41–43, 120, 209–210
National Guard, 174–176
National Rifle Association, 126, 162
nationalism
Christian, 14–15, 18, 108
economic, 14–15
hyperaggressive, 118
see also White Nationalism
nativism, 3–4, 11–12
Nazis, 3–4, 29–30, 118–120, 124–127, 141, 147, 198–199
negative partisanship, 47–48, 127–128, 133, 137, 139–140, 151–153
neo-Marxism, 67
neo-Nazis, 137–138, 147
Netanyahu, Benjamin, 217
New Lost Cause, 65
New York, 93
Newsmax, 92
Noem, Kristi, 34, 84–85, 101

Oath Keepers, 59, 61–62, 111, 117–118, 132
Obama, Barack, 12, 77, 95, 97, 103–104, 105–106, 137–138, 161, 215
and the birther movement, 2–3, 76–77
Obamacare, 215
Ogles, Andy, 160–161
Ohio, 167–168
oligarchy, 2–3

One American News Network, 92
Orban, Viktor, 16–17, 37, 39–40, 119–120, 122, 128, 145, 157, 201, 217
outgroup hostility, 10, 11–12, 56–57, 60–61, 67–68, 79, 82–83, 103–104, 125–126, 157–159

Palestinians, 229, 232
Pallin, Sarah, 195
Pape, Robert, 133–136
partisanship
  and choice of living location, 151
  dysfunctions of, 38–39
  increase in, 54
  negative, 47–48, 127–128, 133, 137, 139–140, 151–153
  turning to enmity, 140–141
patriarchy, 179
Patriot Militia. *See* Militia Movement
Patriot Prayer, 70–71*f*
Patriot/Militia Movement, 58–64, 114
  see also Militia Movement
Paxton, Robert, 119–120
Pearlstein, Rick, 48, 109–110, 220–221
Pelosi, Nancy, 139
Pence, Mike, 48–49, 143–144
Penny, Daniel, 177
Perlstein, Rick, 17–18
Perón, Juan, 123
Perry, Daniel, 177
personality cult, 9–10, 57, 70–75, 181–182, 194–195, 198–200, 226
Piven, Frances Fox, 52–53
pluralism, 85, 87
polarization
  affective, 7–8, 48, 51, 127–128, 131, 133, 137, 151–153, 155
  asymmetrical, 48
  cultural, 150–151
  elite, 48, 155
  mass, 155
  partisan, 104, 155
  political, 9–10, 36, 50–51, 54, 107, 127, 136–137, 149–150, 153–154
  public, 155
  of the Republican Party, 103–105
  Right-Wing, 155
police violence, 87–88, 106, 170–171
policy feedback, 210–211, 215
political science, 42, 204, 206
Polity Project, 156–158
polling results, 205–206
populism, 217
  authoritarian, 113, 141
Posse Comitatus Act (1878), 224–225
poverty
  demonization of, 1
  relational approach to, 1 n. 4
  stigmatization of, 2
power
  abusive/abuse of, 33, 50, 90, 199, 209–210
  authoritarian, 122, 201, 229
  consolidation of, 18, 20–21, 45–46, 145, 224
  constitutional, 20, 225
  embedded structures of, 1
  federal, 164–165, 174–175
  peaceful transfer of, 5–6, 19–21, 62, 68, 73–74, 136–137, 143–144, 186, 196–197, 201, 207, 226–228
  of the people, 142–143
  political, 23–24, 186, 195
  presidential, 5, 10, 16–17 n. 72, 18, 156–157, 185–186, 195, 217, 220, 224–226, 227–229
  sharing, 20, 61–62, 73, 211
  of states, 163–165, 166–167, 174
  White, 16–17
pragmatic experimentalism, 123–124 n. 51
presidential campaigns
  1980, 198
  2016, 3, 10, 27, 29–30, 43, 136, 189–190
  2020, 114–115, 136, 211–212, 217–218
  2024, 15–16, 26, 29–30 n. 129, 37–38, 45–46, 48–51, 62, 63–64, 70–71, 74, 76–77, 84–85, 109–110, 126, 136, 142, 146–147, 181, 182–183, 189–190, 192–193, 196–197, 198–200, 210–212, 222, 224, 226
presidential debate, 61, 76, 111–112, 114–115
presidential elections
  1968, 11–12 n. 49
  1992, 188
  2008, 103
  2012, 97, 103
  2016, 2–3, 5–6, 10, 23–24, 27, 232
  2020, 5–6, 10, 21–22, 29–30, 35–37, 41, 43, 45–47, 48–49, 65, 87–88, 90–92, 97–98, 111, 116–117, 120–121, 129–131, 132–133, 140, 143, 182–183, 197, 207, 224
  2024, 2–3, 5–6, 10, 15–16, 18, 20–22, 23–24, 26, 29–30 n. 129, 35–38, 58, 121, 139, 146, 169, 176, 185–186, 206, 227, 232
  claims of election fraud, 61–62, 93 n. 55, 129–131
presidential immunity, 19–20, 63–64, 122, 146–147, 186, 200–201, 223–227, 229
presidential power. *See* power, presidential
Presidential Records Act, 183–184
progressivism, 15–16
Project 2025, 18–20, 210, 212, 220, 223–224, 225–228
Pro-Life Movement, 53–54, 169

protest movements, 52–53
Proud Boys, 61–62, 70–71*f*, 111–112, 114–115, 117–118, 132, 194–195
Public Debt Act (1939), 215
Putin, Vladimir, 16–17, 122, 217

QAnon, 46–47, 60

race relations, 105–107, 170–173
racial colorblindness, 171
racial denialism, 84–87
racial diversification, 83–84
racial fear, 7 n. 26
racial inclusion, 7, 172
racial justice, 105–107
racial realism, 82–83, 84–87, 107, 109
racism
  changing definition of, 85
  "color-blind"/"laissez-faire," 58, 78
  co-optation of, 29–30
  denial of, 44, 76, 77–78, 79–85, 87–94, 102, 126
  and fascism, 141
  on Fox News, 91–94
  and the new civil war, 66
  opposition to Obama, 2–3
  in presidential politics, 76–78
  and the Republican Party, 103–104, 104*t*
  in Right-wing politics, 77–78
  toward outgroups, 82
  of Trump supporters, 11–12, 14–15, 36–37, 43–44
  and Trumpism, 21, 24, 31, 33, 37–38, 45–46, 56–58, 75, 77–78, 204
  White, 35–36, 171
  Whites as victims of, 58, 95–96
  see also America First Committee; White Nationalism
Raddatz, Martha, 180
Raffensperger, Brad, 129
Ramaswamy, Vivek, 214
Raspail, Jean, 84–85
reactionary movements, 8
Reagan, Ronald, 7, 7 n. 26, 198
Reich, Robert, 140–141
religious fundamentalism, 14–15
reparations, 105–106
Republican National Committee, 193
Republican Party
  2020 Presidential Nomination Convention, 211–212
  2024 National Convention, 211–212
  approach to governing, 220
  causes of, 193–194
  covering Trump's legal costs, 193
  and the Electoral College, 9–10
  extremist views of, 154
  and the Far Right, 145
  and Fox News, 91–93
  and the insurrection, 131
  judges appointed by, 5
  and the MAGA movement, 207–208
  members of Congress, 219–220
  polarization of, 103–105
  and Project 2025, 18
  racism of, 103–104, 104*t*
  radicalized, 153
  remaking of, 10, 22
  support for Trump, 25, 136
  and Trumpist Movement, 53–55, 127–128, 155, 204, 207–209, 208*f*
  Trump's relationship with, 5–6, 209–216, 219–221
  Trump's transformation of, 104–105
Republicans
  Radical, 156
  Racial Extremists vs. Racial Conservatives, 104, 105*t*
Resistance Movement, 232
rhetoric of resentment, 26–27
Rhodes, Stewart, 59, 132–133
Richardson, Heather Cox, 11
Riefenstahl, Leni, 121–122
righteous resistance, 33
Right Wing
  and the anti-Obama movement, 103–104
  and civil war, 153
  and culture war, 149
  extremism of, 50–51
  polarization, 154*f*, 155
  and political violence, 139
  see also Far Right
RINOs (Republicans in name only), 48–49, 54
Rittenhouse, Kyle, 177
Robb Elementary School shootings, 161–162
Roberts, Kevin, 18–19, 226–227
Robinson, Mark, 33
Rockwell, George Lincoln, 126–127
Roe v. Wade, 163–164, 167
Romney, Mitt, 103, 217
Rosenthal, Lawrence, 116
Rufo, Christopher, 170–173
rule of law
  authoritarian disregard for, 38–39
  and the insurrection, 88, 130–131, 139, 231
  and the Left, 49–50
  Trump's disregard for, 33, 36, 61–63, 66, 122, 217–218, 224–226, 229, 231–232

rule of law (*Continued*)
  undermining of, 20–21, 70–71, 88, 111–112, 121, 177, 184, 188, 194, 201–204, 217
Russia, 16–17

Saenz v. Roe, 164–165
Save America super-PAC, 193
Scheppele, Kim, 38–39
Schmitt, Carl, 69–70, 187
Schwerner, Michael, 198
Scott, Phil, 174
Scott, Tim, 180–181
Scottsboro Boys, 106
Second Klan, 12
Second White Redemption, 53
seditious conspiracy, 132–133
Serwer, Adam, 127–128, 176
sexual minorities, 14–15, 86–87
  see also LGBTQ+ community
Sharlet, Jeff, 16–17
Shelley, Mary, 94
"shy Trump voter," 205–206
signaling, 70–71
Silverstein, Michael, 30–31 n. 134
Smith, Jack, 185–186, 200
Smith, Rogers, 142–143
Snyder, Timothy, 73–74, 120, 143, 229
social media, 10–11, 36, 213–214, 232
  dominance of, 27
  memes on, 70–71
  Truth Social, 10–11, 18–19, 44, 196–198
  see also Twitter
social movement theory, 52
socialism, 15–16, 49–50
Soros, George, 121
Stanley, Jason, 119–120, 124–126, 145
states' rights, 66, 175, 198
  and abortion laws, 163–170
Stefanik, Elise, 25–26 n. 110, 66, 101
stereotypes
  gender, 1
  racial, 1
  racist, 76
Stevens, Stuart, 103
"Stop the Steal" campaign, 45–46, 61–62
Stop Woke Act, 171
Streitmann, Laura, 168–169
Sununu, Christopher, 146
Supreme Court
  2024 election ballot, 139
  abortion rulings, 163–166
  Clinton socks case, 183–184
  immigration issues, 174, 229
  power of, 144
  on presidential immunity, 19–20, 63–64, 122, 146–147, 186, 200–201, 223–227, 229
  Trump's appointments to, 169–170

tariffs, 220, 232
Tea Party Movement, 95, 103–104
Teixeira, Jack, 107–108
terrorism and terrorists
  domestic, 23–24, 67–68, 74–75, 114–115, 137–138, 158
  Far Right, 63, 137–138*f*
  protesters and radicals as, 49–50, 87–88
  Right-Wing, 63, 226
  stochastic, 23–24, 32–33, 67–68, 74, 109–110, 131–132, 197–198, 222, 232
Texas
  constitutional sheriffs in, 225
  defending from "invasion," 66, 174–176
  gun control in, 159–163
  "Operation Lone Star," 175–176
Texas Military Department, 174, 176
Tilly, Charles, 52–53
Tops Grocery Store attack, 138–139
transgender rights, 14–15
travel ban, 163–170
Tree of Life Synagogue shooting, 138–139
trolling, 27, 91–92
Trump, Donald
  accused of stealing documents, 41, 93, 136–137, 181, 183–184, 186, 188–190
  admiration for foreign autocrats, 122
  alleged illegalities, 181–183
  and the "America First" slogan, 3–4
  assassination attempt against, 15–16, 32–33, 71–72, 74, 159, 190, 192–193, 222
  authoritarian turn, 15–21
  and the birther movement, 2–3, 103–104
  blind loyalty to, 127, 197, 200–201
  border control, 174
  and the Capitol insurrection, 45–46, 61–62, 111–112, 114, 116–117, 130–131, 139, 143, 200
  Carlson's opinion of, 88–90
  charged with semi-Fascism, 63
  as charismatic leader, 38–39, 190–194, 230
  claiming immunity, 63–64
  claiming victim status, 185–186
  at CNN Town Hall meeting, 212, 217
  constituency of, 14–15, 21–22, 24
  and the COVID-19 pandemic, 60–61, 115–116, 220
  debate with Hillary Clinton, 29–30
  defamation case, 179–180

denying racism, 76, 80–81
as dictator, 16–17, 19–20, 27–28, 36, 44, 63–64, 123, 187, 201, 222–225
election interference case, 197–198
exaggerated rhetoric of, 23
as fascist, 145–147
as heroic outlaw, 69–70, 73–74
history as sex abuser, 47
hush money payments, 68–69, 81, 181, 183, 194–195, 197–198
impeachment of, 139
indictment of, 5–6, 41, 64, 67, 68–69, 74, 81, 136–137, 183–187, 189, 196, 200
and the MAGA movement, 3, 41, 44–45, 46–47, 69, 181–183, 207, 209–216, 220–221
metapragmatic discourse of, 34–36, 123, 198
pardoning Bundy ranchers, 116
pardoning insurrectionists, 66, 121, 147, 226, 227–228
and the Patriot/Militia Movement, 59–61
personality of, 41–42, 43–44, 47–48, 69, 112, 181–182, 209
as president, 99–101, 202–203, 212–213, 214–215, 220–221, 226–228, 230, 232
and presidential power, 5, 15, 16–17 n. 72, 24
and Project 2025, 18–19
promises of revenge and retribution, 8–9, 15–17, 27–28, 38, 45–46, 63–64, 128, 137, 146–147, 182–183, 189–190, 202–203, 212, 214–215, 217–218, 227–229, 232
prosecution of, 193–194
racist behavior of, 76
reelection of, 10, 18, 21–22, 23–24, 37–38, 44, 46–47, 75, 147, 176, 178, 201, 202, 216–218, 224, 227–228, 230
relationship with the media, 10–11, 26
and the Republican Party, 5–6, 209–216, 219–221
rhetoric of, 42
role in Trumpism, 41–47
self-defense efforts, 36
supporters of, 192, 198, 205–206
as threat, 24
transforming the Republican Party, 104–105
uniqueness of, 8–9
use of social media, 10–11, 27
and the White Nationalist movement, 2, 56–57
see also Big Lies; Capitol insurrection; presidential campaigns; presidential debate; presidential elections
Trump, Eric, 193
Trump, Ivanka, 139–140, 188
Trump, Lara, 193
Trump, Melania, 169–170
Trump v. U.S., 224–225
Trumpism
as aberration, 203–204
about rage, 207–208
and affective polarization, 51
as anti-democratic movement, 117–118, 141
and the Capitol insurrection, 133–134
Carlson's commitment to, 88–89
as constitutional crisis, 194
as counter-movement, 53
counter-movement against, 232
cruelty in, 127–128, 176
disaffection of supporters, 13–14
as distinctive discourse, 11, 13, 21–24, 47–48, 53, 91–92, 93–94, 113–114, 158–159, 222–223, 230, 232
drivers of, 37–38, 41
encouraging authoritarianism, 39–40
evolution of, 70–71, 81–82
as extremist movement, 4–5, 8–9, 11–12, 47–48, 58–59, 162–163, 202–203
as fascism, 58–64, 118–122, 141, 145–147, 222–223
as fear-mongering machine, 23–24
foundation of lies, 4
and Fox News, 91–92
future of, 207, 217–218
global allies, 38–40
inciting violence, 139
legalistic maneuvering of, 143
legitimation of, 27, 222
mainstreaming of, 28
as metapragmatic discourse, 24–28, 30–31, 34, 37, 54–55, 67–68, 109–110, 142, 148, 177, 198, 201, 214–215, 229
metapragmatic levels, 25–26
metapragmatics of, 73, 90–91, 96–102, 180–182, 223, 229
normalization of, 29, 70–75, 218, 219–222
opposition to, 231–232
opposition to DEI initiatives, 106
outgroup targeting, 61–62
and the Patriot/Militia Movement, 58–64
as personality cult, 55, 69, 70–75, 181–182, 194–195, 198–200- 226
as political ideology, 13, 21
as political movement, 13, 21, 202, 204–205
and the possibility of a future coup, 136–137
and racism, 21, 24, 31, 33, 37–38, 45–46, 56–58, 75, 77–78, 204
reaction of the Left to, 51
as reactionary movement, 41
representing White America, 105
and the Republican Party, 53–55, 155, 204, 207–209, 208*f*

Trumpism (*Continued*)
rhetoric of, 41–47
and the rhetoric of civil war, 64–68
rise of, 5–13, 38–39
success of, 4–5, 11–12
supporters of, 73
as threat, 112–113, 220–222, 230–232
Trump's role in, 41–47
and the Tucker Carlson show, 89
Trumpocene, 16–17
Truth Social, 10–11, 18–19, 44, 196–198
Tuberville, Tommy, 77–78, 107–108
"Tucker Carlson Tonight," 87–91
Twitter, 10–11, 29–30 n. 129, 44, 71–72*f*, 84–85, 116–117, 120, 196, 214

Ukraine, 217
unitary executive theory, 18, 224
Unite the Right march, 56–57, 80–81, 120, 168
United Constitutional Patriots, 117
US Constitution
1st Amendment, 28
22nd Amendment, 19
amendments to, 167, 230–231
authoritarian undermining of, 119, 145
and civil war, 162–163
creation of, 4, 175
free speech clause, 132
"Full Faith and Credit Clause," 164
insurrectionist boomerang, 66, 139, 143–144
"invasion clause," 174–175
Left distancing from, 49–50, 67
and protection against invasion, 66, 174–175
and the rights of citizens, 163–166, 167–170
and states' rights, 163, 177
Supremacy Clause, 164–165
Trump as threat to, 15–16, 18, 20–21, 24, 37–39, 69–70, 112–113, 130–131
and Trumpism, 5–6, 8–10, 61–62, 73–74, 113–114, 133–134, 142–143, 155–156, 188, 194, 197, 200–201, 210, 216–219, 220–229, 232
weaponization of, 73–74

Vance, J. D., 26, 54–55, 58, 84, 124, 169, 187, 226
Vavreck, Lynn, 153
Vietnam War, 49–50
vigilantism, 173–174, 176–177
violence
alternatives to, 24
anti-government, 36, 61–62
in the Capitol insurrection, 143–144
domestic, 174–175
fascist, 113
glorification of, 121–122
gun violence, 158–163
incitements to, 67–68, 139, 188, 222, 231
justification of, 132–136, 192, 226–227
mass killings, 71–72, 138–139, 159–160, 162–163, 173–174, 176
mob, 91
by the Patriot Movement, 58–59
police, 87–88, 106, 170–171
political, 32–33, 63, 127, 136–137, 139, 146
preference for, 132–139
rationalization for, 74–75
rewarding and encouraging, 23–24, 177
right-wing extremist, 63, 139
support for, 137
terrorist, 109–110
threats of, 144
and Trumpism, 74
by Trump's supporters, 63
at Unite the Right rally, 80–81
use of to maintain power, 131
vigilante, 177
White racist, 94–95
White Supremacist and Militia groups, 111–112
see also terrorism
voter suppression, 232
Vought, Russell, 18

Wallace, Chris, 111
Wallace, George, 11–12 n. 49, 77–78
Walter, Barbara, 156–159
Watters, Jesse, 197–198
Wax, Amy, 82–85
Weather Underground, 49–50
Weathermen, 49–50
Weber, Max, 191–192, 218
Webster, Daniel, 175
welfare
demonization of, 1, 2–3, 16–17, 219
elimination of, 216–217
redistributive, 213–214
social, 64
stigmatization of, 2
work requirements for, 219
welfare rights, 164–166
West, Kanye (Ye), 44–45
Wheeler, Burton K., 124
White Christian culture, 6, 58
White Identity Politics, 95
White Nationalist Movement
and the America First Committee, 3–4
and the birther movement, 76–77
Carlson and, 87–89, 92–93
domestic terrorism by, 23–24

and the Great Replacement Theory, 87, 138–139
and grievance politics, 208, 208*f*
hand signal of, 70–71*f*
and island mentality, 87
and the MAGA Movement, 15, 193–194
and the Patriot/Militia movement, 58–59, 60–61
and racial realism, 157
Trump's relationship with, 35, 56–57, 76–77, 112, 114, 147, 218–219
Trumpism and, 56–58, 71–72, 77–78, 82, 98
"Unite the Right" rally, 80
and White Supremacy, 107–108
White privilege, 58
White Supremacy
as cultural heritage, 6, 81
and domestic terrorism, 137–138
and the Great Replacement Theory, 138–139
and gun violence, 159
called "hoax," 89
and the MAGA Movement, 123–124
and the Militia Movement, 112, 202
and the Nazis, 29–30
and racial realism, 86
and Right-Wing politics, 77–78
Trump's relationship with, 111
and the White Nationalist Movement, 107–108
white triumphalism, 118
White victimhood, 58, 95–97, 97*t*, 99–100*t*, 103
Whitmer, Gretchen, 58–59, 114–115
"woke" appellation, 105–107, 172
Wolf, Naomi, 50
Wolverine Watchmen, 58–59, 115–116
women
and abortion rights, 163–170
anti-liberal, 14–15
demonization of, 179
sexualization of, 179
Women's Movement, 53–54
women's rights, 149
World Health Organization, 168–169

xenophobia, 11–12, 14–15, 18, 85
Xi Jinping, 16–17

Ye (Kanye West), 44–45
Yost, David, 167–168
Youngkin, Glenn, 171